To Ken,
Christmas 1985
With so very much love!
Nat

Sharps Rifles and Spanish Mules

Sharps Rifles and Spanish Mules

The San Antonio–El Paso Mail, 1851–1881

By

Wayne R. Austerman

Texas A&M University Press

COLLEGE STATION

Library of Congress Cataloging in Publication Data

Austerman, Wayne R. (Wayne Randolph), 1948–
    Sharps rifles and Spanish mules.

    Bibliography: p.
    Includes index.
    1. Postal service—Texas—History—19th century.
2. Coaching—Texas—History—19th century.   3. San Antonio (Tex.)—History.   4. El Paso (Tex.)—History.   I. Title.
    HE6376.A1T417   1985   383'.49764   84-40557
    ISBN 0-89096-220-0

Manufactured in the United States of America
FIRST EDITION

Contents

Illustrations

x   Illustrations

Acknowledgments

THE author wishes to acknowledge Dr. Rex Strickland for his generous aid and insightful guidance of my pursuit of this subject. I would also like to express my deep gratitude to Dr. John Loos and Dr. Robert Becker of Louisiana State University for their interest and valuable criticisms. Dr. Becker's intimate knowledge of mules and vineyards has been of particular value.

Sharps Rifles and Spanish Mules

After the Eagle Screamed

Bᴇᴛᴡᴇᴇɴ January and March, 1848, a random glitter of light on the pebbled bank of a California stream and the dry scratch of a quill's point across the face of a parchment sheaf combined to thrust the American people out of a dream of empire and into the dawn of its realization. Blind fortune at Sutter's Mill and astute diplomacy at Guadalupe Hidalgo bound the Southwest irrevocably to the United States from the Rio Grande to the Pacific. John Sutter's luck and James K. Polk's statesmanship guaranteed that the newly won lands would draw legions of men across the wilderness in quest of a golden promise.

Thousands of people sought the quickest routes across the continent as they caught the California virus. The overland trails of the Central Plains attracted most; others braved the jungles of Panama. A few tested Mexican hospitality as they marched from Vera Cruz to Chihuahua. Many, however, chose to travel the plains that reached across Texas from the Gulf Coast to the Rio Grande, for "the distance looked shorter, the climate milder, and the spring came much sooner."[1]

There were no roads worthy of the name on this route, but that mattered little to the men who landed on the beach at Indianola or rode overland across the Sabine. They naturally gravitated toward two points for launching their journeys across the arid plains. San Antonio and Austin were the largest settlements in the state, and natural rivals for the emigrant trade. These twin departure places hosted caravans bound for one vital way station on the trail to California. The old Spanish frontier outpost of El Paso del Norte beckoned to them like a lantern hung in a dark archway.

---

[1] Mabelle E. Martin, "California Emigrant Roads through Texas," *Southwestern Historical Quarterly* 28 (Apr., 1925): 290.

Immutable geographic factors dictated that El Paso should be a funnel for travel to California and for trade with other points in the Southwest. It was at the Pass of the North that the Rio Grande cut through the southern spur of the Rocky Mountains to win a passage to the Gulf of Mexico far to the southeast. For several centuries already, El Paso had served as a stopping place on the Camino Real from Chihuahua to Santa Fe. When the axis of travel shifted in the 1840s, it likewise served a similar role on the road from the Gulf to the Pacific. Once travelers had negotiated the plains that lay to the east and emerged from the Rio Grande Valley, they found that the Gila River's course led them west to the crossing of the Colorado and on to the final hurdle of the Sierras.[2]

The momentum of the California emigration movement built rapidly after the discovery of gold became widely known in 1848. In early 1849 a total of 17,341 people departed New York by sea alone. Nearly one out of every twenty of them was bound for Texas to begin the first land leg of the passage to the west. Many more fortune seekers assembled in New Orleans to secure berths on steamers bound for the Gulf ports. Texas was destined to become a marshaling yard for one of the great American migrations.[3]

The citizens of San Antonio quickly recognized the advantages to be gained from luring the emigrant traffic through their town and raised funds by public subscription for an expedition to blaze a wagon road west to El Paso. Not only would such a road attract the emigrant trains, it would also cut into the rich trade that had formerly flowed largely north from Chihuahua to St. Louis via Santa Fe. Thus, in the summer of 1848 they appointed John C. Hays, a noted surveyor and plainsman, to lead a party west under the protection of thirty-five Texas Rangers commanded by Captain Samuel Highsmith.[4]

Hays and Highsmith rendezvoused northwest of San Anto-

---

[2]Rex W. Strickland, *Six Who Came to El Paso*, 4; C. L. Sonnichsen, *Pass of the North*, 100–24; Ferol Egan, *The Eldorado Trail*, 114–17; Donald W. Meining, *Imperial Texas*, 42.

[3]Martin, "Emigrant Roads," 290.

[4]W. Turrentine Jackson, *Wagon Roads West*, 36–37; Martin, "Emigrant Roads,"

nio on the Llano River in late August and then rode on to the head of the Nueces before striking south to reach a crossing on the Pecos near its union with the Rio Grande. Their bumbling Indian guides led them on a wandering course that cut deep into the trans-Pecos wilderness. After much suffering and a brush with starvation, the expedition crossed the Rio Grande at a rocky ford and stumbled into the border village of Presidio del Norte. The Americans apologized to the Mexican authorities for this trespass and soon moved back across the river for a spell of rest at the trading post of Fort Leaton. After spending ten days recuperating from the journey, the explorers concluded that they were too tired to press on to El Paso.[5]

The dejected men swung northeast from Fort Leaton to seek a pass through the mountains. They found the 150 miles from Presidio del Norte back to the Pecos to be relatively easy going, and Hays felt that it would make a good wagon road at any season of the year. Upon striking the Pecos they followed it south for nearly 70 miles to its junction with Live Oak Creek. From there the expedition rode northeast toward the headwaters of the Concho and San Saba. Their mounts began to weaken, however, and long before they reached the San Saba, Hays elected to swing south for Las Moras Creek and San Antonio. By December the party was back in the town plaza after a journey of 107 days. Even though the expedition had not reached its objective, Hays could still report the discovery of a trafficable road to Presidio del Norte.[6]

Not only private concerns were interested in establishing a safe route to El Paso. During the same month that Hays arrived in San Antonio, Secretary of War William L. Marcy ordered Major General William J. Worth to establish a network of posts on the line of the Rio Grande below that city and to "examine the country on the left bank of the Rio Grande and from San Antonio to Santa Fe."[7]

291; A. B. Bender, "Opening Emigrant Routes across West Texas, 1848–1850," *Southwestern Historical Quarterly* 37 (Oct., 1933): 118–19.

[5] Bender, "Emigrant Routes," 118–19.

[6] Ibid.

[7] Ibid.

The citizens of Austin cooperated with Worth in fielding an expedition to scout a wagon road that would be suitable for the movement and supply of troops as well as for commercial purposes. Dr. John S. Ford of Austin and Major Robert S. Neighbors, U.S. Indian agent for Texas, led the party of four whites and six Indians.

The expedition assembled on the North Bosque and moved northward to Brady Creek. From that point it crossed the lush grasslands that led to the headwaters of the Concho. After some friendly encounters with the local Comanche bands, the explorers struck Horsehead Crossing on the Pecos and pressed on through Carrizo Pass to reach El Paso on May 2, 1849. After a brief rest Ford and Neighbors turned back for San Antonio via the Guadalupe Mountains and the Pecos. Returning to the ford at Horsehead Crossing, they then moved back along the Concho to Brady Creek, and the San Saba and Llano watercourses. On June 2 they arrived in San Antonio. The Austin–El Paso road had been opened with a success that was in marked contrast to the Hays-Highsmith adventure.[8]

Other government-sponsored expeditions had been mounted as well. General Worth ordered lieutenants William H. C. Whiting and William F. Smith of the Corps of Topographical Engineers to embark on a road survey that coincided with the Ford-Neighbors reconnaissance. The two subalterns were to retrace the earlier route to Presidio del Norte from San Antonio to confirm its suitability for wagons. If they found the road to be too rough for wheeled vehicles, they had discretion to return from El Paso by way of the Pecos and San Saba rivers. Worth hoped to see a route established that hugged the international boundary, so that settlers along the road could provide cheap supplies for the army's border stations.[9]

Departing San Antonio on February 12, 1849, the two pathfinders led their detachment northwestward to the German settlement of Fredericksburg, and then beyond to the head-

[8]Ibid., 119–20; Martin, "Emigrant Roads," 292–93; Jackson, *Wagon Roads*, 37–38.
[9]Jackson, *Wagon Roads*, 39.

waters of the San Saba's south fork. Whiting found the San Saba route to be a fine natural road with ample water and shade. As they pressed westward, however, water grew increasingly scarce. By the time they struck Live Oak Creek they were forced to conclude that only the digging of a chain of wells would make it a practical wagon road. After crossing the Pecos and entering the Limpia Mountains, they had a brush with Gomez, a notorious Apache chieftain, but managed to escape his pursuit and rode into Fort Leaton on March 24.[10]

Within five days the engineers continued their journey up the east bank of the Rio Grande. On April 12 they reached the hamlets of Ponce's Ranch, which rested on the American bank of the river, opposite El Paso del Norte. Their arrival sparked much enthusiasm among the inhabitants.

On their return trip they hugged the Rio Grande for 120 miles, following the outward route from Presidio and then swinging east to the Pecos. Descending this winding stream for 60 miles to the south, they crossed over to the Devil's River, which they followed to within a short distance of its mouth. From there they trekked east across the Nueces, Leona, and Frio rivers to San Antonio. They arrived in town after a round trip of 104 days to find that a cholera epidemic had preceded them. General Worth was among the dead. Whiting reported to his successor, Brigadier General William S. Harney, that the return route had been well watered and was much better suited to wagons than the drier territory charted by Ford and Neighbors.[11]

Harney responded to this intelligence by ordering Major Jefferson Van Horn to move his six companies of the Third Infantry to El Paso via the new trail. This would provide a genuine test of the road's utility, as Van Horn's column consisted of 275 wagons and 2,500 head of stock as well as the troops. Lieutenant Colonel Joseph E. Johnston, the senior topographical engineer in Texas, was attached to the caravan with instructions to supervise its march and construct a well-marked road. The trail-worn Smith, a civilian surveyor, and twenty laborers joined him for

[10] Ibid., 39–40; Bender, "Emigrant Routes," 121–23.
[11] Bender, "Emigrant Routes," 121–23.

the mission. A party of California emigrants also followed the column for protection.[12]

The troops left San Antonio late in May, and by June 3 they were camped on the Leona. The road west to El Paso generally followed the Smith-Whiting route, although Johnston made a detour between the Devil's River and the Pecos, and another as they approached the Rio Grande. It was slow going to make the road passable for the heavy freight wagons. Large work parties from the infantry companies spent hours clearing brush and moving rocks in the rougher sections of the trail. The column finally reached El Paso on September 8 after a march of 650 miles in a hundred days.[13]

Captain Samuel French, Van Horn's quartermaster, was relieved to have brought his wagons through, as were the rest of the exhausted soldiers. He was not so tired, however, that he failed to note the strategic advantages enjoyed by the little cluster of settlements:

El Paso, from its geographical position, presents itself as a resting place on one of the great "overland" routes between the seaports of the Atlantic on one side and those of the Pacific on the other. Fourteen miles above, and our territory crosses to the opposite side of the Rio Grande; a little further north and west are the headwaters of the Gila; and, should the route from El Paso to the seaboard on the west present no more difficulties than that from the east, there can easily be established between the Atlantic States and those that have so suddenly sprung into existence in the west—and which are destined to change, perhaps, the political institutions and commercial relations of half the world—a connexion that will strengthen the bonds of union by a free and constant intercourse.[14]

Thomas B. Eastland, one of the emigrants who accompanied the train, was less impressed with both the route and the charms of El Paso. "The road is not a *practicable* one, in any

---

[12] Ibid.

[13] Ibid.

[14] Jackson, *Wagon Roads*, 40–41; U.S. Congress, House, *Report of Captain S. G. French, United States Army, descriptive of the route from San Antonio to El Paso*, 31st Cong., 2d sess., 1850, House Ex. Doc. 1, p. 312.

other than dry weather, and *then* there is great risk of suffering for Water," he wrote. "I am greatly disappointed in El Paso—it is a poor, miserable, dirty town, badly built," complained Eastland, "containing a population of some 5,000 Mexicans, and a few foreigners."[15] Eastland may have been disenchanted with the settlement, but to the other travelers who had already wandered across the parched void beyond San Antonio and Austin, the green valley was a paradise. By that July there were four thousand people with twelve hundred to fifteen hundred wagons camped along the river above and below the town.[16]

They had not made the journey without paying their dues to the desert, although some had come through with surprising ease. The Mays party, which had gone ahead of Ford and Neighbors, departed Fredericksburg in mid-March and reached the Rio Grande north of El Paso after only sixteen days on the trail. Its members reported that "carriages and ladies could have gone over the road." Later groups were not so fortunate. "Most of them were lost, some were on the road to El Paso sixty days, and many were without water for days at a time, and some almost died of starvation."[17]

Although little of the trip was easy, the real killing ground on the road lay between the Pecos and the Rio Grande. A traveler who passed that way in June, 1849, saw "no less than sixty wagons abandoned on the road between the river and this place [the Guadalupes] and that it was really distressing to witness the dead and dying animals strewn along the way." When the pilgrims finally came in view of the fertile valley they felt that "the sight of this little place is truly refreshing to the weary traveler of the plains—indeed, the cool shady avenues, fragrant breezes, delicious fruits, and luxuriant appearance of everything around, make one almost feel that he is transported to the bowers of Eden." The comparison was grandly overstated, but it fully con-

[15] Douglas S. Watson, ed., "To California through Texas and Mexico: the Diary and Letters of Thomas B. Eastland and Joseph G. Eastland, His Son," *California Historical Quarterly* 18 (June, 1939): 124–25.

[16] Sonnichsen, *Pass of the North*, 129.

[17] Martin, "Emigrant Roads," 294–96.

veyed the relief that even the most experienced plainsmen felt when that green notch in the mountains appeared on the horizon.[18]

Even as more emigrants converged on the Pass of the North, yet another military road survey expedition was dispatched across the plains that rolled north from San Antonio. The dust raised by Van Horn's wagons had barely settled before Lieutenant Francis C. Bryan departed the town on June 14, 1849. Leading a party of thirty men and a train of supply wagons, Bryan marched to Fredericksburg and then crossed the Llano and San Saba to gain the headwaters of the Concho. From that point west to Horsehead Crossing the engineer found a well-marked trail in the ruts left by the eager California caravans. Between the Pecos and the Guadalupes, Bryan ran across a string of dry wells dug by the overlanders as they traversed that notoriously parched stretch of country. The army column reached El Paso on July 29 and reported that the route offered no serious obstacles to a properly equipped train.[19]

Bryan's arrival in El Paso marked the close of a significant period of exploration. "Within only a few months in 1849," noted W. Turrentine Jackson, "the United States Army had confirmed the desirability and practicability of two new wagon roads across west Texas that were to remain main arteries of travel until the present time." Both the northerly "upper" road from San Antonio via Fredericksburg and the "lower" road by way of the Leona and Devil's River were to endure as the main routes of commerce through the region until the coming of the railroads in the 1880s. The way had been charted on army maps and marked by the wreckage of emigrant wagons. Whatever the risks and privations involved, large-scale travel to El Paso and beyond was a workable reality.[20]

The wagons continued to roll out of eastern Texas and across the plains. The *Texas State Gazette* of August 25, 1849, advertised the benefits enjoyed by those who chose the route from

[18] Sonnichsen, *Pass of the North*, 128–29.
[19] Jackson, *Wagon Roads*, 42.
[20] Ibid., 43.

Austin to El Paso, although a sister journal had only three weeks before printed grim news of a stranded train whose members faced death from thirst and starvation. By September 1 there was news of still another large party departing Austin for California, and by mid-October the *Houston Advertiser* reported the organization of a commercial trading company that planned to operate a freight line from that city to El Paso. The floodgates were open.[21]

This influx of soldiers, teamsters, emigrants, and merchants was bound to have an impact on the cluster of little villages that straggled along the Rio Grande. Whereas Austin and San Antonio had prospered from filling the needs of the westering parties, El Paso, San Elizario, Ysleta, and Socorro were hard-pressed to meet the demands for food and goods presented by these thousands of newcomers. In 1839 the Santa Fe trader Josiah Gregg had reckoned the population of El Paso at some "four thousand inhabitants, scattered over the western bottom of the Rio del Norte to the length of ten or twelve miles." A decade later the transient population alone exceeded that figure.[22]

The sudden growth brought a host of problems. As early as the summer of 1849 provisions were "scarce—not to be had." The Mexican farmers hoarded their stores of beans, onions, and corn to see themselves through to the next harvest. The surplus was sold for exorbitant sums. Coupled with the shortages and high living costs was the natural friction arising between two groups of people. Many of the newcomers were rough-hewn types who needed only a few sips of the potent local brandy before deciding to reopen hostilities with the nearest Mexican. The emigrants made a bad situation even worse. Many stayed in the Pass area for several weeks to rest and refit for the next leg of the journey. As supplies dwindled and prices soared, some of them turned to theft and bullying the natives. Even the quartermaster stores at Major Van Horn's camp were pilfered.[23]

[21] Austin *Texas State Gazette*, Aug. 25, 1849; Austin *Texas Democrat*, Aug. 4, 1849; *Houston Advertiser*, cited in Austin *Texas State Gazette*, Oct. 6, 1849.

[22] Sonnichsen, *Pass of the North*, 103; Josiah Gregg, *Commerce of the Prairies*, 273.

[23] Strickland, *Six Who Came*, 4–7; W. Eugene Hollon, *The Southwest: Old and New*, 181.

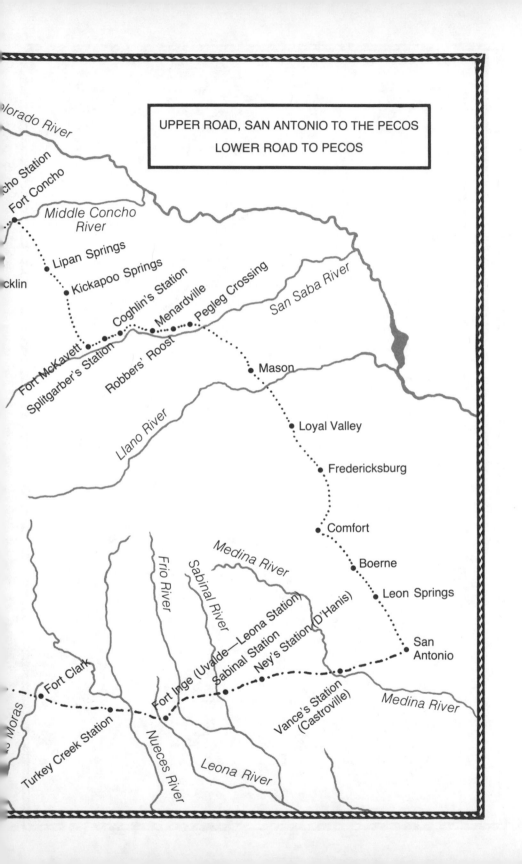

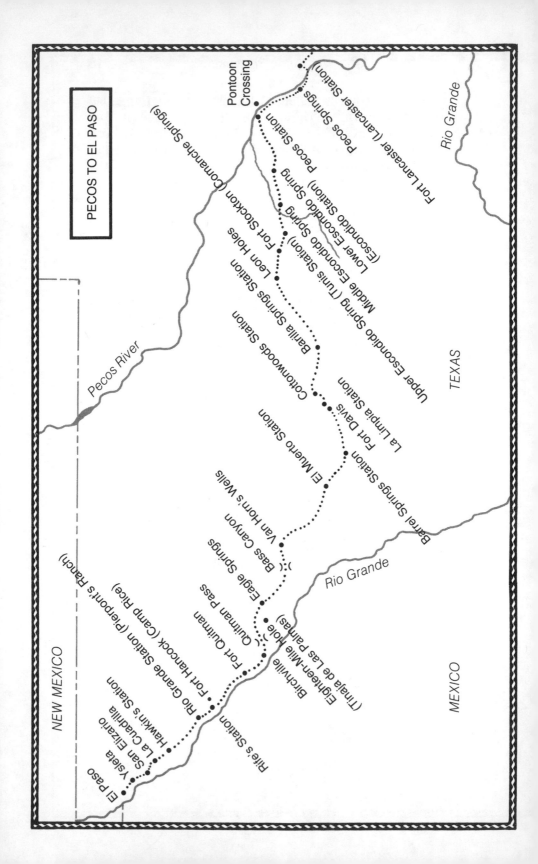

PECOS TO EL PASO

There was obviously a market for virtually anything that could be eaten, worn, or ridden. Enterprising Mexicans and Americans alike gravitated to El Paso to start farms and businesses to meet the demand. Their efforts spurred even greater growth in the population and increased commercial travel along the trails to the eastern settlements. The old Spanish colonial families who formed the gentry of the valley had to make room for a new strain of American merchant princes, as the general store and saloon began to rise in the shadow of the hacienda and mission towers.

Other parts of the nation took note of the new importance of the region as a crossroads. The editor of the New Orleans *Picayune* asserted that the Hays-Highsmith road would shift the flow of the Mexican trade from Santa Fe to Texas, for it made San Antonio the closest American market to Chihuahua. A good road from San Antonio to the Gulf ports would funnel the trade into New Orleans. In Houston an editor foresaw "a snug little fortune" for a local merchant who had departed with a cargo of goods, vowing that he would "not unload them till his wagon arrived in the public square" of El Paso. Prices for such staples as coffee and tobacco were seven to eight times as high there as in Houston. In April, 1850, a San Antonio merchant sent two hundred oxcarts west with goods for the El Paso market. Other businessmen of the town had already departed for New Orleans and New York to purchase bulk lots of supplies for the trade.[24]

The California gold fever had been joined by a trade frenzy that brought flush times to eastern Texas. In 1848 the state had boasted a white population of approximately 116,000 people in addition to 42,000 slaves. Two years before, the stone and adobe village of San Antonio numbered only 800 residents. By 1850 Texas counted 212,592 whites and over 58,000 slaves. San Antonio had grown to nearly 3,500 souls on the official census rolls, although a year earlier one visitor had judged it to be closer to 6,000 inhabitants.[25]

Other men scented opportunity in the wind over the Rio

[24] Ronnie C. Tyler, *Big Bend: A History of the Last Texas Frontier*, 59–62.

[25] Hollon, *The Southwest*, 187; Louis Burkhalter, ed., *A Seth Eastman Sketchbook, 1848–1849*, xxii; Charles Ramsdell, *San Antonio*, 44.

Grande and set up permanent businesses and ranches near El Paso. In June, 1849, young Ben Franklin Coons came south from Santa Fe and established two stores, a blacksmith shop, and a ferry on the river. His settlement became known as both Franklin and Coon's Ranch. Six months before his arrival James W. Magoffin had settled near El Paso. A veteran of the Santa Fe trade, he staked out a plot of ground that was soon dubbed Magoffinsville. Other Americans had already arrived on the scene with Alexander Doniphan and Sterling Price during the Mexican War. Among the remnants of their occupations were such ambitious men as Simeon Hart, Sam Bean, and John Lucas. Before them had come the independent traders like T. Frank White, William T. Smith, and Gabriel Valdez. Others, such as Bradford Daily, who arrived in 1842, and Hugh Stephenson and Price Cooper, who settled there in the 1820s, could claim to be as nearly native as any North Americans could be in El Paso.[26]

In the river settlements the population, both permanent and transient, continued to grow. The Texas legislature took note of the region's expansion when it officially organized El Paso County in 1849. San Elizario acted as the county seat for a unit of land that stretched east to the Pecos and north toward Santa Fe. Even after the Compromise of 1850 required Texas to yield its claim to New Mexico, the new county still encompassed 9,435 square miles. Many men found ample room there for dreams of private empire.[27]

By 1850 there was a pressing need for a system of regular commercial transportation between El Paso and her sister settlements to the north and east. Travelers often brought newspapers and correspondence with them, but only relatively large parties could travel in safety, and their arrivals and departures were unpredictable. Merchants and townspeople alike found the lack of public transportation to be a hindrance to the continued growth of trade and settlement at the border crossroads.

Texans took optimistic notice of a New York entrepreneur when he arrived in San Antonio in June, 1850, and announced

[26] Strickland, *Six Who Came*, 4–12; Sonnichsen, *Pass of the North*, 100–24.
[27] Richard K. McMaster, "The Evolution of El Paso County," *Password* 3 (July, 1958): 120.

that he was establishing "a line of stages on La Vaca Bay for conveying passengers overland to California, via San Antonio and El Paso." Parker H. French, a man of "facile talk, false promises, and fast gun," had come to capitalize on both the emigrants' desire to reach the gold fields and the Texans' hunger for a reliable system of communication between El Paso and Bexar.[28]

Displaying a bogus letter of credit from the Pacific Mail Steamship Company, French tricked over 200 gold seekers into paying him $250 each on condition that he deliver them to California within sixty days after their departure from New York. Upon arriving at Port Lavaca on the Gulf early in June, the greenhorns found that French's stages were actually former circus wagons and a nondescript collection of carriages. The draft stock consisted of a herd of wild mules that had to be broken for harness by the would-be passengers. The silver-tongued French soothed the disgruntled Argonauts and convinced them that after they tamed the animals and outfitted their vehicles, the trip would proceed smoothly.[29]

When he reached San Antonio, French produced his fake letter of credit and obtained drafts on the local banks. The garrison commander was presented with a forged commission naming French an officer in the U.S. Army. Also included were fraudulent orders authorizing him to draw on the quartermaster stores for supplies. Army mules and a herd of beef cattle were also procured on the strength of the documents.[30] The "French California Express Train" departed San Antonio on July 10. By the time the army, merchants, and bankers learned of his swindle, French was well down the trail to El Paso and planning more mischief with his packet of impressive papers.

Grass fires, snakes, prowling Comanches, and personal squabbles marred the train's progress as French pretended to lead it westward. He quarreled constantly with his guides and

[28] Austin *Texas State Gazette*, Sept. 21, 1850.

[29] Strickland, *Six Who Came*, 19–26; Egan, *Eldorado Trail*, 130–37. It should be noted that San Antonio's original Spanish name was "San Antonio de Bexar." The terms "San Antonio" and "Bexar" are thus used interchangeably to designate the same place. This was a common practice of the time.

[30] Egan, *Eldorado Trail*, 132–33.

displayed a monumental ignorance of how to run an emigrant caravan. The expedition stumbled on, its members growing steadily more disenchanted with their glib captain. Soon after crossing the Pecos, French met Franklin Coons and his train of freight wagons. The swindler purchased the entire outfit and its cargo with another draft for nearly $18,000 in nonexistent funds drawn on the unsuspecting steamship line's account.[31]

The train reached the Rio Grande on September 15, and for a few days French impressed the residents of El Paso with his grandiose plans and unlimited supply of credit. James Magoffin accepted his check for a staggering $80,000 worth of mules, while one-fourth of that amount in supplies was gulled from other local merchants. French then made the fatal error of resting three days before moving on for California.

At midnight before the day of his scheduled departure, a haggard courier cantered into El Paso from Bexar. In his saddlebags were letters denouncing French as a fraud and a warrant for his arrest. The imposter and his henchmen scuttled across the river into Mexico. The 250 men he had contracted with levered open his strongbox and found only dust. Outraged but still determined to reach California, they confiscated the train and sold it. Dividing the proceeds, they broke up into small parties and drifted out of town. Some headed west along their originally intended route. Others struck south and west through Mexico. One such group was ambushed near Corralitos by French and his gunmen, but they repulsed the attack and had the satisfaction of shattering the betrayer's arm with a rifle bullet.[32]

Parker French moved off the stage of southwestern history trailing a dark cloud of scandal and deceit behind him. The leading citizens of San Antonio and El Paso were left with thinner wallets and a blighted hope for reliable communication between their settlements. The charlatans and opportunists had enjoyed their day. Now it was time for men to try who were fit subjects for an epic instead of a farce.

[31] Ibid., 133–34; Strickland, *Six Who Came*, 21–23.
[32] Ibid., 24–26.

CHAPTER 2

"Notice to Travelers"

ONE of the few happy ironies of the region's history is that the man who exposed Parker French as a fraud would also be the one who established a regular system of communication across the Southwest. Henry Skillman was the rider who brought the warrant for French's arrest into El Paso in mid-September, 1850. He was already respected throughout the territory, and his grueling six-day ride from San Antonio to alert his townsmen to French's duplicity met with much gratitude but little surprise. Skillman was an accomplished scout and Indian fighter who was continually drawn away from civilization by the lure of wild country and free horizons. A questing spirit with a relish for adventure, he would have been a fit companion to stand by Leif Ericson on the deck of a longship. The most knowledgeable student of his life has called him "a Viking of the wastelands."[1]

A man of high repute among his contemporaries, Skillman is little remembered today, for the record of his exciting life is brief and fragmented. What little is known about him comes from old newspaper files and the accounts of travelers he met in his wanderings. They paint a uniform picture of courage, drive, and endurance equaled by few other men of the time.

Skillman's origins are obscure. He was born in New Jersey sometime in 1814 but spent his adolescence in Kentucky, and he claimed that state as his home. Nothing is known of his immediate family or early life, but between 1839 and 1842 he entered the Santa Fe trade as a teamster and courier on the high plains. He learned how to handle men, wagons, and mules. He also gained insight into the ways and thinking of the Indians. Skillman

---

[1] Rex Strickland, manuscript notes on Henry Skillman, El Paso, Texas. Copy in the author's possession.

developed an uncanny knack for divining when it was time to parley and when it was time to fight.[2]

The outbreak of the Mexican War found Skillman leading a train of freight wagons down the Rio Grande to Chihuahua. When a small army of Missourians marched down the river to seize El Paso on December 27, 1846, Skillman and his teamsters found themselves being mustered into Colonel Alexander Doniphan's ragged legion.[3]

Doniphan launched an invasion of Chihuahua the following February and the newly commissioned Captain Skillman played an important role in scouting the country that lay below the Pass. The wagonmaster distinguished himself at the battle fought on the Rio Sacramento on February 28, 1847, and led the way into the city of Chihuahua. When Doniphan was ordered to march to the southeast and join General Wool's American force at Buena Vista, Skillman returned northward to serve as a scout for General Sterling Price in Santa Fe. He once more distinguished himself when Price emulated Doniphan by marching his own force southward to seize El Paso and Chihuahua again in a pointless campaign that reached its embarrassing climax after the United States and Mexico had signed a peace treaty.[4]

Skillman continued in government service. In April, 1849, he met lieutenants Smith and Whiting upon their arrival in El Paso and served as their guide throughout the rest of the expedition, winning the explorers' unqualified praise. He subsequently joined Lieutenant Colonel Joseph E. Johnston's army engineers as they surveyed the road west from San Antonio.

Following a brief foray into freighting and livestock dealing, Skillman and several associates established an informal courier service between El Paso and San Antonio. The enterprise depended upon private subscribers to sustain its irregular operations. The Kentuckian also served as a special representative for

[2]Ibid.; St. Louis *Missouri Reporter*, May 20, 1846; Houston *Beacon*, Aug. 15, 1851. In a letter dated June, 1853, Skillman stated that he had been a "frontier man" for fourteen years. Martin Rywell, *Sharps Rifle: The Gun That Shaped American Destiny*, 37.

[3]Ralph P. Bieber, ed., *Journal of a Soldier Under Kearney and Doniphan, 1846–1847*, 327–32.

[4]Ibid., 343–46; Frank S. Edwards, *A Campaign in New Mexico*, 110, 175.

John A. Rogers, the U.S. Indian agent in San Antonio. At Rogers's request, this "gentleman of high and respectable character" undertook a census of the Indian bands living along the routes to El Paso and Presidio del Norte. It was a highly dangerous undertaking, but Skillman completed the survey by September, 1851.[5]

During Skillman's temporary service with Rogers, his fellow plainsmen William Alexander "Bigfoot" Wallace and Edward Dixon Westfall continued to carry private correspondence between the settlements. Wallace was already a mythic figure on the frontier. Dubbed Bigfoot for his longstanding feud with a Lipan Apache who left huge moccasin tracks in his path, Wallace had come to Texas from Virginia in 1836 at the age of nineteen. He had sworn to avenge his brother's death in the massacre at Goliad. After seeing extensive service against the Indians and Mexicans, he had joined Skillman's impromptu mail service. Aided by Westfall, a taciturn Kentuckian, Wallace carried the mail between El Paso and Bexar on muleback. Over forty years later he told Frederic Remington that he traversed "a howling wilderness, but always brought it safely through—if safely can be called lying thirteen days by a water-hole in the desert, waiting for a broken leg to mend, and living meanwhile on one prairie-wolf, which he managed to shoot."[6]

In mid-April, 1851, Wallace and Richard A. Howard submitted a bid to the Post Office Department for a contract to operate a mail service between San Antonio, Texas, and Doña Ana, New Mexico, via Eagle Pass, Presidio del Norte, and El Paso. A round trip would be completed every thirty-eight days. The two men calculated that they could operate for $25,000 a year. If the Eagle Pass and Presidio stations were deleted from the

[5] "Journal of William Henry Chase Whiting, 1849," in Ralph P. Bieber, ed., *Exploring Southwestern Trails, 1846–1854,* 304–14, 337–49; Robert Eccleston, *Overland to California on the Southwestern Trail in 1849,* 104–105; *Nacogdoches Times,* June 16, 1849; Austin *Texas State Gazette,* Feb. 23, Dec. 28, 1850; *The Texas Monument,* Aug. 20, 1851; John A. Rogers to Gov. Peter Hansbrough Bell, San Antonio, Texas, Sept. 3, 1851, in Dorman H. Winfrey, ed., *Texas Indian Papers, 1846–1859,* 141–42.

[6] The literature on Wallace is too extensive for detail here. The best biography of him to date is Stanley Vestal's *Bigfoot Wallace.* Also useful are A. J. Sowell's *Early Settlers and Indian Fighters of Southwest Texas;* John C. Duval, *The Adventures of Bigfoot Wallace;* and Josiah Wilbarger, *Indian Depredations in Texas.*

route, the time could be cut to twenty-five days. The government was unimpressed, and the bid was refused as "extravagant and not according to advertisement."[7]

Despite the government's parsimony, El Pasoans continued to forge their own links to the outside world. As early as 1839 trader Josiah Gregg had seen a regularly scheduled mail service in operation between Chihuahua and Santa Fe. The Americans had apparently continued its northern leg after the war, for in May, 1851, the *Missouri Republican* noted that the mail from El Paso reached Santa Fe on April 22, "as usual."[8]

There were other problems to be faced in addition to the Post Office's indifference to the frontier's needs. Unless mail was entrusted to freighters or emigrant parties, whose trains moved at a slow pace, the settlers were left with the alternative of sending it by a single mounted courier, who would rely on his speed to elude the Indians. The problem was that everyone who crossed the wilderness east of El Paso had to stop at the same string of waterholes. Meetings between whites and Indians were inevitable, and the outcome was often fatal for the smaller party. Some travelers lost only their stock. Others were never heard from again after they left the settlements. Survival could hinge upon the whims of the tribesmen.

Early in August, 1851, a rider left El Paso with mail for San Antonio and stumbled into an ambush at Eagle Springs, 116 miles to the east. The braves were in a generous mood and took only his saddle and a small supply of provisions. They then followed him for some distance, playing cat-and-mouse with the nervous courier. Finally their chief gave him an Indian saddle and some food. They left behind them a Texan who was thankful to be alive but sorely puzzled by the Indians' uncharacteristic charity. The incident brought home to all concerned the fragility of the link between the two towns. Henry Skillman decided to set things on a more secure and systematic basis.[9]

[7] U.S. Congress, House, *Report on Mail Contracts, Letter from the Postmaster General, February 6, 1852*, 32d Cong., 1st sess., 1851, House Ex. Doc. 56, p. 391.

[8] Josiah Gregg, *Commerce of the Prairies*, 266–67.

[9] St. Louis *Missouri Republican*, May 19, Oct. 6, 1851; San Antonio *Western Texan*, Sept. 11, 1851.

Soon after rendering his report to Rogers, Skillman left for the Gulf Coast and took a steamer east for Washington, D.C. He wanted the contract that Wallace and Howard had been denied and was willing to make the long trip to lobby in his own cause. He must have found the Texas delegation in Congress on his side. With its support Skillman did not have to tarry long in the sweltering tidewater heat of Washington.

On Saturday, September 20, Skillman signed a contract with Postmaster General Nathan K. Hall. The route, No. 6401, stretched from Santa Fe to El Paso, and then ran east to San Antonio by the lower road. Service was to begin on November 1, 1851, and run until the contract expired on June 30, 1854. Skillman was allotted $12,500 a year on which to run the line and turn a profit.[10]

The *Daily National Intelligencer* broke the news and supplied more details about this new adventure, remarking that "these arrangements will be very welcome to all who have family or business relations in those distant countries, hitherto cut off from any regular channel of correspondence." The journal tempered its congratulations with the observation that "as the transportation of mails through a vast unsettled wilderness, infested by roaming bands of rude and often hostile Indians, must, to afford them the proper protection, be attended with an expense far beyond any possible receipts, the Postmaster General has been induced to enter into these contracts solely, we presume, with a view to the public accommodation."[11]

The newspaper was justified in its concern that this would be an operation of high risks with little chance of ever showing a profit for the government, but it trusted Skillman's abilities, describing him as one "well known on the frontier, and highly rec-

[10] *Daily National Intelligencer*, Sept. 22, 1851.

[11] Ibid. The original mail contracts for this period have been lost. Neither Postmaster General Hall's official letterbook nor his personal papers make any reference to the Texas contracts. The Nathan K. Hall Papers are located in the Miscellaneous Manuscript Collection, Library of Congress, Washington, D.C. The official correspondence of the period can be found in the Post Office Department, Letterbooks of the Postmaster General, Series 2: Records of the Immediate Office of the Postmaster General, Letters Sent, July 21, 1850–August 18, 1882, Record Group 28, National Archives and Records Service. Hereafter cited as RG 28, NARS.

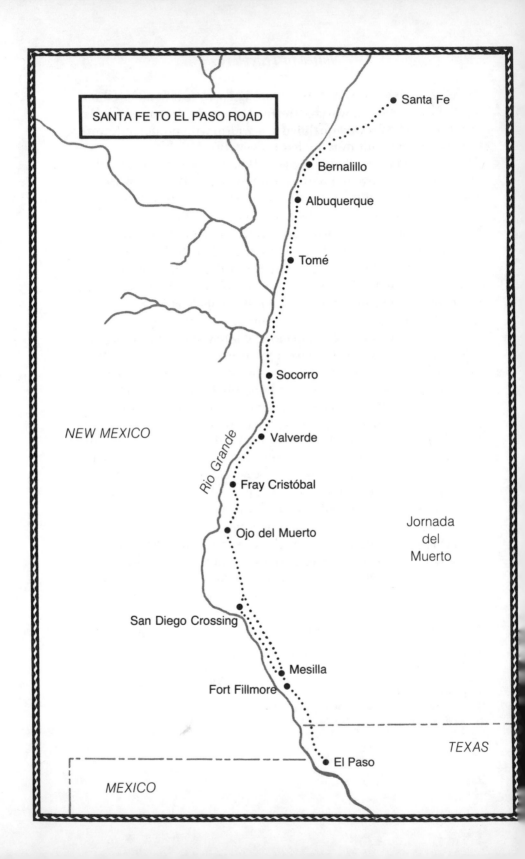

SANTA FE TO EL PASO ROAD

Santa Fe

Bernalillo

Albuquerque

Tomé

Socorro

Valverde

Fray Cristóbal

Ojo del Muerto

San Diego Crossing

Mesilla

Fort Fillmore

El Paso

NEW MEXICO

Rio Grande

Jornada
del
Muerto

TEXAS

MEXICO

ommended as a man of energy, intelligence, and firmness, and he is extensively known and respected by the Indians; so that there are few men well qualified to perform with punctuality and success the difficult duty he has undertaken." [12]

By October 25 Skillman was back in San Antono, where the news of his venture met with warm optimism. The *San Antonio Ledger* praised "this energetic and enterprising frontiersman," declaring that he had "our hearty good wishes for his success in his new enterprise." In Austin the *Texas State Gazette* expressed its gratification over the turn of events, although the editor was doubtless chagrined to admit that San Antonio and not his own town would be the new line's eastern terminus. Still, declared the *Gazette*, "our intercourse with the Territory of New Mexico, as well as with the intermediate country of El Paso, has become of such importance as to demand the attention of the Government, and we trust that before a great while, the mail facilities over this route will be expedited to at least once a month." [13]

This last comment may have been a dig at the relative infrequency of the service. The contract called for the mail to leave Santa Fe on the first of each month and arrive in San Elizario by the eleventh. It would depart that place on the twelfth of every other month and reach San Antonio on the last day of the same month. The westbound mail was to leave Bexar on the first of every other month and pull into San Elizario on the nineteenth. Northbound, it would depart on the twentieth of each month and strike Santa Fe by the end of that month. Santa Fe would be served twice as often as San Antonio, but it was still a vast improvement over the old arrangements. Skillman announced that he would carry the first mail packet west on November 3. By the spring he hoped to have a string of coaches running to carry passengers over the route as well. [14]

Skillman made good time on his first ride, reaching Santa Fe by November 24. The trip had not been without incident, however. He was not far from striking the Rio Grande when he met a party of forty Comanches. "These fellows had just come

[12] Washington, D.C., *Daily National Intelligencer*, Sept. 22, 1851.
[13] *San Antonio Ledger*, Oct. 30, 1851; Austin *Texas State Gazette*, Nov. 15, 1851.
[14] *San Antonio Ledger*, Oct. 30, 1851; Austin *Texas State Gazette*, Nov. 15, 1851.

from a marauding expedition into Durango," reported a Santa Fe correspondent. "They had with them six hundred head of horses, and several captive children. This band was from the Northern Comanche horde, who live in the southeastern part of New Mexico. But recently four Americans have been murdered near the place where Capt. S. met these Comanches. They had been caught and killed asleep."[15] Evidently the Comanches were content with their plunder and did not care to challenge Skillman. He must have pitied the stolen children, but he was in no position to help them. Within a few years some of them were probably shooting arrows at his coaches.

The record suggests that Skillman purchased some equipment for his line while in Santa Fe, for on December 6 he composed an advertisement for publication in the newspapers along the route. The "Notice to Travelers" stated that "the undersigned, Mail Contractor from San Antonio, Texas, to Santa Fe, would respectfully inform the traveling public that he has placed upon the line the best kind of stock and good comfortable spring carriages for the accommodation of passengers." In the schedule that followed Skillman changed his departure date from Santa Fe to the second of each month but otherwise hewed to the same routine. Fares from San Antonio to Santa Fe ran $125; those from El Paso to Bexar were $100. From Santa Fe to El Paso a seat cost $30. All passengers were allowed forty pounds of baggage. Monthly mail service to San Antonio was promised in the near future, as well as a "small train of light wagons."[16]

Skillman may well have acquired his carriages from Jacob Hall, who had been operating a regular stage service between Santa Fe and Independence, Missouri, since 1849. The vehicles purchased in Santa Fe were probably intended solely for the route between that town and San Elizario, for not until January, 1853, did Skillman advertise the departure of "four-horse coaches" from both San Antonio and Santa Fe. Even this was not an accurate indication of when wheeled vehicles appeared on

[15] St. Louis *Missouri Republican*, Jan. 5, 1852. The article quoted a letter from Santa Fe, dated Nov. 30, 1851.

[16] San Antonio *Western Texan*, Sept. 23, 1852; Robert H. Thonhoff, *San Antonio Stage Lines, 1847–1881*, 9–10.

the eastern portion of the line, for there were references to their use as early as January, 1852.[17]

Given the paucity of evidence, it is impossible to say whether or not the "light wagons" referred to in Skillman's original notice described conveyances for passengers or freight. Coaches were readily available in San Antonio at the time he began his operations. The firm of Brown and Tarbox had been conducting a stage service between that city and Houston as early as February, 1847. They also built coaches for their own use and sale to the public.[18]

Whatever the details of Skillman's procurement of equipment, his mail service was as welcome in Santa Fe as it had been in the settlements to the south and east. One resident noted that in addition to the new benefits to be enjoyed locally from its inauguration, "for Texas, and indeed New Orleans, and some of the Southern States, this mail will be a favorable way of communicating with Santa Fe, at least every alternate month." The army welcomed the line's coming also, for it relieved the posts along the Rio Grande in New Mexico from the necessity of maintaining a dispatch service between the garrisons. The forts between Bexar and El Paso could also take advantage of the civilian enterprise. In December, orders were issued at the department headquarters at Fort Marcy, directing that all military mail was to be sent in Skillman's pouches and that escorts were to be provided for the service as required.[19]

Skillman's name was much bandied about by the press, and he deserved full credit for organizing the new express line, but it was no longer a business limited to a handful of adventurers. Other men joined him as outriders, guards, and drivers. Some of

[17] W. Eugene Hollon, *The Southwest*, 198; LeRoy R. Hafen, *The Overland Mail, 1848–1869*, 73. The Austin and San Antonio newspapers of the early 1850s are the best sources for detailing Skillman's activities. Though he was certainly an intelligent person, Skillman left no company records or personal papers behind to aid the historian. Despite his public prominence at the time, he remained a rather enigmatic figure, and not even a photograph of him survives.

[18] San Antonio *Western Texan*, Apr. 1, 1853; Thonhoff, *Stage Lines*, 5–9.

[19] St. Louis *Missouri Republican*, Jan. 5, 1852. The journal quoted a letter from Santa Fe, dated Nov. 30, 1851. The military escorts were the start of an uneven relationship between the soldiers and the stage lines.

his new employees died on the trail before their names could ever become part of the public record. The identities of a few have come down to us. Bigfoot Wallace and Edward Westfall were still with the company. Louis Oge, Tom Rife, Bradford Daily, Benjamin Sanford, Adolph Fry, and a dozen others signed on as well. Most of the rank and file are forgotten now, but in their own time they commanded respect for the risks they ran in performing a vital service for the residents of those isolated frontier settlements.

Despite its promising beginning, the mail company was soon mired deeply in trouble. Beyond Fort Clark on Las Moras Creek, 125 miles west of San Antonio, there were no relay stations for over 500 miles until the Rio Grande villages below El Paso hove into sight. Between that place and Santa Fe there was only a scattering of army posts and tiny villages. The various bands of Indians along the route soon found a coach and its herd of spare animals too tempting a prey to resist.

People along the mail road knew that Skillman was running a risk, but then virtually any business enterprise undertaken in that harsh country was a gamble against the elements and the Indians. Skillman remained in Santa Fe as the new year opened to prepare a depot for the care of his stock and equipment. The mule dealers, carpenters, and wheelwrights of the town counted on profiting from his losses.

There is no record of the first departure of southbound mail from Santa Fe on January 2, 1852, but the second westbound mail from San Antonio must have made it off on schedule, although it never reached its destination. When the mail party was reckoned overdue at San Elizario, a heavily armed search party probed the mountains downriver and found a pile of cold ashes surrounded by charred wheels. A battered hat with a bullet hole in its crown lay nearby. Tucked inside its sweatband were some papers bearing the stage conductor's name.[20]

It would be some time before Skillman learned of the trag-

---

[20] St. Louis *Missouri Republican*, Mar. 27, 1852, quoting a letter from Santa Fe, dated Feb. 29, 1852; Washington, D.C., *Daily National Intelligencer*, Apr. 2, 1852; John S. Calhoun to Luke Lea, Santa Fe, New Mexico, Feb. 29, 1852, in Annie H. Abel, ed., *The Official Correspondence of John S. Calhoun*, 485–87.

edy, for the Apaches next turned their attention to the road between El Paso and Santa Fe. The barren stretch of trail between
the hamlet of Doña Ana and the campground of Fray Cristóbal
lived up to its title, Jornada del Muerto.

At dawn on January 25 the mail party left its overnight
camp at Laguna del Muerto and drove north with an escort from
the Second Dragoons. The whites had gone only a short distance
when they struck an Apache ambush. After a twenty-minute
fight the soldiers and expressmen had to abandon the coach and
retreat southward. Three whites had been killed and another
reeled in his saddle with a wound. Troops from Fort Conrad
mounted an immediate pursuit of the warriors, but they had
vanished into the wastelands with their booty.[21]

That day was a bad one for Skillman. In the evening a band
of Indians slipped past the sentries at nearby Fort Inge to steal a
herd of mules from his new relay station on Leona Creek. A San
Antonio merchant named George Giddings was camped at the
station and lost his stock as well. It would not be the last time
that Skillman and Giddings shared the loss of their property to
the tribesmen.[22]

Skillman departed Santa Fe on February 1 with an escort
and five passengers riding in two ambulances. They reached San
Elizario by the eleventh, and the contractor gave orders to have
the northbound mail leave ahead of schedule in an effort to make
up for the time lost by the earlier coach's destruction. The Santa
Fe mail wheeled out of the settlement early that month and ran
into another Apache ambush at the same site on the Jornada del
Muerto. The escorting troopers repulsed the Indians, but casualties among the coach's team forced them to return to Doña Ana
for replacements before finally reaching Santa Fe on the evening
of the twenty-eighth.[23]

The Apaches kept the western end of the line in turmoil for

[21] Calhoun to Lea, Jan. 31, 1852; Calhoun to Noah Webster, Feb. 29, 1852, *Correspondence*, 473–77, 485–86.

[22] St. Louis *Missouri Republican*, Feb. 24, 1852, citing the New Orleans *Picayune*,
Feb. 14, 1852, and the *San Antonio Ledger*, n.d.

[23] Calhoun to Webster, Feb. 29, 1852; Calhoun to Lea, Feb. 29, 1852, *Correspondence*, 485–89; St. Louis *Missouri Republican*, Mar. 26–27, 1852.

several months afterward by attacking the next coach to traverse the Jornada from El Paso and repeatedly raiding Skillman's corral in the settlement. The El Pasoans petitioned Governor P. Hansbrough Bell to have troops stationed in the valley to deter future raids, for "lives have been lost, and property of great value has from time to time, been destroyed and stolen." Bigfoot Wallace and Preston Pollory, a Skillman employee, signed the petition.[24]

Despite the perpetual turmoil created by the Indians, the mail kept rolling between Bexar and New Mexico. Things quieted down by the spring, but the settlers still kept up their guard. At a meeting in Magoffinsville on July 28 they appointed Skillman, Simeon Hart, James Magoffin, and several other leading citizens to compile a report on Indian depredations. All the men on the panel were individuals of education, property, and influence in the community. Skillman's presence among them was an index to his reputation among a people who were both daring and eminently practical.[25]

There had been a welcome hiatus from the Indian raids for several months, and by August an army officer posted on the route remarked that "to show how small the danger on the San Antonio road has grown, the mail with six men each month passes up and down the Road." As if challenged by this casual attitude, the warrior bands set out to prove that they were still to be feared.

Early in September the Comanches ambushed Bigfoot Wallace's coaches as they wound up the narrow canyon of the Devil's River, forcing the Texans to return to Fort Clark after a bitter fight. Wallace requested an escort from the post commander but was told that there were no troops to spare from the garrison. The expressmen backtracked another forty miles to Fort Inge and received a similar response. The disgusted Wallace sent word to San Antonio from Leona Station that "I will return today

[24]Robert W. Frazer, ed., *Mansfield on the Condition of the Western Forts*, 72; La Grange *Texas Monument*, May 5, 1852, citing the *San Antonio Ledger*, n.d.; St. Louis *Missouri Republican*, May 22, 1852; New Orleans *Picayune*, May 17, 1852; *San Antonio Ledger*, Apr. 29, 1852; Washington, D.C., *Daily National Intelligencer*, May 20, 1852; Winfrey, *Indian Papers*, 159–60.

[25]*San Antonio Ledger*, Sept. 2, 1852; Austin *Texas State Gazette*, Sept. 11, 1852; St. Louis *Missouri Republican*, Aug. 3, 1852.

with three hired men, which makes our number nine, and if we cannot clear the road we shall fight it out with them, and if any are left to make their way to El Paso for the return mail."[26]

Wallace had made it through to the Pass on his second try, but the catalog of troubles continued to grow as the year edged toward its end. Despite the mounting Indian troubles, Skillman kept his coaches moving to provide reasonably punctual and rapid service along the route. The contractor prepared for a major revision of his operations that would require yet another trip to Washington.[27]

He probably left El Paso for the east with the regularly scheduled mail on October 12. Upon reaching the Pecos River he met a party of six Comanches bearing a flag of truce. The Indians claimed that they were bound for Presidio del Norte to do a little peaceful trading. The band's leader was clad in the full regimental uniform of an American army officer, and the braves' mounts were all suspiciously fresh and well-groomed. The Texans suspected that this was part of the same group that had ambushed Wallace the month before, but the Comanches offered no threat at this meeting, and Skillman let them go in peace while he hastened on to the Gulf Coast.[28]

By December 2 he was in Washington to renegotiate his contract with Postmaster General Samuel D. Hubbard. On December 10 the contract was amended to provide a new subsidy of $28,000 a year. Commencing in January, 1853, a mail was to leave both Santa Fe and San Antonio in the middle of each month. The *Daily National Intelligencer* applauded the return of the "steady, energetic, and reliable contractor."[29]

A new contract was probably not the only thing Skillman took home to Texas. During his visit to the Northeast he apparently met a representative of the Sharps Rifle Manufacturing

[26] *San Antonio Ledger*, Sept. 23, 1852; Marshall *Texas Republican*, Oct. 16, 1852; New Orleans *Picayune*, Sept. 28, 1852; Washington, D.C., *Daily National Intelligencer*, Dec. 2, 1852; Wilbarger, *Depredations*, 115–23.

[27] Frazer, *Mansfield*, 74; Annie H. Abel, ed., "Indian Affairs in New Mexico under the Administration of William Carr Lane," *New Mexico Historical Review* 16 (July, 1941): 221, 228.

[28] New Orleans *Picayune*, Nov. 18, 1852.

[29] Washington, D.C., *Daily National Intelligencer*, Dec. 2, 14, 1852.

Company of Hartford, Connecticut. Skillman had seen Sharps rifles in use among the members of the American Boundary Survey Commission when John R. Bartlett led it through El Paso in the fall of 1850, and he was impressed with the weapons' accuracy and rapidity of fire. The Sharps Company had just begun manufacturing an improved model of their carbine for the army, and Skillman managed to purchase a case of ten weapons from an early production lot. The new Model 1851 "boxlock" carbines were solidly built and hard-hitting .52-caliber breechloaders. They would give the mail coaches' guards a welcome advantage over the Indians.[30]

As Skillman returned to the Southwest, he must have felt renewed confidence in his company's future. The Post Office Department had kept its trust in him despite the losses and delays inflicted by the Indians. His fee had been more than doubled, and he had acquired a small arsenal of some of the finest rifles in the world to safeguard his enterprise. The year 1853 promised to be profitable.

Skillman's hopes for the new contract were probably based more on cautious optimism than sober retrospection. The first months of the mail contract had been rocky ones, and nothing had changed to indicate that the situation would improve. The threat of continued Indian depredations persisted, and as the months passed he would face an additional danger from a border dispute between the United States and Mexico that seemed to foreshadow yet another war to determine ownership of the Southwest. The region that Skillman's coaches traversed was a part of the Union, but its population remained essentially Mexican in language, culture, and political sympathy. Suspicion and animosity still colored relations between the land's former stewards and its new masters. Violence was still a real possibility whenever Anglos and Mexicans were thrown together.

Skillman was not one who took frequent counsel of his fears, however, and the mail line continued to operate with increasing regularity and dispatch. Throughout January and February the

---

[30]Wayne R. Austerman, "Arms of the El Paso Mail," *Gun Report* 25 (Jan., 1980): 48–51; Frank Sellers, *Sharps Firearms*, 30, 43–49; Rywell, *Sharps Rifle*, 37; *San Antonio Ledger*, Dec. 30, 1852.

coaches arrived in San Antonio and Santa Fe as expected. The Indians were agreeably quiet that season and would remain so until the spring allowed them to fatten their ponies and range down the plains once again to haunt the emigrant trails. The coachmen enjoyed this respite and managed to improve their time on the road considerably. On March 4 a stage rolled into San Antonio after a record passage of twenty-three and one-half days from Santa Fe, and only sixteen days from El Paso.[31]

This speed depended in part on the new armament carried by the mail's escorts. It was probably on his initial westbound trip after returning from Washington that Skillman first impressed the Apaches with the power of his lethal new weapons. The mail party had crossed the Pecos and forged deeply into what were then known as the Limpia Mountains. A band of Mescaleros attacked the whites as they neared a grove of oaks that garnished the rocky base of a slope flanking the road. The Texans halted and opened fire. The Apaches retired to what they assumed was a safe distance out of range, dismounted, and began to taunt the expressmen. One cocky warrior stood behind his horse, leaned over the saddle, and dared the plainsmen to come out in the open and fight.

Henry Skillman slipped a cartridge in the breech of his new Sharps carbine, trimmed its sights, and aimed carefully. The Sharps barked, and the Apache pitched backward with a bullet through his head. His stunned comrades picked up his body and quickly retreated beyond the reach of Skillman's "medicine gun."

This encounter became a minor legend, and Skillman liked to boast of his feat to his drinking companions at one of the army posts along the route. "He had a good supply of whisky aboard," recalled one, "and repeated the story several times, taking a drink each time. He said he saw the Indian standing there . . . and fired and knocked him ten feet. He then took another drink, and in repeating the story said he knocked him twenty yards. He kept repeating the story and his drinks, each time increasing the

---

[31] San Antonio *Western Texan*, Jan. 20, 1853; *Santa Fe Gazette*, Jan. 29, 1853; New Orleans *Daily Picayune*, Mar. 29, 1853; Ralph P. Bieber, ed., "Letters of William Carr Lane," *New Mexico Historical Review* 3 (April, 1928): 187–94. The January mail left Santa Fe on the morning of the second.

distance he fired and the number of feet he knocked him, and finally closed the recital by saying, 'When I drew a bead on that Indian he was about eleven hundred yards off and was looking over his horse so that I could only see his head, and I took him right between the eyes, and sir, I knocked him more than forty rods.'" Despite Skillman's later boozy hyperbole, it was a shot to be proud of, and the scene of the fight is still known as Skillman's Grove.[32]

The Apaches continued to keep their distance. On April 14 Captain Tom Rife pulled into Bexar from the west after a quiet trip that had shaved even more time off the normal length of the run. He had left San Elizario only thirteen and a half days before, and he brought news that "El Paso bids fair to become the theatre of a speck of war," as Mexican troops were assembled on the south bank of the Rio Grande. Excitement grew in the eastern settlements as word of the mounting threat spread.[33]

The crisis had been gestating since 1848. Men had long discussed the possibility of building a transcontinental railroad across the Southwest. The U.S. Boundary Commission had been dispatched in 1850 with the task of marking the border and exploring a railroad route from Texas to California. John R. Bartlett, the expedition's chief, turned in a lackluster performance but did succeed in discovering that faulty maps and ambiguous wording in the Treaty of Guadalupe Hidalgo had placed the southern border of the United States along a line north of the only passes through the mountains to the east of California that were suitable for a railbed. Bartlett, a Whig appointee, was accused of pegging the boundary too far north in order to prevent the adoption of a southern rail route. The southern Democrats saw a pet dream being threatened and dire consequences for the nation if the boundary line remained unaltered.[34]

The confusion over New Mexico's southern boundary

[32] Zenas R. Bliss, "Memoirs," Zenas R. Bliss Papers, Barker Texas History Center, University of Texas at Austin, 1:244. Bliss was posted at Fort Davis in 1855 and heard Skillman tell the story there.

[33] Austin Texas State Gazette, April 16, 1853; Clarksville Northern Standard, May 7, 1853. For the March mail's arrival see the New Orleans Daily Picayune, Mar. 29, 1853.

[34] William H. Goetzmann, When the Eagle Screamed, 88–91.

aroused the concern of newly appointed territorial governor William Carr Lane. Mexico still claimed sovereignty over the strip of land west of the Rio Grande and generally south of the Gila. On March 13 Lane issued a proclamation in the adobe village of Doña Ana, informing the Mexicans that he would use force if necessary to retain American possession of the disputed territory.

Stung by Lane's belligerence, President Santa Anna ordered Governor Angel Trias of Chihuahua to move troops into the Mesilla Valley to counter any overt actions by the Americans. An advance guard of lancers rode north through El Paso and camped in Mesilla late in March, having passed directly by the nervous Yankee garrison at nearby Fort Fillmore.[35]

On April 24 the westbound mail stage reached El Paso and found Governor Trias on hand with a thousand soldiers. He was headed for Mesilla, and the expressmen pressed on to carry the alarming news to Santa Fe. Skillman must have been upset to find Mexican cavalry deployed along his stage route. Trias had certainly not forgotten that it was Skillman who had twice guided American armies southward from El Paso to seize his capital city.[36]

Fortunately an armed confrontation never took place. Colonel Edwin V. Sumner simply refused to let his troops be used in support of Lane's proclamation. Sumner had been acting governor until Lane's arrival in the territory, and the two men despised each other from the start. Trias showed forebearance as well when he left his army below the Rio Grande and rode into Mesilla with only a small escort. The situation evolved into a game of mutual watching and waiting, although Bradford Daily helped to steel American determination to keep control of the area when his coach carried news into El Paso of a silver strike only fifteen miles west of Las Cruces.[37]

[35] Calvin Horn, *New Mexico's Troubled Years*, 46–47; William A. Keleher, *Turmoil in New Mexico, 1846–1868*, 131; George Griggs, *History of the Mesilla Valley or the Gadsden Purchase*, 57. The mail from Santa Fe passed Fort Fillmore at about this time, according to Griggs's sources.

[36] Abel, "Indian Affairs," 210, 339.

[37] New Orleans *Daily Picayune*, July 20, 1853; Austin *Texas State Gazette*, May 21,

While the border crisis simmered, the stages continued to move between the opposing forces with no interference from the Mexicans. East of El Paso the Indians opened their spring campaign against the whites, with Bigfoot Wallace meeting attacks both going and coming on the April runs.[38]

The next mail into San Antonio was carrying an unusual passenger when it overtook a group of travelers at the Pecos on June 1. German adventurer Julius Froebel recorded that "the mail from El Paso passed us here. Two carriages, each with four mules, coachmen, guard and passengers all fully armed. One of the passengers was a little girl of three or four years old, who— entrusted to the coachman, and with no other companion—was thus sent the 700 miles from El Paso to San Antonio." Froebel was impressed by the Texans' solicitude. "The other passengers, however, joined in taking care of her, and it was touching to see how these rough, bearded men, with their pistols and daggers, supplied the place of a mother's care to the tender little creature."[39]

Skillman had been in Santa Fe that spring, doubtless keeping a wary eye for any sign of a flare-up in the impasse with the Mexicans. On June 21 he took a coach south for the Pass and Bexar. The journey afforded him a chance to check the line's operation while he prepared for another trip to Washington, and a session of lobbying with the postmaster general.[40]

The town that Skillman left was the linchpin of a rich trade with both St. Louis and Chihuahua, but little of the wealth that passed through was reflected in its appearance. Nestled in a valley shaded by mountains whose slopes were dappled with thick stands of cedar and pine, and blessed with the clear flow of a snow-fed stream, Santa Fe itself was decrepit. Its streets were crooked, narrow, and usually choked with refuse. "A wretched

---

June 4, 18, 25, 1853. The *Gazette* of June 18 reported the westbound mail at Live Oak Spring on May 23.

[38] San Antonio *Western Texan*, May 12, 1853; Frazer, *Mansfield*, 74.

[39] Julius Froebel, *Seven Years Travel in Central America, Northern Mexico and the Far West of the United States*, 417.

[40] New Orleans *Daily Picayune*, July 21, 1853.

collection of mud houses, without a single building of stone. . . . The appearance of the town defies description," noted a visitor, "and I can compare it to nothing but a delapidated brick kiln or a prairie-dog town." There were men of property there, of course, and the interiors of their homes were often richly furnished, but the drab adobe construction that predominated in the town made it appear to be a colony of mud daubers.[41]

The town's heart lay in its great plaza. Flanked on all sides by irrigation ditches and shaded by rows of cottonwoods, the plaza was lined by all the important public buildings. Assorted shops, numerous cantinas, and at least six churches vied for patrons on the side streets. When a caravan was in town the plaza throbbed with activity. Everything from Hawken rifles to New England primers could be purchased at a healthy markup in price. Missourian Preston Beck kept a store near the square and served as Skillman's local agent.[42]

Skillman and Beck said their farewells and the coach trundled out of town and swung south for the first leg of a 337-mile haul into El Paso. The road it followed had been opened by Oñate's pikemen over two centuries before and had changed little since then. Rutted and worn by the wheels and hooves of innumerable trains from Chihuahua, the trail snaked down to join the valley of the Rio Grande at the pueblo of Santo Domingo, and then hugged the river's east bank for a passage of over a hundred miles until the ancient camping ground of Fray Cristóbal hove into view, 180 miles from the plaza at Santa Fe. Only a few forlorn hamlets lay in between, with neither a station nor inn on the entire route.[43]

Fray Cristóbal and its namesake mountain marked the northern end of the Jornada del Muerto. Barring sparse seasonal rains to fill the Laguna del Muerto, twenty-six miles below, the next day's travel took Skillman across better than a hundred miles of

[41] LeRoy R. Hafen, ed., *Ruxton of the Rockies*, 180; Gregg, *Commerce*, 102–103; Max L. Moorehead, *New Mexico's Royal Road*, 102–103.

[42] Keleher, *Turmoil*, 128; San Antonio *Western Texan*, Apr. 1, 1853.

[43] Moorehead, *Royal Road*, 106–111; Gregg, *Commerce*, 268–69; Hafen, *Ruxton*, 170–80.

waterless plains, flanked by two mountain ranges, and plagued
with Apache war parties. Once they cleared the Jornada the
travelers joined the river again at Sierra de San Diego. Thirty-
one miles beyond lay the settlement of Doña Ana, and the disputed village of Mesilla, with nearby Fort Fillmore still showing
the flag to Trias's dragoons. The Rancho del Bracito, site of Doniphan's victory in 1846, came up next with its distinctive cluster of
round-topped hills. Thirty-three miles to the south lay El Paso
and a welcome at Magoffinsville, the prosperous hacienda of
Joseph Magoffin.[44]

The stage may have had a minor brush with the Apaches as
it came down the Jornada, for Skillman paused at his friend's
settlement to write a letter of appreciation to the Sharps Rifle
Company. "The ten Sharps' carbines purchased of you were all
put to immediate use in arming my escort," he related, "and for
range, accuracy, and rapidity of firing, they are far superior to
any arm known. They have gone through what an ordnance officer would term a pretty severe field test, without the least in-
jury." Skillman went on to note that "having been a frontier man
for fourteen years, I had occasion to look after a bosom companion to stand by me in case of life or death; and hence I have given
some little attention to the subject of firearms, and I think I can
tolerably well appreciate their excellence; and in my search after
such a comforter, I have found no arm that in all its attributes
begins to compare with the Sharps' arm and for army, navy, caravan or sporting service, it is sure to take and hold the front
rank." The plainsman's testimonial received a prominent place in
the Sharps Company's catalog.[45]

The express did not tarry long at the Pass. By the thirtieth
it was back on the road again, and from that point on to San Antonio the party consisted of its regular complement of "two ambulances, twenty-two mules, and eight men." Since there were
still no stations west of Fort Clark, and safety lay in maintaining
a rapid and regular pace, "the mode of traveling is to divide the
twenty-four hours into three equal parts and travel fifteen or

    [44] Hafen, *Ruxton*, 162–66; Moorehead, *Royal Road*, 11–13; Gregg, *Commerce*,
269–73.
    [45] Rywell, *Sharps Rifle*, 37.

more miles in each division, thus averaging about fifty miles a day."[46]

From El Paso the party bore south past Ysleta and Socorro to San Elizario before finally swinging away from the Rio Grande at a point 104 miles below El Paso. The trail entered the narrow twisting pass that ran for nearly 10 miles through the hogbacked mountains that fronted on the river. Once through that defile, the road forked to the southeast and ran for an equal distance down a broad canyon before heeling east again around the lower end of Devil Ridge. Another 18 miles and a steep ascent up a mountainside carried the mail party into Eagle Springs.

Until they reached the Pecos it would be a journey of long, wearing days spent following the rutted track from one water-hole to the next through rolling plains and gloomy mountain canyons and passes. El Muerto, Barrel Springs, Point of Rocks, Limpia Creek, Wild Rose Pass, and Barilla Springs fell away behind them as they cleared the Limpia range and struck out across the flatlands for two of the richest water sources between the Pecos and the Rio Grande.[47]

At Leon Holes they passed one of the few places of green shade in that greasewood-studded expanse of flatlands. The holes were described by one traveler as "a deep moorland tarn, whither troops of antelopes come over the plains to drink. It is said never to have been fathomed, through sounded with a line of five hundred feet." As welcome as the deep waters were, they were a minor oasis when compared with the liquid riches to be found nine miles to the east at Comanche Springs. One of the largest flows in the Southwest, it daily poured sixty million gallons into the baked earth to make the camping ground one of the most strategic locations on the entire route.[48]

As might be expected, there were frequent encounters

---

[46] New Orleans *Daily Picayune*, July 21, 1853.

[47] Roscoe Conkling and Margaret B. Conkling, *The Butterfield Overland Mail, 1857–1869*, 2: 31–56; Kathryn S. McMillen, "The San Antonio–San Diego Mail Line in Texas, 1857–1861" (M.A. thesis, University of Texas at Austin, 1960), 127–58; Escal F. Duke, "A Description of the Route from San Antonio to El Paso by Captain Edward S. Meyer," *West Texas Historical Association Yearbook* 49 (Oct., 1973): 128–41.

[48] Conkling and Conkling, *Butterfield Mail*, 2:15–21; Carlyle G. Raht, *The Romance of Davis Mountains and Big Bend Country*, 220–21.

there between the whites and Indians. Unwary emigrants were fortunate if all they lost were a few head of stock. A pilgrim who passed the site only a few months after Skillman found the skeletons of five men who had lowered their guard as they enjoyed the cooling waters. Such morbid relics abounded nearby. One cattleman told of how "the bones of a man was found, the guide was acquainted with the man; on the knee cap & foot the muscels still remain, although it has been three years since he was killed." [49]

Skillman may have experienced a guarded encounter with the tribesmen at the watering place, for he subsequently mentioned having met several bands on the road and stated that "their object seemed to be the robbery of parties bound for California." They offered no threat to the heavily armed caravan at that point. [50]

From Comanche Springs the party rode on across an increasingly forbidding landscape dotted with soaring, turreted mesas. The trail led them down a long draw in the lowlands to Upper and Lower Escondido Springs, the last reliable water sources until they gained the Pecos, 402 miles east of El Paso. Aside from the bold, caprock-nippled thrust of Squawteat Peak, there was little to distract the expressmen as they followed the rocky trace through the thin-leafed haze of thorn in the dry creek bottoms, weaving between the sugarloaf hills and wind-scoured mesas that shimmered in the ghost-dance of the empty heat. [51]

When the caravan reached the Pecos, both men and animals drank sparingly of its brackish waters. The river often had a violently laxative effect on those who were unused to the minerals it carried. From the Pecos's west bank the road curved south and east, hugging the river as it flowed fitfully past the mouth of Riffle Canyon to reach Pecos Spring.

[49] J. Evetts Haley, ed., "A Log of the Texas-California Cattle Trail, 1854," *Southwestern Historical Quarterly* 35 (Jan., 1932): 222.

[50] New Orleans *Daily Picayune*, July 27, 1853, citing the *Galveston Daily News*, n.d.

[51] Haley, "Log," 22; Douglas S. Watson, ed., "To California through Texas and Mexico: The Diary and Letters of Thomas B. Eastland and Joseph G. Eastland, His Son," *California Historical Quarterly* 18 (June, 1939): 115, 135.

Not five miles from the spring the road brought them to a ford on the river that cut through the summer shallows. After splashing across the trickle of nearby Live Oak Creek, the rigs and their teams were laboriously maneuvered up the slope of a steep, rock-strewn hill to the crowning bluffs that overlooked the Pecos from the east. Once up on the high ground, the caravan had an easy run across a broad and level tableland to the northeast and then again to the south, until it entered another mountain-lapped valley to arrive at Howard's Well, an excellent campground for water and grazing, but also a favored haunt of the Indians.

More broken country lay to the southeast as the road dipped into a long draw that ran into the Devil's River valley at a point known as the Eighteenth Crossing, and close to a small backwater called Beaver Lake. The river's course flanked the road as it continued southward past Pecan Springs to the landmark of Second Crossing. Leaving the river there, the Texans followed the ruts through a range of rolling hills and stunted limestone peaks, finally reaching one of the most dreaded defiles on the trail. Dead Man's Pass was narrow, rocky, and choked with brush. The forlorn cluster of graves at its southern end told of other travelers who had died there under the Comanche lances.[52]

The dry springs at Palos Blancos and the damp bed of California Creek came up before them as they headed for the Painted Caves and the lower ford of the Devil's River. Once across the river for the final time, they could count on finding a lush haven at San Felipe Springs, where fifty million gallons of water gushed forth each day to sire a creek that ran strongly for a dozen miles to the south before joining the Rio Grande. As always where

[52] McMillen, "Mail Line," 121–30; August Santleben, *A Texas Pioneer*, 100; Jesse Sumpter, *Life of Jesse Sumpter, The Oldest Citizen of Eagle Pass, Texas*, 5; Lt. Colonel Thomas B. Hunt, "Journal Showing the Route Taken by the Government Train Accompanying the 15th Regiment, U.S. Infantry from Austin, Tex. to Ft. Craig, N.M. and Returning to San Antonio July–December, 1869," RG 77, NARS. Howard's Well is located on the Pierce Ranch in southern Crockett County, southwest of Ozona. The steep hill overlooks the present site of Fort Lancaster State Park, east of Sheffield. Modern highway 163 traverses Dead Man's Pass. The modern road route through the Devil's River country north of Del Rio approximates the course of the mail road up to the deserted village of Juno on Highway 163.

water was abundant in that parched country, there was plenty of shade, pasturage, game, and Indian sign.

With the cottonwoods and rippling pools falling behind to the west, Skillman's train pressed on across Sycamore Creek and the Pedro Pinto ford to arrive at Fort Clark and the struggling settlement that had sprung up around Oscar B. Brackett's store. San Antonio lay only a little more than 120 miles away by that point, and little time was wasted at the post. With Turkey Creek and the Nueces falling behind, it was an easy run into Fort Inge and Leona Station. After a pause at Reading Black's store and attendant village, the Texans were ready to start again.[53]

A sandstone shelf carried them across the Frio without wetting the mules' harnesses, and then they breasted the Sabinal to arrive at Hammer's Station and a greeting from the news-hungry settlers of the community. There was a fair amount of other traffic on the road by them, with long trains of freight wagons stretching out across the prairie as they carried supplies to the outlying army posts and frontier villages from Bexar.

A seven-hour drive from Leona Station brought Skillman into the hamlet of D'Hanis, a colony of Alsatian settlers established a decade before. At Joseph Ney's house they picked up fresh teams and quickly left the cluster of stone and picket cabins behind as they crossed the Hondo and then Verde Creek. The next stop was Castroville, the first major town to grow up on the trail west of Bexar. It was an Alsatian colony as well, but unlike D'Hanis it enjoyed an air of prosperous confidence and orderly neatness. The coaches creaked to a halt at John Vance's store and post office to surrender the mail bags, while the stagemen walked across the road to enjoy a hurried meal at the Tarde Hotel. The high-columned verandah that fronted the building and the crisp linen and succulent food of Clarisse Tarde's table told them that they were at last back on the fringes of civilization.

They had barely left Vance's yard when the road dropped

[53] Hunt, "Journal," 32–38; McMillen, "Mail Line," 109–124; Ike Moore, *The Life and Diary of Reading W. Black: A History of Early Uvalde*, 14–16. San Felipe Springs is located on the grounds of the Del Rio Country Club. Fort Clark is a private resort, and Brackettville remains a sleepy adobe village. The town of Uvalde stands a few miles north of Fort Inge.

down to the stony ford on the Medina, snaked through the shallows, and then climbed abruptly up the far bank to lose itself in the rolling hills beyond. The mules settled into an easy rhythm of a pull over a good road that ate up the remaining twenty-four miles into San Antonio. Less than five hours later they thundered into the plaza and slowed their pace as the reins tightened and Skillman brought the train to a slow halt in front of the post office.[54]

The mail's arrival from the border settlements always drew a crowd in Bexar, and one resident noted with pride on this July 10 that Skillman had been only twenty days on the road from Santa Fe, and but twelve days from El Paso. "That is traveling for the mule telegraph—only 1,100 miles!"[55]

Skillman still had many more miles to go on that trip. Leaving the line in his brother's care, he hurried on to the coast and caught a steamer to New Orleans, arriving there on July 20. The *Daily Picayune* hailed him as "the active and indefatigable contractor" and cited his brave exploits on the frontier. Once more he paused only long enough to find transportation to the East and then slipped downriver to the Gulf on another vessel. By early August he was in Washington. It is not hard to imagine the effect he must have had upon the strollers along Pennsylvania Avenue as he stalked through the city on his way to the postmaster general's office. He probably put away his buckskins and dressed as a gentleman of consequence, but there was no mistaking the fact that he was Henry Skillman. Standing six feet tall, and packing 220 pounds of hard muscle and bone on a frame bronzed by the desert sun, he walked with the purposeful stride of a man who made his own luck. Above a full, sandy-colored beard his eyes looked out upon the world with the feral gaze of a prairie hawk.[56]

If he startled the clerks he also impressed Postmaster General Campbell. Skillman spoke to him once again of the line's

---

[54] Hunt, "Journal," 38–41; McMillen, "Mail Line," 99–111; Frederick Law Olmsted, *A Journey Through Texas*, 280.

[55] New Orleans *Daily Picayune*, July 20, 1853.

[56] Ibid., July 21, 1853; Washington, D.C., *Daily National Intelligencer*, Aug. 11, 1853.

progress and the severe losses in men, stock, and equipment that it had suffered. Campbell was sympathetic, although both men knew that the route would never make any money for the government and that the contractor would be lucky to squeak by on even a handsome subsidy. Skillman won his point, however, and Campbell agreed to grant an extension of the contract until June, 1854.[57]

Nothing else is known of Skillman's second trip to the East. The faith placed in him by the government was well justified, but even with its support the plainsman would face increasing odds against his success as Indians and bureaucrats combined to plague his every effort.

[57] Ibid.

CHAPTER 3

A Tangled Weave

Henry Skillman had no way of knowing that the months after his return to Texas would bring recurring threats to his company and himself from a widening circle of enemies. Skillman might have been able to tell what an Indian was going to do before the brave had decided himself, but he still had much to learn about the psychology of the bureaucrat. If he was elated over the extension of the contract with the government, his mood must have been dispelled quickly when he arrived back in San Antonio late that summer. The crisis between governors Lane and Trias was still simmering, but other conflicts had erupted along the stage route in his absence. A clash between the Mexican and American authorities over the disputed ownership of a herd of cattle and the jailing of a Texas stockman led to a brief skirmish at El Paso in mid-July. James Hammock, one of Skillman's veteran drivers, was killed in the foray. To the east, the Mescaleros were plaguing the road. At least one large emigrant party staggered into the Pass minus much of its stock and counting ten men slain by the Apaches.[1]

The situation could have been worse. On August 6, Tom Rife arrived in San Antonio with the western mail, having bluffed his way past a band of Indians en route. He brought exciting news besides that of the common, if regrettable, Indian depredations. James Magoffin was hosting a convention for prospective investors in a railroad that was projected to run from the Gulf of Mexico to the Pacific via El Paso. Magoffin's hacienda accommodated a mixture of visionaries and fortune hunters drawn there by the drum-beating of Senator Thomas Rusk.

In 1852 the Texas legislature had granted charters liberally

---

[1] New Orleans *Daily Picayune*, Aug. 19, 1853; St. Louis *Missouri Republican*, Oct. 6, 1853, citing a letter dated "Maggoffinsville, August 15, 1853."

to companies that were willing to build from any "suitable point" on the state's eastern border to the mountain gap at El Paso. Generous land grants came with every mile of track to be laid.[2] Rusk led the field in his efforts to forge the Texas link in a chain of transcontinental railroads. He alternately badgered and beguiled the directors of the Atlantic and Pacific Railroad Company of New York in an effort to secure their backing. He followed his eastern publicity campaign with a highly touted personal trip to El Paso over the route deemed most likely to be followed across the state by the future railroad. A newspaper editor and several other prominent Texans accompanied Rusk. Amid the hospitality of Magoffin's hacienda they met with local citizens and potential investors from Mexico. Over glasses of the potent Pass brandy they planned the spanning of the continent and forged the linchpin that would bind El Paso to a trail of riches from the Gulf to the Pacific.[3]

By the time Skillman returned from Washington, Rusk was back in eastern Texas to convince the legislature to grant further support to the project. Rusk foresaw the day when Texas would be linked to Illinois, Mississippi, and Louisiana as the eastern terminus of a route that would run west to the Pacific. The smell of money and coal smoke was in the air.

Henry Skillman must have looked upon all this enthusiasm with a doubting eye. Better than any other man in Texas, he knew the nature of the pitiless land beyond the settlements. The project might be pushed through if Rusk ever got together enough men and money for the job, but for the price that would be paid the rails might as well be wrought from California gold as Pennsylvania iron. Still, anything that boosted interest in travel to El Paso was certain to aid the stage line. Full coaches and heavy mail pouches would come in the wake of any effort to bring the railroad to the Rio Grande from the Sabine. Skillman left the prophets to rant and the fools to cheer while he took up

[2] New Orleans *Daily Picayune*, Aug. 19, 24, 1853; St. Louis *Missouri Republican*, Sept. 5, Oct. 6, 1853.
[3] Robert W. Russel, *Improvement of Communication with the Pacific as an Issue in American Politics, 1783–1864*, 125–26.

the reins for El Paso and set his mules to braying in mocking echo of the gullible townsmen.

The autumn passed quietly on the road between Bexar and Santa Fe. Skillman checked his stock and equipment, paid his men, and got the line in order for the winter runs. The mail continued to go through with surprisingly little interference from the Indians. November brought additional evidence of a growing confidence in the state's expansion and prosperity. The *Western Texan* advertised a change in management for the Tri-Weekly Stage Line, which had offered service between San Antonio and Indianola since October, 1852. William D. Skillman, Henry's brother, had taken over the line and promised "comfortable and substantial coaches, good horses, and careful and attentive drivers." Regular connections with steamers for New Orleans were available at Indianola. It was now possible for a traveler to ride completely across Texas in coaches owned by the Skillman brothers.[4]

On November 27, Henry Skillman personally brought the western coach into San Antonio with a distinguished passenger. From August into October, Colonel Joseph K. F. Mansfield had inspected the army posts in New Mexico from Fort Union to the north down the Rio Grande and ended his tour in San Elizario. The Austin *State Times* optimistically reported that "Colonel Mansfield is highly pleased with the trip and the route. His representation of its advantages will doubtless induce the Government to send the trains for New Mexico over this route."[5]

Mansfield's conversations with Skillman, Judge Joel Ankrim, and other citizens of the Pass impressed him with both the perils and promise of life on that frontier. In his official report the colonel urged the reestablishment of a post near El Paso, which had been undefended since October, 1851, when the garrison had marched northward to occupy Fort Fillmore. The settlement and the road that linked it to San Antonio were too important to leave unguarded, for "the trade that is carried on

---

[4] San Antonio *Western Texan*, Nov. 4, 1853.
[5] St. Louis *Missouri Republican*, Dec. 23, 1853, citing the New Orleans *True Delta*, Nov. 12, 1853, and the Austin *State Times*, Nov. 30, 1853.

over this route is great; it is one of the overland routes to California and to Chihuahua, and across this route the Indians travel at different points to commit their depredations on the Mexicans." Mansfield also called for the construction of new posts where the road left the Rio Grande just below El Paso, at the headwaters of Limpia Creek, and at Live Oak Creek, just east of the Pecos crossing. "These points," he stressed, "are selected for the abundance of grazing, wood, and *good* water they afford, and as excellent locations to overawe the Indians." With a nod to Skillman, he added that "by the establishment of these posts too, the mail contractor would be enabled to have relays of mules, and the mail might then be readily carried twice a month with much greater ease than it now can be done once a month."[6]

Mansfield also urged that Santa Fe and El Paso be served by a weekly mail. Skillman's revenues from the government were bound to increase if this proposal was adopted. The trip east from El Paso had obviously afforded the contractor a golden opportunity to win a valuable ally in his drive to obtain proper funding and protection for his operation.

As was so often the case on the mail route, bad news came fast on the heels of the good. A vengeful gang of New Mexicans chose that December to ambush and kill the Mescalero chieftain Cuentas Azules after he left a parley with the commander of Fort Fillmore. Seventeen Indians died in the treacherous attack, and although the mob's leader was subsequently arrested and indicted for murder, the Apaches cared nothing for legal niceties and were soon out for revenge. Not long afterward they caught Bigfoot Wallace's coach on the road, and only a determined show of force by the frontiersman prevented an attack on the mail.[7]

The excitement over the Indian threat had barely receded before an even greater novelty rolled into El Paso on the stage from the east. A. B. Rohman, a local merchant, had left his wife and family in St. Louis when he had gone west the year before. Now Mrs. Rohman, her daughter Amelia, and a niece, Alice

[6]Robert W. Frazer, ed., *Mansfield on the Condition of the Western Forts*, 28–29, 68–69.
[7]Rex. W. Strickland, *El Paso in 1854*, 41; A. J. Sowell, "The Life of Bigfoot Wallace," *Frontier Times* 5 (Nov., 1927): 166.

Samules, stepped down from Skillman's coach in the dusty plaza at San Elizario. If the Austrian-born woman was expecting the Rio Grande to resemble the Danube, she was in for a rude shock. Certainly the raw, arrogant thrust of the Franklin Mountains had none of the cool beauty of the alps near Salzburg. The welcome she and her companions received made up for the bleak surroundings. A white woman was a definite rarity at any time on the border. Many of the men kept Mexican mistresses or married local women and lived happily, but the sight of a European female was still a cheering thing for them. The arrival of three such ladies on the same day called for serious celebration.[8]

The valley must have seemed crowded that January as new arrivals continued to take up space in the settlements. About the same time that the Rohmans appeared, Colonel Edmund B. Alexander led four companies of the Eighth Infantry in from the desert to take up quarters in buildings leased from James Magoffin. In March, Alexander would name the new post Fort Bliss, after an officer of the regiment who died in the Mexican War. The foot soldiers were of little use in patroling the road, but their presence lent an air of order and security to Magoffinsville, and their silver was always welcome in the stores and cantinas.[9]

The new troops and womenfolk were not the end of excitement in El Paso that month. On January 14, Skillman and some of his hands crossed the river to attend a fandango that quickly degenerated into a brawl. Knives and pistols were pulled, and by the time the Texans had escaped back across the Rio Grande at least one Paseño lay dead. There were a few days of tension following this escapade, but Skillman did not seem to have incurred any lasting enmity on the Mexican side of the border. Such affairs were common and the killing was judged as honorable self-defense. Both races in the region recognized a distinction between murder and the settlement of personal disputes.[10]

Certainly the shooting did not harm the contractor's standing among his neighbors. When Skillman approached James

[8] Rex Strickland, manuscript notes on Henry Skillman, El Paso, Texas (copy in the author's possession); W. W. Mills, *Forty Years at El Paso*, 187–88.

[9] Strickland, *El Paso*, 43.

[10] San Antonio *Western Texan*, Feb. 16, 1854.

Magoffin for a loan, he was not refused. On February 4 he mortgaged "100 mules and the four carriages which are now being used in the conveying of the mail from San Antonio to Santa Fe." Skillman also gave "to the said Magoffin a draft on the Post Office Department, being the money due the said Henry Skillman for the last quarter's contract and payable to him from said government on the 1st day of July, 1854, for $7,000." He also sold his house and lot in Concordia to Magoffin as part of the deal. Obviously the losses on the line were beginning to drain Skillman's financial reserves if he was forced to barter future payments from the government to secure enough money to stay in operation.[11]

The funds received from the sale and mortgage came at the right time, for Skillman soon suffered the first losses of the year when the Comanches raided Leona Station late in February and emptied its corral. The stage line was struggling manfully to maintain a reliable service, but visitors to the frontier were sometimes unappreciative of the expressmen's efforts. On April 4, Frederick Law Olmsted, a correspondent for the *New York Daily Times*, met the mail at Fort Inge and left a rather patronizing account of what he saw:

The train consists of two heavy wagons, and an ambulance for passengers, who are carried through to El Paso, seven hundred miles, for one hundred dollars, and found. "Passengers," the contractors advertise, "are allowed forty pounds of baggage, and not required to stand guard." There are four mules to each vehicle, and one spare mule for each team is led.

The train is attended by a mounted guard of six men, armed with Sharp's rifles and Colt's repeaters. Their pay is forty dollars a month. A man is lost on nearly every trip out and back, but usually through his own indiscretion. After passing Fort Inge, there is no change of team for more than five hundred miles. The train usually camps from ten o'clock at night till four in the morning. At eight o'clock, a stop of an hour or more is made, to graze the mules, and for breakfast. Another halt is made between three o'clock and sunset. The average distance accomplished in a day is over fifty miles. No government officer or

---

[11] Deed Record Book A, El Paso County, Texas, 460–61; Strickland, Skillman notes.

functionary goes with the mail. The commander was an old Texas ranger captain, and the guard, we understood, was composed of old rangers. They had, however, so much the appearance of drunken ruffians, that we felt no disposition to join the party.[12]

Like so many other easterners, Olmsted mixed fact and error. Skillman had taken some painful losses in carrying the mail, but he hardly lost a man on each trip. Certainly, men who were veteran rangers had not survived by being careless. Olmsted obviously had no idea that Skillman maintained a station at Fort Clark to the west, and if he did trouble himself enough to speak to the expressmen, he most likely did not refer to them as "drunken ruffians" within their hearing.

Henry Skillman might have altered Olmsted's opinions on quite a few things had they spent some time together on the road, but he had already left the state once again on an urgent trip to Washington. Comanches and journalists were small threats compared to the danger that loomed from the Post Office Department. Early in the year Postmaster General Campbell had called for new bids to cover Skillman's route, to begin service on July 1, 1854. The Texan had already submitted a bid of $50,000 a year for monthly service from San Antonio to Fort Fillmore, with a weekly trip from the army post to Santa Fe and back. Campbell had seen fit to grant the new contract to fellow Pennsylvanian David Wasson on April 22. Wasson, who probably had never been any farther west than his native Levittown, agreed to carry a monthly mail between Bexar and Santa Fe for $16,750 a year.[13]

It was a stunning shock for Skillman, but the game was not yet ended. Wasson had just a little over two months in which to staff, stock, and equip his line. Skillman knew fully well the expense and labor involved in such an undertaking. He might still work out a new deal with the government when the Pennsylvanian failed to meet his obligations. Upon Skillman's arrival back

[12] Frederick Law Olmsted, *A Journey Through Texas*, 286–87; Ike Moore, *The Life and Diary of Reading W. Black*, 44–45. The mail departed San Antonio on Apr. 12.

[13] U.S. Congress, House, *Report on Mail Contracts*, 33rd Cong., 2d sess., 1854, House Exec. Doc. 86, pp. 518, 714.

in Texas on May 30 the *Galveston News* remarked that "it is supposed, however, the contract will again be given to Capt. Skillman, whose capacity to carry it out cannot be doubted, and who has given so many proofs of his ability to meet all the difficulties on this dangerous route."[14]

Skillman took one of his brother's coaches to San Antonio and met with more bad news when he arrived. A new spate of Indian attacks had erupted east of El Paso in mid-May, and the months ahead promised more. The June stages made their runs safely, but all of the company's men knew that more powder would be burned on the trail before summer arrived.[15]

The news of Skillman's troubles met with much sympathy among his neighbors at the Pass. Frederick A. Percy was the community's self-appointed scribe, and in his handwritten newspaper, *El Sabio Sembrador*, he declared, "We had hoped and firmly believed that the present contractor, our worthy neighbor Captain Henry Skillman would have secured the contract, it is to be hoped that he may be continued in this service. If he gets his deserts it must be so." The transplanted Englishman went on to commend "this old Texan . . . warmly, kind, in his friendship, as the tenderest of woman-kind, and yet as fierce in former times on the battlefield, as an uncaged lion."[16]

The old lion was not ready to fall down and die just yet. Still in San Antonio, he was setting in motion a plan to steal a march on David Wasson. Skillman suspected that no matter how much political influence the man had exerted in gaining the contract, he had seriously underestimated the magnitude of his new responsibilities. No one along the route had seen anything of Wasson or his agents. By mid-June it was obvious that he would not be ready to begin service out of either Bexar or Santa Fe on

[14] New Orleans *Daily Picayune*, June 3, 1854, quoting the *Galveston Daily News*, May 30, 1854.

[15] U.S. Congress, House, *Report of the Secretary of War*, 33rd Cong., 2d sess., 1854, House Exec. Doc. 1, vol. 1, pt. 2, pp. 35–36; Strickland, *El Paso*, 12, 24, 43. Cattle man Michael Erskine reported meeting the May eastbound mail near Fort Clark on the twenty-fifth. On June 18 he passed the eastbound coach again 18 miles west of the Pecos. Walter S. Sanderlin, ed., "A Cattle Drive from Texas to California: The Diary of M. H. Erskine, 1854," *Southwestern Historical Quarterly* 47 (Aug. 1959): 400–402.

[16] Strickland, *El Paso*, 36.

time, and Skillman's friends were ready to help him step in and seize the fallen reins.

The designated head of the route was in Santa Fe, and Preston Beck, the Texan's local agent, had already laid the groundwork for decisive action. When Wasson's company failed to pick up the mail on July 1, the postmaster, William A. Miller, followed the normal practice of contracting for the best service available in the absence of the assigned carrier. On July 2 two prominent Santa Fe businessmen, Elias Brevoort and Joab Houghton, signed a contract with Miller for transportation of the mails at $28,000 a year. Henry Skillman was designated their chief agent and carrier.[17]

Back in San Antonio a variant of the same ploy was used when Wasson failed to appear at the post office. Skillman was on hand to inform Postmaster John Bowen that he was "verbally authorized by the department to continue the service until the new contractor should commence." At eight o'clock that night Skillman cracked the whip over his team's ears and wheeled triumphantly out of town. The echoes of that curling lash would be heard in courtrooms and government offices for the next six years.[18]

The mail moved as rapidly as before under the pirated contract, although conditions on the road hinted at both progress and continued hardships for travelers. The army had heeded at least some of Colonel Mansfield's proposals and established new outposts above Fort Clark on the Devil's River and on Live Oak Creek near the Pecos crossing. As Skillman continued his run, he found water and grazing to be scarce. There were at least nine herds of cattle on the road for California that summer, and the expressmen had barely passed one sprawling column of slat-sided longhorns before another hove into view. Skillman wished the drovers well, but he dreaded their company, for cattle inevitably drew Indians in their wake. The dust cloud churned up by their hooves formed a great dun banner that alerted the warriors

---

[17] U.S. Congress, House, *Court of Claims Report No. 266*, 36th Cong., 2d sess., 1860, pp. 2–7, 27; Jack C. Scannell, "Henry Skillman, Texas Frontiersman," *Permian Historical Annual* 18 (Dec., 1978): 24.

[18] *Court of Claims Report No. 266*, 27.

to their presence the moment it rose above the horizon. Already the Mescaleros were gathering their bands in the Limpia Mountains to levy a toll on the herds' passage.[19]

Near El Muerto the coach coming down from El Paso met Skillman's party, and he was happy to learn that his partners in Santa Fe had carried off their roles in the coup. He waved the rig on after briefing the escort on the road ahead of them. By the fourteenth he was filling his casks at Eagle Springs and learning just how rough a trip it had been for many of the cattlemen. The Dunlap herd had lost seven hundred animals for want of grazing, and it weathered an Indian attack in the Limpias. Upon reaching El Muerto it yielded another hundred head to the Apaches. At Eagle Springs, Chief Marcos paid a call and ran off most of the saddle horses, leaving many of the drovers afoot. He attacked another herd that was watering there and captured half of its steers.[20]

Skillman found grisly evidence of the herds' losses when he left Eagle Springs and pushed on through the mountain gaps for the Rio Grande. The road was littered with hundreds of rotting carcasses. Gorged vultures scuttled clumsily out of the way as the coaches rolled by, and packs of wolves trotted brazenly among the gutted cattle. The guards and drivers held bandannas to their faces against the stench while the skittish mules strained in their harnesses to escape this killing ground. Men and animals alike were glad when the river appeared and the air sweetened over the desert. The road ahead lay open for El Paso and Santa Fe.[21]

When Skillman finished his trip late in July he must have felt secure in the knowledge that his enterprise remained un-

---

[19] Strickland, *El Paso*, 44. Strickland mistakenly cites July 1 as Skillman's departure date from El Paso. Traveler James Bell recorded meeting Skillman at Eagle Springs on July 14, while in company with the mail from San Antonio. It could not have taken the eastbound mail two weeks to reach Eagle Springs. Though Bell might have placed Skillman in the wrong party, Postmaster Bowen's register for July stated that Skillman left Bexar with the mail on July 1. J. Evetts Haley, ed., "A Log of the Texas-California Cattle Trail, 1854," *Southwestern Historical Quarterly* 35 (Jan., 1932): 166, 230; *Court of Claims Report No. 266*, 5.

[20] Austin *Texas State Gazette*, July 29, Aug. 4, 1854.

[21] Sanderlin, "A Cattle Drive," 404.

challenged by competitors. Wasson's failure would certainly be reported to Washington. Skillman's deft exploitation of the situation could well lead to cancellation of the Pennsylvanian's contract and an endorsement and extension of Brevoort and Houghton's agreement. The Texan should have been happy, for the line had survived one crisis in July and kept its momentum despite the irregular methods employed to keep it in business. Unfortunately, August saw the beginning of a season of confusion for postmasters and contractors alike. It would have been humorous had not the lives of so many men been at risk as they struggled to carry out their obligations to the government.

On the first day of the month Skillman's road captain applied for the mail bags in San Antonio and was refused. Wasson's agents, Johnson Thomas and George W. Woods, had finally arrived in Texas and presented their credentials to Postmaster Bowen. Their sheaf of documents impressed him more than Skillman's earlier "verbal authorization," and since Wasson was the assigned contractor, Bowen was obliged to recognize only his representatives' authority to receive and carry the mails. Wasson's first coach rolled out of town that evening, leaving Skillman's lieutenant fuming helplessly.[22]

George Woods got a frosty reception when he reached El Paso on the seventeenth. Postmaster Jarvis Hubbell accepted the San Antonio mail but refused to surrender the pouches for Santa Fe. Instead, the mail was handed over to Skillman. Woods was stunned to learn that even if he proceeded north to Santa Fe and returned with that town's mail, the correspondence for San Antonio would still be denied to him. Henry Skillman was still a very popular figure in El Paso. David Wasson's reputation was at best a joke, and Woods and Thomas were complete strangers. The angry couriers returned to San Antonio and swore out a complaint against Hubbell and Skillman with the bemused Bowen.[23]

Thus began five months of wrangling in which political patronage, local loyalties, and the bureaucratic inertia of the government combined to spin a tangled web of conflicting ambitions

[22] *Court of Claims Report No. 266*, 6, 25–28.
[23] Ibid.

and disputed responsibilities for both service and reward. Henry Skillman could carry the mail south from Santa Fe and back from El Paso, as well as taking it on to San Antonio. Wasson's men were recognized as legal carriers only by Bowen, and thus were restricted to the single westward trip, although even then it was only the mail from San Antonio and not El Paso that would reach Santa Fe with them.

Affairs were confusing and frustrating enough that summer when the Indians gleefully got into the act. Captain Louis Oge brought Skillman's coaches into Bexar on August 27; the splintered holes in their sides told the story. The strapping, twenty-two-year-old Alsatian had made good time from El Paso to the Pecos, heading a large caravan that included seven vehicles and thirteen men. A Philadelphia merchant had traveled with them, his mule-drawn hacks laden with $300,000 in specie. The businessman had almost begun to relax by the time they reached Howard's Well. It was a mistake, for as guard James M. Adams recalled, "While halted at the wells, seventy-five hostile Indians put in an appearance, and Oge made quick preparations for defense by running the hacks and stages in a circle and making breastworks of them and the mules and horses." The whites did this just in time, for "the Indians charged at long range, but before they came close enough to do any damage Oge was ready for them, and the battle commenced."[24]

The first volley from the Texans' rifles hit several braves and the raiders "fought shy and circled the wagons many times, yelling and shooting under their horses as they ran. This was kept up for four hours and then they withdrew with considerable loss." The whites were unharmed, but five mules lay dead and several others were wounded. Somehow the men pieced together teams for all the coaches and finished the run into San Antonio. Oge's stalwart defense won him toasts in the town's saloons, but Bowen still refused to have anything to do with Skillman's line beyond accepting the incoming mail.[25]

At this point the contract dispute reached new depths of

[24] Frank W. Johnson, *History of Texas and Texans*, 4:2168; A. J. Sowell, *Early Settlers and Indian Fighters of Southwest Texas*, 2:585.
[25] Sowell, *Early Settlers*, 2:585.

irony. Johnson Thomas had taken a heavy loan from a local merchant in order to put Wasson's coaches on the road. When Oge arrived in town with news of Wood's rebuff in El Paso, it seemed that the loan might never be repaid if the Pennsylvanian lost his contract. George H. Giddings was the worried creditor. He and Skillman were old friends and trail companions. They held no animosity toward each other now, but Giddings knew that he would have to take drastic action to protect his investment.[26]

Even before Woods had returned empty-handed from the west, Giddings had prevailed upon Thomas to certify his brother, Frank, as a courier. On September 1, Frank Giddings and Thomas were ready to carry the next mail, and the merchant had a means of active control over this shaky undertaking.

The two men made the journey with six other travelers, both guards and passengers. James H. Hunter was the conductor, and he took them along at a good clip, passing the frustrated Woods on the road and learning firsthand from him of the obstacles ahead. Their first challenge came not from Jarvis Hubbell, but from the Apaches.

Once again the steep, brushy hills flanking Howard's Well harbored an ambush. Twenty Apaches attacked the camp while the mules were being watered, but luckily only three of the raiders had rifles, and the Texans rallied to break their charge. The Indians made several more rushes but withdrew after Hunter's men killed a few braves. Frank Giddings was a practicing physician, but there was no need for his skills. A dead mule was the caravan's only casualty.[27]

They met Skillman's party on the road during the trip, and both groups must have reflected on the ludicrous nature of their rivalry. Upon reaching El Paso they were again refused the mail, even though Giddings was well known to Hubbell. The young doctor must have stayed behind to check on his brother's store, for it was Thomas who rode on to Santa Fe and made Wasson's

---

[26] U.S. Court of Claims, Deposition of George H. Giddings, *George H. Giddings vs. the United States, Kiowa, Comanche, and Apache Indians*, Records of the Court of Claims Section (Justice), RG 205, NARS.

[27] *Court of Claims Report No. 266*, 6, 9–11, 24–33, 41; Giddings Deposition, *Giddings vs. the United States*; Sowell, *Early Settlers*, 2: 562.

first formal application for the mail there on September 30. Post-master Miller was suspicious, and "as he had not the proper proof to show that he was entitled as agent for said Wasson, or any proof that Wasson had complied with the law in giving bond, &c., and as he had not been known as a mail carrier, I declined to deliver the mail to him." On the same day Skillman's agent got a similar response from Bowen in San Antonio. Giddings and Johnson returned to Bexar with nothing to show for their long trip but a receipt for the mail and a dead mule left to feed the coyotes at Howard's Well.[28]

The farce was repeated by both contractors in October. The month did bring a few hopeful signs for ending the impasse. Postmaster Miller informed his superiors in Washington that Brevoort and Houghton "were ready to relinquish the contract to Mr. Skillman, as they had made the contract for his benefit." The two merchants may have hoped to smooth the way for a de-cision in Skillman's favor, or they may have feared being caught in a welter of fines and lawsuits if Wasson triumphed. Whatever the reasons, their withdrawal cleared the field for the old con-tractor and his rival.[29]

David Wasson finally arrived in San Antonio that month and blandly confessed that he could neither repay his loan nor cover the debts that his creditor had incurred in his name while keep-ing the line in business. It was a sickening shock for Giddings. He was too deeply committed to the enterprise to let it fail and cut his losses, but there was also no assurance that the govern-ment would allow Wasson to keep the contract in light of his slip-shod performance to date. When Wasson offered to transfer the contract to Giddings, the young businessman accepted in the grim knowledge that only by shouldering the full responsibility could he hope to at least break even on what had proved to be a very bad investment.

Things began to look up for Giddings as the year drew into autumn. Henry Skillman had brought in the mail on October 27, and evidently he and Giddings agreed to pool their resources.

---

[28] *Court of Claims Report No. 266*, 6, 10–11, 29–30; Giddings Deposition, *Giddings vs. the United States*.

[29] *Court of Claims Report No. 266*, 29.

The two men knew and trusted each other. Skillman possessed a keen native intelligence but little formal education. Giddings was at ease on the plains and well versed in the mechanics of running a successful business. They complemented each other well, and with Skillman's reputation and Giddings's resources the stage line might yet survive.[30]

There was other heartening news from the frontier that month. Early in September, Major General Persifor F. Smith, commander of the Department of Texas, departed San Antonio to inspect the troops at Fort Inge, Fort Clark, and Fort Bliss. He had already decided to build a new post on the road and ordered Lieutenant Colonel George W. Seawell of the Eighth Infantry to meet him with his command at the Painted Comanche Camp in the Limpia Mountains that October.

Smith reached El Paso and started back late in September. He got a firsthand look at the Indian threat when his escort clashed with the Mescaleros near Eagle Springs. On October 7 he met Seawell in the mountains. The colonel's six companies of infantry had waged a running fight with the Apaches up the length of Limpia Canyon for three days' march. Even after they formally established the new garrison of Fort Davis on October 23, they were incessantly plagued by Apache raids and ambushes.

The fort's presence certainly did not guarantee an end to depredations on the road, but it did offer a welcome refuge for travelers on the long stretch between Las Moras Creek and the Rio Grande. The Regiment of Mounted Rifles joined the Eighth Infantry in patrols of the region. The Apaches soon learned that the bluecoats were there to stay.[31]

With added protection available on the trail and a new partnership based on mutual trust and not strained expediency, Giddings and Skillman readied their first coach for the run to El Paso. On November 1, Frank Giddings and James Hunter led the express out of town with fresh confidence. That same day Philip Broad showed William Miller his credentials as Wasson's agent and the Santa Fe postmaster showed him the door. Ten days later

[30] Ibid.
[31] Barry Scobee, *Fort Davis Texas, 1583–1960*, 5–8; Robert M. Utley, *Fort Davis National Historic Site, Texas*, 5–7.

he confronted Jarvis Hubbell with identical results. None of them knew that Wasson had sold out to Giddings and that Skillman had joined his operation. It was a portent for continued confusion on the line's western section.[32]

Skillman and El Paso merchant A. C. Rand left San Antonio a day behind Giddings and Hunter. Two Mexicans rode along as guards, and a hardbitten character named Jack Gordon was at the reins. An experienced frontiersman and cool fighter, Gordon boasted of having lived with the Apaches for several years in the late 1840s. He had ridden with them on their raids into Mexico and taken his share of scalps and plunder before returning to dwell uneasily among his own people. Gordon was one of those dark spirits who found license as well as freedom on the frontier. His days in Skillman's service were numbered.[33]

The two parties ran into heavy rains east of Fort Inge and the road was reduced to a set of mired ruts, but they pressed on beneath the dripping, slate-gray skies. The weather soon moderated, and on the night of the fourteenth Skillman caught up with Giddings. The next morning they breakfasted at El Muerto. Skillman left before the doctor, promising to wait for him at Eagle Springs. Several miles to the west he met A. A. Lockwood's freight caravan and Bradford Daily's mail coach. El Pasoan Rufus Doane had come down with him to meet Skillman. Price Cooper occupied the driver's box and called down greetings to his old friend. A thirty-year resident of El Paso, he was a good man to have along on any trip into Apachería. Tall, gaunt, hamfisted, hook-nosed, and crowned with a shock of fiery red hair, this craggy Celt was something of a legend among his fellows. Attorney Josiah Crosby knew him as "a brave man, but in no sense an adventurer. He was a quiet, good citizen, always honest, and didn't hesitate when a scrap with the red men was imminent." Cooper, unlike Gordon, was a man who responded to the dictates of life on the frontier with the better side of his nature.[34]

[32] *Court of Claims Report No. 266*, 6, 10–12, 28–32; Giddings Deposition, *Giddings vs. the United States*; New Orleans *Weekly Picayune*, Jan. 10, 1855, citing the *San Antonio Ledger*, Dec. 28, 1854.

[33] Austin *Texas State Gazette*, Jan. 6, 1855; Austin *Texas State Times*, Feb. 3, 1855.

[34] *El Paso Daily Herald*, Nov. 11, 15, 1900; "El Paso Pioneers Sketchbook," Southwestern Collection, University of Texas at El Paso Library, 2.

Doane joined Skillman for the ride into El Paso while Gordon and Cooper exchanged places on the coaches. Daily and the contractor conferred briefly and then they parted. Lockwood and Daily must have passed Giddings soon afterward, although none of them were aware that yet another group of travelers was charting their progress along the road with keen interest.

Giddings was about eighteen miles east of El Muerto when James Hunter spotted fifty Apaches quartering across the plains in an effort to cut them off from the oasis. It was soon evident that they could not outrun the Mescaleros' ponies, and Hunter ordered the train to halt and prepare to fight.[35]

The Indians reined in about two hundred yards away and their chief rode forward, calling out "Amigos! Amigos!" Guard Louis Dickens told him to keep his distance if he wanted to remain both friendly and alive. A short parley followed, and then the warriors whipped their mounts around in a sweeping circle and gained the road in front of the whites' position. Jeering, they lofted a soldier's bloody jacket on a lance point and tossed a crumpled letter down on the ground. A week before, they had killed a dispatch rider west of Fort Clark. The Texans got ready to fight, but the war party turned and sped after Skillman's caravan.[36]

They caught up with him as he stopped to shoe a mule and tried the old ruse of false friendship again. When Skillman warned them to leave, they opened fire. By the time Giddings arrived, the fight was in full sway, with rapid puffs of gunsmoke spurting from behind the stages as arrows rattled against their sides. Hunter and his men raised a yell and charged forward through the circling braves to join Skillman.

"The prettiest part of the fight was now coming on," an El Pasoan reported later, "and the fun was not stopped 'till sundown, having commenced about eleven o'clock in the morning." There were now fifteen men making a stand with the coaches. Skillman organized the defense and set a cool, detached example until an Indian shot his favorite mule and turned the skirmish into a personal contest.[37]

[35] Sowell, *Early Settlers*, 2:563–65; J. Marvin Hunter, "Major James M. Hunter, Frontiersman," *Frontier Times* 38 (Nov., 1950): 44–45.

[36] Sowell, *Early Settlers*, 2:562–65.

[37] Austin *Texas State Gazette*, Jan. 6, 1855; New Orleans *Weekly Picayune*, Jan. 10,

The Mescaleros sent some of their warriors to climb a rise several hundred yards away and began lobbing heavy-caliber rifle bullets into the Texans' position. Mules began to drop, dying or kicking and squealing with wounds. Skillman ordered Giddings to hitch up the teams and pull back out of range while he gave covering fire. "Capt. Skillman has a fine gun, with which he considers he has a 'dead thing' on any Indian at three hundred yards," read a later account, "and in this fight he is said to have killed three in that distance—these were three that he *got* and others that were doubtless killed but not known to be killed." A. C. Rand estimated that he fired only a dozen rounds from his Sharps, but the shots were so accurate that the awed Apaches soon sought cover in the brush.[38]

The Indians renewed the siege from a respectful distance after Giddings gained a better position. They sniped at the frontiersmen until night fell, and then they withdrew. Several mules in the herd of spare animals that accompanied the coaches were dead or wounded, but none of the mail party were killed. Two passengers had been painfully bruised by spent bullets, but that was small payment for survival.[39]

When the expressmen reached El Paso, they got a hero's welcome, but Giddings faced still more frustration. Both Hubbell and Miller adamantly refused to surrender the mail to anyone but Skillman's agents. In Santa Fe, Giddings had not even bothered to mention the transfer of the contract to his brother. Things were confused enough, but even when the haggard physician produced a copy of the original contract and identified himself as a sworn courier, Miller still refused to recognize his authority.[40]

1855, citing the *San Antonio Ledger*, Dec. 28, 1854. Rand's account was carried by the *Picayune*; an El Paso correspondent described the incident for the *Texas State Gazette*.

[38] Austin *Texas State Gazette*, Jan. 6, 1855; New Orleans *Weekly Picayune*, Jan. 10, 1855.

[39] Giddings Deposition, *Giddings vs. the United States*.

[40] *Court of Claims Report No. 266*, 6, 10–12, 28–32. On the same day that Frank Giddings was rebuffed in Santa Fe, the next mail train left Bexar with "two good carriages drawn by four mules, and accompanied by seven men, well armed with rifles, revolvers, 'Arkansas toothpicks,' &c." New Orleans *Daily Picayune*, Dec. 17, 1854. George Giddings did not wait to hear of his brother's success or failure before putting the next coach out on schedule.

Frank Giddings started south with his coach's boot empty
once more, doubtless wishing that an open season could be declared on postmasters as well as Mescaleros. The trip back to
San Antonio did nothing to lift his spirits. The Kiowas and Comanches had descended upon the station near Fort Inge and
driven off the mule herd only a few days after William Skillman
had restocked the corral. They also raided Ney's Station at D'Hanis and made off with its stock. These were staggering losses
for the struggling company at a time when good mules cost
$150 each.

The little hamlet of D'Hanis was ravaged again that month,
this time by a band of white desperadoes. Captain William
Henry, a professional filibusterer and Indian fighter, was leading
a force of volunteers westward with the stated intention of aiding
the army against the hostiles, although he was rumored to be
planning an adventure into Mexico as well. Henry's legion proceeded to get drunk while camped at Ney's Station and shot up
the settlement. After killing a few hogs and riddling Ney's house
with pistol fire, these gallants broke into the letter box and scattered the mail over the prairie. The townspeople complained
that they would rather be left to the Indians' mercies than con-
signed to such protectors.

These depredations must have been disheartening for Giddings, coming as they did at the end of months of wrangling with
the postal authorities. While the raids marked the unhappy ending of a trying year, they also signaled the mere beginnings of his
misfortunes.[41]

[41] Giddings Deposition, *Giddings* vs. *the United States*; Olmsted, *A Journey*, 507.
Reading Black recorded William Skillman's passage through Uvalde on Dec. 5 and 7, as
well as Henry's rowdy progress along the road. Moore, *Life and Diary*, 61–63.

CHAPTER 4

"I'll Be Damned If I'll Die!"

THE man who had taken on the challenge of carrying the mail across the Southwest had never aspired to such a responsibility, but neither was he an individual who shrank from personal risk. Like so many others who were drawn to the frontier, he found that life there honed the edge of his ambition and tempered his resolve.

Born the sixth of eight sons in a family of thirteen children, George H. Giddings began life in Herrick Township, Susquehanna County, Pennsylvania, on July 4, 1823. He sprang from a clan that had westering in its blood. In 1635 another George Giddings had left St. Albans, England, to settle among the saints at Ipswich, Massachusetts Bay Colony. By 1700 the Giddings family was well established in the new country, and its men led the clan south and west into Pennsylvania when New England began to stifle their ambitions.[1]

In 1835 George's elder brother, Giles, went adventuring to the Mexican province of Texas and lost his life with Houston's army at San Jacinto. Another brother, Jabez, left Pennsylvania to settle Giles's estate, and decided to settle in Texas. His success in the new republic lured James and George to the frontier as well. En route both young men were stricken with smallpox while visiting relatives in Kentucky and lapsed into delirium. As George lay wasting away, his uncle and a doctor stood by the bedside and discussed the practicality of sending the boys' bodies home for burial. Young Giddings came out of his coma at that moment, sat bolt upright, and gasped, "I'll be damned if I'll die!"

[1]Frank W. Johnson, *History of Texas and Texans*, 4:1781; Emmie W. Mahon, "George H. Giddings and the San Antonio–San Diego Stage Coach Line" (seminar paper, University of Texas at El Paso Library), 3; Kathryn S. McMillen, "The San Antonio–San Diego Mail Line in Texas, 1857–1861" (M.A. thesis, University of Texas at Austin, 1960), 220–21.

Two months later the brothers reached Jabez's home in Brenham, Texas, and George went to work as a clerk in his law office. By spring, 1846, he had won an appointment as district and county clerk for Washington County, and took his salary in bacon and cornmeal.[2] Giddings soon learned that on the Texas frontier the rifle had more use than the law book, and that June he joined Captain Thomas L. Smith's company of Texas Rangers as they rode in pursuit of Comanche raiders. The newcomer saw his first Indian fight and served as the company's surgeon when he extracted an arrow from a comrade's shoulder with his Bowie knife. Two days later Giddings used the same knife to help scratch out a grave for his patient.

Smith's company volunteered for service when the Mexico War erupted, but the unit got to see little action with Zachary Taylor's army. Giddings was appointed quartermaster officer, a job that garnered him much valuable experience in the logistics of moving and supplying large numbers of men and animals over long distances.

In the spring of 1847 Giddings left the service and joined his brother in surveying land for the German Immigration Company's grant in Llano and San Saba counties. A spell of clerking for the San Antonio mercantile firm of C. J. Cook and A. A. Lockwood followed. The businessmen had stores in both Bexar and El Paso in addition to running a line of freight wagons south into Mexico. Giddings spent a lot of time on the trail with the freighters, learning the vagaries of mules, Indians, Mexican customs officials, and the land itself.[3]

By the early 1850s the Pennsylvanian had amassed enough capital to buy out his employers' interests in San Antonio and El Paso. He added his own store in Fort Clark and stocked them all with everything an emigrant might need as he toiled along the road to Calfornia. Giddings banked on the belief that more gold would probably be spent by people en route to California than

[2] McMillen, "Mail Line," 220–22; Charles M. Barnes, ed., "Memoirs of Colonel George H. Giddings," *San Antonio Daily Express*, May 4, 1902.

[3] Chester V. Kielman and Emmie W. Mahon, "George H. Giddings and the San Antonio–San Diego Mail Line," *Southwestern Historical Quarterly* 61 (Oct., 1957): 220–26; Barnes, "Memoirs," *San Antonio Daily Express*, June 1, 1902.

was ever likely to be panned from the streams of the bonanza fields. Estimates for the cost of overland travel to the Pacific Coast in the 1850s ranged from as low as two hundred dollars for an individual to fifteen hundred dollars for a family. Although freighting costs were high and the danger of losing stock and property to the Indians was always present, Giddings knew that even after the gold seekers were gone there would always be a market for his goods from both travelers and the army posts that were springing up along the trail to El Paso.[4]

Giddings's younger brother, Frank, left his medical studies in Vermont in 1852 and came to Texas to aid in the growing business. Together they moved everything from bolts of cloth to kegs of nails west to stock the shelves of their stores. Then David Wasson's men appeared in San Antonio, and the prospering merchant made his fateful loan to them. Within a few months he was not only a storekeeper but an expressman by default.

As 1855 opened, Giddings began to realize the full import of his situation. Not only would he lose his initial investment and the annual contract fee if the mail service failed, he would also be fined by the Post Office Department if the mail was not picked up and delivered on schedule at both ends of the line. As a businessman he knew the dangers of mixing heavy and often unpredictable operating costs with a fixed amount of operating capital. Any deficit would come out of his own pocket.[5]

The risks were high, but the Giddings brothers still had reasons for optimism. San Antonio was yet enjoying the flush times brought about by war and migration. It was already the most populous city in the state, and Frederick Law Olmsted had found it thriving on his visit the previous year. "The capital owned here," he observed, "is quite large. The principal accumulations date from the Mexican War, when no small part of the many millions expended by Government were disbursed here in payment to contractors." Another visitor remarked that "the Mexican character of this city is fast disappearing under the superior enterprise and taste of its new inhabitants . . . it was a

[4]John D. Unruh, *The Plains Across*, 405–408; Bernard DeVoto, *The Year of Decision, 1846*, 144.

[5]Johnson, *Texas and Texans*, 5:2126.

frontier town which in 1850, had but 3,000 inhabitants . . . great numbers of enterprising northern men and indomitable Germans . . . settled here, swelling her population in five years to 10,000. . . . There is a stir and a vigorous life here that I have seen in no inland city of the old states."[6]

San Antonio held proud place as the Rome of Texas. Its position astride the trade and immigration routes to California and Mexico funneled money and people through it in a steady stream. Commercial travel, whether by the freighters or expressmen, forged links in the lines of communication that bound the city to Austin in the north, and Houston, Galveston, and Indianola in the east. Colonel Saltmarsh, Brown and Tarbox, Harrison and Brown, and other entrepreneurs had all begun stage services between these points in the previous decade. The Skillman's lines had taken the network westward in a great bound to link eastern Texas with El Paso and Santa Fe, thus forming a tenuous spoke to bind the far borderlands to the hub of Bexar's fortunes. In 1851 few men would have wagered on their ability to ride from the mouth of the Trinity to the head of the Pecos in less than a month. By 1855 fewer still would have cared to hazard their fortunes with George Giddings's as he strove to keep the line in operation.[7]

As Indian raids continued to lash his stations to the west that January of 1855, Giddings was forced to confront a basic problem in the terms of his contract with the government. The Post Office Department myopically asserted that a two-horse carriage was an adequate vehicle for delivering the mail on this route. Wasson's contract had been granted on this basis, and since the cost of procurement, subsistence, and replacement of a two-horse team formed part of the basis for computing the contract fee, Giddings's $16,750 per year was judged a reasonable amount by the government. It might well have been a fair and realistic sum for service on a route from Boston to Albany, but it was a pittance when applied to the support of Giddings's line under the conditions he faced. By he end of January his losses to

[6] Frederic Law Olmsted, *A Journey Through Texas*, 152; J. D. B. Stillman, "Wanderings in the Southwest," New York *Crayon* 5 (1855): 67.

[7] Robert H. Thonhoff, *San Antonio Stage Lines, 1847–1881*, 5–11.

the Indians already totaled $12,150. All of this was in excess of normal operating expenses. If the next seven months were to prove as costly as the first, he would be mired even deeper in a losing investment.[8]

The contractor managed to bring some powerful influence to bear on his problem. Former state governor Peter Hansbrough Bell was visiting Washington that month and dispatched a letter to Postmaster General Campbell that bore signed endorsements from both Senator Rusk and Sam Houston. The trio praised Giddings's "great energy and promptness," despite the sad reality that "the service is found exhausting and impracticable." The letter stressed that "it is found necessary from actual experiment to employ on each trip two 4-horse wagons for transportation of supplies, mail, and provender, as also a guard from 8 to 12 men. The commander of the guard receives $100 and the men $40 each per month." In closing, Bell and his associates urged a new contract providing for weekly or semimonthly mail deliveries by four-horse coaches.[9]

While Campbell was musing over Bell's letter, the mail trains were running late as the result of winter weather that grew progressively worse. The January mail did not reach Santa Fe until February 3, and the eastbound coach pulled into Bexar at about the same time. Blizzards that month kept the mail from reaching Santa Fe at all, and the snow east of El Paso was so deep in the mountains that the coaches could not move. The mail went out on pack mules and failed to arrive in San Antonio until the second week in March. In an uncharacteristic departure from its usual cheery boosterism, the *Texas State Gazette* asked:

How is it that we can hear generally much earlier from Santa Fe via St. Louis and New Orleans? No one who wishes to learn from Santa Fe can rely upon the route from San Antonio. It is a foolish expenditure of money for the government to employ at enormous expense, the present mail facilities. We ought either to have a semi-monthly mail or

[8]United States Court of Claims, Depositions of A. C. Hyde, William Ford, William A. Wallace, and Antonio Pina, *George H. Giddings* vs. *the United States, Kiowa, Comanche, and Apache Indians*, Records of the Court of Claims Section (Justice), RG 205, NARS.

[9]Deposition of George H. Giddings, *Giddings* vs. *the United States*.

none; for any longer delay defeats the object for which the mail is established and compels even those in Texas to send their letters &c., by the St. Louis route.[10]

The paper's criticisms were probably aimed more at Campbell than Giddings, but the contractor was sensitive to any such comments, and he must have winced when the *Santa Fe Weekly Gazette* sneered at his coaches as "the Lightning Express Train" and complained that newspapers from New Orleans and Charleston were old even by the standards of the day when they finally arrived.[11] The criticism stung, but Giddings quickly departed on a tour of inspection that would keep him moving along the line between Fort Clark and Mesilla from March into August. He was committed to the enterprise now and intended to spare no effort to make it succeed.

Great efforts had to be intelligently directed, and Giddings knew well that any business was doomed to founder without a firm system of organization. It was impossible for one man to oversee every aspect of an operation that stretched over a thousand miles of desert and plains, especially when he still had another business to run. Responsible and intelligent lieutenants were needed. Many of Skillman's guards and drivers were retained, and Giddings recruited other able hands to serve with him. James R. Sweet continued to act as the company's representative in San Antonio, and Thomas S. Rogers handled affairs at Fort Clark. In San Elizario, Archibald C. Hyde and William Ford, partners in a mercantile firm, were agents for the leg between Fort Clark and El Paso. Price Cooper covered the route from the Pass to Santa Fe. These men were charged with maintaining the schedule, hiring new employees as needed, and replacing stock and equipment when necessary. The job allowed little rest for any of them.[12]

---

[10] Austin *Texas State Gazette*, Mar. 10, 1855; U.S. Congress, House, *Fines and Deductions of Mail Contractors*, 35th Cong., 1st sess., 1854, House Exec. Doc. 81, pp. 36, 64, 95; Giddings Deposition, *Giddings* vs. *the United States*. See the *Texas State Gazette* of May 5, 1855 for other mail notices.

[11] *Santa Fe Weekly Gazette*, Mar. 10, 1855; Morris F. Taylor, *First Mail West*, 210.

[12] Depositions of A. C. Hyde, William Ford, Price Cooper, and George H. Giddings, *Giddings* vs. *the United States*.

Giddings also started a slow expansion of the stations on the road. The relay points at Castroville, D'Hanis, Fort Inge, and Fort Clark were retained, as at San Elizario and El Paso. Others were located at Comanche Springs, Fort Davis, and Eagle Springs, although not all of them would be completely built by the year's end. Rock and adobe were plentiful, but lumber had to be hauled in from the settlements at an exorbitant cost. The average expense of building a station was at least one thousand dollars.[13]

Before he departed San Antonio that March, the contractor purchased a herd of mules to aid in stocking the stations and loaded several wagons with supplies for their staffs. He also prudently sent in another order for more Sharps rifles. Like Skillman, Giddings had been won over by the weapon's accuracy and rapid fire. On February 10 he wrote to the Sharps's makers, saying that "it affords me great pleasure to bear testimony from actual experience to the merits of Sharps' rifle. I have used it for two years, a part of the time over my mail route, and it has proved a saviour to myself and my men, when any other arm would have failed me. As for killing bear, deer, &c., I will pit Sharps' rifle against all other arms known."[14]

Giddings's trip to the west that season was hardly a triumphal procession. Trouble seemed to flare on the line both ahead and behind him as he rode. Indian raids and late mail deliveries cost him both stock and money in the early weeks of 1855. April, May, and June conspired to form a dismal quarter on the calendar, as heavy spring rains mired the roads and kept the creeks in flood, slowing the mail and bringing more fines from the government.[15]

The press continued to complain about the service as well. The *Santa Fe Gazette* charged that "there are two or three screws loose in the Southern mail arrangements, and we hope the Postmaster General will have them looked after." In mid-April the *Texas State Gazette* defended Giddings by alluding to the confu-

[13] Ibid.

[14] Ibid.; Martin Rywell, *Sharps Rifle*, 38.

[15] Giddings Deposition, *Giddings* vs. *the United States*; *Fines and Deductions*, 63, 96.

sion created by the earlier contract disputes, remarking that "during the term of the present contractor, the mail has been delivered to him by the Santa Fe postmaster only once, and the cause is imputed to obstinacy and disinclination to permit the contractor to carry it." The *Texas State Gazette* went on to advocate a semimonthly contract for Giddings, as "the Santa Fe mails would reach Washington City several days earlier than at present. The commerce of the Southern ports of Charleston, Savannah, Mobile, New Orleans, and Galveston demand, at any rate, this extension of service, should it also be granted on the Independence and St. Louis route. We think we shall obtain it." Giddings must have wished that he could fully share the journal's optimism.[16]

That summer continued to tax Giddings's confidence and resolve as conditions worsened on the road. In June the Apaches ambushed a coach on the Jornada del Muerto and killed two of the three men with it. All of the mail was lost in the attack. A few nights later a nervy band of warriors slipped into the Pass settlement and stole all the mules from the corral that adjoined Giddings's store. The line's losses were mounting at a sickening rate. Giddings knew that he could command up to $175,000 in credit with his bankers in New York, but he did not want to be reduced to that expedient. By this time the company's minimum operating expenses were running at $1,000 a month, and the Indians were sending them spiraling higher. If things did not improve soon he would face the choice of either going deeply into debt or siphoning off resources from his mercantile business to support the stage line. No matter what Giddings did, a new dilemma would arise from the ruins of the old.[17]

Giddings started a trip down the eastern end of the line to San Antonio while his men struggled to keep the coaches moving on time. In July he joined Bigfoot Wallace and over a hundred of their fellow residents of Bexar County in petitioning Governor Elisha M. Pease for relief from the Indian depredations. They

[16] Austin *Texas State Gazette*, Apr. 14, May 5, 1855, citing the *Santa Fe Gazette* of the preceding months.

[17] Depositions of Price Cooper and George H. Giddings, *Giddings* vs. *the United States*.

requested the formation of ranger companies in Bexar and Medina counties to patrol the frontier to the north and west. Otherwise, "the tide of immigration, which has so suddenly arrested, will flow backwards, leaving a beautiful, but desolated country to the unchecked wanderings of the savage."[18]

Things did begin to improve on the trail to the west that summer. In July a detachment of the Regiment of Mounted Riflemen mauled an Apache war party as it prepared to lay an ambush on the stage road. Only a few weeks later the First Infantry made its earlier temporary camp on Live Oak Creek a permanent post by establishing Fort Lancaster on the site. While the foot soldiers could pose no serious challenge to the Comanches, their presence and the sight of the flag snapping in the fitful breezes off the Pecos were enough to hearten travelers.[19]

By October the Indian threat had receded temporarily, and a newly commissioned young West Point graduate purchased a ticket west to Fort Davis in Giddings's San Antonio offices. Lieutenant Zenas R. Bliss was appalled at the expense. His fare was fifty dollars, plus another sixty dollars in freight charges for his baggage. The trail-worn rig was a rude step down from the massive Concords he had ridden in the East. "The wagon in which the mail was carried on that trip was called a celerity wagon, for want of a better name, I suppose, as there was very little celerity in its movements," he complained. His misgivings grew as the team was buckled in the traces. The mules were half-broken at best, and they hauled the coach around the plaza several times in a wild display of reluctance before they settled down.

Bliss's companions on the trip were also enough to give him pause. "A German named Broad was in charge of the party, and we had two other men, and a Mexican boy for cook. As we left town a man named Zumbro joined us. He had been in some man's house and the husband returned unexpectedly. Zumbro had

---

[18] "Petition of Citizens of Bexar County to E. M. Pease," in Dorman H. Winfrey, ed., *Texas Indian Papers, 1849–1859,* 224–27.

[19] U.S. Congress, House, *Report of the Secretary of War,* 34th Cong., 1st sess., 1855, House Exec. Doc. 1, pp. 54–55, 136–37; Austin *Texas State Gazette,* Aug. 7, 1855; *San Antonio Ledger,* Sept. 29, 1855; *San Antonio Herald,* Aug. 21, 1855; Giddings Deposition, *Giddings* vs. *the United States.*

jumped out the window with very little clothing on, and he was naturally anxious to spend some time in the country, and as Broad needed a man for the road they soon made a deal and he went with us."

The other two men struck Bliss as being typical frontiersmen. James McFarland commanded respect for his stoicism, as "one or two trips before this he had been shot in the breast by an Indian at Eagle Springs . . . and the wound had not entirely healed." James Hunter was also along on this trip, although it was doubtful that he would accompany the party beyond El Paso, for recently "he had been in a duel with a man in Santa Fe and killed him." The lieutenant wryly noted that "the Mexican boy and myself seemed to be the only ones in the party that had not killed someone and the only ones that no one cared to kill." [20]

The coach bowled along with a six-mule hitch in the lead and a herd of twenty-two other animals trotting along behind to furnish relief teams. "Someone gave Broad a bugle when we started out, and that was blown by someone of the party nearly all day and all night," the subaltern noted with amusement. "We never passed a house without giving them a salute with it, and I have no doubt that we astonished the natives along the road with our music."

The mail party passed D'Hanis and forged on into Indian country, with Bliss watching for signs of the hostiles. "Stages on this road at this time were frequently attacked by Indians, and the guards murdered and the mail captured. For a year nearly half the number of stages were attacked," he related, "but sometimes they succeeded in driving the Indians away and saving the mail." Bliss was increasingly struck by the tragic toll exacted by the tribesmen as the journey continued. "The El Paso road today from San Antonio to California," he wrote many years later, "would appear like one long grave if the innumerable graves had not been leveled by the elements. I do not believe that there is a single water hole or camping ground from one end of the road to

---

[20] Zenas R. Bliss, "Memoirs," Zenas R. Bliss Papers, Barker Texas History Center, University of Texas at Austin, 1:146–48. An abridged version of this document is also available in the library of Fort Davis National Historic Site, Fort Davis, Tex.

the other that has not been marked with from one to fifty graves erected by soldiers or friends over the bodies of murdered travelers."[21]

Broad was always alert to the threat of Indian attack, and the party never traveled at night. Throughout the day the travelers drove for four hours and then rested for two. Camps were seldom made at a waterhole. Once the kegs and canteens were filled, Broad pushed on for several miles to find a concealed campsite. After seventeen days of this routine they rolled into La Limpia, the little settlement that had sprung up around Giddings's station that stood a mile north of Fort Davis. Broad's vigilance had carried them through with only a fleeting glimpse of an Indian at Comanche Springs.

La Limpia was hardly an imposing station with its rude picket walls and dirt floors, but it was the first sign of white settlement any of them had seen since leaving Fort Clark. Two of Skillman's old hands were there to greet them. Both Edward P. Webster and Diedrick Dutchover had ridden with the mail in the early days of the contract, and when the establishment of Fort Davis had brought some tenuous security to the area, they had built a station nearby. In turn, their presence attracted a handful of Mexican farmers and stockmen who provided corn and hay for sale to the fort and station. The Apaches preyed on everyone with grim impartiality.[22]

Lieutenant Bliss could congratulate himself on a safe arrival at his new home, but for George Giddings it was another month of frustration. The unpredictable October weather dumped more rain on the trail, making the journey a slow and exhausting one for the mules and men alike. More delays resulted when the Pecos jumped its banks and halted traffic at the ford near Fort Lancaster. More fines for late deliveries were the result for the company. Giddings prevailed upon a Washington-bound friend,

[21] Ibid., 1:148–54, 241.

[22] Ibid.: Barry Scobee, *Old Fort Davis*, 8, 46, 49–50, 67, 72–73; Barry Scobee, *Fort Davis Texas, 1853–1960*, 23–24, 71, 99, 131–35, 147, 169, 173, 193; Carlyle G. Raht, *The Romance of Davis Mountains and Big Bend Country*, 129–32, 149–51, 185, 204; Wayne R. Austerman, "Identifying a 'Lost' Stage Station in Jeff Davis County," *Password* 25 (Spring, 1980): 3–10.

merchant E. C. Allen, to explain the delays to the Post Office Department. Allen obligingly certified that the mail line had "used all due diligence in order to make schedule time." The last thing the company needed was another heavy fine.[23]

Giddings had no sooner placated the clerks on the Potomac when he had to contend with a new challenge that came in on the north wind. In November, bitter cold swept down across the Southwest, bringing deep snows with it that soon choked the road between El Paso and Santa Fe. Old New Mexicans marked it as the earliest and coldest winter in fifty years, and the snows would continue until well into March.[24]

The stinging cold seemed to invigorate the Apaches. Attacks and ambushes flared at Point of Rocks on the Jornada del Muerto above El Paso, and to the east at Eagle Springs. By Christmas the Indians had also stolen the stock from one of Giddings's freight trains as it camped near Barilla Springs. As the contractor went over his books that December, he must have felt discouraged in looking at the total of debts and losses charged to his new venture. Since assuming the mail contract in October, 1854, he had lost at least 358 head of stock to the Indians and suffered additional property damages to the amount of $54,465. Two men lay buried on the Jornada, and several others had been wounded defending the coaches. At this rate it was costing the company an average of $3,890 a month simply to replace its losses. Employees still had to be paid, animals shod and fed, and stations built and equipped.[25]

Of course Giddings was receiving his contract fee from the government and had even won an increase over the original $16,750 allowance. Governor Bell's lobbying had evidently paid off, for on March 3 Congress had boosted the amount to $33,500 per year and instructed that the sum would cover the period forward to the end of the contract from August 18, 1854. This seem-

[23] *San Antonio Ledger*, Oct. 29, 1855; *Galveston Daily News*, Nov. 13, 1855; Deposition of E. C. Allen, *Giddings vs. the United States.*

[24] John H. Moore, ed., "Letters of a Santa Fe Army Clerk," 1855–56," *New Mexico Historical Review* 40 (Apr. 1965): 158; Hyde, Ford, Wallace, Cooper, Allen, and Giddings Deposition, *Giddings vs. the United States.*

[25] Giddings Deposition, *Giddings vs. the United States.*

ing act of generosity was more than offset by the decisions
rendered by Attorney General Caleb Cushing and Postmaster
General Campbell when Brevoort and Houghton joined David
Wasson in appeals for payment on their nullified contracts. Giddings's pay increase withered away before the government's liberal adjustments in favor of the plaintiffs.[26]

Between January, 1855, and February, 1856, the Post Office
Department punished Giddings for its own sins with a vengeance. On January 17 it awarded David Wasson a total of $1,500
for his sterling services. The money was deducted from Giddings's contract. He could take some comfort in knowing that six
days later Campbell decided to pay Brevoort and Houghton for
their mail deliveries between July 1 and August 31, 1854, based
upon a rate of $24,900 a year. This time Wasson was charged for
the amount due the Santa Feans. On May 19 Campbell dunned
Giddings for $2,029.89 to pay Brevoort and his associate for ser-
vice in the month of September, 1854. The Texan escaped any
more such levies until February, 1856, when the order of January 13 was amended to allow Brevoort and Houghton pay on the
basis of $28,000 per year through September, 1854. This time
Giddings lost $1,467. In addition, the decision of May 19 was
altered to charge him another $1,274 for failure to deliver the
mail from August 18 through September 1, 1854. Then, in a
master stroke of clerical obfuscation, the department fined Giddings $1,365.49 to cover alleged delinquencies from September
1 to October 1, 1854, and followed this ruling by rescinding its
earlier direction to "withhold $2,029.89 for the month of Sep-
tember, 1854, and so much of the one requiring to deduct the
settlement for service prior to 1st January, 1855, as embraces the
$4,195.11 paid to Brevoort & Houghton."[27]

When Giddings received the last of these crazy-quilt ukases,
he must have despaired of ever getting his financial house in order. By then he had seen at least $5,607.37 pared away from his
contract, and it was all due to Wasson's incompetence and the

<hr />

[26] U.S. Congress, House, *Court of Claims Report No. 266*, 36th Cong., 2d sess.,
1860, pp. 24–25; U.S. Congress, Senate, *Annual Report on the Postmaster General for
1855*, Senate Exec. Doc. 1, 1855, p. 326.

[27] *Court of Claims Report No. 266*, 24–25.

confusion it had created with postmasters Beck, Bowen, and Hyde. Even worse, there was no reason to believe that any of the money paid to Brevoort and Houghton would be shared with Henry Skillman. Added to Giddings's contract deductions were the fines levied against him for failing to make scheduled deliveries on time. Deep snows had slowed the mail to the west in February, 1855, costing him $200 in penalties. In April and June the heavy spring rains delayed the mail to San Antonio, and another $650 was slashed from his pay as a result.[28]

When it was all figured together, the losses wrought by Indians and bureaucrats had cost George Giddings at least $60,922.37 in fifteen months of service on the line. In all of Texas in 1855 there were only 1,637 miles of postal coach routes. Giddings's line covered 673 of them from San Antonio to El Paso. The total funds paid by the Post Office Department for all the contractors on these routes amounted to $57,657. It was costing Giddings more in losses, excluding normal operating expenses, to keep his single line in service than the United States government was paying to deliver mail by coach all over the state. As 1856 opened Giddings might as well have been watering his mules with champagne for all the profit he was realizing from his labors.[29]

The young adventurer had been trained in a hard school during his decade on the frontier. The mail company increasingly looked like a failed investment, but Giddings knew that virtually any endeavor that led a man beyond the settlements was fraught with risk. Those that survived were directed by individuals who spent little time taking counsel of their fears. Despite his heavy losses, he still preferred the brassy lilt of his drivers' bugles to the furtive whisperings of self-doubt. The coaches would keep rolling.

Both George and Frank Giddings left San Antonio early in 1856 on a trip that they hoped would help restore their precarious financial situation. They left affairs in the hands of their younger brother, John, who had joined them in Texas several months before. The visit to the East lasted until well into the

---

[28] *Fines and Deductions*, 36, 63–64, 95–96.
[29] *Annual Report*, 374–75.

spring, as Frank traveled to New York to confer with their bankers, while George remained in Washington for a round of lobbying with Congressman Bell and Senator Rusk.

Several other prominent residents of the Southwest who were in the city during his visit added their testimonials to Giddings's petition for an increase in the contract fee. Postmaster Bowen had already sent a letter urging amendment of the contract to support Giddings's added expenses in maintaining four-horse teams on the route. Judge Joel Ankrim filed a deposition outlining the contractor's operating losses and called for additional funds to support the stage line. Captain George Howland of the Regiment of Mounted Riflemen seconded Ankrim's appeal with the remark that "the mail matter is now more than double what it was a short time ago." General Persifor F. Smith's statement stressed the toll exacted on the line's stock and equipment by the rough roads and Indian attacks. He remarked that Giddings had "but two stations for relays from San Elizario to Fort Clark—viz at Fort Davis about 160 miles & at a temporary post on Liveoak Creek—relays must consequently be driven along & are not fresh when harnessed." He added an appeal for expanded service, for "a semi-monthly mail is *absolutely* necessary." Giddings hoped that such testimonials would make some impression on the tightfisted Postmaster General Campbell.[30]

The Texan had a conversation with Rusk that illustrated the continental scope of the senator's ambitions for Texas. Rusk wanted to know why Giddings could not carry the mail beyond El Paso to California. "I told him I could," recalled Giddings. "He then asked me to make an estimate of the cost of carrying it from San Antonio, Tex., to San Diego, Cal. When I made the estimate and submitted it to him, on reading it he expressed doubt at my ability to carry it for double the amount." Rusk promised to secure such a contract for him if he ever applied for it.[31]

Giddings was more concerned with salvaging his operation in Texas than embarking on wider adventures, and he got a sym-

[30] Giddings Deposition, *Giddings* vs. *the United States.*
[31] Ibid.; Clayton Williams, *Never Again: Texas*, 3:154; "The Overland Mail Service to the Pacific," *San Antonio Express*, June 28, 1903.

pathetic hearing from Rusk and the other members of the Committee on Post Offices and Post Roads. On March 17 the contractor presented them with a lengthy memorial that detailed his problems and stated that the minimum of $3,000 per month he was spending to cover losses and meet operating costs constituted a yearly outlay of "at least three times the contract price."[32]

There was no immediate relief available from Rusk's committee, although Giddings knew he had a firm ally in the senator. No doubt Rusk had commiserated with him on February 29 when Campbell issued the order that fined Giddings for late deliveries and deducted funds from his contract to support the settlement with Brevoort and Houghton. It would take time, but with Rusk's help a bill might be steered through Congress that would repair some of the damage done by Campbell's habit of robbing one contractor to pay another for his department's mistakes. All Giddings could do was hope.[33]

The two brothers left Washington and returned home to find that little had changed on the road west to Santa Fe. The weather had temporarily replaced the Indians as their greatest enemy. At least one man froze to death on the run north from El Paso, and Captain John Dusenberry's eastbound coach spent fifteen miserable days on the trail in the teeth of bitter conditions. "The mail party was overtaken by a terrible hurricane on the 15th ult. at Escondido which took off the top of their ambulance," reported the *San Antonio Herald*. "On the 19th between Devil's River and Howard's Canon hail fell to the depth of five inches in twenty minutes. The weather was cold and unpleasant the whole trip." (In the 1850s an ambulance was simply a light passenger wagon. It had not yet acquired a medical connection.) Things were even worse on Dusenberry's return passage to the west. For seventeen straight days his caravan endured rain, sleet, and biting cold. Four mules died of exposure before they reached the Pass. It was business as usual on the mail road.[34]

The warmer weather that followed revived the Indians'

---

[32] Giddings Deposition, *Giddings* vs. *the United States*.

[33] *Court of Claims Report No. 266*, 24–25.

[34] *San Antonio Herald*, Jan. 3, Mar. 8, Apr. 26, 1856; Austin *Texas State Gazette*, Apr. 5, 1856.

deviltry. They were soon raiding the station at Fort Lancaster and attacking one of Giddings's freight columns amid the rumpled wastes east of Eagle Springs. Despite such setbacks, Giddings continued to find some of his strongest supporters among the settlers in El Paso. Henry L. Dexter, merchant, notary public, and tax assessor of the small Anglo community, called a meeting at Ysleta, "for the purpose of taking into consideration the propriety of a tri-monthly mail coach line from San Antonio, by way of El Paso." Dexter optimistically declared the road to be "open and passable at all seasons, with everything to cheer the emigrant and traveler in rich soil and varied landscape." He was not afraid to think in continental terms when the Pass's prosperity was involved. "The establishment of a tri-monthly mail line, on coaches, by this route," he maintained, "would tend greatly, not only to develop the resources of North Western Texas, but of the state—indeed, the whole nation. It would be the first active, progressive step in the establishment of the great Southern Pacific Railroad." [35]

Part of the impetus for Dexter's campaign lay in his dissatisfaction with the circumstance that much of El Paso's mail came in via the northern route that ran over the plains from Independence, Missouri, to Santa Fe. The previous June, Dexter had remarked in a letter to his sister in the eastern part of the country, "In this outside barbarian region we have not daily mails as in your country—recollect, we are somewhat remote from civilization . . . our mails are monthly from either place (San Antonio or Independence) but I prefer the Texan to the Missouri route, having lost a great deal of correspondence by the latter." [36]

When news of Dexter's rally reached Austin, the *Texas State Gazette* announced, "We cordially join our friends at El Paso in asking for this additional service of the Department, and from

[35] Austin *Texas State Gazette*, May 31, 1856; Depositions of Thomas M. Collins, Thomas Rife, and George H. Giddings, *Giddings* vs. *the United States*.

[36] Austin *Texas State Gazette*, Apr. 5, May 31, 1856; Henry L. Dexter to Mary Dexter Roundy, June 7, 1855, Henry L. Dexter Papers, Art Leibson Collection, El Paso, Tex.; Art Leibson, "Early Day El Pasoan Found Things Rugged," *El Paso Times*, Sept. 16, 1957; "A Page from El Paso's Past," *El Paso Today* 30 (Sept., 1978): 16–17; John P. Wilson, "A *Mesilla Times* Returns to New Mexico," *El Palacio* 78 (1972): 2–9; W. W. Mills, *Forty Years at El Paso, 1858–1898*, 177–78.

the state of the mails on the Independence route, it is clearly evident that it is insufficient for the vast amount of mail matter sent over it." The journal took note of similar meetings held in Santa Fe. "By a division of the mail and confining all matter south of Mason and Dixon's line to the San Antonio route," counseled the *Gazette*, "the evils seriously complained of at Santa Fe might be avoided." Dexter had struck a responsive chord in Texan's minds when he called for a mail service that would prepare the way for a transcontinental railroad through the region.

Public enthusiasm continued to grow as Giddings's men shaved hours and even days off the time needed to reach the Pass from Bexar, and did it in the face of continuing Indian raids. By mid-June the army had been forced to increase its patrols on the trail west of Fort Clark, but even the hard-riding dragoons could not be everywhere, nor could they always distinguish between those who traveled the road in peace and those who sought to prey upon them.[37]

That month Frank Giddings took the mail out of San Antonio in company with Thomas O. Wright and another traveler. Wright had made previous journeys with the mail and was well known in San Antonio. The train had a clear passage west to the Pecos. On the morning after they had forded the river, Wright and his companion decided to ride ahead of the coach as it headed for Escondido Springs. Giddings and his crew paused to finish breakfast and followed soon after the two men left camp. Five miles to the west they found Wright and his friend sprawled dead in the trail. Their horses were gone, but neither man had been scalped or mutilated. It was curious behavior for Indians. Giddings buried them hastily and drove on to make a wary halt at the springs. Behind him two lonely piles of stones marked the site of yet another instance of quick and merciless death on the mail route.[38]

July began well despite the memory of the tragedy that lingered from Giddings's journey, but things took a grim cast quickly when Captain Jerry Snyder's coach pulled into Eagle Springs and

[37] *San Antonio Herald*, June 28, 1856; Post Returns, Fort Davis, Texas, citing Special Order 72, Headquarters, Department of Texas, June 14, 1856, RG 94, NARS.

[38] Austin *Texas State Gazette*, Aug 2, 1856; *San Antonio Herald*, Aug. 30, 1856.

found the station house reduced to a pile of charred rubble, while twenty tons of hay smoldered in the feedlot next to the empty corral. Not far away lay the bodies of the three station hands. When a shocked George Giddings arrived a few days later on an inspection tour of the line, he found the scene unchanged, except that the wolves had been pawing at the stones piled over the graves Snyder had dug. It would be months before the station could be rebuilt.[39]

The embers had barely cooled at Eagle Springs before more violence erupted along the route. This time white desperadoes were the transgressors. The previous fall Giddings had fired Jack Gordon from his driver's job after he clashed with James Broad. Gordon drifted west to El Paso, and by November he was leading a gang of thieves in a series of crimes with his partner, a man known variously as William McElroy and William Blair. That month they blew open the safe in the customs house and stole $2,300. The next night they robbed Ben Dowell's store and corral, leaving a taunting note behind before riding north to Las Cruces.[40]

Several of the outlaws were later reported killed by Apaches near Fort Thorn, New Mexico, but Gordon and McElroy remained in the area near El Paso. Dowell's investigations confirmed his belief that these two had been involved in the thefts. McElroy openly boasted that he would kill Dowell someday.

On August 6 Gordon and his partner rode in from the desert to spend the night in San Elizario. They did some serious drinking at William Ford's saloon, unaware that he was a good friend of Dowell. While they discussed their plan to kill the merchant, Ford sent a rider off to warn him. The next morning the two felons rode into the settlement upriver. As Gordon kept watch outside, McElroy strode into Dowell's combination of store, saloon, and billiard parlor. Dowell and his friend, Albert Kuhn, were waiting for him with cocked pistols. McElroy died

[39] San Antonio Herald, July 5, 1856; Hyde, Ford, Rife, and Giddings Depositions, Giddings vs. the United States.

[40] San Antonio Herald, Nov. 27, 1855; San Antonio Ledger, Dec. 1, 1855; Nancy Hamilton, Ben Dowell, El Paso's First Mayor, 19–21.

before he could even get off a shot. Jack Gordon swore vengeance against Dowell and then galloped out of town.[41]

Gordon dropped out of sight after this narrow escape from justice, but his dead partner helped to answer some questions that still lingered from an earlier set of killings. Dowell found a revolver on McElroy's body, and one of Giddings's men recalled that he had seen either Wright or his friend carrying it before their deaths. There could only be one response to such treachery. Every man on the stage line would be after Jack Gordon's head.[42]

Giddings could take some pleasure in the outlaws' defeat, but it was soon dispelled by news from Washington. In May, Congressman Bell's committee had recommended that Giddings receive an extension to the supplementary allowance granted to him in August, 1855, to cover the previous year's service. Three months later Senator Rusk's Committee on Post Offices and Post Roads followed with a motion that Giddings receive a doubled contract fee for his service since 1855. On August 18 Rusk's bill was passed and Giddings seemed assured of receiving $33,500 for the year between August 18, 1855, and August 18, 1856. Then Postmaster General Campbell stepped in and on August 25 ordered that Giddings was to draw only $25,000 a year, which he felt was "a liberal compensation for the service, and a rate at which it can be well and faithfully performed, with profit to the contracting party." He could also cite Attorney General Caleb Cushing's recent opinions on the compensation due Wasson, Brevoort, and Houghton, all of which supported his earlier decisions on Giddings's pay. Thus, although both House Bill 382 and Senate Bill 432 had been passed with the specific aim of aiding Giddings, Campbell refused to spend the funds appropriated for that purpose.[43]

[41] *San Antonio Herald*, Jan. 3, 1856.

[42] Ibid., Aug. 28, 30, 1856; *San Antonio Texan*, Aug. 28, 1856.

[43] U.S. Congress, House, *George H. Giddings*, House Rpt. 170, 34th Cong., 1st sess., 1855, pp. 1–2; U.S. Congress, Senate, *Petition of George H. Giddings*, 34th Cong., 1st sess., 1855, Senate Comm. Rpt. 264, pp. 1–2; Giddings Deposition, *Giddings vs. the United States*.

Giddings was no stranger to frustration, but no sooner had he recovered from Campbell's latest bureaucratic obduracy than another disaster struck on the road west of the Pecos: a band of Indians ambushed Bigfoot Wallace's caravan near Escondido Springs and burned both coaches after capturing the mules. The mail was lost, simply giving Campbell one more excuse to impose a fine. Giddings's fears that it was going to be a costly autumn were confirmed in October when the Mescaleros emptied the station's corral at La Limpia, provoking a futile pursuit from Fort Davis led by Lieutenant Bliss. In November the Apaches nearly overran a party of emigrants camped amid the ruins at Eagle Springs, and another band struck the stage on the Jornada del Muerto. Four Indians died and several passengers were wounded before Price Cooper's crew shot their way clear of the ambush.[44]

Giddings's men would continue to pay in a bitter currency for passage on the road, but at least the year ended without a repetition of the disasters of December, 1855. The first eastbound mail of the new year left the Pass with Giddings riding along with it. The travelers were only a few days out of the valley settlements when the Apaches made an early morning attack on the whites as they camped at Eighteen-Mile Hole. Guard Joseph Hetler and James Cook, the conductor, joined Giddings in directing the defense, but the warriors soon captured all the mules from the picket line and then set fire to the coaches as the Texans' Sharps rifles cracked in the predawn darkness. When it was all over, Giddings could only curse his luck while the guards lifted the hair from some dead braves before rolling their bodies onto the leaping flames. It would not be the last time that expressmen and Indians would clash at the waterhole.[45]

In February a howling blizzard delayed the coaches east of El Paso, costing the line even more penalties. Despite the continuing drain on his finances, Giddings repeatedly tried to improve his service and provide for the comfort and safety of his

---

[44] Wallace and Giddings Depositions, *Giddings* vs. *the United States*; Austin *Texas State Gazette*, Sept. 6, Dec. 13, 1856; John C. Reid, *Reid's Tramp*, 88, 106–124.

[45] Depositions of Joseph Hetler, A. C. Hyde, and George H. Giddings, *Giddings* vs. *the United States*. This oasis was also known as "Cienegas" and "Tinaja de las Palmas."

passengers. By early 1857 he had managed to construct a relay post at Van Horn's Wells. The roughly finished rock-and-adobe station offered crude accommodations, but any mark of civilization was welcome in that wild country. Unfortunately the presence of mules, firearms, and supplies also lured the Indians. The men at the station had to remain alert if they were to survive, for in March the Comanches caught the herd while it was grazing near the station and drove it off in triumph, draining more gold from Giddings's accounts.[46]

Events of far greater significance than the theft of a few mules were unfolding in the East that month. On March 4 James Buchanan, a Pennsylvania Democrat of allegedly prosouthern sympathies, was sworn in as president. This was good news for Giddings, as it meant the end of Cushing and Campbell's influence. Two days later Chief Justice Roger Taney of the Supreme Court handed down the Dred Scott decision and sank his judicial ax deep into the already rotten timbers of the Missouri Compromise.

Other elements were being blended into a political climate that was already riven by sectionalism. In mid-April, 1856, California had dispatched a set of petitions to Congress that bore 75,000 signatures in support of requests for a wagon road and overland mail service from the eastern states. In an effort to avoid a prolonged sectional squabble and keep the Californians happy in an election year, Congress appropriated funds for two post roads. One was to run from Fort Kearney, Nebraska Territory, to the California border via South Pass. The second road would follow the old Gila Trail west from El Paso to the California boundary at Fort Yuma on the junction of the Gila and Colorado rivers. When the mail service came up for discussion, a deadlock ensued. After a year of debate a joint House and Senate conference committee drew up a compromise. The Post Office Appropriations bill for 1857–58 was amended to authorize the postmaster general to "contract for the conveyance of the entire letter mail from such a point on the Mississippi River as the contractors may select, to San Francisco, in the State of Califor-

---

[46] Hyde and Giddings Depositions, *Giddings vs. the United States.*

nia, for six years, at a cost not exceeding $300,000 per annum for semi-monthly, $450,000 for weekly, or $600,000 for semi-weekly, at the option of the Postmaster-general."[47]

This seemed to be a reasonable compromise, but with Buchanan's election the southern Democrats had won a victory. Buchanan offered Thomas Rusk the postmaster general's chair in his new cabinet, but the Texan declined. Buchanan then turned to Aaron V. Brown, a vehemently proslavery Tennessean. Although the legislation gave the contractors their choice of an eastern terminus on the Mississippi, it gave Brown the power to choose the contractor, thus according him de facto authority to select the route.

Congress passed the Post Office appropriations bill on the day before Buchanan took office. On April 20, 1857, Brown advertised for bids on the new route. Fate was about to step into the traces alongside George Giddings's teams.[48]

[47] W. Turrentine Jackson, Wagon Roads West, 161–78; George Minot and George P. Sanger, eds., Statutes at Large and Treaties of the United States of America, 11: 188–90; Ralph Moody, Stagecoach West, 71–73.

[48] Moody, Stagecoach West, 71–73; Mary W. Clarke, Thomas J. Rusk, 201.

CHAPTER 5

"From No Place through Nothing to Nowhere"

AT about the same time that George Giddings was entering the mercantile business in San Antonio, a young New Englander was setting out to make his fortune in California. Unlike Giddings, he did not drift into the express service. It was his chosen profession from the start, and in his brief life he became one of its giants. In 1846 nineteen-year-old James Birch began driving a stage for Otis Kelton, a prosperous Providence, Rhode Island, livery stable owner. Birch was a hard worker, and his efforts were spurred in part by his love for Kelton's young ward, Julia Chase. He was determined to make himself a worthy suitor.

In 1849 Birch left Rhode Island for California, confident that an enterprising young man could soon win wealth by hauling miners and supplies to the gold diggings. By the end of the first year he had established a stage line that ran daily from Sacramento to Sutter's Mill. Each fare brought him two ounces of gold dust.[1]

Birch's business never faltered, and he was soon operating both stage routes and telegraph lines to Nevada City, Nicolaus, Marysville, and Stockton from his headquarters in Sacramento. In October, 1851, he sold his holdings and returned to the eastern states a wealthy man. He built an elegant mansion for Julia Chase in Swansea, Massachusetts, and married her in September, 1852. He had kept his vow to make her a rich bride.

Birch enjoyed an extended honeymoon that winter, and in the spring of 1853 he left Julia behind in Massachusetts while he

---

[1] Alfred D. Galluci and Mary M. Galluci, *James E. Birch*, 1–5; William Banning and George H. Banning, *Six Horses*, 8–14; Mae H. B. Boggs, ed., *My Playhouse was a Concord Coach*, 30, 49–54, 65.

returned to California to rebuild his stage line and telegraph empire. Joining with several other expressmen, he consolidated several large stage lines to form the California Stage Company and won a seat as the firm's first president. As before, everything that Birch touched seemed to prosper. By February, 1855, he was able to step down from the company's helm and leave its affairs in charge of his partners. He returned home to his bride and began planning a new enterprise.[2]

Birch had not been back in Swansea for very long before he departed for Washington, D.C., on the first of a series of trips that saw him deeply involved with members of Congress who held positions of influence over postal affairs. Birch wanted to be engaged from the beginning in the creation of a transcontinental stage line. For the next two years he shuttled back and forth between Swansea and the capital, keeping firm his political and social ties with the leading residents of both cities. The gleam of empire had settled in his eyes.[3]

Birch was ready when Postmaster General Aaron V. Brown advertised for bids on the new California mail route, and along with eight other contractors, he submitted an offer to carry the mail west from the Mississippi. The lowest bid was for $520,000 a year and designated St. Louis as the eastern terminus, with the route following a still unfinished post road from Fort Kearney, Nebraska Territory, through South Pass to California. A staggering bid of $1 million was proposed for one year's weekly service from Vicksburg, Mississippi, to the Pacific over an unspecified route. Birch was unconcerned over these two highly unrealistic proposals, but he was alarmed to hear of another bid submitted by Butterfield and Company. Formed from a union of the Adams, American, National, and Wells Fargo express companies, this new firm was headed by John Butterfield, a personal friend of President Buchanan.[4]

Buchanan and Brown were put in a ticklish position by the

[2] Galluci and Galluci, *James Birch*, 19–30.

[3] Banning and Banning, *Six Horses*, 92.

[4] LeRoy R. Hafen, *The Overland Mail, 1849–1869*, 88–89; Roscoe Conkling and Margaret B. Conkling, *The Butterfield Overland Mail, 1857–1869*, 1:118–19; Ralph

Butterfield and Birch rivalry. A tangle of personal and sectional loyalties were involved that seemed to be beyond hope of compromise. No matter what decision the government reached, a chorus of outraged critics would be waiting to voice their opposition to this latest blow against their interests. Brown had to reconcile both his choice of route and contractor with the desires of his president, the Californians, the North, and the South. His actions proved to be anything but placatory in the tense situation.

When Butterfield proposed to follow a route that would leave St. Louis and follow the Santa Fe Trail as far as Albuquerque before tracing the thirty-fifth parallel to California, Brown proceeded to muddy the issue even more. He announced that neither the route nor St. Louis as the sole eastern terminus was acceptable. Instead, he would contract only for service "from St. Louis, Missouri, and from Memphis, Tennessee, converging at Little Rock, Arkansas; thence, via Preston, Texas or as nearly so as may be found advisable, to the best point of crossing the Rio Grande, above El Paso, and not far from Fort Fillmore; thence along the new road being opened and constructed under the direction of the Secretary of the Interior, to Fort Yuma, California, thence, through the best passes and along the best valleys for safe and expeditious staging, to San Francisco." All of this was in open violation of the congressional directions that accompanied the postal appropriation. Under them, the contractor would have the choice of routes and a terminus on the Mississippi. Certainly the selection of Memphis, Brown's hometown, was not the result of a guileless coincidence.[5]

Brown's capricious alteration of the contract terms earned him criticism on other counts. Many Californians protested that the bulk of all traffic into the state came over the central route that ran via South Pass, and not by way of the arid, Apache-haunted track along the Gila. The road that Brown cited as being under construction by the Department of the Interior had barely been started. Brown rightly responded that the trail from El

Moody, *Stagecoach West*, 73–76; Banning and Banning, *Six Horses*, 93–95; *New York Times*, June 25, July 7, 1857.

[5] Moody, *Stagecoach West*, 73–76.

Paso was the only one that was free of heavy snow and passable all year round, but that did little to still the clamor.

The criticism served to tighten the squeeze of conflicting loyalties placed upon Brown and Buchanan. Birch had entered a bid of $600,000 a year for semiweekly service on the exact route specified by Brown and was confident that he would win the contract. A Californian who met him in New York in mid-May reported him "so sure of getting it that he has ordered the necessary coaches to be built. He says that he will make the trip through in twenty days, and will carry each time twenty passengers, at less rates than now charged by steamers."[6]

Birch's confidence was sadly misplaced, for Brown and Buchanan concluded a compromise that summer that plainly put their interests ahead of his, no matter what his previous understanding may have been with the pair. On June 22, Brown awarded Birch a contract that was essentially a consolation prize. For $149,800 a year he was to commence a semimonthly service for four years between San Antonio and San Diego, California. Thirty days were allowed for each one-way trip, and the service was to begin on July 1, 1857. Brown then awarded a six-year contract for the semiweekly Mississippi–to–San Francisco route to Butterfield at $600,000 a year.[7]

Though June 22 was the official award date for his contract, Birch had actually signed the document on June 12, and he immediately set about readying his new express line for operation. His choice of a man to serve as his chief lieutenant must have come as a surprise to many people. Isaiah Churchill Woods had known Birch during his early days of staging in California. At the time Woods was a director of the local branch of Adams and Company's banking and express business. With Woods's dedicated help the concern flourished, and he was soon a junior partner and prominent citizen of San Franciso.

Woods was a talented and diligent servant of the company, but like all men he was hostage to the economic vagaries of the day. In February, 1854, word reached California of a depression

[6] Boggs, *Concord Coach*, 275; *Sacramento Union*, June 18, 1857.
[7] Hafen, *Overland Mail*, 84–92.

in the East. Rumors flared and quickly spread. In the blaze of panic that followed a run on both local banks degenerated into a frenzied stampede. By February 23 Wells Fargo and Company was managing to weather the storm, but Adams and Company had closed its doors. The panic flowed across the state, and mob violence erupted against banks and express offices in several settlements. The Adams firm went into receivership, and Isaiah Woods fled the country on a ship bound for Australia.[8]

It was never determined if Woods had been guilty of criminal conduct or had simply yielded to the fear that as junior partner he might be made the scapegoat for the company's failure. The San Francisco branch of the business had been solvent, but the weak standing of the parent office in St. Louis had caused a rapid drain on its funds. Whatever the truth of the matter, Woods took the blame when the company folded. After a sojourn in Australia he traveled to Europe and then returned to the United States to seek a new start in New York City.[9]

James Birch met him there as he prepared to start his new company. The New Englander did not share the widespread distrust of Woods that persisted in California, and he valued his abilities as both an organizer and promoter. It was proof of his trust that he gave Woods cash and certificates of deposit worth $20,000. The grateful Woods quickly assumed his new responsibilities and set out to put the coaches on the road by the scheduled time. On June 15 he dispatched agent James Mason to San Antonio from New York with orders to purchase stock and equipment with which to take the first contract mail west on July 9. Five days later he sent detailed instructions to his brother-in-law, Robert E. Doyle, in San Francisco. Doyle was to organize and equip the first eastbound mail to start from San Diego on July 24. He was appointed superintendent of the line west of Tucson, Arizona Territory, to the Pacific Coast.[10]

Woods lingered briefly in New York to settle some related

---

[8] Alvin F. Harlow, *Old Waybills*, 141, 157–67.

[9] Isaiah C. Woods, *Report to Honorable A. V. Brown, Postmaster General, on the Opening and Present Condition of the United States Overland Mail Route Between San Antonio, Texas and San Diego, California,* 1–3.

[10] Ibid.

business before departing for San Antonio on June 24. Traveling by way of Chicago, Cairo, and New Orleans, he arrived in the Crescent City on the night of July 3 to find a telegram from Birch waiting for him. His employer was leaving New York on a mail steamer and planned to meet Woods in San Diego after he came overland on the new mail road. It was the last communication that Woods ever received from Birch. Neither man could have guessed of the tragedy that lay ahead.[11]

By July 7 Woods had landed in Texas at Indianola, but he arrived too late to catch the stage to San Antonio. He had hoped to reach the town before the first Pacific mail departed, but the delay kept him from arriving in Bexar until the afternoon of the eleventh. Much to his relief, he learned that Mason had succeeded in outfitting a party for the trip. Amid great excitement he had presented his credentials to the postmaster and collected the mail pouch for San Diego. On July 9 the coach swung out of the plaza to the cheers and applause of a large crowd. Sheriff Thomas McCall was at the reins as far as the city limits, when he relinquished his seat on the box to Mason and wished him a swift passage to California.[12]

Woods spent that Sunday resting from his trip, and early Monday morning he sought out George Giddings and appealed for his aid in organizing the line for continued operation. Giddings must have been skeptical of Woods's chances for success, but he guided him around town and gave him the benefit of his advice as the Californian purchased more stock and supplies, hired men, and rented a corral and office. Giddings could tell a trail-seasoned mule from a green one, and his familiarity with Bexar's citizenry lent prestige to Woods's activities while insuring that he hired only capable and honest men.[13]

On July 16 Woods made one of his wisest decisions when he hired Henry Skillman and Bigfoot Wallace to help get the next

---

[11] Ibid.

[12] Ibid.; *San Antonio Express*, Feb. 13, 1949; New Orleans *Daily Picayune*, July 18, 1857. The *Picayune* stated that Mason left on the tenth, accompanied by Texan W. L. Baylor and Samuel A. Ames of Massachusetts, along with two Missourians, W. C. Benton and A. W. Beardslee.

[13] *San Antonio Express*, Feb. 13, 1949.

mail party through the wilderness. Skillman was to serve as conductor of the mail slated to depart on July 24. He was to take the
coach through to the Pima Indian villages west of Tucson. On
July 19 he dispatched Wallace westward to Fort Lancaster with a
supply train and a remuda of twenty-seven mules to stock the
relay stations en route to the Pecos. Nine of the animals were to
be left at Fort Clark, and another eighteen were to be held at
Lancaster. Skillman could thus push his own teams hard during
the first several days and make good time, secure in the knowledge that fresh ones would be waiting for him at the posts.

Three days after Wallace's train had left town, Giddings's
regular mail from El Paso came in and the driver told a relieved
Woods that "they had met our mail of July 9 getting along safely
though slowly." During all of his hurried preparations for the
next mail's departure he had felt the nagging fear that some disaster might have claimed Mason's train.[14]

Henry Skillman saw to it that nothing delayed the caravan
that he was to lead out of town that Friday. Promptly at 6:00 A.M.
he cracked his whip and the team leaped forward in the traces as
the coach and its outriders swept across the plaza to begin the
first day's race with the westering sun. Five men went with him,
all heavily armed and well equipped for the exigencies of the
trail. They were provisioned for thirty days' travel to the Pima
villages on the Gila. The mules were in good trim and ready for
hard service. If any gave out along the way or were stolen by
Indians, Skillman carried six hundred dollars in gold to buy replacement stock. Woods must have felt a thrill of pride as he
watched the bearded plainsman lead his little band out of San
Antonio that morning. No surer hand ever held a pair of reins
than Skillman's, and he knew that this mail would be brought
through against any odds.[15]

With Skillman safely away, Woods could turn his attention
to the problems that still remained. Despite Giddings's aid and
the dispatch of buyers into the surrounding countryside, he still
had trouble purchasing enough stock to support the company's

[14] Woods, *Report*, 4–7.
[15] Ibid.

continuing operation. Keenly aware of Birch's admonition to push the new line to "an early and vigorous success," Woods met with Giddings only two days after Skillman's departure and proposed a merger of the two stage companies. "The bringing of this property under my superintendence," explained Woods, "in conjunction with the stock I had already purchased, would enable me to perform our mail service of twice a month and also Mr. Giddings' contract of once a month, with less stock than if the two lines had been run separately." [16]

Giddings considered the offer for several days. The line had become a crushing financial burden during the past three years, and little had changed to indicate that it might ever clear a profit. Under Woods's terms he would retain his original San Antonio–Santa Fe contract and assume additional duties as superintendent for the route east of Tucson. Thus the losses to his contract would be partially borne by Birch's company, while he retained both a salary from Woods and the payment for his original service. On July 29 he made a binding agreement with Woods and added his holdings to those of the San Diego Mail. Giddings's fortune was firmly tied to that of a man who was already doomed. [17]

Woods had no sooner shaken hands with his new partner than he began preparing yet another supply train for departure from Bexar on July 31. Three coaches, thirty-eight mules, and seventeen men were assembled on the plaza as he checked the stowage of saddles, harnesses, ammunition, kegs of nails, spare mule shoes, and two tons of supplies for the journey to San Diego.

The caravan left on schedule, and the next day Woods followed it on Giddings's El Paso coach. Before leaving he had organized the mail party for August 9 and instructed Giddings to accompany it as far as El Paso, remaining there to supervise affairs while he was in California. Woods had also solicited the army's aid to speed his coaches' passage through Indian country. On July 21 Brigadier General David E. Twiggs, the department commander, issued a special order instructing the garrisons along the stage route to furnish Woods with escorts upon his request

[16] Ibid.
[17] Ibid.

and "give protection to any horses or mules he may leave at their posts." The expressman used Twiggs's order as a carte blanche to request any sort of assistance from the army. This presumption was to create grave problems for him in the months ahead.[18]

The mail stage quickly overtook the supply train, and they traveled in company for the first several hundred miles. They met Bigfoot Wallace on the road beyond Castroville under a sky that drizzled rain upon their slickers and serapes. All that now remained of the supply train he had captained consisted of the haggard Wallace and his companion, who sported a wounded arm in a sling. Soaking wet and mounted on borrowed army mules, they looked their roles as heralds of disaster.

Wallace tersely informed Woods of what had happened when the train entered the Devil's River country north of Camp Hudson. The men were fifteen miles above the post and nearing the upper crossing on the river when the Comanches boiled out of the heavy brush that flanked the road. Wallace and a young adventurer from New Orleans, William Clifford, were on the box, and the other four men rode herd on the mules that trotted along a good distance ahead. The screaming braves went after the stage, and the terrified team bolted into a mesquite thicket, running in a circle until a sudden jolt snapped the pole. Wallace threw down the reins and jumped clear, calling on Clifford to join him. The milling warriors cut off the Louisianian as they sprinted for the remuda, and Wallace saw him go down beneath a lance. Gaining the mule herd, Wallace leaped astride an animal and told the guards to ride for their lives. The raiders were too numerous to risk making a stand, and the Texans cut through the brush in a desperate race for Camp Hudson. The Comanches were content to loot the coach and round up the mules, letting the whites escape without pursuit.

Wallace cantered into the army post several hours later and found that a patrol of the Second Cavalry had just arrived from Fort Clark. Its commander immediately left in hopes of punishing the Indians, while an infantry escort accompanied Wallace

[18] Ibid., 4–9; Special Order No. 91, Headquarters, Department of Texas, July 21, 1857, Post Returns, Fort Davis, Texas, Aug. 1857, RG 94, NARS.

back to the ambush site. They buried the mutilated remains of Clifford and hauled the wrecked coach back to Camp Hudson. The Comanches had escaped with twenty-one mules and all the supplies that they cared to take before destroying the rest. A box of goods bound for Fort Lancaster was also lost, but luckily it was the only piece of mail on the coach.[19]

The cavalrymen caught up with the braves later and in a skirmish recaptured the mules, but by that time most of the animals were lamed or wind-broken and useless for stage work. It was a painful defeat for Woods, but he knew that his men had been lucky to escape with only one casualty. Just a few days before, the same war party had ambushed Lieutenant John B. Hood and a patrol of the Second Cavalry several miles north of where they met Wallace. The troopers had taken and given heavy casualties in the fight before cutting their way free, and the Comanches were understandably hungry for revenge when they attacked the expressmen.[20]

Woods sent Wallace and his men back to San Antonio to await further orders while he pressed on to Uvalde and Fort Clark. At the army post he paused to write a progress report for Birch. The loss of Wallace's mules had obliged him to draw on his account at the Bank of Manhattan for a three-month note totaling $5,000 to cover Giddings's expenses in filling the company's corral in San Antonio as well as for the emergency purchase of new stock. Anticipating Birch's approval, he sent the draft back to his bank in San Antonio along with the letter, which was to go by steamer from Indianola to Sacramento. This was only the beginning of a series of tangled financial transactions involving the infant company. Woods had acted in good faith, but events would conspire to defeat him.[21]

The caravan made good time up the Devil's River and into Fort Lancaster on the Pecos, arriving on August 8. Woods was happy to hear that Skillman had purchased two extra mules there

---

[19] Woods, *Report*, 4–9; *San Antonio Herald*, Aug. 5, 1857; New Orleans *Weekly Picayune*, Aug. 13, 1857.

[20] John B. Hood, *Advance and Retreat*, 12; Washington, D.C., *Daily National Intelligencer*, Aug. 28, 1857.

[21] Woods, *Report*, 8–9.

and proceeded swiftly on his way. Woods quickly followed Skill-man's trail across the Pecos and gave his teams little rest until they arrived at Fort Davis. Upon reaching La Limpia he hastened over to the post and called on its commander, Lieutenant Colonel George W. Seawell. Woods hoped to purchase fresh animals in the settlement adjoining the post, but there were none to be had for any price. Impressing Seawell with his mission's importance, Woods secured the loan of thirty-six army mules for his use as far as El Paso. Three soldiers would accompany the mail train and bring the animals back to Fort Davis when it reached the Pass. The forty-two mules in the original remuda would be left in Seawell's charge. It was another action that would plague the company in the months to come.[22]

By the next day, August 13, Woods was on the road again. He met Giddings's eastbound mail at the fort before his departure and sent part of his escort back with it as far as Fort Clark. The superintendent forged on with his new teams at a brisk clip. Three days later Woods arrived in San Elizario after having fought his way upriver through mired roads and sheets of driving rain from the summer thunderstorms. On reaching Fort Bliss he flashed his credentials before the post commander and soon had an army blacksmith at work repairing a damaged wagon while he and his men canvassed the settlements for fresh mules. Only a few were to be had at any cost, and Woods knew that the next mail was already on the trail west from San Antonio. It would need new teams upon arrival at El Paso also. The only solution was to keep fourteen of the army mules while sending the rest back to Fort Davis with the troops. Colonel Seawell might have accepted the necessity of this action had not Woods sent him a false report stating that the rest of his animals had strayed from the party's camp and were lost. Seawell was a grizzled old regular and quickly classified Woods as a simple horse thief.

While part of his caravan proceeded fifty miles upriver from El Paso to await the incoming mail from California at Fort Fillmore, Woods headquartered himself in Giddings's store and continued to buy as much stock and as many supplies as he could to

[22]Ibid., 10–14.

sustain the line in his absence. Giddings soon joined him with the San Antonio mail. He brought bad news. Senator Thomas Rusk, the company's greatest political ally, had shot himself in a fit of depression only a few weeks before. A mocking fate had dictated that the weapon he used in his suicide was a Sharps rifle. Both Woods and Giddings knew that their enterprise would feel Rusk's loss keenly every time it had to deal with the government. No man had held a deeper appreciation of the stage line's importance as a vanguard of progress in the Southwest than the skilled and articulate senator.[23]

The two men shook off their gloom and continued with the task at hand. While Giddings assumed charge of affairs in El Paso, Woods picked up the California mail and was on the road before dawn on August 22. He rendezvoused with the rest of the party at Fort Fillmore and made a precarious crossing of the Rio Grande before striking off to the north and west to leave the river and head for Cooke's Spring, forty-eight miles beyond.[24]

When Woods left the Rio Grande behind him, he was entering new territory as far as the mail line was concerned. The emigrant trail to the west of El Paso offered as many dangers and challenges as that to the east. There would be no easy passage for anyone who traveled it, as Woods soon learned.

Cooke's Spring, the Rio Mimbres, Cow Spring, Hawk Spring, Stein's Peak, and a dozen other landmarks fell behind them as the caravan breached the limits of Apachería again. At Stein's Peak, Woods had a nasty scare when his party found the stripped hulk of Skillman's coach sitting in the trail. He feared the worst for a moment and then noticed that a broken rear wheel had been carefully propped up on a pyramid of rocks. There were no bullet or arrow scars on the rig's body, and Woods noticed that the front wheels and pole were missing. Skillman had jury-rigged a light cart and continued his journey after caching whatever supplies and equipment he could no longer carry.[25]

[23] Ibid., 14–15.

[24] Ibid.; Mary W. Clarke, *Thomas J. Rusk*, 210–15.

[25] Woods, *Report*, 16–17; Roscoe Conkling and Margaret B. Conkling, *The Butterfield Overland Mail, 1857–1869*, 2; 108–39; John R. Bartlett, *Personal Narrative of Exploration and Incidents in Texas, Mexico, California, Sonora, and Chihuahua, Con-*

A relieved Woods cheered his crew on and drove to narrow the gap between the two parties, making a nervous run through the Chiricahua Mountains and Apache Pass to reach Dragoon Springs, an oasis only a little more than a hundred miles from the settlement at Tucson. By that time, unknown to Woods, they had been passed by the returning Skillman as he followed a side spur of the main trail. Having safely reached the Pima villages at Maricopa Wells, he was making good time back to El Paso.

By August 29 the caravan had forded the San Pedro River and was closing on Tucson when Woods saw several men approaching on muleback. They were the first eastbound mail couriers from San Diego, riding twenty days out from the coast. Woods was glad to see them but chagrined at some of the news they bore.

Before leaving New York in late June, Woods had sent full instructions to Doyle in San Diego on the dispatch of the initial eastern mail. The letter did not reach him until July 13, leaving him only five days to assemble all the required equipment in San Francisco before shipping it down the coast to San Diego. Doyle worked frenziedly but had trouble finding enough stock to support the line's beginning in San Diego. July 24 came and passed with Doyle still hunting for more mules. He finally put a small party of riders on the road on August 9, having sent other men ahead with relays of fresh animals as far east as Fort Yuma. The couriers had ridden beyond that point to meet Woods nearly forty miles east of Tucson. Since they had already missed their rendezvous with Skillman and were not adequately equipped to make the rest of the journey into El Paso, Woods had them join his train for the meantime.[26]

The mail party finally reached Tucson, and Woods purchased more stock to replace the exhausted teams. Knowing that the Indian threat decreased markedly west of the settlement, Woods reorganized his outfit for the dash to California. With only three

nected with the United States Boundary Commission During the Years 1850–1853, 1: 219–43, 361–71; Gerald T. Anhert, *Retracing the Butterfield Overland Trail through Arizona,* 16–25.

   [26] Woods, *Report,* 17–19; Conkling and Conkling, *Butterfield Mail,* 2: 140–57; Anhert, *Retracing,* 25–49.

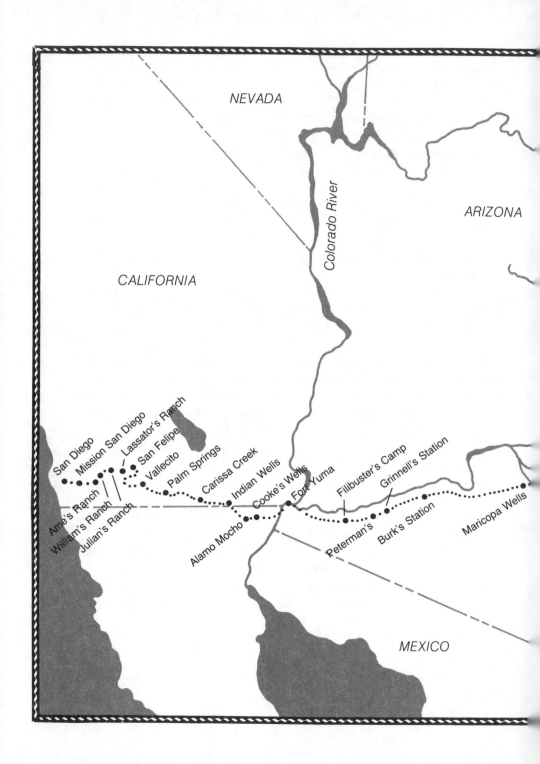

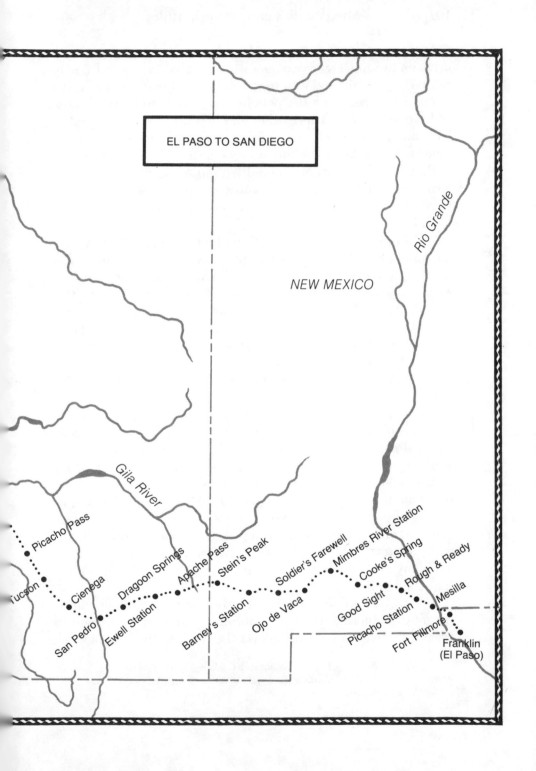

men as escort, one carriage, and a dozen mules, he proposed to drive on to San Diego. Two men were ordered to proceed slowly to Maricopa Wells and wait there for the next mail from San Antonio. Upon receiving the pouches they were to make all possible speed for Fort Yuma, 180 miles beyond. Woods planned to have another team of men waiting there for them. He took another pair of riders with him as he departed Tucson on the thirtieth. These hands were charged with picking up the next California mail at Maricopa Wells and escorting it back to Tucson, where the rest of the original party would be waiting to carry it to El Paso.[27]

Within two days Woods had reached Maricopa Wells, arriving just in time to be a nervous spectator as the local Pimas and Maricopas waged a pitched battle with the neighboring Yumas, Mojaves, and Tonto Apaches. The battle raged around the whites' camp all that day, with scores of warriors dying within pistol-shot of the carriage. The Texans took great pains to remain aloof during the fighting, for Woods had no desire to antagonize any of the rival tribes in the region. After resting his teams he drove on, leaving three men behind to build a corral and station building near the waterholes.[28]

The next day Woods met another mail party from San Diego. It had left the coast only nine days before, but he knew that it was already too late for it to make the right connections to the El Paso mail. The riders at Maricopa Wells had orders to wait no longer than sunset that day before heading back to Tucson, as the train had to depart in time to reach Mesilla and pick up the mail of September 9 from San Antonio. Woods told the Californians to return to Fort Yuma and prepare to make a quick march with the next mail from San Diego upon its arrival at the post. With any luck they could carry it on to Maricopa Wells within the scheduled time.

It was a period of mounting anxiety for Woods. The closer he got to California, the more confusion and disarray seemed to plague the eastbound couriers on the line. As time grew more

---

[27] Woods, *Report*, 19–20; Conkling and Conkling, *Butterfield Mail*, 2: 158–62; Anhert, *Retracing*, 50–67; Bartlett, *Personal Narrative*, 2: 210–8.

[28] Woods, *Report*, 19–20.

and more precious, even the road seemed to mock his efforts to steal a march on the clock. Oatman Flats and the Gila Crossing came up and then fell away as they drove onward along a trail that was often mired and scored by gullies from the heavy summer rains along the river. Time and again Woods and his men stripped off their clothes and wrestled the mules and carriage free of the mud's sucking grip. Filthy and deathly tired, they reached Jaeger's Ferry on the east bank of the Gila at eleven o'clock on the morning of September 4. On the high ground across the river Woods could see the flag hanging limply from its staff above Fort Yuma's parade ground. San Diego lay only 160 miles to the west of that bright splash of color, but the road to it still ran for most of the way over utterly barren desert and mule-killing mountains.[29]

The mail party did not linger by the crossing. Picking up the settlement's mail for the west, Woods ferried the outfit across before dawn the next day and then whipped the team on for Cooke's Wells and Alamo Mocho. An all-night pull took them across the worst portion of the great Colorado Desert, but there was still hard going left. They battled the heat and wretched road all day long on the sixth, only to pull into Indian Wells and find a dry waterhole. "The want of water left us no resource but to push on for Carrissa [*sic*] Creek, thirty-two miles more," Woods recorded with weary resignation. "We traveled all night and reached Carrissa Creek about sunrise in the morning."[30]

Another searing day brought the mules close to exhaustion, and only a few of the animals were fit to continue without proper rest and feed. Woods and a companion took the strongest mounts and left the carriage and most of the herd behind under guard as they struck out in the saddle to try and cross the mountains that loomed ahead with a cruel grandeur. Once they reached Vallecito Springs it was not much farther to Lassator's Ranch, a station established by Doyle at the existing settlement. The road grew worse, dipping and twisting through a maze of dry washes and

[29] Ibid.; Conkling and Conkling, *Butterfield Mail*, 2:163–81; Anhert, *Retracing*, 67–89; Bartlett, *Personal Narrative*, 2: 203–10.

[30] Woods, *Report*, 20–22; Conkling and Conkling, *Butterfield Mail*, 2:210–34; Bartlett, *Personal Narrative*, 2:111–56.

sandy hills before leading them to the wells. Beyond that point it began to climb up into the mountains through even more rugged country. By the time they reached the ranch, both men and mounts were staggering and reeling with fatigue.

The next day was a long but satisfying one for Woods. Mounted on a pair of horses, the two men picked their way through the mountain valleys and down the western slope to the rolling expanse of the coastal plains. At ten o'clock that night they cantered into San Diego. The first mail to come through from Texas to California on schedule had arrived after thirty-eight days of perilous carriage. Its arrival was heralded only by the bitter echoes of anticlimax.[31]

In San Diego, Woods was able to piece together the full account of his company's maiden effort on the new mail route. As he fully expected, it was a narrative mixing triumph with frustration. The mail that had left San Antonio with James Mason on July 9 had reached Cooke's Spring without mishap, to be overtaken there by Henry Skillman with the mail of July 24. The two trains traveled in company as far as Maricopa Wells, arriving there on August 20. Skillman halted to wait for the mail from San Diego, while Mason took both parties' satchels and drove on to California, reaching San Diego on August 30.[32]

Mason and his trailworn crew received a grand welcome. The *San Diego Herald* reported that "the event naturally created the greatest enthusiasm among our people, and was hailed with a salute of one hundred anvils, the firing of crackers, and the general congratulations of the citizens. It was looked upon as the most important event which has ever occurred in the annals of San Diego, and undoubtedly constitutes an epoch in the history of the Pacific coast of the Union."[33]

Mason had undoubtedly met the tardy California mail of August 9 on the trail and knew that it would probably not make the scheduled rendezvous with Skillman at Maricopa Wells, but there was nothing he could do about it and trusted that his superintendent would rectify matters when he learned of it. Upon

[31] Woods, *Report*, 22.
[32] Ibid.
[33] *San Diego Herald*, Sept. 5, 1857; *Sacramento Union*, Sept. 12, 1857.

Woods's arrival, they set about taking up the slack in the company's operations.

Woods knew that the line was off to a shaky start with both of its initial deliveries coming in behind time, and they could ill afford to continue running up a list of fines with the Post Office Department. With Rusk dead, the Texas route had lost a powerful supporter, and its detractors would seize upon any failure by Birch to pressure Postmaster General Brown into annulling the contract. Woods could not permit the mails to run late for two months in succession.

Isaiah Woods had not been in town for twenty-four hours before he threw himself into a reorganization of his western base of operations. Early on the morning of September 9 he sent two men off for Fort Yuma with the mail. Each party that had been posted in succession at the fort, Maricopa Wells, and Tucson would carry the pouches eastward to the next relay of couriers and then return with the San Antonio mail over its allotted portion of the route. Thus Woods hoped to sustain the momentum of a swift passage at least between San Diego and Mesilla. Giddings's line from El Paso to Bexar was already well established, and Woods knew that only the Indians and the weather posed obstacles in that quarter.[34]

Woods faced a major handicap in his efforts with the absence of James Birch. Apparently confident that the line was off to a good start, he had decided not to wait in California for Woods's arrival. On August 20 Birch departed San Francisco aboard a mail steamer bound for Panama. After a journey over the isthmus he would board another ship for the voyage north to New York. Woods was chagrined to find him gone when he reached San Diego. During the trip from San Antonio he had incurred several debts in purchasing equipment, hiring men, and contracting for the construction of stations. He had promised to honor all these debts upon his return from California. Giddings also used Birch's and Woods's names in maintaining his portion of the line. Woods's earlier experiences in California did not help him in obtaining credit, despite the universal respect

[34] Woods, *Report*, 22.

that Birch's name commanded. The *Sacramento Union* welcomed him back by sneering that "the reported return of I. C. Woods, the great Adams and Co. defaulter, will create no slight sensation throughout our State, although the indignation once felt against him will be somewhat modified by the fact that some of those who came after him in the management of those concerns have dealt as extensively in robbery as he did, although under the shield of the law."[35]

At times Woods must have felt that only Sarah and Emmett Doyle retained any great faith in him as he struggled to clear his name and safeguard Birch's investment. Trading heavily upon his patron's credit, he continued his efforts to keep the company in business. On September 13 he sent a party of men on a five-day expedition into the mountains in search of an easier route through the eastern passes. Fortunately the people of San Diego were still enthusiastic about the mail service, and the county surveyor accompanied the men as they marked out a better trail for the coaches to follow.

By October 17 Woods had succeeded in breathing new life and purpose into the faltering operation. Charles McLaughlin, his agent in San Francisco, had sent new supplies and equipment southward on a steamer, and Woods had bought more mules as well as signing contracts for hay to be delivered to the stations at Vallecito and Carissa Creek. A coach, supply wagon, and herd of mules had also been dispatched for Maricopa Wells. There had been a brief pause to celebrate during this busy period when the fifth mail party from San Antonio rolled into town on the evening of October 5. The *San Diego Herald* was agreeably surprised at the speed of its travel, for "in the extraordinarily short time of 26 days and 12 hours, the shortest time on record. . . . The mail came from the Pimo Villages in 4 days and 6 hours, and from the Colorado River in 48 hours." In less than three months the line had put five parties over the route and cut their time from fifty-three days on the first run to less than half of that by the latest arrival.[36]

[35] Ibid., 22–23; *Sacramento Union*, Sept. 29, 1857.
[36] Woods, *Report*, 22–23; *San Diego Herald*, Oct. 5, 1857.

Woods was quick to capitalize on the favorable publicity and boldly followed after the *Herald's* article with advertisements in the state's newspapers:

Office of the San Antonio and San Diego Mail Line—This line is now ready to ticket passengers through from San Francisco to New Orleans, via San Diego, Fort Yuma, Tucson, Mesilla, Fort Fillmore, El Paso, and San Antonio, as well as to all intermediate stations. Also to Santa Fe and Albuquerque, (New Mexico). For rates of passage, and further information, apply at the office of the company, Kearny Street, (opposite Plaza.)

> C. McLaughlin, Agent
> R. E. Doyle, Superintendent
> Western Division [37]

Woods's advertising received another boost on October 18, when the next Texas mail arrived in equally rapid time with four paying passengers on board. The *Sacramento Union* relented in its criticism of Woods and reported that "the way mails are much increased. The entire road is now stocked with four hundred animals, twenty-five coaches and seventy-five men (messengers and guards). With this outfit they can accommodate passengers through to New Orleans by this route. The fare from San Diego to New Orleans is $200, which sum includes meals on the route." [38]

Skeptics might still sneer that Birch's line ran "from no place through nothing to nowhere," but there was no denying that the mails were being carried forth in greater speed and efficiency with each train that arrived or departed San Diego. The day before the sixth mail arrived, Woods had put the cap on his organization of the company's western division.

Woods sent two coaches out of town with full teams and loads of equipment. One was to run between Carissa Creek and Fort Yuma; the other was slated for the route between Yuma and Maricopa Station. On October 22 two more coaches and fourteen pack mules left San Diego for Carissa Creek, where they would await Woods's arrival in a few days. This contingent consti-

[37] Woods, *Report*, 23–24.
[38] Ibid.

tuted a supply train for the maintenance of all the stations beyond the mountains. The next day Woods left with the regular
mail party. He could have no way of knowing the disastrous
news that awaited him at Fort Yuma. Ten days before, an event
had transpired that would nearly destroy everything he had labored so diligently to achieve, and leave him struggling once
again to protect his fortune from a harsh fate and public charges
of fraud and dishonesty.

CHAPTER 6

Hard Passages

W HEN Isaiah C. Woods left San Diego for El Paso on October 23, 1857, he had no intimation that the weeks ahead would bring him both a bitter personal defeat and many threats against the mail company. Although the venture would survive, it would continue to wage a desperate battle against both debt and the Indians. Much of the burden in this struggle would be borne upon George Giddings's broad shoulders.

Traveling with Robert Doyle, Woods moved rapidly along the trail, reaching Carissa Creek in four days. The supply train and twelve men were waiting there, along with three coaches and a herd of seventy-four mules. The mail party left Fort Yuma the next day but lost several days' travel in the desert when the mule herd stampeded and scattered into the wastes.[1]

On November 2 a frustrated Woods pulled into Fort Yuma and met the westering mail party. It carried horrifying news. James Birch had been lost at sea when the steamer *Central America* went down in an Atlantic storm on September 13. With Birch dead, the company's future was in question. The news quickly spread through Colorado City, the village adjoining the fort. The contractors whom Woods had hired to supply his stations clamored for immediate payment. Woods assured them of the line's continued solvency and pledged to settle all his debts upon reaching San Antonio. He immediately sent Doyle home to San Diego to weather the storm that would break when news of Birch's death reached California.[2]

Doyle was already too late. On October 23 the *Sacramento Union* received word of the disaster by telegraph from the coast

---

[1] Isaiah C. Woods, *Report to the Honorable A. V. Brown, Postmaster General, on the Opening and Present Condition of the United States Overland Mail Route Between San Antonio, Texas and San Diego, California*, 24.

[2] Ibid.

and gave full play to it. The next day the paper published an account of the formal signing of Butterfield's new California mail contract. The implications were clear for Doyle and Woods. James Birch's name and reputation could have competed with Butterfield's. With Birch gone and Woods's character still suspect for many Californians, the company's credit would no longer stretch very far beyond El Paso.[3]

Shaking off his fears, Woods left Fort Yuma on November 7 with two coaches and a large mule herd. One coach and a relay team remained at the post. On November 9 he reached the Gila and was surprised to find that frontiersman Joseph Peterman had already built a sturdy house and corral there in expectation of obtaining the company's patronage. Woods agreed to make it a station on the line and contracted for supplies. The optimistic Peterman planned to dig irrigation ditches from the Gila and bring several hundred acres under cultivation within a short time. Woods must have been heartened to find someone who still believed in the company's future. Two other men at the station informed him that they also planned to open stopping places along the river to serve his coaches. Woods praised their ambition but discreetly refrained from mentioning Birch's death to the entrepreneurs.[4]

Woods had no way of knowing it, but as he rode east along the rutted track things were beginning to look better for the mail company. At Maricopa Wells he found the station in good order, if a bit crowded. The crew had erected a brush hut and corral. Most of the hands still slept outside, for the cabin already hosted a mail party waiting to go on to Tucson, another relay team bound for Fort Yuma, the resident agent, three passengers for Tucson, and seven through passengers for California. Crowded in with them were the station's cook and several other travelers who had paused at the waterholes. Six months before, the site had hosted only Indian villages. Now it was showing signs of becoming a permanent white settlement. Woods held an amiable conference with the local Pimas, distributed gifts, and promised to purchase their corn for his stock.[5]

[3] *Sacramento Union*, Oct. 23, 1857.
[4] Woods, *Report*, 24–25.
[5] Ibid., 25–26.

The Pimas never posed a serious threat to the stage line, but the Tonto Apaches were already making their presence felt in the area. A young New Yorker named Silas St. John was taking a herd of mules east from Fort Yuma to Maricopa Wells even as Woods paused there. A veteran of Birch's service in California, he was accompanied by two other company hands on the journey. On reaching the Gila they were warned by another party of whites that a large band of Tontos was watching the river crossing.

St. John knew that it was his job to deliver the mules and not to fight Apaches. Cutting overland across a waterless stretch of desert on a thirty-six-hour march, he brought the herd safely into Maricopa Wells. For St. John it was only the start of a long, weary autumn in Woods's employ.[6]

Maricopa Wells was far behind Woods by the time the mules arrived. On November 16 he met the mail from San Antonio just west of Picacho Pass, and by midnight on the next day he had reached Tucson and found the relay team from Mesilla waiting for the Pacific mail.

Woods had picked up the California mail bags when they reached Maricopa Wells on the eve of his departure and took them on from Tucson with sixteen men and three coaches on the nineteenth. En route to Mesilla he met the advance guard of a government road-building expedition that would soon be plagued by charges of mismanagement and corruption. Its tenuous association with George Giddings in El Paso would draw the mail company into the line of fire when the government launched an investigation. All of this was still in the future when Woods encountered the surveyors and noted their presence as another good omen for the growth of travel and settlement along his mail route. Not long afterward, he met the San Antonio mail of November 9 driving hard for Tucson.[7]

Upon gaining Mesilla early on the twenty-sixth, Woods sent the San Antonio mail eastward and began an assessment of the company's condition from that point south to the settlements below El Paso. He was pleased with Giddings's energetic work on the eastern division of the line. When they met in the Pass

[6] James M. Hunter, "The San Antonio–San Diego Mail Route," *Frontier Times* 25 (Nov., 1947): 57–58. Hunter's article was based upon St. John's unpublished memoirs.

[7] Woods, *Report*, 26–27.

settlement of Franklin, he was pained to tell the Texan that, having missed Birch in California, he had no funds with which to cover the debts Giddings had incurred in his name. Although Woods attempted to pay some of the local bills with his personal drafts, the next mail from the east practically destroyed his standing as a good credit risk. Dated November 20, the notice in a San Antonio newspaper had been entered by Abner Barrows, the company's newly appointed agent for Texas. It informed the public that Mrs. Birch had transferred the mail contract to her old guardian, Otis H. Kelton. He now held title to "all the stock of the mail line and post routes from San Antonio, Texas, to San Diego, California, and from El Paso to Santa Fe, in Texas, so far as the said James E. Birch, deceased, has any interest in the same." [8]

Woods's authority was completely revoked and his public standing demolished by Barrows's declaration that "all contracts and acts made by any person otherwise than those I may appoint, touching the interest of said routes, will be treated as a nullity." The same mail pouch carried a letter to Giddings from Barrows, informing him that Kelton had named him the new agent for Texas and directing the merchant to continue all operations as before. Woods was ignored. Julia Birch's motive in transferring the contract was unknown. She may simply have wished to dispose of a potential drain on her husband's estate. Kelton's offhand dismissal of Woods must have reflected his deep distrust of the man, although no specific reason was cited. Whatever the reasons behind it, Barrows's notice threw the company into confusion. [9]

Despite his loss of authority, Woods still had to meet a payroll and honor his debts. Giddings could not possibly assume the full burden, and if Woods reneged on the payments his creditors might seize the company's property. Since neither Mrs. Birch nor Kelton had sent him instructions or written revocation of his authority, Woods decided to bluff his way through the debacle. He applied to El Paso merchant Simeon Hart for a loan to sustain operations until he could reach New York and obtain more finan-

[8] Ibid.
[9] Ibid.

cial support as well as his reinstatement in the business. Hart realized the significance of the mail line to El Paso's future growth and lent him $10,000. Hart also urged his fellow merchants to accept Woods's personal notes. With Hart's aid, the company restored its credit completely in the region of the Pass.

Simeon Hart's generosity had temporarily saved the stage line, but both Giddings and Woods realized that many questions remained unanswered. When the coach left San Elizario on Christmas Day, they were both aboard. Only an interview with Barrows or Kelton could bring things back into clear perspective for them.[10]

The coach bore south along the river for the mountain-hemmed notch of the Cañon de los Lamentos. There on a rise above the Rio Grande stood the new station of Birchville. The mail of December 9 from Bexar waited in the brush-walled corral. The coach had been caught in a snowstorm west of Fort Davis, and the conductor had turned back to the post after the cold began to cripple his team. Begging the use of a light carriage from the garrison, he had taken six of his strongest mules and battled the weather to reach the rude shelter of Birchville.

Woods and Giddings did not let the snowy trail delay them. With a coach, four passengers, four guards, and twenty-two complaining mules, they entered the narrow pass to the east, trusting that the cold would keep the Mescaleros close by their campfires and out of mischief. On the twenty-ninth they reached Fort Davis and found that Colonel Seawell was ready to roast them over a slow blaze.[11]

Still angry over Woods's misappropriation of his mules, the colonel had few civil things to say to the contractors. Woods and his partner met with the post quartermaster, Lieutenant Thomas Jones, and inquired about a letter of instruction that had been sent from Fort Davis to Forts Bliss and Fillmore in reference to Woods's activities. In his conversation with Jones, and in a subsequent report to the postmaster general, Woods claimed that Sea-

[10] Ibid., 28.
[11] Ibid.; Col. George W. Seawell to Aaron V. Brown, June 23, 1858, Seawell to Sen. William M. Gwinn, July 13, 1858, Post Correspondence File, Fort Davis National Historic Site, Fort Davis, Texas.

well had directed the subaltern to order the other posts to the west to recover the army mules and deny the mail line any further assistance. It was a tense meeting. Jones attempted to explain that he had issued the letter on his own initiative, and that while he had called for the mules' return, he did not order any punitive measures to be directed at Woods. The Californian angrily refused to look at Jones's copy of the correspondence, remaining adamant in his belief that Seawell was conducting a vendetta against him.[12]

Both of the contractors got a frosty reception when they called on Lieutenant Zenas R. Bliss while in search of a hot meal after their frigid ride from Birchville. "They came just after breakfast," recalled Bliss, "and I had some other provender, buckwheat cakes, but there were not enough of them. Giddings complained at the short allowance. I was pretty much disgusted with this party, as I was not acquainted with either, but I had seen Giddings before." Woods made an ill-advised attempt at humor with the lieutenant. "When they left Woods asked me, if I ever went to San Antonio, and I told him I had not been there in some years, but hoped to go sometime." The contractor turned to Giddings and told him to "chalk his hat," and let Bliss ride for free on his next trip to the settlements. Sometime later Bliss was posted to Camp Hudson and took leave to visit San Antonio. The stage conductor refused to give him a pass but said that he could seek a refund upon arrival. "When I reached San Antonio, I spoke to Giddings and asked him if he remembered what Woods . . . had said." Giddings's response infuriated him. "He replied, 'Oh yes, do you know Woods well?'. I said no, that I had never seen him but twice in my life. 'That is what I thought,' he replied. 'He is the greatest joker you ever saw, and he was just joking when he said that, and he would be awful mad if I did not collect your fare.'" Bliss was understandably irritated and decided that "if they ever came to my house again, I would practice some little joke myself and send them elsewhere for breakfast."[13]

If his reception at Fort Davis had clouded his spirits Woods

[12] Woods, *Report*, 28.

[13] Zenas R. Bliss, "Memoirs," Zenas R. Bliss Papers, Barker Texas History Center, University of Texas at Austin, 2:185–86.

gave no sign of it. He remained determined to keep the mail moving. Before leaving the fort he met an extra coach and team bound for Birchville. When the blizzard halted the earlier coach, the conductor had left the newspaper mail behind at the local station to lighten the load. Woods stowed it in the rig's boot and ordered the driver to send it forward from Birchville promptly upon his arrival. A fine for unsatisfactory service could easily result from another late delivery.[14]

The two harried men passed New Year's Day on the road and reached Fort Lancaster on January 3. Bad news met them there as well. The tireless Silas St. John had left El Paso ahead of them with three coaches full of western mail and passengers. On reaching Fort Lancaster, he found that the Comanches had stolen all of the station's mules. The caravan had to go on to Fort Clark before obtaining fresh teams. It met high water on the Sabinal and Nueces, delaying the mail's arrival in San Antonio by ten days. En route from Lancaster, St. John had met a band of forty Apaches. The Indians attempted to approach the whites under a spurious flag of truce, but they departed hastily when St. John's escorts raised their Sharps rifles and thumbed back the hammers. It was a rough passage, and when the mission towers of Bexar finally appeared on the horizon, the passengers gave a prayer of thanks.[15]

Woods and Giddings could only wish St. John well when they learned of the theft at Fort Lancaster. Collecting the mail, they set out before noon on the third and soon ran into their own difficulties. In high summer the country around Fort Lancaster rolls away with a sort of parched grandeur, but in mid-winter the leonine bluffs overlooking the Pecos seem to creep closer and glower down on the lonely outpost. The winds that slide down the river from the New Mexico highlands lose none of their bitter edge as they near the Rio Grande. When the coach left Lancaster that day, the sky was the color of a spent rifle ball and the mules snorted at the damp promise of more snow in the air. Nine miles out from the post the flakes were falling so heavily that the driver could not see beyond his leaders. Woods had him

---

[14] Woods, *Report*, 29.
[15] Ibid.; Hunter, "Mail Route," 57–58; *San Antonio Daily Herald*, Dec. 31, 1857.

take refuge in a narrow canyon. The men huddled in the coach while the storm clawed at the leather side curtains, piling the snow deeply around the mules' hooves as they huddled on their tether ropes in the lee of the rig.

The dawn broke clear and cold with the sun stoking the whitened ground into a dazzling shimmer with its chill fire. Woods knew that the mules' stiffened muscles would never move the coach very far through the drifts that covered the road ahead. He sent two men eastward on muleback with the mail pouches for Fort Clark, while another pair of riders backtracked to beg more mules from Fort Lancaster. Woods led the half-frozen team slowly back toward the Pecos. The coach finally creaked into the station late that night.

Woods spent the next three days resting the team and wait-ing for some of the snow to melt. On the seventh he and Gid-dings left with another party under escort to Camp Hudson. That evening they met the mail of December 24 from Bexar. The conductor reported that the Medina had been in full flood at Castroville for several days, barring all traffic across the ford. Later he had been stranded for two days by the same blizzard that had halted Woods. The mules needed no urging from their driver to seek the corral at Fort Lancaster. Woods wished them luck and drove on to reach San Antonio on the seventeenth. His two riders had arrived safely eight days before.[16]

The next morning Woods received written revocation of his authority from Julia Birch in a letter dated October 26. It was not unexpected, but the loss of his job was still a wrenching blow. Leaving the company in Giddings's charge, he departed for the East to report to Postmaster General Brown and seek a posi-tion in the new organization.[17]

Woods had not been gone for long when more grim news filtered into San Antonio from the frontier. The Mescaleros had raided La Limpia and emptied its corral. Giddings sent another fifty-two mules westward to make up the loss. The Indians also launched a raid on El Muerto, catching the mail party in the sta-

[16] Woods, *Report*, 29–30.
[17] Ibid.; *San Antonio Daily Herald*, Aug. 29, Sept. 8, 9, 23, 25, 26, 1857.

tion when they struck. After a fierce fight the whites were forced to abandon the station and most of the stock to the Apaches. Two coaches were burned down to their axles, but the mail was saved. William Ford, Giddings's El Paso subcontractor, came down the line soon afterward and surveyed the damage with guard Thomas Collins. They reported the station was a total loss.[18]

Attitudes among the expressmen toward the Indians at this point ranged from guarded indifference to consuming hatred. Ford remarked: "It was no part of my business to kill Indians, and we were not hunting for them. I always made it a rule if the Indians let me alone I let them alone." Veteran Texas Ranger and driver Tom Rife had a different philosophy: "Whenever we got the drop, we used it."[19] The Apaches returned Rife's hostility in full measure, and before January was out they launched a third raid on Van Horn's Wells. This time it was a victory that cost much and gained them little.

Twenty-three-year-old Light Stapleton Townsend served as station chief at Van Horn's Wells that winter. Normally he drove for Giddings, but he had injured his arm in a fall several weeks before and was given the lighter duty at the station until it healed. He had already seen enough violent death on the line to realize that driving a stage or running a station was often simply a choice between occupying a moving target or a stationary one. If a man spent enough time in that country, he was bound to clash with the Mescaleros eventually.

Like most Texas frontiersmen he had to have been something of a fatalist. Already that month Townsend had seen the smoke curling above El Muerto to the east, and he knew that his station could well be next. All he could do was keep his men alert and stack a rifle and cartridges ready beside each loophole. There were only three other men at the station. All of them were Mexicans. José Lopez, Townsend's assistant, was an experienced Indian fighter. Another hand, a mixed-blood from Chi-

---

[18] U.S. Court of Claims, Depositions of William Ford, Thomas Collins, and George H. Giddings, *George H. Giddings* vs. *the United States, Kiowa, Comanche, and Apache Indians*, Records of the Court of Claims (Justice), RG 205, NARS.

[19] Ford and Thomas Rife Depositions, *Giddings* vs. *the United States*.

huahua, had a furtive air about him, and Townsend knew that he would bear watching should trouble erupt.[20]

The signs were mixed that evening as Townsend secured the station for the night. Contractor George Lyle had come safely through that morning and delivered twenty-five tons of hay to the ricks outside, where another fifty tons of forage were already stored. The mules were tethered in their stalls and the massive double gate was shut and barred at the corral's entrance. Townsend's main concern was for the stage that had been due in from the east that afternoon. It was badly behind schedule and he kept his ears pitched throughout dinner for the brassy ring of the driver's bugle.

The men gathered in one of the two rooms that flanked the gate for a card game that night. By twelve o'clock Townsend had won all the money in camp and there was still no sign of the stage. Apprehensive, they doused the lights and prepared to go to sleep. Townsend was sitting on his bunk with one boot off when he heard a crackling roar outside and shafts of yellow light spilled through the loopholes, bathing the room in an eerie glow. He realized at once that the hay was on fire and shouted at Lopez to open the gate and drive the stock to safety. The Mexican had one door open when a sheaf of arrows whistled by him. "Los Indios!" he yelled, and slammed it shut while more arrows rattled against the thick timbers.[21]

The four men stood to their loopholes and watched for a muzzleflash or fleeting form in the darkness beyond the glare of the leaping flames. The Apaches shrieked and howled while their arrows beat like hail on the adobe walls of the station and musket balls cratered the spaces around each rifleport. Thick smoke billowed through the station as Townsend and his comrades kept firing and tried to ignore the sound and smell as the flames torched the hay stored on top of the stables and twenty-six mules died in screaming agony. Coughing and retching, the Texans fought desperately to hold the Mescaleros at bay as they

[20] Everett E. Townsend, "An Old Texan," *West Texas Historical and Scientific Society Publications* 33 (Dec., 1930): 48–50.

[21] Ibid., 50.

swarmed around the buildings and over the walls. One brave crept along the base of the house and tried to shoot in through a loophole. Townsend thrust the muzzle of his Sharps out through a chink in the wall until it touched the Indian's side and then squeezed the trigger.[22]

By this time the Apaches had fired the room opposite the gate and were climbing onto the roof of Townsend's stronghold, attempting to dig a hole through the mud-and-wattle ceiling. Lopez cooly stood on a bench beneath the sound of their digging with his shotgun cocked and ready. Suddenly a large stick broke through the ceiling and was wrenched around to enlarge the opening before being withdrawn. The Mexican raised his weapon, and when an Indian put his eye to the hole, Lopez saluted him with a charge of buckshot. The blast threw the Apache off the roof and his headless body fell next to the brave Townsend had slain.

The Texan had been watching the Chihuahueño during the fighting. Several times he had heard him call out to the Apaches but could not understand what he was saying. Finally he lost all trust in the half-blood when he saw him pass something out through his loophole. Townsend told Lopez what he had seen, and the Mexican knocked the traitor down with the butt of his gun, telling him that he would blow the half-blood's head off if he raised it from the floor. Townsend never made reference to the man again in his account of the raid, but he noted cryptically, "This cooked his goose, for they had no more trouble with him."[23]

The fighting continued all night, and as their ammunition began to run low, the defenders estimated that they had killed or wounded at least a third of their attackers. It had now become not just a raid for loot, but a grudge match. The Mescaleros had lost too heavily and only Townsend's scalp would satisfy them.

The sky was beginning to lighten outside when Townsend heard the Apache chieftain call out in English, "Luz Lightie, come out; we are your friends and won't hurt you." The station hands were not about to fall for so clumsy a ruse, but Townsend

[22] Ibid.
[23] Ibid., 51.

kept the Indian talking while he and Lopez located his position and took steady aim upon it. The white man called out a question and the Apache exposed himself for a few seconds to reply. Both men fired together, "scattering his brains over the ground."[24]

This coup threw the warriors into momentary confusion, and the expressmen bolted out the door for a nearby arroyo. They had fewer than a dozen rounds of ammunition left, but the Apaches mounted only a token pursuit. They were discouraged by their losses, and the chief's death was obviously a sign that their medicine was weak.

When the Indians had gone, Townsend and his companions headed east down the road toward Fort Davis. All of them were black with soot, exhausted, and parched with thirst. They did not go back to the station for fear that some braves might remain there in ambush. After marching a few miles, they met the tardy coach and returned to the scene of the raid with it.

All the Apaches were gone, taking their dead and wounded with them but leaving numerous pools of blood behind to testify to their losses. The station was a blazing hulk, and in the ashes of the stalls white bones gleamed obscenely through the smoking mounds of charred meat. Wolves trotted through the brush nearby, tantalized by the aroma but wary of the men who poked about the ruins. Townsend leaned tiredly on his Sharps and concluded that survival was triumph enough for him.[25]

The losses west of Fort Davis served only to convince Giddings that his own investment as well as Simeon Hart's must be protected. He knew little of Otis Kelton but was certain that he could not manage a stage line from an office in the East. In February, Giddings left San Antonio after receiving news of an Apache raid on Birchville. Traveling to Washington, he presented his case to Brown and conferred with Julia Birch's attorney, who agreed that he had a legitimate claim on control of the contract. Clifford, the lawyer, advised Kelton to cede the contract to Gid-

[24] Ibid.
[25] Ibid. Townsend survived this and many other adventures until his death in San Antonio at the age of ninety-three on Sept. 23, 1928.

dings, thus freeing himself of what was increasingly seen as a bad risk in light of the line's repeated losses. The contract officially changed hands with Brown's assent on March 11, 1858.[26]

This move did not solve all of Giddings's legal problems. That spring marked the end of a quarter-year's service, and a $37,450 payment was due the company. Congress had neglected to pass the appropriations bill during its previous session, and the mail contractor received certificates of indebtedness from the Post Office Department in lieu of cash. The certificates were nonbankable and Giddings found that speculators in New York would pay only sixty to ninety cents on the dollar for them. Disgusted, he took them home with him in the hope that the San Antonio banks would honor them in full.[27]

Upon his arrival in Bexar in mid-April he found that things had gotten even worse in his absence. More Indian raids had lashed the western stations, and a personal tragedy had struck. Since August, 1856, Frank Giddings had served as the line's El Paso agent and manager of his brother's store, while pursuing his own medical practice. One night he was caught in the middle of a gunfight in Ben Dowell's saloon and a bullet ripped into his head. His killer fled into Mexico.[28] The news shook Giddings when it reached him in San Antonio. The mail company seemed to have become as much a curse as merely an unprofitable investment.

Despite his grief and the line's shaky financial status, he had little choice but to continue the business. His perseverance won him praise in the local press. The *Daily Herald* remarked that "the more we see of the management of this line the more we are convinced that it is conducted with energy and ability, and is destined to become a great thoroughfare to the Pacific." With some exaggeration the editor held that "not a single failure has taken place upon it; but on the contrary it invariably arrives in-

[26] *San Antonio Daily Express*, May 18, 1902; *Sacramento Union*, April 3, 1858; *San Antonio Daily Herald*, Apr. 1, 1858. For the last mails' arrival in San Antonio see the *Daily Herald*, Feb. 23, Mar. 6, 9, 1858.

[27] *San Antonio Daily Express*, May 18, 1902.

[28] *San Antonio Daily Herald*, Apr. 1, 15, 1858; *San Diego Herald*, June 10, 1858; W. W. Mills, *Forty Years at El Paso, 1858–1898*, 181.

side of the scheduled time." The California papers were not so supportive. Though it praised the company's promptness and efficiency, the *Sacramento Union* complained that the route "terminates . . . too far south for the use of the people of North California and Oregon. By the time a man from Shasta County could reach San Diego, he could be nearly to Salt Lake, on the great emigrant line of travel."[29]

Other journals found points to pick over in the line's performance. Because of problems with stock, water, and the availability of coaches, the company had been requiring passengers to ride muleback over the hundred-mile stretch of the Colorado Desert. That imposition, as well as the management's primary concern with moving the mail rapidly even at the expense of the passengers' comfort and convenience, led to criticism in the California papers. Travelers were cautioned to expect a rough passage, and one editor provided them with an itemized list of necessities for the jaunt:

One Sharp's rifle and a hundred cartridges; a Colt's Navy revolver and two pounds of balls; a knife and sheath; a pair of thick boots and woolen pants; a half dozen pairs of thick woolen socks; six undershirts; three woolen overshirts; a wideawake hat; a cheap sack coat; a soldier's overcoat; one pair of blankets in summer, and two in winter; a piece of India rubber cloth for blankets; a pair of gauntlets; a small bag of needles, pins, a sponge, hair brush, comb, soap, etc., in an oil silk bag; two pairs of thick drawers, and three or four towels.[30]

All of this baggage could be expensive. Each passenger could carry thirty pounds for free, but any overage cost a dollar a pound for the entire trip, or forty cents through to El Paso. A ticket for the San Diego–San Antonio passage cost two hundred dollars. Travel from El Paso to Bexar was half of that amount, with the leg to Tucson requiring fifty dollars more. A ride between intermediate stations along the route cost fifteen cents per mile.[31]

[29] *San Antonio Daily Herald*, Mar. 6, 1858; *Sacramento Union*, Apr. 29, 1858.
[30] Ralph Moody, *Stagecoach West*, 86.
[31] San Antonio Daily Herald, July 10, 1858.

Expensive and uncomfortable as it might be, Giddings knew that he held a virtual monopoly on commercial travel along the Gila route until the Butterfield company began its operations. And although his passenger traffic was not heavy along the entire road, it was reasonably steady. Telegrams from as far north as New York notified the line's New Orleans office to secure seats on the stage, and at times extra coaches had to be put on to accommodate the travelers. Giddings kept Doyle as his agent on the Pacific end of the line, and Woods remained as general superintendent, with permanent offices in the American Coal Company Building, 50 Exchange Place, New York. Merchant Benjamin R. Sappington handled affairs in Bexar during Giddings's absence. All of these men aggressively advertised the company's service, stressing the speed and security of travel on the coaches.[32]

Giddings probably tried to put on a good face before the public after his disappointment in Washington and the shock of his brother's death. Any sign of doubt or discouragement on his part might send his creditors into court and permanently dry up what was left of his credit resources. He left San Antonio for El Paso in mid-April and spent the next six months supervising operations from the border town. The Comanches celebrated his return by attacking Lancaster Station just before his arrival on the ride west. Giddings managed to remain grimly philosophical about the incessant depredations. "The first question we used to ask when the mail came in was, 'Where did the Indians hit us last?' I used to tell my men that good news would keep and to give me the bad news first," he recalled years later. He had long since learned that this was a business in which the ledgers were filled with long columns of red ink, and good news was as rare as a sweet-tempered mule.[33]

Giddings had been in El Paso only a short time when two travelers arrived in San Antonio and booked seats on the stage. One was a government agent who was investigating the mail

[32] Giddings Deposition, *Giddings* vs. *the United States*.

[33] *San Antonio Daily Herald*, Apr. 15, 23, 29, May 4, 7, 11, 14, 18, 22, 1858; Giddings Deposition, *Giddings* vs. *the United States*.

company's alleged role in a major scandal. The other was an optimistic investor in an Arizona mining venture. He would keep a diary of his journey that still endures as the finest primary account of the stage line's operations ever written by a passenger. Giddings would never meet the diarist, but he would see more than enough of his traveling companion in the weeks ahead.

The journey's chronicler proved to be a young Ohioan with the improbable name of Phocion R. Way. An engraver by profession, he had decided to try his luck in the Arizona mines, and he eagerly anticipated his first taste of frontier life. Arriving in San Antonio from one of the Gulf ports on May 21, he learned that the next westbound coach left at two o'clock on the following afternoon. So many people had purchased tickets that two coaches had to be laid on to accommodate all of them plus the mail bags. Way would ride his coach all the way to Tucson, and the trip gave him an often startling initiation into life in the West.[34]

As the rig rolled farther beyond the Sabinal and Frio, Way realized that he was entering an entirely different type of society from that he had known among the stolid townsmen of Cincinnati. His companions were truly "citizens with the bark on." In Uvalde most of the travelers slept outside on the ground in preference to the station's beds. Way found out why when he awoke in the morning as host to an army of hungry fleas. At Fort Clark he gained an insight into the temperament of many frontiersmen.

There are a good many border men living here and they are decidedly a hard looking set. They are generally fine specimens of the physical man, but the life which they lead is of constant danger and makes them bold and reckless. They seem to place no value on human life, and apparently think no more of shooting a man who offends them than they would of shooting a horse or dog. They had a quarrel here last night among themselves, caused by the partaking too freely of rotgut whiskey. One of them drew his pistol and fired at another, but fortunately missed him. Another big rough looking fellow (one of our escort) lost his revolver and tore a shirt all off our landlord because he could not find it, and swore he would have it before morning or have

---

[34] William A. Duffen, ed., "Overland via 'Jackass Mail' in 1858: The Diary of Phocion R. Way," *Arizona and the West* 2 (Spring, 1960): 35–37, 41, 42.

brains for breakfast. One of our party, an old frontier man, took offense at what he said and could hardly be prevented from shooting him. Every man, no matter what his business, goes well armed at all times. You can form some idea from this what a place I am in.[35]

By the time they reached Fort Lancaster, Way had endured more rowdy antics from the denizens of the border settlements, survived a brutal hail storm, and braced himself for an expected Indian ambush on the Devil's River that mercifully never materialized. Tired and anxious, he was completely taken aback by the last mile of the journey into Lancaster. The road snaked down the face of the precipitous bluffs over a bed of loose gravel and keg-sized rocks. The passengers dismounted and helped to clear away some of the worst debris while the rig's rear wheels were locked and the driver coaxed the skittish team along, his language profane and endearing by turns. The last half-mile of trail took them an hour to negotiate, and Way welcomed the stiff drink that awaited him at the post sutler's store.[36]

The remaining miles into Comanche Springs and Fort Davis were a blue haze of heat, dust, and discomfort. The day before they reached Fort Davis, the weather changed and the chill winds of a late norther hunted them through the Limpias on the last day of May. Way found the mountains a "grand, sublime" sight, but he was sobered by the ruins at El Muerto and a brush with a prairie fire to the east of Eagle Springs. The threat of Indian attack mounted as they drew closer to the Rio Grande. "Even while I am writing this I may be a mark for some Indian's rifle. . . . We will have to keep close watch. . . . We walk about with our arms, we sit down with them by our sides, and we sleep with them," one day's entry recorded. The novelty of danger was beginning to wear thin for the Ohioan.[37]

Their luck held good into Birchville, which Way described as "2 or 3 adobe houses and a corral for confining horses and mules." It was a bleak place, but a cup of coffee and some fresh mutton struck him as "a great luxury" after so many days of salt

---

[35] Ibid., 43–44; *San Antonio Daily Herald*, May 29, 1858.
[36] Duffen, "The Diary," 45–52.
[37] Ibid.

beef and brackish canteen water. The fresh eggs Way devoured for breakfast were certain signs that they were nearing civilization.[38]

The travelers changed to light wagons with two-mule teams at Birchville and forged upriver along a wretched road, which delayed their arrival in El Paso for most of the rest of the evening and night. Way had time for a brief nap in the settlement before he boarded the coach again for the run to the west. They left Fort Fillmore late in the afternoon of June 6 and picked up a herd of relay teams along with a mounted escort of six men. After another pause at Mesilla the next morning, they were ready to start the drive under conditions that angered Way. He penned a bitter denunciation of the line's management in his journal. "The company should have sent another carriage," he fumed,

but it was not done; in fact, the company have deceived us and acted shamefully from the start. They told us that the two carriages we started with would go all the way through to San Diego, and both of them have been taken from us. We left the last one at Fort Fillmore and have an old wagon in its place. The one we have is strong and would do very well, but we should have another; it is not sufficient. The mules we have now are good, but those we have had were poor broken down things; and what is worse than all, they tell us now that the wagon will go no further than Tucson, and consequently those unfortunate fellows who are going through to San Diego will have to ride mule back from Tucson and keep up with the mail which is also packed on mules, and travels day and night. The poor fellows will have to travel 500 miles over a barren desert and I am afraid it is more than they can stand. It is a gross imposition that should not be born [sic] and the public should know it. They paid their money with the full understanding that they were to be taken through in an ambulance. The men employed along the line are fine fellows, and of course they are not responsible for this. This is an important route and will be much traveled, and [the] Government should see that it is properly managed.[39]

It had not dawned on Way that running even a rudimentary mail and passenger service across that harsh land was an expensive proposition. From speaking with his fellow travelers and the

[38] Ibid., 52–53.
[39] Ibid., 147–52.

escort, he had learned that "the mail company is much in debt. They owe the men several months' wages and are greatly in debt the whole length of the line. Their credit has nearly run out, and if they do not square up before long their employees [will] take their property from them. People have had great confidence in them, but their conduct has nearly destroyed it."[40]

Unpaid or not, the expressmen still strove to meet their schedules, and drove on all night to reach Cooke's Spring and the Mimbres Crossing by the end of the first day's run. Soldier's Farewell and Stein's Peak soon came up and were left behind. There was a brief but peaceful encounter with some Apaches en route, but once Apache Pass and Dragoon Springs were cleared it was a free drive into Tucson on the eleventh. The California mail was waiting for them there, and Way voiced another protest over the "most rascally imposition" that required westbound passengers to ride muleback for the remaining distance to Fort Yuma and San Diego. He felt lucky that his mining interests drew him south to Tubac and ended his journey with the stage line.

While Phocion R. Way had not been entirely happy with Giddings's struggling service, he had confided his grievances mainly to his private journal. One of the passengers he had left behind in El Paso was there for the specific purpose of collecting evidence against the company for its possible prosecution by the government. Welcome B. Sayles, a confidential agent for the Post Office Department, was on loan to the Department of Interior that spring to investigate a problem that involved both organizations.

The reasons behind Sayles's investigation stretched back to the spring of 1857 when Secretary of the Interior Robert McClelland had named James B. Leach to command an expedition to construct a wagon road from El Paso to Fort Yuma. Leach was an experienced surveyor and engineer with frontier service behind him in the Mexican War. The problem was that Leach selected a personal friend to serve as his chief assistant. That man was David Churchill Woods, and his presence on the expedition

[40] Ibid.

drew Giddings and his company into a quagmire of rumored corruption and charges of guilt by association.[41]

The survey and construction project began under the aegis of McClelland's successor, Jacob Thompson, and he charged Leach with making the most efficient use of his $200,000 budget, as no future funds for the project were anticipated. The expenditure of this money soon became the object of official concern, as Leach proved to be either a woefully poor administrator or a dishonest servant of the government.

Woods and Leach made a purchasing tour through the Northeast to outfit the expedition before traveling to their operational base at Memphis, Tennessee. The construction team and surveyors were lavishly equipped by the time they departed Memphis in late June, 1857, and headed for Fort Belknap, Texas. Leach reached El Paso by late October, but Woods and the ox-drawn supply team remained behind on the trail, pausing to winter at Fort Belknap. Woods left the team in the hands of an assistant and returned east to New York for some undisclosed business. He did not return to Fort Belknap and start the train west again until six months had passed, finally bringing it into El Paso on June 25, 1858. Nearly half of the wagons lay abandoned on the road behind him by that time. Although Leach had begun work on the new road in Woods's absence, it had been a lackluster performance on both their parts.[42]

Secretary Thompson was alarmed not only by Leach's poor progress but by his sloppy handling of the expedition's finances. Drafts drawn by him flowed into Thompson's office, but there were few properly verified vouchers to document the expenditures they represented. On top of this came a report from Fort Davis that Leach had been gambling and drinking heavily while encamped there. Another informant charged that some of the expedition's equipment had been diverted to the San Antonio—

[41] W. Turrentine Jackson, *Wagon Roads West*, 176, 220–22.

[42] Ibid., 223–25. Maj. James Scott, government postal agent, was reported in San Antonio in late July for an inspection tour of the mail line. No other references to his activities have been found. *San Antonio Herald*, July 31, 1858. For the June and July mails see the *Herald*, June 8, 19, July 1, 8, 13, 23, 1858.

San Diego Mail Company. Thompson conferred with Postmaster General Brown, and Sayles was dispatched westward to investigate both Leach and Giddings.[43]

Sayles found nothing to substantiate the initial charges against Leach or the mail company. On reaching the surveyor's Mesilla headquarters, he examined his books and the real trouble began. They were so poorly kept that Sayles ordered Leach to dissolve the expedition. While Sayles returned to Washington, Leach and his chief engineer were to go over the road to San Diego with a small party to make some final repairs to the construction already under way.

When he reported to Secretary Thompson, Sayles received authority to continue his probe and enlisted the aid of the U.S. attorney in New York. Sayles located David Woods's agent, Charles F. Whitcomb, and extracted a full confession from him. Woods had allegedly instructed Whitcomb to have merchants sign blank vouchers that would be forwarded to him with only penciled entries for the amounts paid in the margins. Sayles dug into Woods's personal dealings while he had been traveling with Leach. At least a dozen businessmen from Vermont to Tennessee charged that the amounts they received in payment were less than those entered upon the expedition's vouchers. The more Sayles investigated, the more damning the evidence he found.[44]

The stage line's involvement in the Leach scandal raised some unanswered questions. The most intriguing of them dealt with the exact relationship, if any, that existed between David C. Woods and Isaiah C. Woods. Giddings's superintendent was never linked to the investigation at any time in Sayles's reports, yet the similarity of names raised questions. Isaiah was still bitterly resented in some circles in California because of the Adams Express Company failure. The California newspapers announced David C. Woods's appointment to the Leach expedition without a trace of rancor or even editorial comment. Leach, like Woods, was a California resident, and it stands to reason that his as-

[43] Jackson, *Wagon Roads*, 228–29.
[44] Ibid., 229–30.

sistant also lived in the state. David and Isaiah could very well have been related, but the evidence permits only conjecture on this point.[45]

Leach's relations with the expressmen were better documented but failed to show any evidence of collusion to defraud the government between him and Giddings. Sayles's investigation established that although items such as grain had been bought from Giddings in El Paso in the amounts of $8.00, $300, and $573.78, only one overcharge of $227 was found, hardly proof of Giddings's doing anything illegal. He was a relatively small supplier of goods when compared with other merchants who traded with Leach. James Dawson, one of Giddings's accusers, was listed as the recipient of $5,477.98 in a single payment. The most curious transaction tied to the stage line took place in San Diego when Leach disposed of the expedition's property. Earlier, in El Paso, Simeon Hart had offered him $900 for each wagon with harness and six-mule team. Leach had refused that offer, only to sell them to Robert E. Doyle in California for $600 a set. He claimed that Doyle was acting for Hart, but Sayles disagreed, also noting that Woods still remained on the payroll at the date of sale, despite a previous order that he be discharged. The most damning item in the vouchers was a payment to Doyle for grain to feed the mules. It was made six days after he had purchased the government stock. Doyle may well have been out to profit at the government's expense, but the evidence was weak at best, and Giddings could not be blamed in any event.[46]

David Woods was eventually arrested and charged with theft and fraud, but neither he nor Leach was ever brought to trial on the strength of Sayles's findings. Difficulties in recruiting witnesses and a dawning realization of the political embarrass-

[45] *Sacramento Union*, Sept. 1, 1857.

[46] Jackson, *Wagon Roads*, 231–32; M. A. Kinnon to Jacob Thompson, Sept. 15, 1858; Welcome B. Sayles to Albert H. Campbell, Dec. 20, 1858; J. D. Fuller to Thompson, June 14, 1860; James B. Leach to Thompson, June 20, 1858, Pacific Wagon Road Office, El Paso–Fort Yuma Road, Letters Received, Interior Department Records, RG 48, NARS.

ment that would attend such an event caused the government to drop the entire issue.

The whole affair came to a messy and puzzling end. Giddings was never even remotely considered for prosecution after the initial phase of the investigations ended. The mail company emerged undamaged from the scandal, although Giddings might have wryly noted that the question of what constituted misuse of government funds and authority remained curiously undefined. Sayles himself had reportedly used part of his time in New Mexico to supervise the operations of his jointly owned silver mine near Las Cruces.[47]

Despite the anxiety that he must have felt during the investigation, George Giddings had survived the attacks on his reputation and the company still held its contract to carry the mail. After so many encounters with both savages and bureaucrats in the past few months, he knew that to have endured this long was a victory in itself. With the government placated, he could turn his attention to more conventional problems. He still hoped that some profit, however small, might be wrung from the company. He was mistaken in his optimism, but there could be no turning back. The advance agents of the Butterfield Company had already appeared in the Southwest and were preparing the road for its operations. Giddings could not afford to have his line suffer by comparison with the newcomer, for many influential men in the government already felt that one mail company in service along a southwestern route was enough. Two might easily lead them to conclude that the results did not justify the expenditure of public funds. Giddings faced the maddening paradox of having to strive mightily simply to retain the right to keep himself exhausted and in debt.

[47] Darliss A. Miller, "Carleton's California Column: A Chapter in New Mexico's Mining History," *New Mexico Historical Review* 53 (Jan., 1978): 23. Zenas R. Bliss commented on Sayles's passage through Camp Hudson. Bliss, "Memoirs," 2:180–82.

CHAPTER 7

Omens and Rivals

THE summer of 1858 found the El Paso mail in a curious state of equipoise. Having weathered the storms of its first year of transcontinental operation, Giddings's service had proven that time and distance could be mastered across those arid reaches if men were willing to accept the challenge. The problem was that the contest never ended, for the challenge was renewed with the completion of each journey into San Diego or Bexar. The Post Office Department awarded no laurels for bringing the mail in on schedule month after month. That was an expected part of the contract obligation, even if at times the government was casual about paying Giddings for his services.

Balanced against the obstacles and cost was the potential for what this often beleaguered enterprise could achieve as the first ripple in a wave of travel, commerce, and settlement that could wash through the region on a rising tide of prosperity. When Isaiah C. Woods told Postmaster General Brown how "our line is already forming the basis of a new state, rich in minerals halfway between Texas and California," he was exaggerating, but he was also saying exactly what both of them wanted to hear. The mail company's value lay as much in its role as a seedbearer for other enterprises as in any revenues generated for its proprietors or the government. It symbolized the entire nation in that it was still in the harsh dawn of growth and the costs exacted by this process were gladly wagered against the promised rewards. The deeper men reached into their pockets to feed this dream, the stronger grew their incentive to make it a reality.

This realization must have moved George Giddings to invest even more of his dwindling resources in improving the mail line that spring and summer of 1858. At great expense, he set about rebuilding his ruined stations and ordered the construction of a string of new ones. His two supply trains snaked up and

Bigfoot Wallace

Edward D. Westfall

George H. Giddings

Louis Oge

James M. Hunter

James Birch

Parker Burnham (*Courtesy El Paso Public Library*)

Ben Ficklin

Francis C. Taylor

William Mitchell
(*Courtesy Mrs. M. C. Bennett,
Marfa, Texas*)

Bethel Coopwood

Eli Bates and F. C. Taylor at the reins. (*Courtesy Fort Concho Museum*)

Jim Spears (*left*) in the mid-1870s. (*Courtesy Fort Concho Museum*)

A mail station in the Concho River country. (*Courtesy Fort Concho Museum*)

The crossing on the Pecos.

Howard's Well as it looks today.

El Muerto Canyon, 1985.

Ruins at the Head of Concho.

Entering Bass Canyon from the east.

Quitman Pass today.

Modern view of the stage road through Quitman Canyon from the slope of Devil Ridge above Tinaja de las Palmas.

down the road with loads of building materials and provisions for the hardy crews of men who dared the Indians while they piled rock, molded adobe bricks, and raised the walls in defiant hopefulness at El Muerto, Van Horn's Wells, and Eagle Springs. Other miniature fortresses were laid out at scattered sites to the east. The Comanches and Mescaleros watched with great interest. The young braves exulted over the promise of more loot and scalps. The older warriors counted the loopholes in the walls and remembered what men like Townsend and Lopez could do with a rifle and a fair mark to fire upon. To the west of El Paso their cousins marked the locations of other new stations, as the Butterfield Company added its relay points to the few that Giddings had already built. Not since the army had thrown its first feeble line of posts across the Southwest had the Indians seen so many whites make camps on the road and settle in with every sign that they intended to stay.

George Giddings must have experienced a few pangs of envy stirring within himself as he saw Butterfield prepare to launch his operation with the backing of $2 million in capital stock. No expense was being spared to have the coaches rolling by the government's deadline that autumn. The company had purchased over fifteen hundred horses and mules, 250 coaches, a fleet of freight and water wagons, and all the other myriad items of equipment needed to run a stage line in the wilderness.

Approximately eight hundred employees were already at work surveying the route, digging wells, and building the 141 stations that marked the 2,800 miles between St. Louis and San Francisco. Arcing down from the twin terminals at Memphis and St. Louis, the road passed through Fort Smith, Arkansas, before leaping the Red River to enter Texas and strike the plains that rolled away to Forts Chadbourne and Belknap. From those stations it led on across the barren stretches between the Concho and the Pecos to strike the ford at Horsehead Crossing. Hugging the west bank at the Pecos, it wound northward before veering almost due west to trace the Texas and New Mexico border. Once clear of the massive notch of Guadalupe Pass, the trail slashed across the desert to reach the sanctuary of Hueco Tanks before intersecting Giddings's route at El Paso.

El Paso marked the division point between the eastern and western legs of the line, and from there to California, Butterfield's coaches shared the road with the San Antonio company. A million dollars had already been sunk into this venture to guarantee its success, yet comparatively little of it had flowed into Texas. The route passed well beyond the state's northwestern line of settlement and avoided all of the major population centers to the east. The company was of virtually no commercial value to Texas.[1]

Only El Paso enjoyed a flush of prosperity as the market expanded for stock and supplies with the coming of Butterfield's agents. The company began construction of a large station in Franklin that dwarfed Giddings's neighboring structure. It gave further impetus to the process begun by Skillman and Giddings. "The stage company primed a pump which continued to flow. Money came to town," remarked a modern historian of the city. "People followed the money."[2]

The Anglo and Mexican population of the Pass settlements swelled, and men began to remark on El Paso as a place with a future. Unfortunately, precious few of the newcomers qualified as men of substance. Along with the stage drivers, hostlers, and company agents came the prostitutes and professional gamblers. At least a score of cardsharps resided in town at one point, and a traveler reported that as much as $100,000 might change hands in the cantinas on a single night.[3]

Bad men and good, they all spent their silver in the Pass and gave the area's economy a badly needed boost. Before the end of the year, surveyors had marked out lots among the rambling collection of adobes that composed Franklin, and there was a real estate boom among the wealthier residents as they banked on

[1] Roscoe Conkling and Margaret B. Conkling, *The Butterfield Overland Mail, 1857–1869*, 1: 103–49; LeRoy R. Hafen, *The Overland Mail, 1849–1869*, 79–99; J. W. Williams, "The Butterfield Overland Mail Road across Texas," *Southwestern Historical Quarterly* 61 (July, 1957): 1–19; Oscar O. Winther, "The Southern Overland Mail and Stagecoach Line, 1857–1861," *New Mexico Historical Review* 32 (Apr., 1957): 93–97; Rupert N. Richardson, "The Southern Overland Mail, Conveyor of News, 1857–1861," *West Texas Historical Association Yearbook* 34 (Oct., 1958): 25–37.
[2] Donald W. Meining, *Imperial Texas*, 61; C. L. Sonnichsen, *Pass of the North*, 143.
[3] Sonnichsen, *Pass of the North*, 143.

the hope that the stage lines would eventually draw the railroad after them. The population remained a mixture of men who had prospered and those who aspired to seize their own share of the promised wealth. Both groups contained individuals who had originally come there to begin life again after some disappointment. It was appropriate that young Anson Mills conducted the town's first survey and helped to build the Butterfield station. The Hoosier lad had been expelled from West Point after failing a mathematics course. Too ashamed to return home, he had struck out for Texas. Giddings's stage had carried him to El Paso on May 8, 1858. Mills and many others arrived in this place of new beginnings carrying dreams that had been spun on the spokes of a Concord's wheels.[4]

However promising things were in El Paso, whatever profits Giddings's store earned there were offset by the mounting losses on the road to the east. The rain storms rolling over the plains that season had brought good pasturage for the Indians' ponies, and the tribesmen were eager to strike at their old quarry. By the end of May they had struck La Limpia again. The raid prompted a dogged pursuit by the troops at Fort Davis, which resulted in the destruction of an Apache camp in the Guadalupe Mountains.[5] It was welcome news for Giddings.

Soon afterward he learned that Isaiah Woods had returned from Washington. He met with his employer in El Paso for a conference. There were rumors afoot in the capital that part of the mail service might be terminated in the fall. Nothing was definite yet, but Giddings knew that it would be prudent to prepare for the worst and began planning his own trip back to the East.[6]

The mail still went through without interruption, and the *Daily Herald* never missed a chance to praise the company. It published a letter from a New Orleans admirer who predicted how "the very first Rail-way which shall connect the Atlantic and the Pacific in the iron bonds of continental commerce, travel and social intercourse will be led to adopt this as . . . the great national . . . route in the future of our expanding Republic." He

[4] Ibid., 144.
[5] *San Antonio Daily Herald*, July 13, 1858.
[6] Ibid., Aug. 7, 1858.

stressed that "the splendid success of the San Diego Mail Line, may yet determine questions of magnitude, and lead to results of the highest importance to our whole country."[7]

Hyperbole was counterbalanced by the cold reality of what was happening along that great projected national road. Cattlemen and emigrants bound for the west suffered from the wave of Indian raids that scourged the trail that summer. Giddings's men brought a grim story of death and plunder into Bexar with nearly every trip they made from the west. Their reports underscored the longstanding vulnerability of all who traveled on the El Paso road. Comanche Springs was the point of intersection between that route and the great war trail that lanced deeply into Mexico from the Comanches' home ranges to the north. General David E. Twiggs, the department commander in Texas, had already ordered his officers to permit Giddings to build his stations under their garrisons' protection, but a post was still badly needed at Comanche Springs. Twiggs confessed that the mail's passage alone required that the road be well guarded, "*but I have not the force to do it,*" he complained to the War Department.[8]

Twiggs's admitted impotence added a fillip of urgency to Giddings's inspection of his stations when he passed over the route in August with Woods and Captain Tom Rogers. Ford and Hyde were already reconstructing the station at Eagle Springs, although no one cared to wager on how long it might survive this time around. Van Horn's Wells and El Muerto were also operating again, and another stronghold had sprung up at Barrel Springs to the east. Giddings had taken still more risks when he planted a new station in the heart of Limpia Canyon, fourteen miles north of Fort Davis, dubbing it Cottonwoods. It sat with almost pathetic defiance in a meadow hemmed on all sides by the mountains., The other new station to the northeast in Barilla Canyon was equally vulnerable.[9]

[7] Ibid., July 23, 1858.

[8] Ibid., Aug. 21, 1858; Post Returns, Fort Davis, Texas, citing Special Order No. 50, Headquarters, Department of Texas, June 1858, RG 94, NARS; T. N. Campbell and William J. Field, "Identification of Comanche Raiding Trails in Trans-Pecos Texas," *West Texas Historical Association Yearbook* 44 (Oct., 1968): 128–44.

[9] U.S. Court of Claims, Depositions of A. C. Hyde, William Ford, Josiah Crosby, Parker Burnham, and George H. Giddings, *George H. Giddings* vs. *the United States,*

Beyond Comanche Springs, the contractor found the rafters going up at Escondido Springs, the site of one of Bigfoot Wallace's earlier Indian fights. The brush was thick along the creek, and he cautioned the hands to clear it away so that possible attackers might be deprived of cover. The scene was much the same at Howard's Well and Beaver Lake. The men worked eagerly to raise the walls and took pains to site their loopholes carefully, knowing that even the smallest stone hut offered better protection than the wooden sides of a wagonbox.

The stations were expensive undertakings for a man who was already financially strained. The scarcity of wood suitable for construction in the western reaches of the state and the steep cost of freighting and labor under such conditions boosted the cost of building even these rude shelters to painful levels. A station and corral might cost from $1,000 to $1,500 to build, with another $500 going for equipping, provisioning, and arming its staff. Added to this was the cost of the prodigious quantitites of feed needed for the stock each month. With hay at $50 per ton and grain at $3.00 a bushel, it did not take the fifteen to thirty animals kept at each station very long to eat their way through a stiff sum. Forage for the mules was often difficult to get even when it was affordable. "At times you couldn't put value upon hay," remarked a station chief, "for it was impossible to get a man to go out and cut it, and they wouldn't cut it for $50 an hour; I know of three instances where men were killed by the Indians while cutting hay." Capping it all was the expense of procuring what often proved to be the most expendable item in the company's inventory: the mule. The beast was sturdy enough to endure hard work and lean rations, but his appeal to the Indians made him fill too many lines of losses in Giddings's ledgers. At $160 to $175 a head for the big Texas- or American-bred mules, and slightly lesser amount for the Spanish variety, the teams did not come cheaply.[10]

The new stations quickly assumed an importance far beyond their role in the company's operations. Giddings estimated that

---

Kiowa, Comanche, and Apache Indians, Records of the Court of Claims (Justice), RG 205, NARS.

[10] Burnham and Giddings Depositions, *Giddings* vs. *United States.*

at least two thousand wagons passed each station every year. Spaced an average of twenty-five miles apart from Bexar to El Paso, they served as havens from Indian attack and supply points for all the travelers on the road. People who ran short of provisions in the wilderness would often become desperate enough to seize them at gunpoint if necessary, and Giddings found it safer and more profitable to keep extra supplies on hand at the stations to meet this demand. "The weary emigrant will no longer be left to protect himself against the incursion of the Indians night after night, and with nothing to subsist his teams on, be compelled to spend a whole summer in making the trip to the Pacific," exulted the *Sacramento Union* as it praised both Giddings and Butterfield's efforts. "He will camp under the roof of the mail station, or the settlers in the vicinity, feed his teams with grain and hay, rest safely, and travel farther in one day than he now does in two." El Paso attorney Josiah Crosby summed up the impact of the stations more succinctly when he recalled after the coming of the railroads that while "none of them were Fifth Avenue hotels . . . the establishment of a stage station was of great importance, and every citizen was interested in it."[11]

The stations served a subtler purpose as well. The influence of law and government did not spread very far beyond the line of settlement on the frontier. The state of Texas had few officials beyond the occasional county judge or Ranger captain to make its authority felt beyond Austin and San Antonio. The stationmasters and line agents in those isolated regions often assumed the role of public official simply by virtue of their association with the United States mail. They usually doubled as postmasters without benefit of either salary or legal appointment. Aside from the army, the expressmen were the only representatives of the federal government that most people on the frontier ever saw. It was not surprising that they were called upon to perform other duties far afield from that of moving the mail. Law enforcement was a desperate problem in those unsettled times, and the stations sometimes became embryonic courthouses, with their residents serving as magistrates and jurors.

[11] *Sacramento Union*, Mar. 5, 1859; Crosby Deposition, *Giddings* vs. *the United States*.

Captain Albert Brackett of the Second Cavalry recalled that in August, 1858, his company had been on the march to Camp Hudson from a post to the east when a traveler camped overnight with the column. The next morning he had disappeared along with an army mule. Upon arriving at Sabinal Station, Brackett found the mule in the stage company's corral. The thief had sold it to the expressmen and quickly moved on. "A party of citizens at once pursued and captured the thief, and hanged him to the nearest tree in accordance with the *lex loci* of Texas," the captain noted grimly. Lieutenant Zenas R. Bliss also remarked in his memoirs of how "the Overland Mail Company had a store at Brackett[ville] at the time I was there, and Tom Rogers was their agent. He was also Justice of the Peace. . . . I was told that a man was shot in a row in some saloon, about midnight. His friends went down and called Rogers up from his bed; he organized his court, tried the murderer, acquitted him, and the man was back dealing monte, or some other gambling game in an hour or two from the time he shot the victim." Rogers may have displayed a rather casual sense of discrimination between homicide and the settlement of an affair of personal honor, but the mail station staffs still served as cadres for the often summary, but always recognizable, workings of justice and civil government on the frontier.[12]

George Giddings had little time to ponder the larger implications of his business as he strove to keep the company running on schedule and operating on the slim funds that sustained its precarious existence. Arriving in San Antonio on September 7, he took stock of his finances and concluded that help was needed if he was to remain solvent enough to keep his stores open and the coaches on the road. In March, the Post Office Department had remitted $1,900 in appealed fines that dated back as far as February, 1855, but that sum would barely cover the cost of rebuilding one of his ruined stations. Leaving his brother James to aid Woods in running the line, Giddings journeyed north to Washington. As he prepared to leave San Antonio, a re-

---

[12] George F. Price, comp., *Across the Continent with the Fifth Cavalry*, 66–67; Zenas R. Bliss, "Memoirs," Zenas R. Bliss Papers, Barker Texas History Center, University of Texas at Austin, 2: 91.

markable phenomenon appeared in the night sky. Donati's Comet blazed through the solar system in a spectacular display of celestial majesty that kept both the expressmen and their Indian enemies gazing skyward in awe each evening for the next two months. Giddings might have taken it as an omen of some sort, for any indication that his luck was destined to change for the better would have been welcomed.[13]

The contractor had already received one portent for good luck that fall when a detachment of Eighth Infantry under Captain Arthur T. Lee established a new post on the Rio Grande only a few miles north of Birchville. Not only would it help to restrain Indian depredations in the area, but the garrison brought added income to some of Giddings's associates. His San Elizario subcontractors, A. C. Hyde and William Ford, had foresightedly joined Jarvis Hubbell in filing a claim on the land that was shortly afterwards occupied by the army. The government initially agreed to pay Hyde an annual rent of one thousand dollars, but his claim to the tract was challenged by Anson Mills, triggering a legal battle that would rage for over a decade and influence the politics of the Pass settlements as they grew.

Whatever the local political and economic overtones of its founding, the new post, Fort Quitman, had been badly needed. Its presence gave a measure of security to travelers in the area beyond Fort Davis. The nearby Cañon de los Lamentos became known as Quitman Pass. The mountains that surrounded it also took the post's name, and the canyon on their far side that ran the length to Devil Ridge became known as Quitman Canyon. It mattered little to the Mescaleros. They had never heard of the dead general from Mississippi whose name graced the outpost, but it was not long before they learned that the troops were there to stay.[14]

Giddings's new stations and the fort were heartening signs

[13] Giddings Deposition, *Giddings vs. United States*; *San Antonio Daily Herald*, Sept. 8, 1858; William H. Hilton, *Sketches in the Southwest and Mexico, 1858–1877*, n.p.; *Harper's Weekly*, Sept. 25, Oct. 9, 1858; U.S. Congress, House, *Report on Delinquent Mail Contractors*, 35th Cong., 1st sess., 1857, House Exec. Doc. 81, pp. 36, 63–64, 95–96.

[14] George Ruhlen, "Quitman's Owners: A Sidelight on Frontier Reality," *Password* 5 (Fall, 1960): 54–56; James C. Cage, *Fort Quitman*, n.p.

of progress on the trail that autumn, but they were far over-shadowed in the public's mind by the beginning of service on the Butterfield line. On September 15 coaches left both St. Louis and San Francisco in a race to beat the schedule that allowed them twenty-five days to make the trip. In his determination to succeed, Butterfield had offered high wages to all the experienced men he could find and even managed to enlist some of Giddings's old hands. Bradford Daily signed on as a driver, and Silas St. John joined as a stationmaster. Henry Skillman had already built a station for Butterfield on the west bank of the Pecos, and he took the reins of the first westbound coach at Horsehead Crossing to drive it all the way into El Paso without relief.[15]

The Butterfield coaches rolled across the desert without hindrance on that first trip and reached their destinations well ahead of time. President James Buchanan sent the company a personal message of congratulations and predicted that it was the vanguard of a new period of progress for the nation. George Giddings's pioneering transcontinental operation remained a poor relation to the Post Office Department, as Butterfield's better financed and heavily promoted company made itself synonymous with the idea of overland stage travel in the Southwest.[16]

While Giddings was shuttling back and forth between New York and Washington in a desperate bid to acquire enough money to stay in business, his new stations furnished continuing amusement for the Indians. Escondido Springs and Lancaster Station both felt the sting of raids as corrals were emptied and haystacks erupted into flames. Giddings decided to abandon the Escondido site and made plans to build another station to the northeast at a point where the road veered west from the Pecos. It would be a risky move as well, but the run from Fort Lancaster to Comanche Springs was too long and punishing to the teams to leave them without a halting place.[17]

The company's men had learned to take such things as In-

[15] Conkling and Conkling, *Butterfield Mail*, 1: 90, 94, 127–29, 375; 2: 61, 141–46, 370–71; *San Antonio Daily Herald*, Oct. 8, 1858. St. John almost died in a treacherous attack by some Mexican employees at his Arizona station.

[16] Hafen, *Overland Mail*, 94–95; *Sacramento Union*, Oct. 14, 1858; *New York Herald*, Nov. 19, 1858.

[17] Burnham Deposition, *Giddings* vs. *the United States*.

dian raids in their stride, and the loss of stock and stations had by then become something that was looked upon simply as part of the risks that came with the job. Certainly traffic on the route did not slacken at all. The San Diego mail arrived in San Antonio on the morning of October 21 with Captain Holliday at the reins and several passengers from Arizona aboard. They reported that the trail was crowded with cattle drovers bound for the west.

Another traveler arrived with the El Paso stage early in December, and though he voiced warm approval of the line's efficiency, he and his companion were ironic symbols of the issue that was already pulling the mail companies into the sectional tug-of-war between North and South. Solomon C. Childers spoke "in the highest terms of the San Antonio and San Diego Mail Line—the stages being comfortable, the drivers accommodating and the conductors a capital set, particularly our friends, Frank and Thomas." The *Daily Herald* noted also that Childers was a professional slave-catcher. He had gone south to Chihuahua to capture and bring back a "valuable negro" who had run away from his Anderson County master. If men were still looking for omens after the comet's fiery passage, there was one to be found standing in the dust of the plaza, clad in rags and shackles.[18]

The year ended on an old note of tragedy and senseless destruction. Tom Rife drove the stage into Eagle Springs on a frosty December night, his team guided up the rocky slope of the trail by the lurid beacon of a burning station. A dead Mescalero lay near the corral. Not far away were the scalped and mutilated bodies of two whites. One of them was Chips, the stationmaster. A Mexican hostler crept out of the brush nearby and told Rife and his escort how the Apaches had overrun them that evening and stolen the mules after looting the buildings. It was not long before Hyde and Ford were once again stubbornly hauling timber and supplies down the road from San Elizario to plant yet another station by the springs that flowed from the honed mountain's flank.[19]

The bad news did not travel eastward quickly enough to ruin Giddings's New Year, but the federal government had al-

[18] *San Antonio Daily Herald*, Oct. 23, Dec. 8, 1858.
[19] Burnham, Rife, Hyde, and Ford Depositions, *Giddings* vs. *the United States*.

ready succeeded in marring the holiday for him. He had gone to the capital in hopes of receiving fairer treatment from the Post Office Department. What he got was the back of its bureaucratic hand. In October the government revoked Giddings's authority to carry the mail north from El Paso to Santa Fe and granted a new contract for the service to Thomas F. Bowler for $16,250 a year. Bowler evidently had problems maintaining his operation, for early in June, 1859, Simeon Hart bought him out and used his equipment to continue running the line. Hart and Giddings may have been partners in this action, but the sale was made in Hart's name for the sum of $11,800. The loss of the route hit Giddings at a particularly bad time that autumn.[20]

This blow was swiftly followed by yet another when Postmaster General Brown terminated Giddings's route between El Paso and Fort Yuma, claiming that it constituted a needless duplication of the Butterfield service over the same road. Brown made no offer of compensation for this arbitrary alteration of the contract, but he did increase compensation on the remaining legs of the line from $149,800 to $196,448 a year. Thus, by October 23 Giddings had the authority to carry the mail between San Antonio and El Paso, and from Fort Yuma to San Diego on a weekly basis. This meant the loss of his stations on the discontinued portion of the route, as well as the expense involved in shifting the men and stock to the operational segments of the line.[21]

A frustrated Giddings consulted with Senator William Gwinn of California and explained his desperate financial situation. In addition to the contract reductions, Congress still neglected to appropriate funds to make good the certificates of indebtedness he had been issued the past March. By October the payments for three-quarters of a year's service were due, and the contractor was issued another sheaf of the virtually worthless documents. Gwinn was approaching a reelection campaign and

[20] Hafen, *Overland Mail*, 74–75; Rex W. Strickland, *Six Who Came to El Paso*, 38, 85; U.S. Congress, House, *Offers and Contracts for Carrying the Mails*, 36th Cong., 1st sess., 1859, House Exec. Doc. 86, p. 85.
[21] U.S. Congress, Senate, *Memorial of George H. Giddings*, 36th Cong., 2d sess., 1860, Senate Misc. Doc. 15, pp. 1–3; Giddings Deposition, *Giddings* vs. *United States*.

knew that a failure of either the Butterfield or Giddings mails could hurt him politically.

Gwinn took Giddings to see August Belmont, a noted New York financier, who was in Washington attempting to win a position as minister to Belgium. The senator used his influence to obtain a loan from the banker. Belmont agreed to give Giddings ninety cents on the dollar for his certificates, which totaled over $200,000, in exchange for 7 percent interest and Gwinn's personal guarantee that Congress would make the postal funds appropriation by January 1, 1859.

Much relieved, Giddings hurried to New York with a letter from Belmont that instructed his bank manager to pay the contractor the amount agreed upon between them. Things did not go smoothly. Giddings found a flinty-eyed old capitalist with the wildly inappropriate name of Christmas mounting watch over Belmont's vaults. The banker refused to believe that his employer had authorized the loan and snorted at the idea that Congress would ever back the certificate with anything besides more promises before the year's end. To get his money Giddings had to agree to pay the man an additional 1 percent commission on the loan. It was pure extortion on Christmas's part. The disgusted Texan left wishing that he could someday introduce Christmas to Chief Gomez or one of his Mescalero cousins in the Limpia Mountains. They could show even a New York banker new ways to skin a man.[22]

When Giddings returned to Washington he found the House of Representatives deadlocked in a battle over the selection of a new speaker. Business dealing with other matters was sidetracked until the contest was settled. It was obvious that no funds would be forthcoming before January. The contractor returned to New York and asked Christmas to extend the deadline for payment. He refused and threatened to sell some additional securities that Giddings had left with him as collateral. Such an action would wipe out everything he had, and a desperate Giddings turned to his uncle, Moses B. Bramhall, who headed another New York bank. Bramhall immediately drew up a note for

[22] Charles M. Barnes, ed., "Memoirs of Colonel George H. Giddings," *San Antonio Daily Express*, May 18, 1902.

his nephew to sign and gave him a personal check or the amount
due to Belmont. Giddings stalked into Christmas's office and
tossed the draft on his desk, demanding the return of his note
and securities. Christmas was dumbstruck at first. When he recovered from his surprise he swore that the expressman was a
born financier and offered him a job with the bank. Giddings refused and collected his papers. After delivering the certificates
to his uncle he left New York for the more congenial company of
his mules.[23]

He had barely arrived back in San Antonio in mid-January
before Isaiah Woods returned to Washington to mount watch on
the company's political well-being. Certain northern congressmen were mustering opposition to Brown's continued support of
the southern overland mails, and a legislative struggle seemed to
be coming.

Giddings found that the new weekly mails were running out
of San Antonio on schedule despite the rather abrupt alteration of routine that the change required. The Indians had taken
note of the more frequent traffic on the road and responded by
stepping up their raids. Comanche Springs and Barrel Springs
were hit, and the new station at Beaver Lake on the Devil's
River was completely destroyed late that month.[24]

Coming on the heels of the Indian attacks was still another
wrenching decree from the Post Office Department. On January
28 the postmaster in New Orleans announced that henceforth
Giddings would be required to carry the western mail from the
Crescent City to San Antonio via Indianola at no charge to the
government. Although the stage line did maintain a branch route
to Indianola, as had Skillman's company before it, the existing
contract made no provision for carrying the mail on that road. It
must have occurred to Giddings that Brown might well be trying
to drive him out of business. His failure would quiet northern
criticism in Congress and throw more business to the Butterfield
line. President Buchanan's friendship with Butterfield was well
known, and whatever helped his company would also benefit
Brown's hometown of Memphis. None of this could be proved, of

[23] Ibid.
[24] Burnham and Giddings Depositions, *Giddings* vs. *United States*.

course, but there seemed to be some deliberate aim behind all the arbitrary penalties that had been inflicted upon the San Antonio company.[25]

The news from Washington told Giddings that the overland mail was definitely becoming a political issue. Republicans in the Senate were opposing any further extension of the mail contracts or road-building projects beyond the Mississippi unless the routes were clearly specified in advance. Brown's granting of the Birch and Butterfield contracts throgh Texas in 1857 were cited as proof of undue southern influence in these matters. One senator specifically denounced the El Paso mail route as a stalking horse for the transcontinental railroad. There was also talk in the Senate Finance Committee of withholding funds from the postal appropriation to kill the San Diego mail service, while leaving the Butterfield contract intact.[26]

As depressing as these reports were, Giddings knew that he would have to rely on his uncle and Woods to look after their interests in Washington, for the simple maintenance and operation of the line consumed all of his attention. There was some satisfaction to be found in knowing that unlike congressmen and bankers, the enemies he met on the frontier could be neatly dispatched with a rifle ball when they tried to bar his way.

February offered him a few small triumphs on the road as the Indians found that they could no longer prey on the whites with their accustomed success. On the fourth a Mescalero band clashed with some freighters and soldiers a mile and a half from Fort Quitman. Their chieftain, José María, died in the skirmish, and the teamsters gleefully hung his body from the limbs of a cottonwood tree that grew by the road. The Apache twisted slowly in the fitful breezes off the river, his sightless grin greeting each stage that came down the trail. The drivers cracked their whips in mocking salute as they passed, happy to have met at least one friendly Apache on their journey.[27]

[25] Giddings Deposition, *Giddings vs. United States.*

[26] *Congressional Globe*, 35th Cong., 1st sess., 1859, pp. 262–63, 305–307; *San Antonio Daily Herald*, Feb. 11, 1859.

[27] U.S. Congress, Senate, *Report of the Secretary of War*, 36th Cong., 1st sess., 1859, Senate Exec. Doc. 2, p. 360.

Only a few days after the Indian's death an infantry detachment camped at Comanche Springs to secure Giddings's station against further raids. Reinforcements were soon sent from Fort Lancaster, and construction began on a permanent post that was to be called Camp Stockton. The troops had been there only a few weeks when, in mid-February, a Comanche war party approached the station and found itself looking down the muzzles of the troopers' muskets. The braves meekly withdrew and skirted the springs as they headed north on some fierce errand. At about the same time, army patrols from Fort Inge and Fort Bliss were claiming victories over the hostiles in several small actions to the west and east.[28]

The good news of that month was capped on the twenty-third when a telegram arrived from Isaiah Woods, informing Giddings that the move to kill the mail route had been defeated and that there was some discussion of increasing the service over it. The *Daily Herald* praised Giddings for his efforts and criticized the preference shown to Butterfield. It subsequently published a letter from a Fort Yuma correspondent who remarked that "the Butterfield Company are in a bad way. . . . Their expenses are perfectly frightful. . . . The San Antonio and San Diego Mail enabled them to start their line here by loaning them barley to stock their Gila road, and thereby got the credit of acting generously by them and having been badly repaid. The San Antonio and San Diego line are doing well, and have a No. 1 credit here." The residents of San Antonio were not about to see their link to the Pacific abolished without mounting a determined defense of it.[29]

Woods's report of quiet on the legislative front was succeeded in March by additional decrees from Brown's successor. The Tennessean had died unexpectedly that month, and Joseph Holt took office as postmaster general. Though Holt came from the same state as Brown, he showed no preferences in his obsessive drive for departmental economy. His ax was already whetted for use on the San Diego mail. On March 12 he an-

[28] Ibid., 361.
[29] *San Antonio Daily Herald*, Feb. 24, Mar. 1, 2, 1859.

nounced that Giddings's service between El Paso and Comanche
Springs would be terminated on May 1. The contract fee would
be reduced to $53,726 a year to reflect the cut in performance.
The Butterfield Company had decided to shift its route south
from Horsehead Crossing to join the El Paso road at Camp
Stockton. This made Giddings's service beyond that point redun-
dant in Holt's eyes. Congress did not help matters when it once
again failed to pass a postal appropriations bill. Moses Bramhall
stepped in and sought to prevent Holt from using this as an excuse to revoke the entire contract by declaring that his nephew
was willing to continue performing the service without pay until
the funding problem was settled. Holt left Giddings hanging in
limbo by replying on March 30 that he "would prefer that the
order of October 27, 1858, should be partially suspended until
Congress meets." The context of this note to Bramhall did not
make clear whether Holt meant to restore the contract between
El Paso and Fort Yuma, or if he was thinking of scrapping the
remaining western and eastern legs as well. Anything Giddings
did at that point was a gamble.[30]

On April 3, Bramhall sent a message to Holt protesting any
further alterations of the contract and arguing that its manifest
value to the region required that it be left intact for the public
good. Eleven days later Holt graciously explained to Giddings
that he had ordered his service reduced by twenty-eight weekly
trips per year, effective June 1, 1859, and that his pay was fixed
at $120,000. When Giddings again offered to continue his nor-
mal schedule of weekly mails pending the subsequent appropriation of funds, Holt coldly informed him that if he attempted
to do so all of the postmasters on the route would be ordered to
deny him the post bags.[31]

Perplexed and confused, Giddings took stock of his situation
once more. Under the previous agreement he had provided
weekly service from San Diego to Fort Yuma, and from San Antonio and El Paso. The mail from Bexar to San Diego was picked

---

[30] *Memorial of George H. Giddings*, 3–4; Giddings Deposition, *Giddings* vs.
United States.

[31] Giddings Deposition, *Giddings* vs. *United States*.

up from the Butterfield line at Fort Yuma and El Paso for delivery during that company's regular semiweekly runs. Now Holt had ordered that after June 1 Giddings could perform only twenty-four trips a year, two a month, and he would suffer a cut in pay from $196,448 to $120,000. He was still in business, but at the cost of absorbing an impending loss in yearly revenue of at least $76,448 even before the losses from Indian raids were considered.[32]

Despite Holt's persistent assaults on the mail company and his mounting personal debts, George Giddings's friends and associates remained firm supporters. His uncle sent his son, Moses Bramhall, Jr., to Texas to aid the company, and the citizens of San Antonio closed ranks behind him in the fight to keep the line operating. Surprisingly, there was no decline in business along the route. Passenger traffic actually increased throughout March and April, although many patrons reached their destinations with more of the now familiar accounts of sudden death on the trail, as on March 23 when the coach for El Paso met a band of warriors at Pecos Spring and drove them off with a volley from the guards' Sharps rifles. Another clash followed the next month at Barrel Springs when the Apaches tried vainly to seize the station's stock. The *Daily Herald* closed its account of the affair with warm words for the company.

Our Overland Mail can no longer be considered an experiment. Those who two years ago said it was impossible to carry a mail through from this city to the Pacific in thirty days, are not satisfied unless it comes to them inside of twenty days; which it often does. Every Monday evening, as regular as clockwork, this mail arrives; in fact it is considered the most regular in its arrivals and departures of any mail that comes into our city, and though not due until Thursday of each week, it has not failed to arrive on Monday for the last four months.[33]

Some of the turmoil had passed on the road by mid-May when Bishop George F. Pierce of the Methodist Church departed San Antonio for California on Giddings's stage. He left a

[32] Ibid.
[33] *San Antonio Daily Herald*, Mar. 30, Apr. 13, 20, 1859.

highly readable account of his journey, which stressed both the dangers of the road and the courtesy and kindness extended to him by the mail company. Like so many travelers from more civilized portions of the country, he was by turns impressed and appalled by the land he traversed in the mail rig. At one point the cleric pronounced the Pecos River region to be "the very nakedness of ruin." The trip had contained much discomfort and disillusionment for Pierce by the time he reached El Paso, but he little realized how lucky he had been in arriving safely at the Rio Grande. On the same day that his coach had paused at Eagle Springs a band of two hundred Comanches had waged a running fight with soldiers from Fort Stockton that continued for over ten miles on the trail. Had they met the mail party, Pierce's scalp might have ended up lashed to the haft of a lance.[34]

Despite the continuing danger and privation that attended stage travel through the region, the residents of El Paso recognized that the mail line was "daily contributing, in a great measure to the settlement, improvement and progress of this remote section of the American Union." They stated their feelings in a formal letter of protest against the cuts in Giddings's contract. Hart, Crosby, Hyde, Ford, and all the other prominent citizens who signed the accompanying petition appealed for a restoration of the weekly mail service and tactfully reminded Holt that El Paso had gone solidly for Buchanan in the 1856 election. The letter might have been written in the sand for all the good it did the contractor.[35]

As spring slid into summer there was no reply from Holt to the El Pasoans' appeal. On June 1 his promised reduction in service took place. This action occurred despite appeals from citizens in Austin and San Antonio that the stage line was of "incalculable importance" to both Texas and the nation. General Twiggs joined in the campaign to aid Giddings by protesting to the secretary of war of the command's dependency on the line "for the regular transmission of all military as well as civil corre-

<hr />

[34] George G. Smith, *The Life and Times of George Foster Pierce*, 377–95; *San Antonio Daily Herald*, May 21, 25, June 9, 1859.

[35] *San Antonio Daily Herald*, May 25, 1859.

spondence with the western posts." Twiggs's superiors forwarded the letter to Holt with the request that he devote his
attention to the problem created by his curtailment of service on
the route.[36]

Appealing to Holt was about as rewarding as preaching the
gospel to a Comanche. In June the warriors struck a station at
Mud Creek, west of Fort Clark. The Mescaleros plagued Cottonwoods Station above Fort Davis, while other bands shadowed
the coaches on the road east of Comanche Springs. Giddings's
supply trains were kept continually on the move to replace the
stock and other property claimed by the raiders, causing the
ever-optimistic *Daily Herald* to laud the enterprise as one "truly
worthy of the men, and the age."[37]

The Indians found that resistance to their forays was stiffen-
ing that August between Comanche Springs and El Paso. Butterfield's line shifted its route down from the Horsehead Crossing to
join Giddings's road at the army post guarding the springs. The
details of the agreement are not documented, but the Butterfield organization evidently consented to share the use of Giddings's stations to the west and aid in their defense. Giddings
may have gained additional benefits by contracting to furnish
stock and supplies to Butterfield as needed. Over it all, however,
hung the possibility that Holt would move to bar him from the
route beyond the junction of the two lines.[38]

Despite the prospect for more trouble from the Post Office
Department, the addition of more men to that section of the
road took some of the burden off the shoulders of Giddings's
often beleaguered station hands. When the Apaches attacked El
Muerto on September 1, they served notice on both companies
that the autumn would be costly. Ten braves ran off part of the
stock and forced the whites to barricade themselves in the station until the westbound stage came along.[39]

[36] Giddings Deposition, *Giddings* vs. *United States*.
[37] *San Antonio Daily Herald*, July 1, 16, 27, 1859; Giddings Deposition, *Giddings*
vs. *United States*.
[38] Conkling and Conkling, *Butterfield Mail*, 2: 13–56.
[39] *San Francisco Bulletin*, Sept. 20, 1859.

The depredations continued as the Mescaleros struck at Barilla Springs on October 1 and Van Horn's Wells, while the Comanches were repulsed at Leon Holes, ten miles to the west of Comanche Springs. The fight at Van Horn's Wells proved costly for the Mescaleros, for they charged into an ambush that had been craftily laid by Adam R. Johnson, one of a brave trio of Texan brothers who worked for Butterfield. Such victories were a tonic for the expressmens' morale, but they were infrequent. The initiative usually rested with the Indians, and it took a special kind of nerve to live under the shadow of the lance for month after month.[40]

With stalwarts like the Johnsons manning the stations beyond the Pecos, the stage lines experienced little trouble as the fall of 1859 passed. In October the San Antonians fired another protest off to Washington, decrying the injuries done to the region's settlement and commerce by the restrictions placed on Giddings. Isaiah Woods had returned from the East sometime in September, and he counseled Giddings that Holt remained fanatically devoted to a program of economy in his department. Since June the company had abided by the postmaster general's orders and operated a semimonthly mail, but by late November it was apparent to Giddings that he could make weekly trips for the same expense required for the less frequent ones and doubtless increase his passenger receipts as well. With the tacit consent of the postmasters on the route, he ignored Holt's directive and began making weekly runs again on the twenty-seventh. At the same time he made arrangements with the Texas Steamship Company to carry eastbound passengers on to New Orleans. With this link assured, Giddings could offer passage from the

[40] *San Antonio Daily Herald*, Oct. 27, 1859; Barry M. Scobee, *Fort Davis, Texas, 1583–1960*, 26–27. Troops from Fort Davis mounted a futile pursuit after the Barilla Springs raid. The army's account of the affair mentioned stock belonging to the "St. Louis and San Antonio Stage Lines," thus indicating that the two companies were sharing the station. The *Daily Herald's* article cited raids on Van Horn's Wells and Limpia Station during the same period. Many of the incidents that occurred on the road during this time remained undocumented either because the white participants did not survive, or they did not reach a settlement with a newspaper while the news was still current. Superbly detailed accounts of the Johnsons' exploits can be found in Adam R. Johnson, *The Partisan Rangers of the Confederate States Army*, 15–16.

Rio Grande to New Orleans in ten days, and to California within twenty-three days of Louisiana.[41]

Woods and Giddings ranged up and down the line that winter, making certain that the schedules were being met and urging their men to shave even more hours off the journey. They had taken the worst that the Indians and the government had to offer and survived. They had learned well the old frontier maxim that to endure was to prevail, and with that knowledge came the gritty, stubborn sense of hope that was as vital for men in that country as powder and ball. As the two weary gamblers sat in the coach and watched the sullen monochrome of the winter sky roll past, they waited expectantly for those clouds, like the cruel months past, to chase themselves into ragged tatters.

[41] *San Antonio Daily Herald*, Oct. 25, Nov. 10, 24, Dec. 1, 9, 14, 17, 30, 1859; Giddings Deposition, *Giddings* vs. *United States*.

CHAPTER 8

The Flame and the Talons

SOMETIME in early January, 1860, the El Paso mail coach thundered into the station at Comanche Springs and rocked to a halt with the mules wheezing and blowing in the frosty air. Steam rose in pungent clouds from their sweating backs while their chill breath spurted in wraiths before them like welcoming ghosts. A few of them groaned and nickered impatiently, waiting to be unhitched, rubbed down, and fed. There were no answering brays from the corral. The Kiowas and Comanches had struck a few days before and driven the stock away from under the very nose of the nearby fort's garrison.[1]

It was a fitting beginning for the year to come. George Giddings had kept his men and coaches on the road throughout that winter, never relaxing in his efforts to keep the mail, passengers, and contract safe from the Indians and Joseph Holt. As the months ahead would prove, fortune and politics often conspired to reward heroic efforts with little but tragic results.

In San Antonio, Giddings instructed his employees and tried to set affairs in order before departing on still another trip to Washington for what he anticipated would be another painful interview with the postmaster general. Isaiah Woods had left for the East earlier, and he reported that Congress was taking its usual lackadaisical approach toward paying the mail contractors while bickering over a widening variety of sectional issues. It was an election year, and both parties sensed crisis in the wind. Following John Brown's raid on Harper's Ferry the previous October, the South had been swept by a fear of northern conspiracy. The Alabama legislature had gone so far as to authorize the

---

[1] U.S. Court of Claims, Deposition of George H. Giddings, *George H. Giddings vs. the United States, Kiowa, Comanche, and Apache Indians*, Records of the Court of Claims Section (Justice), RG 205, NARS.

governor to call a secession convention if a Republican should win the presidency in November, 1860. The Congress that assembled in November, 1859, was "in reality as much a presidential nominating convention as it was a legislative body." Neither party controlled the House, and thus another battle was certain to rage over the election of a presiding officer. Virtually all legislation would be tabled pending its outcome. Following that affair would be an internal struggle between northern and southern Democrats, while the Republicans rooted around in search of corruption and incompetency in the Buchanan administration. Scores of other mail contractors were already in Washington, vying with Woods to influence Congress into passing a bill to honor the Post Office Department's debts. The city was a cauldron of bitterly competing interests whose shouts and clamor added to the rising volume of sectional hysteria. Giddings could well guess that under such circumstances his contract could easily be seized upon as either a target of opportunity by the Republicans or a sacrificial lamb by Holt.[2]

When he arrived in town he found that Holt had already drawn another arrow in his fiscal bow. On February 4 he decreed that on the first of April the San Antonio company would lose the western leg of the route between San Diego and Fort Yuma. Its pay would be reduced to $91,305. The order meant that Giddings would either have to sell all of his property on that division or bear the expense of shifting it eastward to El Paso. In either case, he had less than two months to adjust his operations to this latest sweeping change.[3]

On February 1 the House of Representatives finally elected a speaker, but the postal funding bill remained stalled as the legislators considered more important matters. Giddings and Woods could only fume at the continuing delay.

While the contractors were watching Congress for signs of action, Joseph Holt responded to his mania for economy by taking

[2] Roy F. Nichols, *The Disruption of American Democracy*, 270–79.

[3] U.S. Congress, Senate, *Memorial of George H. Giddings*, 36th Cong., 2d sess., 1860, Senate Misc. Doc. 15, p. 6; U.S. Congress, House, *Abstract of Offers for Carrying the Mails*, 36th Cong., 2d sess., 1860, House Exec. Doc. 73, pp. 437, 441; Giddings Deposition, *Giddings* vs. *the United States*.

a knife to the Texas line once more. In March a horrified Giddings learned that he would lose the service on the route between El Paso and Fort Stockton on May 1. Payment for operations on the surviving portion of the line would fall to $53,726.[4] By that point the Texan had given up all hope of dealing directly with Holt. He immediately petitioned Congress for the restoration of the original schedule and payment granted to the company in its 1857 contract, plus a grant of the back pay due him for the government's arbitrary and illegal alteration of the agreement. He also requested an extension of the contract for another four years. Copies of the memorial were printed and circulated through Congress while he waited for the House Committee on Post Offices and Post Roads to take action. The days passed with no end of the delay in sight, and Giddings returned to San Antonio as the spring approached.[5]

Despite the grim prognosis, Giddings continued to treat the stage company as a long-term investment. Before leaving for the East he had loaded thirteen freight wagons with supplies and sent them over the route to stock his stores and stations for the expected upsurge in travel that the warmer months would bring. The coaches continued to blaze along the rutted trace in increasingly better time. On March 7 the El Paso mail reached Bexar in four days and seventeen hours. Giddings had earlier purchased a herd of blooded horses from a Kentucky dealer and distributed them at certain key stations. The horses lacked the stamina and strength of mules and drew unwelcome attention from the covetous Indians, but they made better speed on a dry road.[6]

Even with a team of "smoking grays," as the local papers called the new animals, the coach could not move fast enough to suit Lieutenant Bliss that April when he rode into town from Camp Hudson. "The stage was crowded, every seat was taken," he found, "and a boy of about twelve years of age, a passenger, had no seat. He was of German descent, and had been captured

[4] Giddings Deposition, *Giddings* vs. *the United States.*
[5] Ibid.
[6] *San Antonio Daily Herald*, Mar. 8, 1860; Deposition of Parker Burnham, *Giddings* vs. *United States.*

by the Comanches in the northern part of Texas." Bliss took pity on the lad and let him sit on his lap as the rig drove south from the post. The child soon fell asleep and Bliss's arm became cramped from supporting him. When he moved it the boy awoke suddenly and began to curse so fluently that even the lead mules cocked their ears in interest. "Nothing in the English language was too vile for him to use in his rage against me for waking him," the subaltern recalled in disgust. The youngster had been traded to the Apaches by his captors and then ransomed to Kit Carson in New Mexico. By that time the child hated all whites and wanted only to be left with the tribe. "He was the hardest case for his age that I ever saw and was better suited by nature to be an Indian than anything else," reckoned Bliss. The tow-headed Apache and the officer parted without sorrow when they reached San Antonio.[7]

Unlike Bliss, George Giddings was happy to carry any paying passenger on the coach that spring, as his line shrank in April and then more in May to cover the final meager span between San Antonio and Fort Stockton. The evidence suggests that although he had to yield the mail to Butterfield's men at Comanche Springs, he kept his vehicles on the road with passengers and freight to El Paso, for his crews continued to man the stations west of the juncture of the two lines beyond the Pecos. Oddly, the most successful Indian attack of the season was against the station in San Elizario, the center of population among the Pass settlements. The Apaches brazenly rode into the outskirts of town and put a torch to the building while they stampeded the teams from the corral. Agent Hyde reported that the structure was destroyed by the fire.[8]

The warriors on the lower road were in a frolicsome mood as well. The Comanches and Kiowas plagued the region east of Fort Davis with renewed persistence. On May 7 they clashed with a detachment of troops at Leon Holes, and on June 23 they stormed into Howard's Well. The station was ready for them, and as long as the rifles kept barking from the loopholes they were

[7]Zenas R. Bliss, "Memoirs," Zenas R. Bliss Papers, Barker Texas History Center, University of Texas at Austin, 2:5–6, 190.

[8]Giddings Deposition, *Giddings* vs. *United States.*

able to steal only one horse. The frustrated braves threw dirt and stones down the well's shaft in an effort to block it. They soon left to cause devilment elsewhere. Several trains had already been ambushed on the road south of Fort Lancaster, and the braves haunted the area for several weeks.[9]

Giddings seemed to be holding his own against the savages that season, but the bad news from the East was unrelenting. By May the Democrats had destroyed their party's hopes for winning the fall elections, and the Republicans were backing Abraham Lincoln. Talk of secession was rife in the South. Congress had never gotten around to appropriating any money for Giddings's back pay, much less replying to his memorial. When the legislative session ended he was still holding nothing more valuable than Holt's certificates. He used these as security on additional loans from several New York banks at interest rates of 1.5 percent per month on each transaction.[10]

Giddings had gone back to Washington to lobby for aid from the government as his financial crisis intensified. The Butterfield Company's representatives were there as well. They sensed that trouble was approaching in the South and wanted Holt to let them shift their route out of Texas to a more northerly line of passage. Giddings learned of their plans, and when he returned home he began anticipating a resurgence of his own company's fortunes.

A re-expansion of the stage line would demand even more money to support it, and Giddings tried to use all his resources to generate more capital. In October he bid on a contract to freight supplies from Indianola to eleven army posts in Texas and New Mexico. He had already begun pressing the army to pay rent on the land occupied by Fort Stockton, for he had filed a claim on the survey for his company prior to the construction of the post. Giddings had originally offered the government free occupancy, but now he was forced to seek compensation for the land's use. The matter dragged on unsatisfactorily for months.

[9]U.S. Congress, Senate, *Report of the Secretary of War*, 36th Cong., 2d sess., 1860, Senate Exec. Doc. 1, p. 38; Clayton Williams, *Never Again: Texas, 1848–1861*, III, 211, 217.

[10]*The Case of George H. Giddings*, 9–10.

While Giddings fretted over his rent and the loss of his quarter-master freighting bid, A. C. Hyde journeyed to Austin, where he served in the state legislature. Working with an ally, he agitated for aid to Giddings's company, meeting with much sympathy but no material support.[11]

Whatever money Giddings managed to raise was soon exhausted by the continuing losses he suffered. Events crowded in upon each other as the year passed into autumn. Between the time Lincoln was elected and South Carolina mustered her secession convention, the Indians struck La Limpia, Van Horn's Wells, and Beaver Lake stations. In December the Comanches atacked Leon Holes again and captured the stock. The Mescaleros were active as well, attacking El Muerto and killing Henry Ramstein, the German emigrant who ran the station.[12]

The tough old German's scalp was still drying on a hoop as his adopted nation began tearing itself apart. Both Butterfield and Giddings watched in grim impotence as their companies were trapped in the web of madness spun by the North and South. The Texan hoped somehow to weather the crisis that was building by establishing a sound relationship with the new administration in Washington even before Lincoln took office. Despite South Carolina's bolt from the Union on December 20, he felt that some means might yet be found to avert a civil war and calm the passions that had been whipped to a frenzy by the recent election. Giddings was in Washington by shortly after New Year's Day. On January 9, 1861, Mississippi seceded, followed by Florida, Alabama, Georgia, and Louisiana within seventeen days. While the country waited to see how the new government would confront this challenge, events in Texas conspired swiftly to undercut Giddings's prospects for a new contract.

On January 28 a secession convention met in Austin to frame a proposed withdrawal from the Union for presentation to the voters. The measure was overwhelmingly approved by the pub-

[11] George H. Giddings to Maj. D. H. Vinton, Oct. 20, 1860, Records of the Quartermaster General, Letters Received, RG 92, NARS; Williams, *Never Again*, II, 212; Austin *Texas State Gazette*, Oct. 29, 1860.

[12] Roscoe Conkling and Margaret B. Conkling, *The Butterfield Overland Mail, 1857–1869*, 1:128, 391–93; Bliss, "Memoirs," 2:11–14.

lic on February 23, with over forty-six thousand ballots favoring secession to less than a third that number in opposition. By March, Texas was in the Confederacy and the staunchly Unionist governor, Sam Houston, had been forced to resign from office. Giddings's employees were caught up in the political fervor of the times as well, and not all of them agreed on which course the state should take. As early as April, 1860, A. C. Hyde had joined other moderates in organizing the San Jacinto Convention, which resolved that "the time has now arrived when all conservative men of whatever section who love their country should unite on a common platform . . . for the perpetuity of the Union." The convention urged the nomination of Houston as "the peoples' candidate" for the presidency. As it turned out, Houston narrowly missed becoming the Constitutional Union party's nominee the following month, losing to John Bell of Tennessee by only a few votes.[13]

Other men linked to the stage line were strongly prosecessionist. Lieutenant Bliss indignantly recorded the activities of two zealots who operated a station thirty-six miles north of Fort Quitman. "Lying Bill" Smith and George Lyle declared their establishment a polling place during the vote on secession and registered a massive turnout. Smith facetiously noted in his report that it was "not a very good day for voting, either," which angered Bliss, for "there were but two men at that place that had a shadow of a right to vote, and yet they cast six hundred votes for secession. This was common talk and considered a good joke."[14]

Giddings had never been a political activist. Like most prudent businessmen, he probably opposed any radical action that would disrupt the normal climate for prosperity. A man holding a government mail contract could hardly be expected to favor his state's withdrawal from the Union, but in Washington he knew that all Texans might be tarred with the same brush of treason.

[13] Louis J. Wortham, *A History of Texas: From Wilderness to Commonwealth*, 4:292–96.

[14] Bliss, "Memoirs," 2:232. For a general treatment of the secession crisis in Texas see Charles W. Ramsdell, "The Frontier and Secession," in *Studies in Southern History and Politics*, 63–82.

Ironically, the rebellious spirit that was loose back home actually proved to be an aid in gaining him access to the most influential people in the new government.

Several years before Giddings had unknowingly made a fateful decision when he engaged Montgomery Blair, a Maryland attorney, as his lobbyist in the capital. When Lincoln selected Blair as his postmaster general, things finally began to turn in Giddings's favor. On March 1, 1861, Congress made a special appropriation for $70,000 in back pay for the contractor at Blair's request, and within two weeks Giddings had the cash in hand. The Butterfield contract for service through Texas was annulled at the company's own initiative on March 2, and the line began preparing to move its operations to a northern route over the Central Plains to California. Giddings received a new contract to link San Antonio and Los Angeles with his coaches from April 1, 1861, to June 30, 1865.[15]

Montgomery Blair expected something in return from Giddings for his beneficent influence. One afternoon in mid-March the Texan paid a call at the Post Office Department to say farewell, as he planned to leave for San Antonio that night. Blair stunned Giddings when he told him to delay his departure because President Lincoln wanted to see both of them that evening.

Feeling that he was being drawn into something that was far beyond his depth, Giddings accompanied Blair to the White House that night and was introduced to Lincoln and his cabinet. The president took a seat beside the nervous expressman and spoke of the confidence that Blair and Congressman Galusha A. Grow of Pennsylvania had in his loyalty and ability. After questioning him briefly about his family background and business enterprises, Lincoln told Giddings why he had been summoned. "I have sent for you with an object. I wish an important secret message delivered to Governor Houston of Texas," explained the president. "Before reading it and confiding in you I must first swear you in as a member of my cabinet, all of whom are sworn

---

[15] LeRoy R. Hafen, *The Overland Mail, 1849–1869*, 213–17; Conkling and Conkling, *Butterfield Mail*, 2:325–28; Giddings Deposition, *Giddings* vs. *the United States*.

to secrecy and not to divulge anything taking place at this meeting. This I must do before entrusting you with this message. Hold up your right hand."[16]

At first Giddings thought he was being made the butt of some elaborate joke, but when he saw that Lincoln was serious, he took the oath of secrecy in dazed apprehension, fearful of what he was committing himself to in the cause of an already bitterly divided nation. Lincoln's message to Houston called for him to lead a counterrevolution in the Southwest. The deposed governor was offered a general's commission and authority to assume command of all federal troops in the state while rallying the Unionist faction in a campaign to pull Texas out of the Confederacy.[17]

Giddings quickly grasped the implications of this message for both himself and the nation, but he cautioned Lincoln that it would be better to use an army officer as his courier. "If those Texans caught a regular United States Army officer with that document in his possession," replied the president, "they would hang him." Giddings protested that they would hang him just as quickly but consented to attempt the mission, not aware that Lincoln had earlier sent a similar message to Houston with an officer who had been politely rebuffed.

The new cabinet member remained in the White House conference until midnight, listening to the debate on the likelihood of war with the South. Secretary of State William H. Seward felt that conflict was inevitable, but Lincoln and several others hoped to achieve some sort of compromise. They assured Giddings that he ran no risk in accepting the new mail contract. The morning found him southward bound, his exhausted mind struggling with contending thoughts that were colored by hope, pride, and anxiety.[18]

Giddings arrived in Austin sometime in late March and approached Houston with the government's proposal. After conferring with four of his closest advisors, Houston concluded that to

[16] Ida M. Tarbell, *Life of Lincoln*, 2:20–23.
[17] Ibid.; Charles M. Barnes, ed., "Memoirs of Colonel George H. Giddings," *San Antonio Daily Express*, May 18, 1902.
[18] Barnes, "Memoirs."

accept Lincoln's offer would guarantee that Texas would be the arena for any future civil conflict. Not even the most ardent Unionists in the state were willing to bring such misery upon their people. Houston refused the commission and Texas remained with the Confederacy. Seeking to avoid one tragedy, he contributed to another. More Texan blood would be shed in the fields and mountains of Tennessee, Virginia, and Pennsylvania than had ever been lost in the struggles against the Comanches and Mexicans.[19]

George H. Giddings boarded the stage in Austin and arrived home in San Antonio on March 28, wisely saying nothing of his meeting with Houston and cheerfully announcing the commencement of his new contract. No blame or suspicion was attached to him for doing business with the U.S. government. There was still an air of unreality about the national crisis, and even the devoted secessionists often assumed that southern independence would be achieved without prolonged conflict. Both the state and Confederate authorities were content to let the postal service function without interference until the governments in the South and North could negotiate a treaty dealing with the issue.[20]

Though Giddings may have found himself caught in the limbo between evolving relationships and volatile circumstances that marked life in the Confederacy at that point, there was no

---

[19] Marquis B. James, *The Raven*, 336–37; Llerena B. Friend, *Sam Houston*, 340–47. The entire Lincoln-Giddings-Houston affair remains cloaked in mystery and poorly documented. Tarbell's account of the White House meeting varied in several details from Giddings's recollections. Tarbell's work has no notes or bibliography, and so later researchers cannot evaluate her sources. Both she and Giddings were imprecise about the date of the Lincoln interview. Friend placed the meeting with Houston in Georgetown, Texas, between Feb. 23 and March 2, 1861. Lincoln did not take office until Mar. 4, and Giddings was back in San Antonio by Mar. 29. It would have been impossible for him to have met Houston at the date given in James's account. Friend estimated that Giddings may have met with Lincoln as late as Apr. 12, but this is clearly incorrect. Lincoln had meetings with his cabinet on the night of Mar. 3 and the evening of Mar. 9. There were similar meetings on the mornings and afternoons of Mar. 14 and 23. No record exists of Giddings's presence at these conferences. The context of Giddings's remarks indicated that it took place after his special appropriation was conducted on Mar. 13. See C. Percy Powell, *Lincoln Day by Day*, 3:24, 27–28, 30.

[20] San Antonio *Alamo Express*, Mar. 29, 1861; Alex L. ter Braake, *Texas: The Dream of Its Postal Past*, 134–39.

question of where he stood with his old enemies on the El Paso road. The news he received of their actions during his absence was almost enough to make the threat of civil war pale by comparison. Giddings had barely left for Washington in December before a campaign for plunder started that stretched over the following weeks like the livid welt of a fresh scar. Leon Holes was hit in a costly raid, and soon afterward the Mescaleros made a determined assault on the new station at Fort Quitman. Giddings had shifted his men and stock there from Birchville in hopes of gaining better protection, but even the presence of the troops did not deter the Apaches from emptying the line's corral after a bitter fight that lasted for several hours.[21]

Hard on the heels of this affray came a Comanche assault on Howard's Well that destroyed the station and two coaches. The staff were lucky to escape with their lives. Then came a truly staggering blow upon Pecos Station that January. A large war party caught one of Giddings's supply trains in camp at the relay point, and the Comanches thundered down on the whites one morning in a shrieking wave. The Texans fought hard, but when the raid was over the Indians had succeeded in running off over a hundred mules while the shattered camp blazed behind them.[22]

In mid-February, 1861, General Twiggs surrendered all military property in Texas to the rebel authorities, and the Union garrisons began their withdrawal from the frontier as the dusty blue columns marched for the coast and a return to the loyal states. On March 4, Lieutenant Bliss led his men out of Fort Quitman and headed east for San Antonio. The next morning he met the stage at Eagle Springs and received orders to return to the post and await the arrival of the command from Fort Bliss. The Mescaleros watched all this countermarching with keen interest.[23]

By early April, Giddings was ready to travel west and set his new operation in order for the coming months. One of his first tasks upon arriving in San Antonio had been to send a new crew

---

[21] Depositions of Price Cooper, Joseph Hetler, George Koalhaus, and A. C. Hyde, *Giddings* vs. *United States.*

[22] Depositions of Samuel Schutz and Parker Burnham, *Giddings* vs. *United States.*

[23] Ibid., 2:236.

of men to operate the station at Turkey Creek. A Mexican hostler had sunk a hatchet into the stationmaster's head and fled with his money. At the same time Indians were plaguing the roads in the region between D'Hanis and Uvalde. An organized band of traders operating in Mexico was prompting the warriors to make their raids to steal stock for sale below the border.[24]

At least Giddings did not have to contend with interference from his fellow whites as well. The Butterfield Company began cutting back its services across Texas just in time, for the state authorities were growing increasingly suspicious of the northern-owned line's activities. Confederate sympathizers had already interfered with the mail's passage at Tucson and Fort Smith. The last eastbound coach cleared El Paso on March 9 and reached Missouri on the twenty-first. As Giddings rode west that spring, he heard stories of the company's mounting financial distress and planned to strengthen his own battered resources by capitalizing on Butterfield's misfortune.[25]

When the El Paso stage left San Antonio on April 1, both George and James Giddings were aboard. Nine days later they reached Fort Stockton, and the younger man rode ahead to the Pass while George remained behind to meet one of Butterfield's agents. He planned to buy the company's stock and property on the line to the west for as little as possible. Giddings spent a week waiting for the man, and when he failed to appear he moved on to El Paso, arriving there by April 19. He consulted with James, and they decided to attempt to put the first mail of their new contract over the road as soon as possible. George returned to Fort Stockton to await the Butterfield man while James began mustering a crew for the run to California. Giddings was mercifully unaware that it was the last time he would ever see James alive again.[26]

At Fort Stockton he finally made contact with the other line's agent and closed a deal for much of the stock, equipment, and property left on the route from Comanche Springs to Cali-

[24] San Antonio *Alamo Express*, Mar. 8, 27, 29, 1861.

[25] Conkling and Conkling, *Butterfield Mail*, 2:325–27; Hafen, *Overland Mail*, 217.

[26] Kathryn S. McMillen, "The San Antonio–San Diego Mail Line in Texas, 1857–1861" (M.A. thesis, University of Texas at Austin, 1960), 201.

fornia. The Butterfield Company undoubtedly took a loss on the sale, but it could not compare with the ones the Texan would suffer before that spring was over.

Giddings finished his business at the post by early in May, and with Parker Burnham at the reins he boarded the coach for El Paso. On the way he had one of his closest brushes with death in many years of travel over the plains. They were about three miles east of Barilla Springs when a Mescalero war party howled down upon them and loosed a volley of arrows and musket balls at the startled team. Burnham and guard Jim Spears were on the driver's box, lashing the mules forward at a dead run while taking snap shots at their pursuers. Giddings and the other passengers opened fire from within the coach.

It was a scene that could have been lifted from the canvas of Frederic Remington's *Downing the Nigh Leader*, as men, animals and coach merged into a dusty blur of frenzied motion. Burnham threw a quick glance over his shoulder and recognized the Indians as Chief Nicolas's band of Mescaleros. On earlier occasions Nicolas had come into Fort Davis to parley with the whites, and Burnham had caught the Indian casting admiring glances at his healthy mane of coppery red hair. Any one of the twenty-five braves chasing the rig would delight in running the edge of his knife around the crown of Burnham's skull to claim such a handsome trophy.[27]

As Burnham raised his whip to urge the mules to greater speed, an arrow thudded into his hip. Seconds later another barbed shaft sliced into his neck. Dazed with pain and slipping into shock, he let Spears take the reins while he collapsed in the storage boot beneath their feet. The mules hardly faltered as they took the curve in the trail and started upslope for Barilla Springs. Three of them already had arrows jutting from their heaving flanks. The Mescaleros were suffering as well. The Texans had emptied four of their saddles during the chase, and the warriors screamed in frustration when the coach hurtled through the gates of the station to safety. One of the mules dropped dead

[27]Burnham Deposition, *Giddings vs. United States*; *El Paso Herald*, Aug. 3, 1917; Washington, D.C. *Rural Free Delivery News*, Apr. 21, 1917; Charles M. Barnes, ed., "Memoirs of Colonel George H. Giddings," *San Antonio Daily Express*, June 1, 1902.

in the traces as they halted, and two others died of their wounds that afternoon, as the whites continued to battle the Indians from the corral's walls. Nicolas and his band finally gave up and left. Later that day Burnham's comrades held him down while the arrows were cut from his wounds. He was a strong man and recuperated quickly, but he left Giddings's company soon afterward for less dangerous service in a Confederate cavalry regiment.

The stage moved on to Fort Davis as soon as the trail appeared to be free of Apaches, passing by the wreckage of an emigrant wagon at Northern Point of Rocks and the graves of a family slain by Nicolas only a few weeks before. The troops had already left Forts Davis and Quitman, and such sights were going to be even more common on the road in the years ahead.[28]

Giddings left Burnham at La Limpia to recover from his injuries; he drove cautiously through the mountains, pausing at each station to check its supplies and warn the hands to remain more alert than ever now that the army had left the frontier. When Giddings climbed down from the rig in front of his store at the Pass, the clerks' faces told him that something was wrong. Travelers coming in from Tucson had brought the news. James Giddings was dead. The Apaches had wiped out his entire party near Stein's Peak. George had become inured to tragedy during his years on the road, but this loss staggered him. Two of his brothers had now died in the company's service, but the line was no closer to being a successful and stable business than it ever had been.

Giddings fell ill as he organized a strong force to ride west and bury the bodies. The next stage in from San Antonio brought even more bad news. Fort Sumter had been fired upon and Lincoln responded with a call for troops to suppress the southern rebellion. For a decade the wild tribes had done their best to destroy the stage line. Now it appeared that the job would be done by a few South Carolina militiamen in Charleston harbor.

While Giddings lay sick he pondered the price he had paid

[28] San Antonio *Alamo Express*, May 3, 1961; Burnham Deposition, *Giddings* vs. *United States*. For a fuller account of Burnham's service with the line, see Wayne R. Austerman, "Parker Burnham, an Expressman of Old El Paso," *Password* 27 (Spring, 1982): 5–14.

for his ambitions and wondered what action to take next. As more news came in about the circumstances of James's death, it became clear that his fate had been sealed many months before when a young army officer, Lieutenant George N. Bascom, had led a patrol out of Fort Buchanan to punish the Arizona Apaches for the kidnapping of a white child and his mother. Bascom singled out Cochise's band, which had been peacefully trading with the stage station in Apache Pass. Early in February, 1861, Bascom betrayed the Indian during a parley and told Cochise that he would be held hostage until the captives were freed. The enraged chieftain slashed his way through Bascom's tent with a knife and escaped under fire. Six other braves were seized and bound. The next day Cochise captured the mail station's staff and attacked a small wagon train west of the pass, taking still more prisoners.[29] A few days later Cochise offered to exchange his captives for Bascom's, but the lieutenant refused to negotiate and shooting broke out. Reinforcements arrived from Fort Buchanan and the Indians faded away into the mountains, leaving the charred bodies of their prisoners behind them. Bascom's rash actions had ignited a major Indian war. Within two months more than a hundred whites would die at the outraged Indians' hands. No traveler, train, or settlement could feel secure in the wake of Bascom's justice. The six braves hanged by Bascom in retribution would be avenged many times over that year.

The Indian attacks on the road had become commonplace by the time James Giddings reached El Paso in April, but he was determined to put the mail through and reorganize the network of stations that his brother had acquired from Butterfield. On the advice of Nelson J. Davis, the other line's bookkeeper in the settlement, he decided to join forces with a party of Butterfield hands who were collecting the unsold stock and property remaining on the road to California. Giddings traveled with them, carrying both the St. Louis and San Antonio mail bags on this opening run.[30]

[29] Giddings Deposition, *Giddings* vs. *the United States*; Paul I. Wellman, *The Indian Wars of the West*, 288–89; Dan L. Thrapp, *The Conquest of Apacheria*, 16–17.
[30] Thrapp, *Conquest*, 16–17; Robert M. Utley, *Frontiersman in Blue*, 162–63.

On April 21 he arrived in Mesilla and gathered his company for the trip. There were only four men besides himself in the party, but all were heavily armed and expecting a fight before the journey was done. The express was approaching Stein's Peak at dawn on the twenty-eighth when it rolled into Cochise's ambush. Edward Briggs and Anthony Elder died in the first volley, as the stage was literally riddled with arrows and bullets. The driverless team bolted from the road and ran for nearly a mile and a half with the braves in pursuit. The rig capsized near the mountain's base. Giddings, Sam Nealy, and Michael Niese crawled from the wreckage and took cover.[31]

The trio fought ferociously, killing several Indians before they were overrun. They were then slowly tortured to death. The Apaches had already demolished the nearby station and left all the bodies where they had fallen. The carnage had just begun on that ravaged track through the desert, and even before George Giddings had recovered from the shock of James's death, the Apaches struck again. On May 17 another mail party left Mesilla for the Pacific. Six guards rode with the coach. Behind them came a large caravan of a hundred men, two hundred animals, and a score of coaches and wagons. They were the remaining Butterfield employees in El Paso and Mesilla, headed for California with the line's unsold property. Giddings and Henry Skillman followed the column with twenty-five men and a herd of their own stock to replenish the stations on the route.[32]

The mail party pulled quickly ahead of the two slower trains and made good time until it ran into Cochise at Cooke's Spring. Here, also, he had destroyed the station and laid an ambush for the incoming coach. When the fighting had ended, twelve more white men lay dead in the brush. By that time the Apaches had struck almost every station on the line between that point and Tucson. In quick succession Mimbres River, Cow Springs, Soldier's Farewell, Barney's Station, San Simon, Apache Pass, Dra-

[31] McMillen, "Mail Line," 202; George W. Baylor, "Tragedies on the Old Overland Stage Route," *Frontier Times* 26 (Mar. 1949): 125; Eleanor Sloane, *The Butterfield Overland Mail across Arizona*, 16–18; James H. Tevis, *Arizona in the '50s*, 218.

[32] *Mesilla Times*, May 17, 1861; Depositions of Charles O. Brown and Joseph Hetler, *Giddings* vs. *the United States*.

goon Springs, and San Pedro went up in flames. More than thirty men died in the onslaught, and tons of forage were destroyed along with at least six coaches. Over a hundred horses and mules swelled the Indians' herds as booty, and the savages made off with scores of Sharps rifles and Colt revolvers. With such weapons they would be ten times as aggressive and dangerous as before.[33]

Skillman and Giddings halted at each killing ground to bury the dead and to salvage what they could. The contractor was probably too numbed by grief and shock to feel much of anything, as the losses in men and property mounted with each station that they visited in this macabre pilgrimage. It was early June, 1861, and the end of the most savage eight weeks in the history of the El Paso mail. It only remained for the Mescaleros to the east to add one final bloody punctuation mark to this terrible chapter.

Giddings left Skillman in Mesilla as they returned eastward and arrived in El Paso looking worn and haggard. On the next Fourth of July he would be thirty-eight years old. Within the past three years he had buried two brothers and amassed a list of debts and property losses that must have approached $400,000. He had little to show for it besides a mocking piece of paper that bound him to four more years of service to a nation at war with itself.

Somehow Giddings found the determination to carry on through the chaos and desolation he had witnessed. Henry Skillman took charge as superintendent of the company's western division from Mesilla to Los Angeles. His brother, William Skillman, acted as agent in New Mexico. On June 1 the *Mesilla Times* had cheerfully announced that "Mr. G. H. Giddings is using his characteristic energy to get the line in thorough working order. Notwithstanding civil war and Indian massacres, . . . the mail now leaves this place every Sunday, and El Paso Mondays and Thursdays for San Antonio." The journal promised that Skillman would soon have semimonthly service available to Cali-

---

[33] Charles M. Barnes, ed., "Memoirs of Colonel George H. Giddings," *San Antonio Daily Express*, May 4, 1902.

fornia. Eight days later another wildly optimistic advertisement promising service to the west ran in the paper over Isaiah Woods's name. It was the last time that the Californian's name was publicly linked with the stage line, and from then on he dropped from sight in the Southwest. The circumstances of his departure from Giddings's company remain obscure. It may well have been that he sensed another failure in the making like that of the Adams firm and wished to avoid being linked with it.[34]

Giddings had not been back in El Paso very long when he prepared to return to San Antonio and learn what measures were being taken by the Confederate authorities to provide a postal service for the frontier settlements. The line to Bexar had been spared the devastation inflicted on the route beyond Mesilla, and the coaches still ran on a regular schedule, bringing keenly anticipated bits of information to the news-starved border dwellers. The road hosted occasional emigrant trains as well. One of them was camped at Fort Stockton that month when the westbound stage passed through. Led by Noah Smithwick, a shrewd old plainsman, it was composed of Texas Unionists who were giving up their homes to join the old government's cause in California. "I do not remember how often the trips of the stage were made," Smithwick remarked in his memoirs, "but I remember how eagerly the stage was watched for, and how breathlessly we listened for the latest news of the war that was only just beginning to take shape."[35]

The news from the East forced many others to make decisions about where their loyalties lay. Major James Longstreet had already resigned his commission as an army paymaster at Albuquerque and taken his family south down the Rio Grande to El Paso, where they sought transportation to San Antonio and New Orleans. He found the settlement on the American side of the river firmly in the hands of the secessionists. "All was enthusiasm and excitement," Longstreet noted, "and songs of 'Dixie and the South' were borne upon the balmy air."[36]

[34] *Mesilla Times*, May 17, June 1, 8, 9, 1861.
[35] Noah Smithwick, *The Evolution of a State*, 339.
[36] James Longstreet, *From Mannassas to Appomattox*, 30–31. The details and se-

Longstreet had done a tour of duty at Fort Bliss in the mid-1850s and enjoyed the friendship of many of the local settlers at the Pass. They persuaded him to leave his family in their care while he took the stage to Bexar ahead of them to make arrangements for travel up the Gulf to New Orleans. His wife and children could follow in the company of a slower, but safer, train of freight wagons. Longstreet consented, and after making certain that his family was comfortably lodged, he visited his old friend from his San Antonio days at the stage line's office in Giddings's store.

Their reunion was as genial as it could be under the circumstances. Longstreet must have noticed more than a few gray hairs in Giddings's temples. It had been thirteen years since they had ridden together against the Comanches near Bexar, and Giddings had spent much of that time on the trail with his freight wagons and stages. The keen ambition of earlier days had been tempered by hardship and tragedy into grim determination and stoic endurance.

Longstreet found that they would be sharing the coach when it left and welcomed the chance to renew his friendship with the man who had saved his life in that skirmish so long ago. They were joined by two young northerners who were posing as resigned army officers headed home to offer their services to the Confederacy. Longstreet knew of their disguise and vouched for them to the authorities in El Paso. Lieutenant William H. Jackson of the Regiment of Mounted Riflemen also boarded the stage with them. Like Longstreet, he had quit the old army and was bound for Tennessee to fight for the Confederacy. Jackson was well known on the frontier for his courage, having once killed a grizzly bear from the saddle with a single saber stroke. The red-haired lieutenant was a good man to have along on a trip through Indian country.[37]

---

quence of events in the company's history during the spring of 1861 are confused and indistinct. Contemporary accounts and the depositions contained in Giddings's court brief are often fragmentary and contradictory as well. The author has attempted to reconcile these discrepancies and present an account based upon the most probable pattern of movement by Giddings and his men.

[37] Ibid., 30–31; Giddings Deposition, *Giddings* vs. *the United States*.

The stage left El Paso that morning in early June and coursed downriver to change teams at San Elizario, Smith's Ranch, and Fort Quitman without incident. The mules threaded their way into the thorned gullet of Quitman Pass and then struck south down the broad canyon that separated Devil Ridge from the ranges fronting on the Rio Grande. The first day's travel lay behind them as the team began its long pull up the gradual, mile-long ascent into Eagle Springs on an unseasonably chilly morning. Driver David Koney paused briefly as they approached the station to blow his bugle, the notes slanting cleanly uphill through the crisp desert air. There was no answering call from above.

A grisly but not entirely unexpected sight met the travelers' gaze as the rig wheeled into the station's yard. The fire had burned itself out in the adobe husk of the storage rooms and house. The hayricks and stables in the empty corral still had a few stubborn sparks dancing over their ashes, but there was nothing of substance left to burn. Nearby lay the twisted and blackened bodies of the two station hands. Koney estimated that the Mescaleros had been gone for only a day at most.[38]

Longstreet, Jackson, and the other two passengers stepped cautiously down from the coach and mounted watch as Giddings and Koney buried the dead and surveyed the damage. The rocky slopes that looked down on them from three sides could still harbor an ambush. All of them must have given a few moments' thought to what might have happened if the mail had left El Paso a day earlier and pulled into the station just in time to be caught in the raid. In his reminiscences Longstreet recalled only how "the ride of our party . . . through the Indian country was attended with some risk, and required vigilance to be assured against surprise." It was a radical understatement of the situation, even for the stolid Longstreet.[39]

There was little conversation in the coach as it left Eagle Springs and entered the long canyon that led to Van Horn's Wells.

[38] Dabney H. Maury, *Recollections of a Virginian*, 124; Ezra J. Warner, *Generals in Gray*, 152–53; Deposition of David Koney, *Giddings* vs. *the United States*.

[39] Longstreet, *To Appomattox*, 31.

Giddings and his companions remained alert, but there was no sign of the Indians. The Mescaleros had been temporarily placated and were busy barbecuing a mule and boasting over their scalps in some high rancheria as the stage crept eastward.

Fort Davis and La Limpia were quiet when the rig pulled in, although it was just a matter of time before trouble would erupt at that haven as well. Only a few settlers and stage men remained to confront the warriors around the empty post. Even the later arrival of Confederate troops would do little to pacify the region.

As they bore north up Limpia Canyon, past the ruins of Cottonwoods relay station, and then wheeled east toward Barilla Springs, Giddings might have recalled a common sight in those mountains during high summer. Quite often a coach would find itself enveloped in a drifting pall of smoke as a grass fire swept down on one of the draws to the north. Behind the billowing cloud the passengers could see the scarlet line of flames sweeping ahead of the wind toward the Limpia. Above the smoke and greedy little blaze a brace of hawks would swing in lazy circles, patiently waiting for a rabbit or mouse to break from cover as the fire roared closer. Giddings could feel a stir of sympathy for the doomed creatures. He knew what it was like to be caught between the flame and the talons. As the stage rolled on for San Antonio he could feel both drawing still closer.

CHAPTER 9

Thrones for the Ravens

T HE summer of 1861 marked the end of one time of trial and the beginning of another as the El Paso mail was pledged to the service of a struggling new nation. The waste and destruction created by the Civil War would be visited upon Texas in lesser measures than those inflicted upon many other regions of the South, but the continuing conflict with the Indians taxed the resources of a state whose people had now to contend with the threat of invading armies from the North. For many Texans, not the least of them George H. Giddings, the war marked not so much the start of a crisis as its prolongation and enlargement.

When Giddings reached San Antonio that June, his life seemed to reflect the greater disarray of the Union. The mail line that had first involved him as an investor and contractor by default in 1854 had come to dominate his existence in the years since. It had proved to be a cruel master. Even before the disastrous events of that season, the enterprise had brought few benefits and many sacrifices to him. The mail service had claimed the lives of two of his brothers, and the end of the last bloody wave of Apache raids had left him poorer by an estimated $229,300 for the whole span of the contract. No value could ever be assigned to the loss of the forty-four men whose bones were turned beneath the earth from the Devil's River to the Gila.

Some of the burden of worry may have lifted from Giddings's shoulders when he met his young wife and two infant daughters at their home in San Antonio. With Emma's aid he began to take stock of his affairs in planning for what was at best an uncertain future. His assets consisted of the surviving line of freight wagons and his stores in Bexar, Brackettville, and El Paso. The mail contract had been doomed by the secession of Texas. Beyond El Paso the damage done to the line was enough to cripple its operations on the leg to California. What South

Carolina had begun in December, 1860, the Apaches helped to
finish by that following June.[1]

It was a time for Giddings to make some hard decisions. He
had already received a letter from the Confederate government,
informing him that none of his services on the old contract route
would be recognized beyond July 1, 1861. Neither payment nor
legal authority to carry the mail would be granted after that
date. He was free to bid on a new contract when the San Antonio
postmaster advertised for other carriers. The letter put his dilemma in very stark terms. If he hoped to salvage anything from
the stage line he would have to win a contract with the Confederacy. If he chose to return to the North he would have to sell
his property at a loss and possibly risk its confiscation by the
state authorities. The ties of business and friendship formed during the past fifteen years would also be severed. "I had been a
Union man and my interests were almost entirely with its government, but I saw it was plainly my duty to join the Southern
cause and cast my fortune with it," recalled Giddings many years
later. "My family were in Texas and the South."[2]

Having made his decision to serve the Confederacy, Giddings lost no time in taking a stage to the Gulf, where he caught
a steamer to New Orleans. Arriving in Richmond, he sought an
interview with President Jefferson Davis. An appointment soon
followed as a government purchasing agent empowered to buy
and export cotton to finance his procurement operations in Mexico. Even at that early date, the Brownsville-Matamoras region

[1]U.S. Court of Claims, Deposition of George H. Giddings, *George H. Giddings
vs. the United States, Kiowa, Comanche, and Apache Indians*, Records of the Court of
Claims (Justice), RG 205, NARS. Virtually nothing is known of Giddings's private life
beyond what was recorded in contemporary newspaper accounts and court records. His
personal papers were destroyed when the San Antonio River flooded part of the city in
1866. Louise Giddings Brusse of Brenham, Texas, once held a collection of the surviving
family records and papers, but since 1960 the bulk of it has been scattered or lost. The
memoirs Giddings dictated to journalist Barnes of the *San Antonio Daily Express* in 1902
revealed little personal information and contained some factual errors. These were to be
expected from an old man who was recalling the events of fifty years past.

[2]Charles M. Barnes, ed., "Memoirs of Colonel George H. Giddings," *San Antonio Daily Express*, May 18, 1902. Lincoln's earlier trust in Giddings must have given
Giddings's conscience a few twinges when he joined the Confederacy, but on a purely
practical basis he had little other choice.

held obvious promise as an entrepôt for supplies from Europe to fuel the South's war effort. Eventually he got a ship for use in running the blockade with cargoes for Cuba and the Bahamas. Almost inevitably he was drawn back into the express business as the infant Confederate Post Office Department labored to create a mail service from the remnants of the old system. A man with Giddings's bitterly won experience would be invaluable to this effort in the trans-Mississippi South.[3]

Giddings was fortunate in that Jefferson Davis had made a wise choice in appointing Texan John H. Reagan as his postal chief. This able and energetic administrator eventually shared a rare distinction with Stephen R. Mallory, the Confederate secretary of the navy. They were the only officers to serve in the same posts throughout the war. Reagan's steady hand was an asset to a department that was sired by crisis and born of extemporization.

Reagan's task was enough to daunt the most dedicated reformer or revolutionary. His response to the challenge was characterized by a blend of bold effrontery and cool pragmatism. Soon after his appointment on March 6, 1861, he sent an agent north on a secret recruiting tour. The man carried letters from Reagan to serving members of the U.S. Post Office Department, offering them positions in his service. Several experienced men accepted, giving Reagan a skilled nucleus of personnel to staff his organization. This preemption by subterfuge of trained people was aided by the Confederate Congress on March 15, when it authorized Reagan to retain in office all postmasters and other employees currently serving in the old organization until new appointments could be made. Five days later Reagan ordered his postmasters to seize all U.S. funds and property at their offices and submit inventories to him at once. It was an astute performance for a former one-term congressman from a backward frontier state.[4]

[3]John H. Reagan to George H. Giddings, May 25, 1861; Reagan to H. L. Radoz, May 25, 1861, Records of the Confedreate States of America (Pickett Papers), Office of the Postmaster General, Letters Sent, Mar. 7, 1861–Oct. 12, 1863, Container No. 98, Manuscript Division, Library of Congress, 24–25.

[4]John H. Reagan, *Memoirs with a Special Reference to Secession and the Civil War*, 124–35; Walter F. McCaleb, "The Organization of the Post-Office Department of the Confederacy," *American Historical Review* 12 (Oct., 1906): 65–69; Cedric O. Reyn-

Reagan and his subordinates had no period of transition to enjoy when they took office. In February, 1861, the U.S. Congress had directed the postmaster general to end service on all routes rendered insecure by the secession crisis, and by May 28 all contracts in the areas concerned were canceled. Reagan's department was to assume full control of the southern postal service no later than June 1, and the entire organization needed to be self-supporting by March 1, 1863, as required by the Confederate Congress. Both the burdens of war and the dictates of economic necessity compelled Reagan to place his operations on a sound footing as soon as possible.[5]

Recognizing the scope of his task, Reagan not only retained the existing postmasters whenever possible but also ordered that all contractors who had been carrying the mail before the war should continue to do so after forwarding a report on the number and nature of the route each followed. At least in theory, Giddings and all the other mail carriers in Texas could keep operating with some hope of payment. They could draw further comfort from the resolution passed earlier in Austin by the state secession convention. Its committee on postal affairs drafted an ordinance declaring that the state government "guarantees and will make good, with the contractors of carrying the mails in the same, so much of their compensation as may be repudiated by the government of the United States and which the Confederate States may not adopt." It thus appeared that Giddings would receive some financial aid even during that time of ruin and confusion.[6]

Reagan was particularly quick to act in establishing a new mail system for Texas. As early as March the department was advertising for bids and negotiating contracts for the 2,207 routes

olds, "The Postal System of the Southern Confederacy," *West Virginia History* 12 (Apr., 1951): 200–210; L. R. Garrison, "Administrative Problems of the Confederate Post-Office Department, I," *Southwestern Historical Quarterly* 19 (July, 1915): 111–13; Henry P. Beers, *Guide to the Archives of the Government of the Confederate States of America*, 387–91.

[5] LeRoy R. Hafen, *The Overland Mail, 1849–1869*, 288–89.

[6] McCaleb, "Organization of the Post-Office," 72–73; Alex L. ter Braake, *Texas: The Drama of its Postal Past*, 133–34, 175; Robert H. Thonhoff, *San Antonio Stage Lines, 1847–1881*, 19–22.

in the Confederacy. Several of the contracts offered for service in the Southwest seemed to have been based on wildly optimistic estimates of both the South's political prospects and the expressmen's capabilities. Route No. 8571 called for monthly deliveries in El Paso and San Francisco, California. No bids were entered on this contract for reasons well understood by the Texans. Other advertisements listed routes from Fort Clark to Comanche Springs, Fort Davis to Presidio del Norte, and San Antonio to Eagle Pass and El Paso. All went unanswered.[7]

Events in Texas were moving faster than Reagan's efforts to create a new postal system. The state had already raised an expeditionary force to seize New Mexico and Arizona for the Confederacy. Early in July, Lieutenant Colonel John R. Baylor and the Second Texas Mounted Rifles arrived in El Paso. By the month's end he had snapped up the Union garrison at Fort Fillmore and declared Mesilla to be the new capital of the Confederate Territory of Arizona, an expanse of territory that stretched from the thirty-fourth parallel south and west to the California border on the Colorado River. As military governor of this wastelands empire, Baylor had succeeded in extending the Confederacy's frontier almost to the Pacific while fulfilling the old expansionist dream held by so many Texans. Prosouthern elements in California took heart, while Unionists in Colorado Territory pondered a possible threat to their rich silver mines.[8]

The prospect of a southern window on the Pacific did not seem entirely farfetched, for only a week before the capture of Fort Fillmore, Robert E. Doyle had managed to send a final mail through to Mesilla from San Diego, the coach still sporting the title of the San Antonio and San Diego Mail Company on its doors. While Giddings was occupied in Richmond, his assistants tried to keep the line running from the Texas end. The mail link to California was operated entirely out of the company's pocket and in clear defiance of the Union authorities in the state, but

[7] Route Book, Texas, 1861–62, chap. 11, vol. 26, pp. 115–16, 127–28, 139, 569, 573, 795, Records of the Confederate States Post Office, RG 109, NARS. Hereafter cited as Confederate Records.

[8] Martin H. Hall, *Sibley's New Mexico Campaign*, 25–28; Jerry Don Thompson, *Colonel John Robert Baylor*, 24–49.

the gamble seemed worthwhile, as small Confederate units reached Tucson to the east and Baylor prepared to move against Santa Fe.[9]

The Confederate advance to El Paso had already created another tragedy that served to remind southerners and Unionists alike that they traveled through that country only at the pleasure of the Apaches. Young Emmett Mills, a Butterfield employee, and six other northern loyalists decided to try to reach California before they were imprisoned by the rebels in El Paso. The fugitives commandeered one of Giddings's rigs and struck out for the west late in July. On the twenty-first they rode into an ambush about a mile beyond Cooke's Spring. The combined bands of Cochise and Mangas Coloradas pursued the coach to a nearby hilltop, where the whites endured a desperate siege for three days before the Apaches finally killed the last of them. The episode had cost the Indians heavily as well and seemed to augur yet another round of bloodletting for those who dared to leave the settlements and brave the trail to California.[10]

Henry Skillman recognized the increased risks involved, but they did not deter him from taking another mail party out of Mesilla with a small escort. Acting as superintendent of the company in Giddings's absence, he intended to, in the words of the *Mesilla Times*, "withdraw the stock from the line for the present, and until Indian affairs become quiet in the Territory." The journal stressed its desire that "the service on this route will be early resumed." An accompanying advertisement reflected its optimism. William Skillman was listed as chief agent for the company and departmental postmaster. He promised arrivals and departures for Santa Fe, El Paso, San Antonio, and California on both a weekly and biweekly basis. There is no record of Henry Skillman's return from California on that final trip, but he was soon back on the Rio Grande. The last mail south from Santa Fe reached Mesilla on August 17, but "it had been overhauled by the U.S. authorities, and the letters opened and read. . . . The Indians captured the mail again on the Jornada, and scat-

---

[9] Hall, *Sibley's Campaign*, 27–29; *Mesilla Times*, July 20, 1861.
[10] W. W. Mills, *Forty Years at El Paso, 1858–1898*, 53, 185, 195–96; *Mesilla Times*, July 27, 1861.

tered it over the ground. It was collected again, and finally reached here, much of it without envelopes."[11]

By mid-August Giddings was back in San Antonio and ready to assume his duties as a mail carrier for the Confederacy. On August 28 he signed a contract for C.S. Mail Route No. 8075, which called for service twice a week between San Antonio and Mesilla via Fort Clark and Fort Davis. From Mesilla he was to run coaches west to Tucson, Fort Yuma, and San Diego every two weeks. The payment was backdated to April 1, 1861. Though the contract as originally advertised had offered $175,000 a year for the San Antonio–Mesilla portion, and an additional $75,000 for the leg to California, the final agreement authorized only $60,000 a year for the entire route, perhaps in recognition of the conditions then prevailing west of Mesilla. The amended contract was valid until June 30, 1865.[12]

The coaches would keep rolling now under the full sponsorship, if uncertain funding, of the Confederate government. The stamps on the letters may have changed, but the dangers of the road remained much the same, with the odds running even more heavily against the expressmen. The Mescaleros who haunted the trails west of Fort Davis remained just as restive as their kinsmen on the Gila, and the mail line made the intimate acquaintance of one of their chieftains in a piece of tragicomic Confederate diplomacy.

When Baylor marched on El Paso that summer, he posted companies of his regiment at the forts along the road from San Antonio. The Indians did not hesitate to capitalize on the war between the whites, and policing the mail route soon became a major concern for the troopers. The Mescalero bands of Nicolas and Antonio gave them particular trouble in the area around Fort Davis. It would require a major campaign to clear the hostiles from the mountains, and Baylor had no men to spare for

---

[11] *Mesilla Times*, Aug. 17, 24, 1861.

[12] Mail Contracts, Texas, 1861–63, chap. 11, vol. 13, p. 215: Henry St. George Offutt to George H. Giddings, July 12, 1861; Offutt to John R. Baylor, Sept. 14, 1861; Offutt to Postmaster, El Paso, Texas, Sept. 14, 1861; Offutt to Simeon Hart, Sept. 14, 1861, Contract Bureau, Letters Sent, 1861–64, chap. 11, vol. 31, pp. 220, 342; Route Book, Texas, 1861–62, chap. 11, vol. 26, pp. 795–97, Confederate Records, RG 109, NARS.

such a task. Patrick McCarthy, the sutler and postmaster at Fort Davis, hit upon the idea of making allies of the Apaches. It proved to be an expensive mistake.[13]

McCarthy persuaded Nicolas to visit the fort under a flag of truce. The suspicious Indian was awarded gifts and told that "the head chief of the soldiers was at El Paso, and that he would welcome him as a brother, make a great feast, have a smoke, and make a treaty." The Mescalero's natural caution was soon overcome by his bravado. The next morning McCarthy and Nicolas boarded the stage for El Paso; the incredulous driver lashed the team forward, stifling an urge to reach for his Sharps. It was the first and last time one of Giddings's coaches made the run to the Rio Grande without fear of attack.

At Fort Bliss the Apache received a royal welcome. Baylor, McCarthy, and James Magoffin held a formal banquet for him, and each delivered a speech that reeked of amity and fraternal love. It must have been a tasteless meal for Baylor, who looked upon all Indians as vermin to be exterminated. When the whites had finished their orations, a pokerfaced Nicolas arose and declared, "I am glad I have come. My heart is full of love for my pale-face brothers. They have not spoken with forked tongues. We have made a treaty of peace and friendship. When I lie down at night the treaty will be in my heart, and when I arise in the morning it will still be there. And I will be glad I am at peace with my pale-face brothers. I have spoken."[14]

Magoffin responded to this pronouncement with a toast to "Nicolas, our friend." The next day Baylor loaded the stage with more gifts for his new ally and wished him a safe trip home while Magoffin gave the Indian a farewell embrace. Nicolas again pledged his eternal friendship and boarded the coach with McCarthy.

The journey back was quiet and McCarthy was napping in his seat as the rig approached Barrel Springs. Nicolas leaned over, jerked the Irishman's revolvers from their holsters, and vaulted out of the coach to hit the ground running. He was soon lost in the brush as McCarthy shouted curses after him.

[13] Hall, *Sibley's Campaign*, 45; Thompson, *John Robert Baylor*, 25–26.
[14] Thompson, *John Robert Baylor*, 69–71.

Soon afterward Nicolas's braves stole a herd of cattle near Fort Davis and lured a pursuing army patrol into an ambush that wiped out all of Lieutenant Reuben E. Mays's detachment. Only their Mexican guide escaped to carry the news of the tragedy back to Fort Davis. The Mays debacle in early August marked the start of a new season of plunder on the El Paso road. Baylor reported that "from this point on outrages were committed frequently; the mails were robbed; in one or two instances the passengers were found hanging up by the heels, their heads within a few inches of a slow fire, and they thus horribly roasted to death. Others were found tied to the wheels of the coach, which had been burned."[15]

The summer of 1861 continued as a prolonged exercise in horror. The new mail contract seemed to be merely an extension of the old nightmare for Giddings. Even the Apaches could overplay their hand, however, and that bloody August saw a costly repulse for the tribesmen.

Captain James Eli Terry and four companions took the mail south from the Pass that month. He loaded the mail on pack mules and counted on making a swift run to Fort Davis, although reports from the east described the Apaches as being "bold and plentiful" on the road. The Texans dropped down past Fort Quitman and cleared Quitman Pass without trouble, but the Indians were already planning their attack.

The riders turned southeast down the long corridor of Quitman Canyon and approached the heel of Devil Ridge, where the oasis of Eighteen Mile Hole promised fresh water. Without warning, fifteen mounted Apaches charged out of the brush and bore down on them, while another large party of braves appeared on foot. Terry elected to abandon their animals and seek cover on top of a hill that jutted from the nearby ridgeline. They barely beat their pursuers to the high ground and whirled about to pour a volley of rifle balls and buckshot into their ranks that literally eviscerated one warrior and dropped several more with wounds.

For the rest of the day and through the night Terry's men

[15] Ibid.; George W. Baylor, "Memories of Old Days," *El Paso Herald*, Dec. 18, 1899; Carlyle G. Raht, *The Romance of Davis Mountains and Big Bend Country*, 148;

kept the Indians at bay with the lethal reach of their Sharps rifles. Two of the guards kept the braves' heads down with rifle fire while the others saved their loads to repel a rush if it came to that. By dawn the next day the Apaches had picked up their dead and departed. The Texans edged warily down the hillside and began the long walk into Eagle Springs. The Mescaleros let them proceed unchallenged, for as Terry put it, "the crowd they had left were just in the right humor to make a wicked fight, and many a warrior would have been laid out before the stage guard would have been destroyed." [16]

The Apaches may have been chastened by this repulse, but the Kiowas and Comanches continued to infest the road to the east of Fort Davis. In mid-October, Bigfoot Wallace led a party of militiamen into a fight a few miles outside of Sabinal. They killed one warrior who mockingly carried a U.S. flag into battle. The raids had their effect on the mail service, for on November 2 the *San Antonio Herald* gave notice that the stages from El Paso and Fort Clark arrived "every Friday irregularly." [17]

The coaches were a welcome sight to the bored and lonely soldiers who manned the forts to the west. They looked forward to the newspapers and information that travelers brought from the settlements, but they were seldom able to secure the road for their safe passage on any permanent basis. Proof of this came as the new year opened with bitter weather and a resurgence of Indian attacks. An icy winter storm scoured the bluffs around Fort Lancaster, and on January 13 the stage from El Paso clattered into the station at a dead run. The driver reported that the Comanches had burned out Pecos Station on the river above. He did not mention any survivors, and the post commander did not bother to send a burial detail out to the ruins. The wolves

Barry Scobee, *Fort Davis Texas, 1583–1960*, 44–45; C. L. Sonnichsen, *The Mescalero Apaches*, 101–104; Robert M. Utley, *Fort Davis National Historic Site, Texas*, 17–18.

[16] George W. Baylor, "Tragedies on the Old Overland Stage Route," *Frontier Times* 26 (Mar., 1949): 125–27; U.S. Court of Claims, Deposition of James Eli Terry, *George H. Giddings* vs. *the United States, Kiowa, Comanche, and Apache Indians*, Records of the Court of Claims Section (Justice), RG 205, NARS. Terry's statement was taken in 1892 and conflicted with some of the details he later related to Baylor. The *Frontier Times* article reprinted an earlier newspaper piece published near the turn of the century.

[17] *San Antonio Herald*, Nov. 2, 1861.

would have done their work long before the men could arrive.[18]

The station's loss did not halt Giddings's coaches, but the new Confederate commander in the Southwest, Brigadier General Harry H. Sibley, was busily creating the final threat to the mail line as his campaign against the Union forces in the theater lurched into motion. The alcoholic Sibley faced an able opponent in Colonel Edward R. S. Canby. When their forces collided at Valverde Ford on the Rio Grande, Canby retired to nearby Fort Craig and let Sibley proceed up the Rio Grande to march on Santa Fe. By March 13 the rebels were in the territorial capital. Elated by his triumph, Sibley decided to march eastward to seize Fort Union. On the way he met a fresh Union force of New Mexico militia, trained regulars, and Colorado volunteers. The battle at Glorietta Pass ended in Sibley's defeat, and the Texans' withdrawal carried them all the way back to El Paso as Canby gathered his strength for a riposte.[19]

The Union forces were now on the offensive, with still another army under Brigadier General James H. Carleton closing in from California via Tucson. Sibley prudently planned a retreat to San Antonio. The Texan dream of empire had been shattered and El Paso would be yielded to the enemy. In mid-May the first elements of the defeated army marched south from the rapidly emptying settlements. Giddings must have felt that he had been granted a new contract just so his coaches could play the role of chariots for Sibley's pharaoh. A female correspondent for the *Herald* boarded the stage on May 17 and recorded her impressions of the line as the Confederacy's western flank crumbled behind her.

"The roads were impassable," she wrote, "the mail stations washed away . . . San Elizario has become an island." Heavy

---

[18] W. W. Heartsill, *Fourteen Hundred and 91 Days in the Confederate Army*, 49–50. For other comments on the mail see the *San Antonio Herald*, Jan. 4, 25, Mar. 15, 29, and June 21, 1862.

[19] Hall, *Sibley's Campaign*, 51–201. Troops at Fort Lancaster, Camp Hudson, and D'Hanis noted the mail's passage in January through April. Heartsill, *Fourteen Hundred Days*, 51–55, 64–66, 75. One of Sibley's officers mentioned the "next stage to San Antonio" from El Paso on May 31, 1862. See Martin H. Hall, "An Appraisal of the 1862 New Mexico Campaign: A Confederate Officer's Letter to Nacogdoches," *New Mexico Historical Review* 51 (Oct., 1976): 35.

spring rains had inundated the valley, making for sloppy traveling in the lowlands by the river, but "Mollie" had nothing but
praise for the expressmen.

We came by stage, and although we were traveling alone, in a wild
Indian country, a woman, and unprotected, under the hottest sun that
ever shone, our journey was made pleasant and very comfortable. In
the first place, we had premium drivers and conductors—men who
handled their reins and managed their teams with skill, whose eyes
were ever on the alert for danger, whether by Indians or unavoidable
accidents, who guard with true courage and bravery all that is con-
signed to their care, and who, although cut off from civilization, are
capable of exhibiting the most profound regard for the presence of a
lady. . . . Many families from El Paso are on the road coming to San
Antonio. Franklin is almost entirely deserted.[20]

The ride to Fort Davis gave continuing evidence of the damage wreaked on Giddings's operations. Eagle Springs was still
deserted, its waterhole clogged with debris. At Van Horn's Wells
the station lay in ruins after an attack mounted by the Apaches
that winter. The raiders had polluted the water with dirt and
sheep carcasses. El Muerto still provided sweet water, but the
station there had been abandoned. Sibley's army continued its
piecemeal retreat through that summer. In August the last troops
departed Fort Davis, leaving Diedrick Dutchover and a few
helpers in charge of the post and stage station.[21]

Dutchover's loyalty to the company almost proved fatal. Not
long after the garrison's departure Nicolas stormed into the empty
settlement with his braves and began looting what had been left
behind. For two days and nights Dutchover, his family, and four
station hands took refuge on the top of a parapeted roof while
the Apaches vandalized the fort. When they left, the whites set
out on foot for Presidio del Norte, leaving behind one man who
was sick and dying. On the day after they left, a stage pulled into
the wrecked station. It arrived safely in San Antonio on August
16. Four days later Union troops occupied El Paso, to remain for
the duration of the war.

The invaders quickly sent patrols eastward to inspect the

---

[20] *San Antonio Herald*, July 5, 1862.
[21] Hall, *Sibley's Campaign*, 208–26; Raht, *Romance of Davis Mountains*, 149–50.

posts abandoned by the rebels. On August 23 a detachment of the First California Cavalry probed the road as far as Fort Davis. They buried a corpse found at the stage station, hoisted the Union flag on the post's staff, and then withdrew, skirmishing with the Apaches en route. The Indians seemed to have emerged as the only real winners in the past year's struggle.[22]

A month later a band of paroled Confederate prisoners was escorted as far as Fort Quitman and then released to make its way back to San Antonio. Lieutenant Edward L. Robb was appalled at the desolation he saw on the road. "Not a stand we pass but what some men have been killed by Indians," he confided to his journal. "These valleys & mountains are full of Apaches. Dead oxen & horses, remains of wagons are scattered all along the road. Not a stick of timber is to be seen. Everything betokens a God forsaken country." At Fort Davis he found "some of the ·hair of a man who had been left probably to die. The worms were thick where his body had lain." The soldier shared the same thought that had come to so many earlier travelers along that road. "It is astonishing how men for a Pittance of 30 or 40 dol pr month will risk their lives in these dreary places."[23]

The Confederates passed on, leaving the wind to keen through the broken rafters and charred walls. From the Rio Grande to Fort Clark, Giddings's stations endured only as thrones for the ravens. When the last companies of Sibley's army reached San Antonio, Giddings set about reorganizing his company in the face of this latest disaster. The troops had stripped the line of all stock and transport during the retreat, but the contractor was able to regain most of his property after an appeal to the general. That autumn he made another trip to Richmond, although it probably dealt as much with his cotton sales and arms procurement activities as with the status of his mail contract. By the end of November, Giddings was ready to pick up the reins once again.[24]

[22] Raht, *Romance of Davis Mountains*, 149–50; Scobee, *Fort Davis*, 50–51; *San Antonio Herald*, Aug. 16, 1862.

[23] Ruth W. Hord, ed., "The Diary of Lieutenant E. L. Robb, C.S.A., from Santa Fe to Fort Lancaster, 1862," *Permian Historical Annual* 18 (Dec., 1978): 71–72.

[24] *San Antonio Herald*, Nov. 29, 1862; Charles M. Barnes, ed., "Memoirs of Colonel George H. Giddings," *San Antonio Daily Express*, May 11, 1902.

The postal authorities had understandably curtailed the route west of El Paso in February, 1862, reducing Giddings's compensation accordingly. The line remained intact as far as Fort Clark after the fall of El Paso, and by the autumn of 1864 coaches were still running as far as Uvalde, 40 miles to the east of Fort Clark. The route had been further shortened becuse "there are no troops at Fort Clark, and it is considered hazardous to go there with any kind of a conveyance whatever." Giddings and Benjamin R. Sappington took up the slack on this route by winning a contract for the branch line from Uvalde to Eagle Pass in December, 1863. This section of the line earned praises from the Post Office Department, for passengers coming in from Mexico paid for their tickets and postage in silver coin, thus making the route doubly valuable to the government by bringing in badly needed specie, the only one to do so, "perhaps in the whole Confederacy."[25]

Giddings had earlier been granted contracts on lines running east and south from San Antonio. Some of these were held jointly with the firm of Sawyer, Risher, and Hall. By 1864 Giddings held complete or partial interest in lines running out of San Antonio to Corpus Christi, Helena, Goliad, Victoria, and Brownsville. Service on these routes was executed with varying degrees of success, owing to the shortage of manpower and equip-

[25]Curtailment of the route west of El Paso was noted in the official records. Records of the Confederate States of America (Pickett Papers), Office of the Postmaster General, Letters Sent Book, Mar. 7, 1861–Oct. 12, 1863, Container No. 98, Manuscript Division, Library of Congress, 365. The San Antonio postmaster reported on Aug. 15, 1862, that the last mail had left El Paso on July 14. On Sept. 2 he stated that "two mails, however, were sent up as far as Forts Stockton and Davis. Since 1st Aug., only to Fort Clark." On Sept. 25, 1862, the Post Office Department authorized payment to Henry Skillman on the route from El Paso to Mesilla, to date from Nov. 1, 1861 through June 30, 1862, "subject to fines and deductions." Route Book, Texas, 1861–62, Notations to Contract No. 8076, chap. 11, vol. 26, pp. 795–96. In a confusing bit of bureaucratic shuffling, the contract number on Giddings's route was changed from 8076 to 8565 on Jan. 25, 1862. No explanation was given for this decision. Bartholomew Fuller to Postmaster, El Paso, Texas, Jan. 25, 1862, Inspection Office, Letters Sent, June 1861–Feb. 1862, chap. 11, vol. 44, p. 430. For comments on the Uvalde–Eagle Pass route see E. L. Derry to James H. Starr, Jan. 10, 1865; Giddings to Starr, Dec. 28, 1864; Morris R. Reagan to —— ——, Sept. 21, 1864; Schedule Book, Route No. 50, Feb. 13, 1865, Mail Contracts, Texas, nos. 1–133, Box No. 2, Confederate Records, RG 109, NARS.

ment created by the war, coupled with the unreliability of several of the subcontractors involved.[26]

The routes became increasingly important as the Union blockade tightened along the Confederacy's coastline. Although with luck the blockade runners might reach the Gulf ports of Indianola and Corpus Christi, Brownsville became the major supply point for the trans-Mississippi South. Neutral ships unloaded war material at Matamoros, Brownsville's sister port in Mexico, and the cargoes were lightered across the Rio Grande to Texas. A brisk traffic had already existed between San Antonio and Alleyton, the terminus of the coastal Buffalo Bayou, Brazos and Colorado Railroad. Stages from Brownsville connected with lines serving Corpus Christi, Goliad, Victoria, and San Antonio at the railhead. With El Paso in Union hands and the Mississippi barred by the fall of Vicksburg in July, 1863, trade and travel in Texas followed the San Antonio–Indianola–Brownsville triangle.[27]

Even this residual communications network did not remain undisrupted for long. Stage operations in southern Texas were rudely altered in November, 1863, when a northern expeditionary force landed at Brownsville and advanced up the Rio Grande for several hundred miles. Giddings responded by recruiting an independent cavalry battalion in the Eagle Pass area and joining Colonel John S. Ford's command in a year-long campaign to dislodge the Federals and liberate Brownsville. Giddings rendered valuable service to Ford and aided in giving a stinging defeat to the enemy at Palmito Ranch, an action fought five weeks after Appomattox.[28]

Giddings's preoccupation with events to the south of Bexar did not mean the end of all communication with El Paso. A col-

[26]Route Book, Texas, 1861–62, chap. 11, vol. 27, pp.76–77, 83–85, 120–21; Henry St. George Offutt to George H. Giddings, Apr. 10, 1862; Offutt to Postmaster, San Antonio, Texas, Oct. 23, 1862, Contract Bureau, Letters Sent, 1861–64, chap. 11, vol. 32, pp. 428, 587; Offutt to Postmaster, San Antonio, Texas, May 14, 1863; Offutt to Giddings, Mar. 20, 1863, Contract Bureau, Letters Sent, 1863–64, chap. 11, vol. 33, pp. 228, 300, Confederate Records, RG 109, NARS.

[27]Thonhoff, *Stage Lines*, 19–22; ter Braake, *Postal Past*, 156–57.

[28]John S. Ford, *Rip Ford's Texas*, 347–75, 384–90; W. J. Hughes, *Rebellious Ranger*, 211–13, 220, 227–29; Marcus J. Wright, comp., *Texas in the War, 1861–1865*, 33, 126–27.

ony of Confederate sympathizers still resided in Paso del Norte, just across the river from Fort Bliss, and they kept alive the hope of a southern resurgence in the region. They were also a useful source of intelligence for the authorities in San Antonio. Henry Skillman was their chief courier and agent. He had remained behind when Sibley's army left, and for almost two years thereafter he plagued the Union forces at the Pass with threats and rumors of raids and invasions while maintaining his courier service not only from San Antonio to El Paso, but possibly even to California as well. Although many of Skillman's activities were only sketchily documented and he had no official contract to carry the mail, his efforts deserved to be chronicled, for he continued to keep the line open at a time when the danger was greatest and the hope of compensation was virtually nonexistent.[29]

El Paso had quickly felt the sting of occupation by a conquering army when Carleton's Californians entered the cluster of settlements on August 20, 1862. The leading citizens of the American community had already fled eastward or across the river into Mexico. James Magoffin, Ben Dowell, Josiah Crosby, and Simeon Hart were on the road for San Antonio. Less prominent Confederates stood watch on the river as the Stars and Stripes fluttered up the staff at Fort Bliss. Though few in number, and hampered by Mexican attitudes that ranged from mild indifference to open hostility, the exiles posed a genuine threat to continued Federal control of the border.[30]

In December, Major William McMullen of the First California Infantry arrived to take command of the garrison and reported that affairs were in a state of great confusion. "The Texans living in El Paso [Juarez] are organized with the intention of attacking this place and preventing the destruction of property on the approach of the enemy," he wrote. "Skillman was . . . last seen below San Elizario, apparently greatly elated and he promised to be back in a few days." The plainsman had sown a healthy crop of rumors in his passing, for McMullen was informed that

[29] Jack C. Scannell, "Henry Skillman, Texas Frontiersman," *Permian Historical Annual* 18 (Dec., 1978): 27–30.

[30] C. L. Sonnichsen, *Pass of the North*, 157–58.

"one thousand Texans are said to be at Horse Head Crossing under the command of ——— Scurry. There are many other rumors too ridiculous to mention. . . . It is my intention to leave here with Cos. D & K Wednesday morning for San Elizario to prevent the removal of grain into Mexico." Despite his professed disdain for the wild stories, the major was convinced that "the first point of attack is intended at Franklin."[31]

Skillman's continuing presence in the area and his unchallenged ease of movement kept the Unionists on edge. In November he had been reported at El Paso with the advance scouts of an army that was being assembled at Las Moras Springs. The six thousand men under Baylor were to wrest the Pass away from Union control. So alarmed were the bluecoats that the commander in Mesilla dispatched a patrol led by scout Bradford Daily, Skillman's prewar companion, to probe the country around Horsehead Crossing that December. The prospect of a dual Confederate drive up the Pecos and the Rio Grande was given real credibility by the scout's purposeful wanderings.[32]

Skillman's unhindered passages across the Rio Grande from Mexico irritated the Union commander in El Paso, and he stationed troops at several points along the river on its southern side, thus triggering a diplomatic crisis with the governor of Chihuahua that further strained relations along the border. Skillman's forays gave the Confederates something to cheer about after a bleak year on the frontier. The *Dallas Herald* gleefully reported the consternation he had created in the Union ranks and forecasted the bluecoats' immediate retreat into northern Arizona when the Texans launched a counteroffensive.[33]

The plainsman's courier service and scouting expeditions continued into the spring of 1863, causing the Union forces to

[31] C. L. Sonnichsen, "Major McMullen's Invasion of Mexico," *Password* 2 (May, 1957): 38–39.

[32] Brig. Gen. James H. Carleton to Brig. Gen. Lorenzo Thomas, Dec. 5, 1862, *War of the Rebellion: A Compilation of the Official Records of the Union and Confederate Armies*, ser. 1, 15:604–607.

[33] Sonnichsen, "Invasion of Mexico," 40–43; Col. James R. West to Maj. David Ferguson, Jan. 3, 1863; Luis Terrazas to Brig. Gen. James H. Carleton, Apr. 11, 1863, *Official Records*, ser. 1, 15:635–36, 701; *Dallas Herald*, Feb. 23, 1863.

send patrols as far east as Fort Stockton to search for signs of the rumored army that he was leading back across the wastes to reclaim the Pass. This "crafty disseminator," as one Union officer called him, kept the enemy in constant fear of such an invasion for nine months. Such a force never materialized, but Skillman's persistent travels told General Carleton that the Texans still had designs upon the region.

Early in March, 1864, Carleton's spies informed him that Skillman had returned from San Antonio and was en route to Presidio del Norte. Captain Albert H. French and twenty-five troopers of the First California Cavalry departed San Elizario on April 3 with orders to kill or capture the scout. Twelve days later the Federals found Skillman's camp a mile below Presidio. In the predawn hours of April 15 the Union soldiers crept up around the sleeping rebels and French called out a demand for their surrender. Skillman rolled to his feet, ready to fight, and French killed him with one shot. In the volley that followed, another Texan died and two others were mortally wounded. A third wounded man and a comrade escaped across the river while French captured four more stunned Confederates.

French found evidence that Skillman's activities as a spy and courier had been far more extensive than the Union authorities had ever suspected. His dispatch pouch contained a letter from a southern officer to his sweetheart, a resident of Sacramento, California. Evidently Skillman was either bound for the Pacific or had connections with a secret network that would carry the letter west from El Paso.[34]

It was still several hours before daylight when the dazed prisoners buried their companions by the cold ashes of their last campfire. They wrapped Henry Skillman in his blanket and laid him beneath the same hard earth that had been host to the bodies of so many of his companions since 1851. A legend had passed, and even the staunchest Unionist in El Paso, W. W. Mills, was moved by his death, recalling Skillman as "the Kit Carson of this

---

[34] Col. John S. Ford to Capt. Edmund P. Turner, Feb. 9, Mar. 9, 1864, *Official Records*, ser. 1, 53:967–68, 34:1033; Raht, *Romance of Davis Mountains*, 151–52; Mills, *Forty Years*, 85–87; Aurora Hunt, *The Army of the Pacific*, 75, 175–78; Richard H. Orton, *Records of California Men in the War of the Rebellion, 1861 to 1867*, 73–74.

section. He was highly esteemed, almost beloved, by the people of the valley, both races."[35]

The most immediate effect of Skillman's death was the end of regular communication between San Antonio and the Confederate colony on the Rio Grande. A firm assertion of Union control over the region west of Fort Stockton followed. Beyond this was the palpable sense of a time closing. Henry Skillman had been one of the most noted figures in the Southwest for nearly two decades. A man of limited formal education but armed with a keen intelligence and a healthy sense of ambition, he had linked El Paso to the growing American settlements to the north and east, thus breaking the old Spanish-hewn yoke that for centuries had bound trade and travel firmly to the road between Chihuahua and Santa Fe. What had long been merely a stopping place on the Camino Real felt the dim stirrings of its destined growth to a city when Skillman's coach first rolled to a halt in the fragrant shade by the river.

This "Viking of the Wastelands" had written his name boldly across that wild country like some noble rune. Paul Horgan would have numbered Skillman among the company of what he called "a wild strain," and dubbed him "an American original, as hard as the hardest thing that could happen to him."

The hardest thing had passed for Henry Skillman. Few easy triumphs were left to his successors.

[35] Mills, *Forty Years*, 85–87.

CHAPTER 10

Coopwood's Try

FOR most southerners the Civil War ended only one week short of a full year after Henry Skillman's death. In Texas the conflict continued through May, 1865, until Colonel John S. Ford's command on the lower Rio Grande learned from the Union force it had just defeated that Lee had surrendered the month before. Ford's men cased their tattered standards and melted away into the brush country of southern Texas. All over the state Confederate troops were helping themselves to whatever government property remained in the warehouses and depots before heading home.

The civil government and military command structure quickly collapsed in the confusion. Governor Pendleton Murrah and most of the senior Confederate officers left in the region headed for refuge in Mexico. The last vestiges of authority began to disappear, and discharged soldiers, deserters, and desperadoes of every stripe haunted the roads. On June 19 General Gordon Granger landed in Galveston with an army of occupation and declared that all slaves in the state were free. Soon multitudes of confused blacks wandered throughout eastern Texas, tasting both freedom and destitution as they blindly searched for the anticipated riches of emancipation.

Granger issued other proclamations that nullified all acts and laws of the Confederate government, thus accelerating the state's slide into anarchy. In Austin a mob looted the treasury, while in the smaller settlements gangs of rowdies bullied the defenseless citizens. Banditry was rife. A stage driver traveling from Rio Grande City to San Antonio reported that he was stopped by road agents an average of every five miles during the trip.[1]

[1] Rupert N. Richardson, et al. *Texas: The Lone Star State*, 266–67; Charles W. Ramsdell, "Reconstruction in Texas," *Columbia University Studies in History, Econom-*

Order of a sort began to return as Union troops fanned out from the coastal ports and marched to garrison the interior. Martial law followed their columns, and its imposition sparked mixed feelings of relief and resentment among the population. In July provisional Governor Andrew J. Hamilton took office in Austin and began the task of bringing Texas under control, if not of immediately restoring it to the Union. He inherited a state in which the normal problems attending settlement and frontier defense were exacerbated by a collapse of the government and economy. Political and racial animosities were already spreading through Texan society like a malignant tumor. The old classic conflict among Anglos, Indians, and Mexicans was enlarged to include blacks, Yankees, rebels, and scalawags.

The restoration of the postal service was not Governor Hamilton's ranking concern, but its loss was soon felt as life began to return toward normal. Military couriers were the only postal messengers available in many areas, and the surviving mail lines offered only uncertain schedules. Galveston had no official postal facilities until November, 1865. The Union occupation government announced that "reasonable bids" for temporary service over the old routes would be accepted by the Post Office Department for contracts lasting until December 31. Proposals would also be considered for permanent service contracts to become effective on January 1, 1866.[2]

Dr. James H. Starr, former Confederate postal agent for the trans-Mississippi department, called for "an early restoration of mails within that region under the authority of the United States," and proposed using his records of the postmasters, routes, contractors, and their fees as a guide to establishing the new postal network. The Union authorities ignored this piece of effrontery, but also failed to act swiftly in restoring the system. As late as December 5 the Galveston *Tri-Weekly News* complained that no mail had been received from Houston for the previous ten days.[3]

ics and Public Law 26 (1910): 55–84; Allen C. Ashcraft, "Texas in Defeat: The Early Phase of A. J. Hamilton's Provisional Governorship of Texas, June 17, 1865 to February 7, 1866," *Texas Military History* 8 (1970): 199–219.

[2] Ashcraft, "Texas in Defeat," 199–219.

[3] Alex L. ter Braake, *Texas: The Drama of its Postal Past*, 164–66.

The Galveston journal sent a reporter to meet the U.S. mail agent in New Orleans, and he learned that no regular contracts would likely be awarded until June, 1866. The temporary carriers were doing a slipshod job in the meantime. Their obligations were so loosely defined that the *News* complained that they run "whenever they choose to run, and the only difference appears to be the larger amount of pay they receive for mail than for freight."[4]

The situation began to improve as various private express companies were organized in the fall of 1865, but San Antonio remained without a link to the west. There was neither official sanction nor profit in a route to El Paso. The road remained unprotected, for the Union troops were assigned the task of policing the settled areas of the state while also making a show of force on the border against the French puppet government in Mexico.[5]

El Paso, for all of its isolation from its sister city, was solidly linked to other portions of the nation. As early as July, 1864, the El Paso, Santa Fe and Kansas City Stage Line had begun operations between the Missouri and the Rio Grande. Coaches ran from the Pass to Santa Fe twice a week on the new line.[6]

El Pasoans might have counted themselves lucky to be in such regular touch with civilization to the east, but they could well have done without some of its influences. The settlement had been occupied by Union troops for almost three years when the war ended and had thus gained an early taste of what the rest of the state would face during Reconstruction. The Unionist faction that had been expelled in 1861 returned to settle old scores and lost no time in turning the tables on the secessionists. El Paso County lost its civil status, and all the local and district courts were abolished.

The entire region and its inhabitants were ripe for punishment and plunder. In December, 1865, Joab Houghton, the un-

---

[4] Ibid.

[5] B. W. Aston, "Federal Military Reoccupation of the Texas Southwestern Frontier, 1865–1871," *Texas Military History* 8 (1971): 123–25.

[6] *Santa Fe New Mexican*, July, 22, 1864; *Santa Fe Weekly Gazette*, Nov. 4, 1865; *San Antonio Tri-Weekly Herald*, Nov. 11, 1865.

tutored judge of New Mexico's Second Judicial District, began seizing property in the county. A strong Unionist, his earlier partnership with Henry Skillman did little to moderate his views when it came to persecuting rebels. The holdings of Simeon Hart, James Magoffin, Josiah Crosby, A. C. Hyde, George Giddings, and most of the other prominent residents of the Pass quickly fell under his gavel. Houghton's assistant, U.S. Marshal Abraham Cutler, served the papers on each case of delinquent back taxes and assorted other offenses. His authority placed him in a very lucrative position, as the seized properties were sold for ridiculously low sums to the resurgent Unionists. The civil authorities could count on the support of the local military garrison in enforcing their decisions.[7]

James Magoffin and Simeon Hart braved the Apaches to ride to Austin in search of some redress for Houghton's judicial pillage of their holdings, but few of the ex-Confederates in the settlement held much hope for their chances of success. In terms of ease and speed of communication, Austin and San Antonio were far more distant than Santa Fe and St. Louis. It had been fifteen years since El Paso had been so far removed from her sister towns in the state. As long as she remained without a reliable means of commercial transportation, her political and economic isolation from the rest of Texas was the dominant fact of life in the community. All of the region east to the Pecos was in real danger of becoming a satellite of New Mexico.[8]

George Giddings would have been the logical candidate to reopen the line of communication between El Paso and Bexar, for he had both a personal motive and the fund of experience necessary to command such an operation. Giddings was not about to be drawn back into the express business, however. He had learned his lesson under two governments and wanted no more of such a risky and thankless endeavor. Despite his war record, he had been promptly paroled by the Union government, and he won a contract to procure, forage, and freight sup-

[7] Edward D. Tittmann, "The Exploitation of Treason," *New Mexican Historical Review* 4 (Apr., 1924): 128–45; Morgan Broaddus, *The Legal Heritage of El Paso*, 79–84.

[8] Broaddus, *Legal Heritage*, 79–84; *Santa Fe Weekly Gazette*, Feb. 10, 1866, citing the New Orleans *Daily Picayune*.

plies to the army posts within the state. There was some initial bad feeling against him for doing business with the invaders, but when several prominent former Confederate officers publicly defended him, the animosity died away. The Texans were beginning to realize that even a conquering army had to eat. At least they could make the Yankees pay for the exercise of their power.[9]

All over the eastern portion of the state men began piecing their lives and fortunes together again, seeking to salvage a new beginning from the rubble of their hopes. There was no proud talk of a Texas route for the transcontinental railroad, or of expansion into New Mexico and Arizona, for the modest accomplishments of survival were enough to satisfy most men who had already passed through the fires of war. Few of them could blame Giddings for making a realistic adjustment to the situation. With over fifty thousand Union troops stationed in the state during the immediate postwar period, there was a ready market for beef, horses, and grain. Stockmen, freighters, and merchants could reasonably hope to benefit from the army's quartermaster contracts and the payrolls for the soldiers.[10]

Within a year of the war's end, Houston and San Antonio were beginning to show some of their old vigor and even a shade of returning prosperity could be hoped for. To the west things remained just as grim as ever, with the struggling settlements cut off from communication with the east, and starved for news and trade.

With Giddings loath to become involved again, the El Paso road lay open to anyone else possessing the enterprise or foolhardiness to challenge its cruel stewards and numbing distances. Sometime in the opening weeks of 1866 a man who had plenty of energy but no experience at running a stage line decided to try his luck at carrying the mail. Although he would maintain the service only briefly and with an uneven record of performance, he did succeed in reopening scheduled communication with the country beyond San Antonio and El Paso for the first time since the summer of 1862.

[9]Charles M. Barnes, ed., "Memoirs of Colonel George H. Giddings," *San Antonio Daily Express*, May 4, 18, June 1, 21, 1902.

[10]T. R. Fehrenbach, *Lone Star: A History of Texas and the Texans*, 393–408.

Bethel Coopwood had amassed a wealth of experience in a variety of occupations. Born in Lawrence County, Alabama, in May, 1828, Coopwood resided in Mississippi for a time before moving to Texas in 1843. After brief service on border duty during the Mexican War, he began studying law. At some point he became a convert to Mormonism and journeyed to Utah. He was quickly disillusioned by the Saints' intolerance of other beliefs and led a company of dissenters out of the colony only a few steps ahead of angry orthodox gunmen.[11] Coopwood settled in San Bernardino, California, in 1854 and practiced law as well as dealing in land. His duties as assistant district attorney for the county and naturally combative temperament earned Coopwood several enemies in the volatile community. On at least two occasions he exchanged gunfire with rival attorneys and political opponents.

When the secession crisis divided the nation in 1861, Coopwood rode east to El Paso and arrived in time to organize a volunteer company for service in Baylor's New Mexico campaign. His unit rendered valuable service to the Confederacy throughout the doomed foray along the Rio Grande.[12]

By 1866 Coopwood had joined hundreds of other Confederate veterans in attempting to win a new start in San Antonio. Even in that time of hardscrabble depression, the old Spanish town continued to enjoy comparative prosperity and offer opportunity to men who were not afraid to take a risk. The previous December had seen moves made toward reopening the trade with Chihuahua and El Paso, although a mail service remained to be organized. The roads to the west were still thick with thieves and riffraff of various descriptions.[13]

In January the transportation prospects brightened when August and Christian Santleben opened a coach mail service to Fort Clark and Eagle Pass. A round trip took place every six

[11] *San Antonio Daily Herald*, Feb. 2, 1866; *Austin Statesman*, Dec. 29, 1907; Martin H. Hall, *The Confederate Army of New Mexico*, 344–46.

[12] Hall, *Army of New Mexico*, 344–46; *San Antonio Daily Herald*, Sept. 13, 1862; Wayne R. Austerman, "'Old Nighthawk' and the Pass of the North," *Password* 27 (Fall, 1982): 115–32.

[13] *Santa Fe Weekly Gazette*, Feb. 10, 1866; *San Antonio Daily Herald*, Nov. 11, Dec. 19, 1865.

days, and a through ticket cost $200. Eventually the brothers ran lines to Laredo and Monterrey, Mexico.[14]

The Eagle Pass coaches had not been running for a month before Bethel Coopwood announced the opening of a freight line to El Paso and Chihuahua. The mule train would be accompanied by an ambulance with space for passengers. The ink was barely dry on this initial advertisement when he advised the public that a passenger train composed of "good coaches with seats for fifty persons with good provisions and baggage wagons, will leave San Antonio, Texas on the 15th day of April next." The train would give passage to Guaymas in Sonora, Mexico, and Los Angeles, California, via El Paso, Mesilla, and Tucson. A through fare to either destination ran $200. Coopwood's exact status as a government contractor remains undocumented, but the mail went with his coaches when they departed.[15]

Coopwood's travel arrangements were definitely innovative. His freight line relied on pack mules to the exclusion of the lumbering Mexican carts or Anglo wagons. Beginning in March he acquired a growing herd of camels that had survived from several large lots of the beasts that the army had imported for field testing in the Southwest during the 1850s. He planned to use them with his California caravans, although the camels apparently proved to be uncooperative after their long vacation from labor. Coopwood eventually began selling them to circuses and any other gullible buyers that he could find. Certainly none of the mail line's passengers ever had to ride atop one of them, and the mules' reactions to the ill-tempered bactrians must have been noisy and violent.

As April approached, Coopwood received mixed reports on conditions to the west. As early as February 27 a scheduled mail began running from Mesilla to San Bernardino. Several private parties had also traveled eastward from El Paso, and although they found lush pasturage and abundant water west of San Felipe Springs, the Indians were more aggressive than ever. In February and March the Apaches killed fourteen men near San Elizario and skirmished repeatedly with a wagon train at Eagle

---

[14] August Santleben, *A Texas Pioneer*, 40; *San Antonio Daily Herald*, Feb. 20, 1866.
[15] Robert H. Thonhoff, *San Antonio Stage Lines, 1847–1881*, 22–23; *San Antonio Daily Herald*, Feb. 2, 9, 16, 20, 1866.

Springs. Near Fort Quitman the road was littered with the wreckage of another small train that had been looted and burned after the Mescaleros butchered the teamsters. The bands around Fort Davis were using the old ruse of displaying a white flag to lull the travelers' suspicions.[16]

Bethel Coopwood sent his first mail out from San Antonio on April 24. Forty mounted men under the command of Captain Theodore A. Wilson and Samuel R. Miller rode with the coach. Among the passengers were James Magoffin and Simeon Hart, fresh from a meeting with Governor Hamilton. They had persuaded him to grant them authority to reorganize El Paso County's government and issue commissions to a new slate of civil officers. Armed with such powers, Magoffin and Hart hoped to restore some of the old antebellum political establishment and halt the confiscation of so many southerners' property.[17]

The stage and its escort rolled on without hindrance as the outlying villages of D'Hanis, Uvalde, and Bracketville fell behind them. The cloud of outriders kept the road clear of any threat until they crossed the Pecos at Fort Lancaster and closed on the abandoned station at Escondido Springs. The Mescalero chieftain Espejo and his lieutenant, José Cigarito, lay in ambush there with a large war party. When the firing started, Wilson and Miller led the caravan up to the crest of a nearby hill and threw a skirmish line out around the coach and supply wagon. The Apaches swept forward, only to recoil from the withering fire the Texans poured into their ranks. Guard Robert M. Keating recalled that many of the escorts carried repeating rifles, weapons unfamiliar to the Indians, and the braves broke in confusion as forty carbines rimmed the hillside in a continuous sheet of flame.[18]

Espejo fell back and tried the old ruse of a white flag and calls for a parley. The expressmen replied with more firing, and after a siege of two days the frustrated Mescaleros finally rode off and let the coach take the road again. It arrived in El Paso on

---

[16] Chris Emmett, *Texas Camel Tales*, 126–55; *San Antonio Daily Herald*, Mar. 5, 20, Apr. 20, June 21, 1866; *San Antonio Daily Express*, Dec. 23, 1868; *Santa Fe Weekly Gazette*, Mar. 3, 1866.

[17] Broaddus, *Legal Heritage*, 85.

[18] *San Antonio Daily Herald*, May 4, 1866; Austerman, "'Old Nighthawk,'" 128–29.

May 6 and the citizens celebrated their first regular communication with the eastern settlements in nearly four years. Magoffin
had barely paused to beat the dust from his coat before conven-
ing a public assembly to announce the county's reorganization.
When he began to appoint new civil officers, the local military
commander refused to recognize his authority and barred the
men from taking office.[19]

While politics simmered in El Paso, the mail line struggled
to establish itself under conditions that were as bad as any ever
faced by Skillman and Giddings. Ironically, it was not clear yet
whether Coopwood would even continue to carry the post bags
on his new route. Even as Wilson and Miller were battling Espejo, another contractor, Frederick A. Sawyer, arrived in Austin
from Washington with an authorization to carry the El Paso mail.
His one year's service was to begin on July 1, 1866. Sawyer was a
partner on the established east Texas stage line of Sawyer, Risher,
and Hall. It is possible that Coopwood had been acting as his
agent from the start, for there was no perceptible change in his
operations after the Sawyer contract was announced. Whatever
his exact status, the company continued to function under Coopwood's name.[20]

It took some time for the first eastbound mail to be organized in El Paso while the newspapers were discussing these
new developments. Other coaches left San Antonio on May 8
and June 11. The *Herald* remarked on June 19, "The only mail
routes that run with any regularity now are those going westward. The Eagle Pass mail arrives every Saturday; . . . when the
El Paso mail arrives there is no telling, but it departs every
Monday morning." Coopwood's delay in moving the mail eastward sparked a meeting of the city's merchants to petition the
government for improved service.[21]

Actually the initial coach for the east was already on the
road when the townsmen met in Bexar. Captain James Holliday
brought it into San Antonio on June 29 after a quiet trip. The
next mail to follow was not so fortunate. Conductor Tom Davis

[19] Broaddus, *Legal Heritage*, 85; *San Antonio Daily Herald*, July 26, Aug. 8, 1866;
Santa Fe Weekly Gazette, May 19, 1866.
[20] *San Antonio Daily Herald*, May 1, 1866.
[21] Ibid., May 4, June 10, 1866.

led the party out from El Paso on July 1. Davis was a northerner and relatively inexperienced on the frontier. Two Mexican guides accompanied his small party, but he largely ignored their advice until it was too late.

Davis's caravan reached the eastern end of Limpia Canyon early on July 7, and met Espejo and a band of a hundred braves. The whites foolishly stopped to talk when the Indian flourished a white flag, and shooting broke out. The Texans made a run for Barilla Springs and had just reached the abandoned station when the coach's pole snapped, leaving the vehicled immobilized. The men took cover just as the Mescaleros thundered up the slope behind them. For almost twelve hours the fight flared around them until night finally brought an end to the braves' attacks. Davis had suffered a crippling leg wound and advised his companions to slip off through the brush and escape while he kept the Apaches occupied.

Two days later Robert Keating and the mail from the east pulled into Comanche Springs and found the six exhausted survivors of the Davis party. The men had walked all the way from the mountains to reach the oasis and were in a state of collapse. They were loaded in the coach and taken back to San Antonio, where their account of the attack sent a surge of anxiety through those who were about to head west.[22]

Keating and his comrades started out for the Pass once more, fully expecting to face a desperate fight in the Limpias. They edged into Barilla Springs to find the coach destroyed but the mail bags left intact. Keating saw what was left of Davis. "He had shot himself as the Indians were coming up to scalp him. We found the top of his head and part of his body and buried it," the guard recalled with grim clarity. The next coach down from El Paso met them on the road and Keating sent the mail bags on to San Antonio with it while they hurried west for the Rio Grande.[23]

Bethel Coopwood took the loss without faltering. He doubled his escorts but kept the schedule intact. The San Antonio newspapers joined him in urging the army to station troops at all

---

[22]Ibid. July 20, 22, 24, 1866; *Galveston News*, July 26, 1866; Austerman, "'Old Nighthawk,'" 129–30.

[23]C. G. Raht, *The Romance of Davis Mountains and Big Bend Country*, 156–57; Austerman, "'Old Nighthawk,'" 129–30.

the old posts along the road. The line of travel had to be secured if the state was to prosper. The annual trade from Chihuahua alone brought $800,000 into the local economy. Texas merchants calculated that there were 250,000 people in that market, and all of them were eager for American goods. If the stages and freight wagons could not move in safety, trade would cease quickly.[24]

Sawyer, Risher, and Hall were supposed to have taken over the route on July 1, but Coopwood continued to send out his men that month. Late in August he announced a new weekly trip from both ends of the line, and on the nineteenth his new superintendent, Holliday, took the mail into El Paso "without accident or molestation." Holliday skirmished briefly with some braves on the return trip, but the company suffered no losses.[25]

Coopwood's rigs continued their runs without further interference until mid-November. He then began transferring the line to Sawyer and his partners. Holliday joined the new company as their agent and supervised the transition. The mail was still moving as Bethel Coopwood left the express business after only eight months' experience. He had quickly learned that it was a business of high risks and sparse rewards. It was doubtless a relief for him to leave the field to others who could more easily bear the costs involved. If his venture had not flourished, it had at least endured long enough to allow his successors to sustain its momentum.[26]

Sawyer and company quickly took control of the line and spared little effort in their attempt to improve its service. "The mail contractors are busy putting on stock, repairing stations, etc.," commented the *Daily Herald*, "to secure speedy and uninterrupted communication between this city and El Paso, by a weekly line of coaches." The army and the stage lines made the local stock dealers happy that autumn. Sawyer had to have teams for his relay stations, and the cavalry's remount officers were buying horses at $139.50 a head. Mules, also, were in demand, as the tempo of trade and travel increased.[27]

[24] *San Antonio Daily Herald*, July 24, 27, 31, 1866.
[25] Ibid., Aug. 19, Sept. 19, 1866. A westbound mail left San Antonio on Aug. 15. See the *Daily Herald*, Aug. 16, 1866.
[26] Ibid., Oct. 21, Nov. 11, 27, 1866.
[27] Ibid., Dec. 4, 1866, Jan. 24, 1867.

Sawyer lost some of those costly animals in mid-February, 1867, when his men ran into trouble west of Fort Clark. Captain James Cook led the escort out of Las Moras Springs on the eleventh. They had not gone far when fifty Kickapoos swung out into the road and forced the whites to make a stand. The fighting continued all night in fitful bursts. In the morning the coach had to be abandoned when the expressmen beat a retreat to Fort Clark after another two hundred warriors appeared on the scene. The Indians taunted their enemies in English as they drove the stage off in hooting triumph. Four days later another coach struck an ambush two miles from Fort Lancaster, and everyone aboard died.[28]

As the weeks passed, more trouble settled on the line. No mail made it through to San Antonio at all from March 16 to March 30. Those of the fourth and eleventh remained in the station at Piedras Pintas, above Fort Clark, and the *Herald* charged the company with negligence in its delay of deliveries. The pouches finally arrived on April 10 after a nervous passage.

A subsequent delivery on May 8 brought news of some excitement over gold and silver strikes in the El Paso area and a sober warning to the current perils of travel. The *Herald's* correspondent claimed that "as it is now, no sane man would venture or ship goods to the Rio Grande without a very strong party and that well armed; as there is no doubt or question, but that the Indians are in large force about Lancaster and on the Pecos River." The writer estimated that six hundred Kickapoos as well as Comanches and Apaches were ranging the road and complained that the mail received there in early April was the first one to arrive from Bexar in over a month. That day, Sawyer announced that service beyond Fort Clark had been suspended until the Indian threat receded.[29]

The situation remained threatening throughout the spring and summer. In June some freighters found traces of a camp along the Pecos that must have hosted over a thousand Indians. Evidently the hostiles were massing for raids south into Mexico,

---

[28] Ibid., Feb. 24, Mar. 3, 1867; *Dallas Herald*, Mar. 16, 1867. This incident was not cited in the Bexar newspapers. It may have been a garbled account of Cook's earlier encounter.

[29] *San Antonio Daily Herald*, Apr. 2, 10, May 8, 1867; *Freie Presse feur Texas*, May

for in late June, Holliday brought in the mail from Fort Clark and reported no signs of Indians to the east of the post.

Conditions to the west did not seem to be improving. The black troopers of the Ninth Cavalry were now manning Fort Davis and Fort Stockton. Their patrols into the surrounding country put the tribes on notice that the army was back. As the summer slipped away, the public became more impatient with Sawyer's inactivity. The *Daily Express* complained that "a mail from this place to Franklin is imperatively needed, and there is no excuse now that the route is well guarded by soldiers, why the mails should not be immediately established." Weeks passed with no renewal of service, and the journal scored the contractor again, pointing out that from November, 1866, through May, 1867, only twelve through trips had been made on the line. Sawyer had assumed the contract in July and assigned it to a subcontractor, claimed the *Express*. He had yet to put a mail through. It was an intolerable situation, for with the recent gold discoveries in Arizona, San Antonio was being deprived of any regular connection with that market. "If the El Paso mail was making regular trips between this city and Mesilla," groused the paper, "all the gold produced in that section would find remittance to this place for exchange, and thousands of dollars worth of business could be made between the two points. Our city is suffering from the withdrawal of this service."[30]

The citizens of San Antonio would not have to wait much longer for the mail to start moving again. In late September a young Virginian arrived in town to take charge of the floundering stage company. Bearing a philosopher's name and the look of a buccaneer, he set quietly to work at building a professional express service in the place of Coopwood and Sawyer's brave makeshift.

9, 1867; Frederick C. Chabot, comp., "Texas Mail Service and the San Antonio Post Office," Manuscript, United States Postal Service Library, Washington, D.C., 170.

[30] *San Antonio Daily Herald*, June 13, 1867; *San Antonio Daily Express*, Sept. 12, 24, 1867. The *Santa Fe Gazette* reported receiving mail from Texas early in August with dates to May 25. It reported that the Indians had halted service between San Antonio and El Paso. *Santa Fe Gazette*, Aug. 10, 1867.

CHAPTER 11

The Brash Reinsman

Few men could have brought a deeper fund of knowledge to their job than the one who succeeded Bethel Coopwood as chief of the El Paso mail line. Benjamin Franklin Ficklin already lived through enough adventures to fill the lives of three men before he arrived in San Antonio that fall of 1867. The rebellious son of a Baptist minister, he had been expelled from the Virginia Military Institute for a long list of disciplinary infractions, and was reinstated and permitted to graduate only after returning from distinguished service in the Mexican War.

The restless young Virginian had taught school briefly after leaving the academy but soon departed his home state to work for an Alabama express company. By the early 1850s he was in California, where he impressed one of the new state's senators with his bold scheme for a transcontinental courier service. By the spring of 1857 the wandering southerner was serving on a government-sponsored expedition to survey a wagon road from South Pass in the Rocky Mountains to Salt Lake City in Utah Territory.

Ficklin performed praiseworthy work on the expedition, but its task was interrupted by the outbreak of a war between the Mormon settlers and the U.S. government. Ficklin found himself serving as a scout and courier for Brigadier General Albert Sidney Johnston's Army of Utah. Had it not been for the young surveyor's heroic efforts at bringing in supplies through the snow-choked mountains, many of the troops might have starved to death before the campaign's end.[1]

[1]Susan Miles and Mary Bain Spence, "Major Ben Ficklin," *West Texas Historical Association Yearbook* 27 (Oct., 1951): 58–63; J. Evetts Haley, "Ben Ficklin: Pioneer Mail Man," *Shamrock* (Spring, 1959): 8–9; B. M. Read, "Ben Ficklin 1849 and the Pony Express," *VMI Alumni Review* (Summer, 1973): 13; William H. Ellison, ed., "Memoirs of Hon. William H. Gwin," *California Historical Society Quarterly* 19 (Sept., 1940): 262;

By February, 1859, Ficklin was in Fort Leavenworth, Kansas, where he joined the newly organized Leavenworth and Pike's Peak Express Company, a stage line designed to link Denver with the Missouri and Kansas settlements, as well as extending a mail route to Salt Lake City. When the company went bankrupt in October, 1859, owner William Russell financed a new line with a loan from his partners in the still-flourishing freight company of Russell, Majors, and Waddell. Ben Ficklin came aboard as route superintendent on the Denver–Salt Lake City leg of the Central Overland and Pike's Peak Express Company.

The new concern was plagued with thievery among its employees along Ficklin's stretch of the road, and with the willing help of a cold-eyed gunman named Jack Slade, the Virginian mercilessly purged the company's roster of the dishonest and incompetent. He did not hesitate to use powder, lead, and a length of rope to restore honesty and efficiency to the stations on the route.

Although Russell's stage line continued to lose money, he was determined to win a monopoly on the government mail contracts in the Rocky Mountains. On January 27, 1860, he announced the formation of the Pony Express service from St. Joseph, Missouri, to Sacramento, California. The line was to commence operations on April 3, and Ben Ficklin was tapped to serve as general superintendent. Frenzied activity filled the next two months as Ficklin struggled to establish relay stations, hire employees, and equip the company with the needed stock and equipment. The first rider vaulted into the saddle at St. Joseph just as promised on April 3, 1860. A haggard and irritable Ficklin was present at the ceremony. He thrust a twenty-five-cent piece into the courier's hand as the moment of departure neared. The startled rider asked him what he was to purchase with the coin. "For you to buy a rope and hang yourself if you don't make the correct time," Ficklin snarled in reply.[2]

W. Turrentine Jackson, *Wagon Roads West*, 191–99; LeRoy R. Hafen and Ann W. Hafen, *The Utah Expedition, 1857–1858*, 122, 343–44.

[2]Raymond W. Settle and Mary L. Settle, *Empire on Wheels*, 43–89; Frank A. Root and William E. Connelley, *The Overland Stage to California*, 216–17; Lew Callaway,

The Pony Express captured the country's imagination from the start, and Russell gained the mail contracts he coveted, but he soon became jealous of Ficklin's managerial ability. He accused his lieutenant of wasting the firm's money, and a feud erupted between them. By July, Ficklin had been forced to resign from the company. It was shabby treatment for a man who had given as much to the job as he had, but Ficklin took it in stride. Throughout the rest of 1860 and into the next spring, he joined Hiram Sibley and Jeptha Wade in a bid to establish the Pacific Telegraph Company.

The rising threat of civil war drew Ficklin back to Virginia, and he spent the next four years as a Confederate purchasing agent in Europe. Between trips overseas he managed to perform several secret missions behind Union lines and saved Thomas Jefferson's Monticello from sale for unpaid taxes. Caught in Washington in the wake of Lincoln's murder, he was arrested and spent two months in prison before the authorities accepted the word of some northern friends that he had not been involved in the conspiracy.

Ficklin returned briefly to Alabama to explore the possibility of starting a stage line there but found that the railroads had eliminated the need for such a service. From Alabama he went back to Washington in search of another project suited to his talents. As he made the rounds of Congress and the Post Office Department, he learned of the turmoil surrounding the mail routes in the Southwest. Ficklin sensed that in Texas there was a place for his hands on the reins of a challenging new endeavor. He was not yet forty when he bid for a contract to carry the El Paso mail. He had less than four years left to live when he won it.[3]

It was typical of Ben Ficklin that he entered the adventure

"Joseph Alfred Slade: Killer or Victim?" *Montana* 3 (Jan., 1953): 9; George A. Root and Russell K. Hickman, "Pike's Peak Express Companies: Part II—The Solomon and Republican Route—Concluded," *Kansas State Historical Quarterly* 13 (Nov., 1944): 211–42; Miles and Spence, "Major Ben Ficklin," 67–68; Raymond W. Settle and Mary L. Settle, *Saddles and Spurs*, 32–33, 164–65.

[3] Frank Vandiver, *Ploughshares Into Swords: Josiah Gorgas and Confederate Ordnance*, 90–95; Susan Miles, "Ben Ficklin," *San Angelo Standard-Times*, Mar. 14, 1971; William F. Zornow, "Jeptha H. Wade in California: Beginning the Transcontinental Telegraph, 1860–1861," *California Historical Society Quarterly* 29 (Dec., 1950): 355.

that would be the climax of his career by a path that remains only dimly marked for his biographers. The circumstances surrounding his involvement in the El Paso stage lines are simply undocumented. The original mail contracts have not survived, and the postmaster general's reports for the immediate post–Civil War years uniformly omit any listing of the routes offered for bids or the services authorized upon them. It is possible that, as an ex-Confederate in a time when the nation was still bitterly divided, Ficklin chose to serve as an agent for a known Unionist who applied for the contract or simply acted as a silent partner until it was granted.

The hazy outlines of the situation suggest that Ficklin joined Frederick P. Sawyer in the service he had been authorized to begin in July, 1867. Sawyer resided in Georgetown, D.C., and reportedly enjoyed some political leverage, as his brother, Philetus, served Wisconsin in the House of Representatives. Some accounts credit Sawyer with taking an active role in the line's operation, while others state that he remained in the East while Ficklin took charge of affairs on the road. Sawyer remains an even more elusive figure than the Virginian, and the details of his background and activities still defy exposure. The surviving accounts of the company's service make it clear that Ficklin bore the brunt of the responsibility for its operation in the field. No one on its payroll ever had reason to doubt that Major Ficklin was in command after the fall of 1867.[4]

When Ficklin arrived in San Antonio he found the populace eager to see him transform the lackluster mail line. He had been in town less than a month when the *Express* praised his business skill, even before the first coach had left for El Paso.

Mr. Ficklin is an old stage man over the Salt Lake route and understands the business perfectly; he is also able to carry out all he assumes to do; he has no connection with Hall, Risher, & Co. It will be a couple of months before the route will be in complete running order, and mails will not be very regular until that time. Mr. Ficklin speaks in perfect confidence of his undertaking; his contract is for a weekly service

[4]W. W. Mills, *Forty Years at El Paso, 1858–1898*, 138; Barry Scobee, *Fort Davis Texas, 1584–1960*, 53; C. G. Raht, *The Romance of Davis Mountains and Big Bend Country*, 154–55, 190; Miles and Spence, "Major Ben Ficklin," 72.

but we hope it will be changed to a tri-weekly to make connections with the tri-weekly service from Mesilla to California.[5]

On September 30 Ficklin and party left town with the first mail for El Paso. Because the new route was not entirely organized yet, he planned to continue following the old road via Fort Clark, San Pedro Springs, and Fort Stockton into the Limpia Mountains. The Kickapoos were still raiding along the border, but Indian attacks were no novelty to the new superintendent. He had already seen the worst that the Cheyennes and Utes could do.

There is no record of Ficklin's arrival in El Paso. He must have traveled slowly, checking the stock and stations along the line, for by October 11 he was only a day's ride north of Howard's Well. Luck was with him on that opening trip, for he narrowly missed being caught in the disaster that befell his second mail from San Antonio.

The mail bags were stowed on pack mules driven by two of Ficklin's hands. They were escorted by four troopers of the Ninth Cavalry from Camp Hudson. The six men ran into a large band of Kickapoos a few miles north of Howard's Well on the evening of the eleventh and were quickly overrun. Two soldiers died in the shooting, and the rest fled on foot. The two couriers escaped into the brush, but the Indians captured the pack mules and other stock. Ficklin had paid the first of many tolls for passage on that road.[6]

The mail accompanying the contractor must have reached the Pass safely sometime soon after the second party's defeat, for by November 9 Ficklin was back in San Antonio, and the *Express* proudly announced that "the mail route is now a fixture." Soon afterward Ficklin departed on a brief trip to Washington, during which he won an expansion of the contract to provide tri-weekly service on the line. While he was gone his men had several more brushes with the Indians, including a running fight into Eagle Springs and an abortive ambush west of Fort Lancas-

[5] *San Antonio Express*, Sept. 30, 1867.
[6] Ibid., Oct. 21, 1867; *Santa Fe Gazette*, Nov. 30, 1867; William H. Leckie, *The Buffalo Soldiers*, 84–85.

ter on the Pecos. Not long afterward, driver Henry W. Daly and agent Jim Spears took a coach down the winding, rock-strewn trail that hugged the bluffs above Fort Lancaster with a pack of Commanches howling at their heels all the way into the station.[7]

Spurred by reports of these depredations, Ficklin left San Antonio to check on the situation himself soon after his return from Washington. On January 13 he appeared at Fort Davis in a light buggy. His unexpected arrival and audaciousness in traveling without an escort "created quite a stir" at the post, in the words of one resident. It was hardly a recommended form of travel even for those whose luck had carried them as far as Ficklin's had. The upsurge in traffic on the road had simply made the Indians bolder. When a company of the Ninth Cavalry reopened Fort Quitman that month, it fought a dozen skirmishes with the Mescaleros in only a few weeks.[8]

The contractor probably did not tarry for long on the western reaches of his line, for the government had ordered a series of major alterations in the company's service. Not only was Ficklin to put three mails a week into Bexar and El Paso, but on March 1 he was to shift his route from the old lower road to a new one that ran northwest from San Antonio via Leon Springs, Boerne, Fredericksburg, Mason, and the newly established post of Fort Concho to a junction with the earlier route at Fort Stockton. Branch lines also sprouted from the main trunk. A triweekly run to Castroville, Fort Clark, and Eagle Pass was scheduled, and a second line ran bravely south from Fort Davis to supply Presidio del Norte with its first regular mail service. The *Daily Herald* was excited over Ficklin's expansion but warned the public, saying, "Before the . . . route can be traveled over with anything like regularity and safety, the government will have to provide for the more efficient protection of the frontier."[9]

[7] Henry W. Daly, "A Dangerous Dash Down Lancaster Hill," *Frontier Times* 30 (Apr.–June, 1953): 166–69; *San Antonio Daily Express*, Nov. 9, 1867; *San Antonio Daily Herald*, Dec. 4, 1867, Jan. 5, 8, 1868; *Tri-Weekly Austin Republican*, Jan. 7, 1868; Leckie, *The Buffalo Soldiers*, 85.

[8] *San Antonio Daily Herald*, Feb. 9, 1868; George Ruhlen, "Quitman: The Worst Post at Which I Ever Served," *Password* 11 (Apr., 1960): 54–64.

[9] *San Antonio Daily Herald*, Feb. 20, Mar. 27, 1867.

Though the shift in operations must have created some problems for Ficklin, it also had benefits. Unlike his predecessors, the new contractor ran a line that passed through or near an extended belt of settlement before entering the wilderness. The counties ranked to the northwest of San Antonio were older and more populous than the ones traversed by the earlier stage lines to El Paso. Not only was that entire tier of settlement afforded a scheduled mail and passenger service, but the towns and ranches along that leg of the route also permitted Ficklin to economize. The settlers could be contracted to act as keepers for his stations, thus sparing him major outlays for additional relay points along the lower reaches of the new route.

Conditions changed drastically once the stages struck west from Fort Concho, however. There were no settlements between that post and Fort Stockton, 150 miles distant. Some of the old Butterfield stations between the Concho River and the Pecos could be rebuilt and utilized, but from there to El Paso the road remained barren of habitation aside from the old stations and army posts. Ficklin would meet the challenge posed by the government's shifting of his route, but during the interim his service would be seriously disrupted, leaving him open to later charges of gross inefficiency.

Moving with his customary dispatch, Ficklin established a relay station on the brushy banks of the river not far from Fort Concho and began transferring stock and equipment to the new route in the rolling hills above Bexar. He managed to juggle both the operation of the old route and establishment of the new one successfully for a time. The *Daily Express* remarked that the El Paso and Eagle Pass mail "is fast assuming system and instead of a nuisance is becoming an accommodation." The citizenry expressed enthusiasm for the restored service by circulating a petition that requested even more frequent mail deliveries and increased funding from the government for Ficklin's business. The San Antonians were joined by the residents of Mason and Fredericksburg, and the *Daily Herald*'s editor gave his support to the campaign, saying with engaging frankness, "We are somewhat selfish, and as our daily subscription list has been considerably augmented since the establishment of those tri-weekly western mails, we can reasonably hope that with quicker time, another impetus will be given."[10]

By mid-April Ficklin was already sending his coaches over the northern road, with arrivals in San Antonio scheduled for every Tuesday, Thursday, and Saturday at 6:00 P.M., and departures listed on Monday, Wednesday, and Friday at 8:00 A.M. In an unwarranted burst of optimism the *Herald* assured passengers that "every stage will be amply protected by military escorts while passing through the Indian country, making the line safe both for passenger travel and mail transportation." In truth, Ficklin's relations with the army were often nearly as bitter as those with the Comanches.[11]

That spring proved to be as difficult a period as he had ever experienced in the business. Only two mails made it through to Bexar in the month of April, the earliest one, on the eighth, being the first through mail received over the new route. The line was obviously running behind schedule, but the public was assured that "the route is now being stocked with good animals and nice new coaches, making regular tri-weekly trips. From the well known activity and long experience of the manager, Mr. B. F. Ficklin, the best results must ensue; renewed life and vigor given to our valuable western trade and greatly enhanced value to our immense tracts of vacant lands."[12]

The month of May served as a capstone for his mounting difficulties. The Kickapoos nearly captured the stage from Fort Clark on the night of the eleventh, but even before then Ficklin had clashed with an even more potent enemy in the guise of the U.S. Army. Not long after establishing his new station near Fort Concho, Ficklin became involved in a running feud with the post commander. Its origins were unclear. One version of the affair relates that Ficklin approached the officer and requested that the garrison's blacksmith shoe a herd of mules that was being

[10] *San Antonio Daily Express*, Mar. 26, 28, 1868; *San Antonio Daily Herald*, Apr. 7, 1868. The *Daily Express* of Feb. 22 cited a letter from the Post Office Department that identified Eli Bates as the new contractor. He was acting as Ficklin's agent.

[11] *San Antonio Daily Herald*, Apr. 10, 14, 15, 18, 1868.

[12] Ibid., May 25, 1868; *San Antonio Daily Express*, Apr. 12, 20, 1868.

driven west to stock the stations down the line. The cavalryman replied that if the blacksmith was willing and had time to perform the task after completing his normal duties, it was agreeable to him. The farrier spent the next four days shoeing the animals. When the job was done, Ficklin offered him a dollar tip for his work. The indignant smith demanded full payment for the task. Ficklin had understood that the post commander was having the job done as a courtesy to the mail company and was furious when the officer sided with the artisan and required him to pay twenty-five dollars for the work.[13]

Major George C. Cram, the officer involved, gave another version of the source of his antagonism toward Ficklin. According to the major, Ficklin and "those in his employ, have, by the connivance of persons in the Military Service, been using public forage and other public property for private purposes." Cram stated that Ficklin had defied his authority "in a grossly insolent and disrespectful manner" when he questioned the contractor's credentials as an authorized mail carrier.[14]

There probably would have been little love lost between the Yankee and the ex-Confederate under the best of circumstances, but Ficklin's quick temper and willful determination made a clash inevitable when the two met. On one occasion a stage driver complained that the post adjutant habitually delayed the coach by failing to have his mail packet ready on time. Ficklin issued standing orders for the men to maintain their schedules whether the army's mail was delivered or not.

The next time the adjutant was late with his packet, the stage departed just as Ficklin had instructed. Major Cram stopped the rig and put two of the Virginian's men in the post guardhouse. Ficklin immediately stormed into Cram's office and confronted him in a manner that the major claimed was impossible to "sanction or sustain." Ficklin used language to address the major that he normally reserved for his mules. Cram lost his

[13] *San Antonio Daily Herald*, May 13, 1868; *San Antonio Daily Express*, May 14, 1868; Miles and Spence, "Major Ben Ficklin," 75; Susan Miles, "Until the Flood: 1868–1882," *Edwards Plateau Historian* 2 (1966): 17.

[14] Maj. George C. Cram to Col. Edward Hatch, May 9, 1868, Letters Sent, Fort Concho, Texas, RG 98, NARS.

temper, and when Ficklin offered to take his employees' place in the guardhouse, the officer was quick to oblige him. Cram informed his superiors of what had happened, adding that "the Mail Company will have to have a new superintendent or this post a new commanding officer unless Mr. Ficklin's future conduct and bearing is radically changed on his future appearance here." Cram did not know it, but he had far overreached himself when he threw Ficklin behind bars.[15]

Cram's superior, Colonel Edward Hatch, was reluctant to interfere with the Post Office Department's affairs and ordered Ficklin's release. The prisoner refused, saying that he would remain in jail until the matter had been brought to the government's attention. This was just what Hatch did not want.

Judging by the tenor of the correspondence that flowed between Hatch and Cram in the following weeks, the postmaster general's reaction to the incident was heated enough to melt both their sabres within their scabbards. Ficklin was released at once and Cram soon received orders for another post. He retired five months later. Ficklin and Sawyer obviously had some influence in Washington.[16]

The Cram-Ficklin affair lasted until July, when the two men that the major had originally arrested filed suits against him for $50,000 each. Relations had been badly strained between the expressmen and the army. During his initial clash with Ficklin, the angry cavalryman had sent orders to his picket posts on the El Paso road, directing them to ignore the contractor's authority as a mail carrier. Ironically, Ficklin had already furnished water barrels to one of these isolated stations near the head of the Concho. He wondered if the troops would be permitted to aid his coaches in case of Indian attack. Cram also requested that the authorities in San Antonio refuse payment to Ficklin for the transportation of government personnel, since he refused to let his rigs enter the limits of the post at Fort Concho. Officers arriving there for duty were obliged to secure their own transpor-

---

[15] Cram to Hatch, May 25, 1868, Fort Concho, Letters Sent.

[16] Miles, "Until the Flood," 17; Stephen W. Schmidt, ed., "Fort Concho, 1868–1872: The Medical Officer's Observations by William M. Notson," *Military History of Texas and the Southwest* 12:147.

tation from the station to the post, a distance of several miles. In many respects it had been a petty clash of egoes, but Ficklin had won. By doing so, he had demonstrated that no one interfered with his affairs with impunity.[17]

The stage line came under attack from a different quarter even before the feud with the army had cooled. A diverse group of El Pasoans issued a letter of protest over the erratic mail service from San Antonio. Citing the failures of previous contractors, they scored Ficklin's inability to deliver the mail on his supposedly triweekly schedule any more often than five times in the six weeks preceding April 28. The complainants requested an immediate government investigation into affairs on the line.[18]

There was no disputing the charges of irregular service into El Paso during that spring, and the formal letter of protest had been preceded by other complaints from the settlement. Yet Ficklin had some loyal defenders, and they willingly replied to the criticism of his efforts. Early in May a Fort Davis resident informed the *Daily Herald* that only two mails had reached the post during April. The delay was due to the company's lack of stock on the new route down from Fort Concho, and not through any lack of diligence on Ficklin's part. "He is a live, thoroughgoing, energetic man," asserted the correspondent, "a regular old 'Virginia never-tire,'—and through our confidence in him, we hope to get our mails and your popular paper every week."[19]

The *Daily Express*, in a rare agreement with its rival, chimed in with an exoneration of Ficklin, stressing that the shift in route and its attendant disruption of service had not been by his choice. Added to this handicap was the jump in prices for stock and forage as both the army and the mail company competed for these commodities on the local market. "Mr. Ficklin has shown unusual tact and energy in preparing for a speedy perfection of this route," the journal concluded, "making it cheaper, safer, and more comfortable than ever before." Not to be outdone in any

[17] Cram to Hatch, May 18, 1868; Cram to Lt. J. G. C. Lee, May 25, 1868; Maj. Wirt Davis to Capt. Joseph Rendlebrock, May 12, 1868, Fort Concho, Letters Sent; J. Evetts Haley, *Fort Concho and the Texas Frontier*, 157, 211.

[18] *San Antonio Daily Express*, May 27, 1868.

[19] *San Antonio Daily Herald*, May 25, 1868.

display of public spirit, the *Herald* later welcomed the news of Major Cram's involvement in the suits brought against him with criticism of his conduct and an oblique suggestion that most of the poor service on the mail route stemmed from his interference with Ficklin.[20]

It was good to have the press on his side, but Ficklin knew that kind words had never been legal tender. He vindicated the journals' faith in him on June 12 when the first mail to arrive on schedule pulled in from El Paso, although this triumph was counterbalanced by news of a Comanche attack on a station and another Kickapoo assault on the Eagle Pass stage. Such disruptions kept another mail from reaching Bexar until July 16.[21]

As if Ficklin did not have enough to worry about, there was another minor clash with the military that month. Colonel Wesley Merritt, post commander at Fort Davis, charged that stage driver John Clark had "recently armed and gave such advice to a man mounted on a gray horse," while at Barrel Springs. The rider was wanted for murder in Travis County, and the colonel charged that Clark was "surely a criminal and connected with the gang of murderers and horse thieves that infest the border country. He should be arrested and tried." Ficklin's response to this charge went unrecorded, and Clark probably remained a free man. In those unsettled times in an occupied state, the man who was marked as an outlaw by the authorities sometimes enjoyed the support of other defiant Texans as he sought to elude the bluecoats.[22]

Ficklin and Merritt both had reasons for other concerns that summer as the Indians continued to strike along the mail road, stealing stock from Fort Stockton, rigging ambushes in Quitman Canyon, and skirmishing with freighters. The stage line received some more welcome publicity as fall approached, when the *Daily Herald* sent reporter H. G. Logan on a trip to

---

[20] *San Antonio Daily Express*, May 8, 1868; *San Antonio Daily Herald*, July 28, 1868.

[21] *San Antonio Daily Express*, June 12, 17, 18, July 16, 1868; *San Antonio Daily Herald*, June 17, 1868.

[22] Col. Wesley Merritt to Lt. Col. Charles E. Morse, July 31, 1868, Letters Sent, Fort Davis, Texas, RG 98, NARS.

Fort Davis. The paper praised Ficklin's "Lightning Line," noting that the coaches had been running on time since September 1, with only six and a half days required for the 650-mile passage. Logan's periodic dispatches from the road gave his townsmen a diverting account of conditions on the frontier and the pleasures of travel in Ficklin's coaches.

The journalist found the road above San Antonio rough and sloppy after a spell of heavy rains, but the good company of route agent James McLeod made the time pass pleasantly as they braved the cold winds and high fords on the trail into Fredericksburg. After a brief pause at the gracious Nimitz Hotel, one of the most welcome landmarks on the entire road, they pressed on through the hill country to such settlements as Loyal Valley, Hedwig's Hill, Fort Mason, and Menardville to reach Fort McKavett on the high banks of the San Saba.

From that post they swung northward to the beleaguered station at Kickapoo Springs, pausing only long enough to change teams while McLeod had his men check the loads in their carbines and take positions on the coach that gave them good fields of fire. Too often the station hands or incoming stages had found the surrounding brush thick with Comanches.

The fresh team made good time over the next ten miles into Lipan Springs, where a rock house and corral lay tucked in the lee of a thick stand of trees that ringed another spring-fed pool. Off to the northwest the dark shoulders of a pair of twin peaks rose against the horizon. That landmark signaled an early end to the leg of the trip into Fort Concho and Ficklin's station, nineteen miles away.[23]

Lipan Springs fell away as the leaders bent into their harness and settled into an easy canter that carried them through a level plain, studded with prairie dog towns and herds of skittish

---

[23] *San Antonio Daily Herald*, Oct. 20, 30, 1868; Kathryn T. Carter, *Stagecoach Inns of Texas*, 103–104; E. B. Potter, *Nimitz*, 23–25; N. H. Pierce, *The Free State of Menard*, 101–102, 126, 187; Margaret Bierschwale, *Fort McKavett, Texas Post on the San Saba*, 17–18, 51–53. Kickapoo Springs is located on the Mathews Ranch in the extreme southeastern corner of modern Tom Green County. Lipan Springs currently hosts a ranch, located on FM 1223, roughly 15 miles south of San Angelo's city limits. Both sites can be marked on the United States Geologic Survey Map Sheets, *Kickapoo Springs 1970, Eola, Susan Peak*, and *Wall 1957*. Hereafter cited as U.S.G.S. Map Sheets.

antelope. Just at dark after a week of slow travel on the mired roads, Logan's coach rolled into Concho Station. He paused for five days to get some rest before catching another rig west for Fort Stockton. The weather had cleared and he was the only passenger on the light, two-mule hack. His driver tucked the mail bags under their seats and began the forty-hour drive into Comanche Springs. They would halt only long enough to change teams and grab hasty meals at the stations ahead.

They followed the ruts of the old Butterfield road down the north bank of the Middle Concho to skirt the Twin Mounds and bear a little south of due west for twenty-three miles to reach Camp Johnston, one of the prewar stations refurnished by Ficklin. The current residents and army guards kept a close watch on the mesquite thickets that lapped the grassy flat occupied by the house and corral. Up until this point Logan had been traveling on or within the line of settlement. Now he was probing the eastern flank of Comanchería, and trouble could wait at any bend of the road ahead.[24]

The rig bore on as the driver kept the mules dancing in the traces to cover the nineteen miles into the cavalry picket post at Camp Charlotte. Logan kept an alert eye on the low, barren hills to the north and south that marked their progress down Centralia Draw's broad trough. He was relieved when they reached an open meadow just east of the union of Kiowa Creek and the Middle Concho and saw the stockaded redoubt that sheltered the small outpost's garrison.

Darkness came on soon after the team had splashed across Kiowa Creek and started the ten mile pull to Head of Concho Station. The skeletal ruins of the old Butterfield post rose starkly amid the brush a short distance below Ficklin's house and the adjoining structure of Shellenbarger's store. Logan and his companion wolfed down some antelope steaks and cups of strong coffee, while the hostlers harnessed a new brace of jacks to the rig.

The journalist tried to nap as the hack cleared the Concho

[24] *San Antonio Daily Herald*, Oct. 30, Nov. 3, 10, 1868; U.S.G.S. Map Sheets, *San Angelo South 1957, Knickerbocker 1957.*

and trundled on past Mustang Holes, nine miles out from the river. They passed several herds of cattle bedded down in the shelter of a nearby ridge, part of the increasing traffic on the trail to New Mexico that had been blazed by Charles Goodnight and Oliver Loving two years before. Mustang Holes marked the only break in the landscape for almost a dozen miles until Centralia Draw began to narrow as they approached Flat Rock Ponds. These shallow limestone basins pocked the roadside for several hundred yards until the ground softened and the cactus and mesquite took hold again.[25]

In less than an hour they wound through the catclaw and sage to enter the lines of another army outpost at a place known variously as Middle or Centralia Station. Though the mail company had not yet built a house and corrals there, it did keep the troops supplied with water. It was good to know that some help was available between the Concho and the Pecos when the coaches hit the dry stretch on the plains.

The army camp also marked an important dividing point on the trail. Ficklin's earlier service had sent the coaches almost due west from this milepost for the narrow mountain pass of Castle Gap and the ford at Horsehead Crossing on the Pecos. The army had made an attempt to secure the old route during the spring of 1868, when troops took station at Horsehead Crossing, Castle Gap, and China Ponds, an oasis located ten miles to the east of the pass. In April cavalry patrols began scouting the country southwest of the road to find a new route to the river. By June Ficklin had begun building a corral and ferry approximately two

[25] Roscoe Conkling and Margaret B. Conkling, *The Butterfield Overland Mail, 1857–1869*, 1:351–64; Haley, *Fort Concho*, 155; Lt. Col. Thomas B. Hunt, "Journal Showing the Route Taken by the Government Train Accompanying the 15th Regiment, U.S. Infantry from Austin, Tex. to Ft. Craig, N.M. and Returning to San Antonio July–December, 1869," RG 77, NARS; U.S.G.S. Map Sheets, *Arden 1972, Mertzon 1972, Mertzon SW 1972, Wallace Draw 1972, Bradford Draw 1973, Causey Draw 1973, Moore Hill, Stiles 1970, Garrison Draw 1970*; Adam R. Johnson, *The Partisan Rangers of the Confederate Army*, 30–32; Kenneth F. Neighbours, "The Expedition of Major Robert S. Neighbors to El Paso in 1849," *Southwestern Historical Quarterly* 58 (July, 1954): 48. Both the Head of Concho and Mustang Holes sites are located on the Rocker B Ranch. Operated by D. W. Herrman, the ranch lies just off Route 163, about 18 miles north of Barnhart, Tex. Flat Rock Ponds rests in Centralia Draw, a short distance west of Stiles, in central Reagan County.

and one-half miles downriver and on the eastern bank across
from Giddings's old Pecos Station. In August an infantry company arrived on the site from Horsehead Crossing to establish a
picket post, "where the new road leaves the Pecos River." The
troops erected rock breastworks and houses, dubbing their new
station Camp Melvin. It was at Middle Station that the road
swung southwest to run for thirty miles before sweeping down
off the high rimrock bluffs to reach the river at this new crossing
place.[26]

The leg from Middle Station to Camp Melvin covered more
of that bleak, raw country. The only break in the landscape came
a little better than halfway to the Pecos when the road ran by
Flat Rock Holes. A broad shelf of rock lay like a giant's fallen
shield, its surface scribed with Indian petroglyphs and pocked
with shallow depressions that held small amounts of rain water
in the wet seasons.

Logan's ride had been fairly tranquil from Fort Concho to
Camp Melvin. It was only another fifty miles from the river
crossing to Comanche Springs, but he found his heart in his
throat several times during the last hours of the drive. Part of
the trouble lay with his driver, who delighted in relating the
grisly history of every landmark in sight. "It affords no consolation to a passenger for the driver to point out by the wayside
graves of unknown parties killed by the Indians," he protested,
"—to designate the exact spot within two hundred yards of the
road, where three mounted warriors stood and watched the
stage pass by only four days previously." "At times he feared they
would meet the braves again. "Still less agreeable is it, while
traveling through a thicket in the night, to have gentle mules,
which were never known to 'shy' at anything dead—only the living—tuck down their ears and pitch out of the road at a fearful
rate." Logan knew too much about the risks involved to be com-

---

[26] Hunt, "Journal," 7–10, 28; Grover C. Ramsey, "Camp Melvin, Crockett County,
Texas," *West Texas Historical Association Yearbook* 37 (Oct., 1961): 137–46; Clayton W.
Williams, "That Topographical Ghost—Horsehead Crossing!" *Permian Historical Annual* 17 (Dec., 1977): 37–56; U.S.G.S. Map Sheets, *Rankin NE 1970, Cedar Canyon
1970, Indian Mesa NE, Iraan 1967.*

fortable when the team took fright at an unseen something in the darkness. "Such facts as these," he admitted, "with the further information that an instance occurred some time ago, when a lone Indian, standing at the side of the road ran his lance through two men sitting together, —will, I think, unsettle the nerves of anybody, 'until he gets used to it.'"[27]

After a safe arrival in Fort Stockton, Logan took another week to fill a dispatch to the *Herald* with comments on the garrison and news of the passing traffic. When he finally reached Fort Davis on November 8, he had experienced yet another anxious ride with Ficklin's coach. Upon entering Limpia Canyon he passed by the site of Davis's fatal encounter with the Mescaleros. The details of the incident were still fresh in his mind, and the driver was worried over their failure to meet the eastbound rig on schedule. The two hacks should have passed each other by ten o'clock that morning. Five hours later there was still no sign of the other vehicle. Both men were relieved when it finally pulled into sight and halted for a brief conference.

The driver had lost time while waiting for the El Paso coach to arrive at Fort Davis. He finally left without the mail, fearing that the Indians had cut the road to the west. Logan's man shared his concern, and after wishing each other good luck the two parties drove on. Half an hour later they saw a cloud of dust boiling up from the road ahead and feared the worst, only to relax when agent Jim Spears cantered up on a lathered horse and paused to talk for a moment. The El Paso coach had finally reached Fort Davis several hours before, and he was trying to overtake the eastbound express with the missing mail bags. Spears was running a terrible risk by traveling alone through those moun-

[27] Seymour V. Connor, "The Mendoza-Lopez Expedition and Location of San Clemente," *West Texas Historical Association Yearbook* 45 (Oct., 1969): 7, 14; Clayton W. Williams, "Excerpts from the Diary of George Wedemeyer," *West Texas Historical Association Yearbook* 46 (Oct., 1970): 158, 162; S. D. Myres, ed., *Pioneer Surveyor—Frontier Lawyer*, 101. Both of the rock basin watering places east of the Pecos are known variously as "holes" and "ponds," resulting in much confusion for the modern researcher. The site nearest the Pecos is located 5 miles east of Rankin, Tex., and a short distance south of Highway 67, at a dirt road-crossing of the Atchison, Topeka, and Santa Fe Railroad line, U.S.G.S. Map Sheets, *Rankin, Rankin NE 1970*.

tains, but he knew that a late mail delivery meant a stiff fine for the company. Logan did not envy him his responsibilities as a line agent.

Spears rode onward down the canyon while their team trotted south past Northern Point of Rocks and took the climb up to the mouth of Wild Rose Pass without breaking stride. They were bowling along at a fine rate on the easy downslope when the hack suddenly lurched drunkenly and squealed to a stop. A pin in one of the axletrees had snapped, and it took the driver an hour to fashion a makeshift replacement. A very apprehensive Logan stood guard as the minutes crawled past. He hefted his carbine uneasily while scanning the heights about them. "I had an excellent opportunity to survey the situation," he stated wryly in a dispatch to his editor. "I tried to do so complacently, but for my life I couldn't." [28]

The driver's handiwork held for the distance into Fort Davis, and Logan had a week in which to calm his addled nerves in the sutler's bar. In three weeks on the road he had gained a genuine respect for the men who ran the stage line, and he transmitted his feelings to the *Herald's* readers. True, the journey had usually been uncomfortable, and often dangerous, but this was to be expected. The images that lingered in the minds of the public were those of bluff James McLeod keeping his passengers cheerful while the cold rain beat at the side curtains, and brave Jim Spears spurring after the errant coach with the precious mail bags slung from his saddle. Ben Ficklin's company had unwittingly scored a publicity triumph when Henry Logan purchased his ticket in San Antonio. There could be no better way to open the line's second year of service.

Logan's praise of the company was partly balanced by news of continuing trouble along the line. Early in November twenty braves had raided Kickapoo Springs and captured the mule herd. The next day they returned to skirmish with the station hands. The same war party later clashed with some ranchers, losing one warrior and the captured stock. James McLeod acquired the dead buck's shield, which was ornamented with two white wom-

---

[28] *San Antonio Daily Herald*, Nov. 10, 13, 17, 1868.

en's scalps. If there were any Indian-lovers in Bexar, he advised the *Herald*, send them to Concho Station to see the savages' handiwork. Other bands prowled the roads to the south, ambushing travelers and striking the smaller settlements. Despite their presence, the El Paso mail reached San Antonio without interference on the tenth.[29]

It was mid-November before the journalist started back from Fort Davis. As the hack left the Limpias behind and rocked across the greasewood plains, he was treated to an awesome sight. Each night flights of meteors streaked across the autumn sky in a spectacular display. Ficklin might have taken it as a good omen as 1868 slipped toward its end. To the Indians the phenomenon resembled nothing so much as the sparks that leaped forth when the blade of a scalping knife was drawn across a whetstone. It would be a season of many coups.[30]

[29] Ibid., Nov. 10, 13, 1868.
[30] Ibid., Nov. 20, 24, 1868.

CHAPTER 12

The Knives of Winter

Optimism and endurance were two of Ben Ficklin's strongest traits. The man who could strike out into a frozen wilderness with only the map of the stars to guide him, or invest his fortune in the preservation of a dead neighbor's home while a nation crumbled about him, had to possess full measures of both qualities. Ficklin's resiliency and buoyant faith in himself came to the fore once again as the winter of 1868 hurled new obstacles in the path of his ambition.

The autumn had ended on a promising note when Henry Logan arrived back in San Antonio. He continued his series of articles on the stage line while making some trenchant remarks about the government postal system. He deflected much of the rising criticism away from Ficklin's operation. After characterizing the Virginian and his employees as thorough professionals, Logan questioned why the frontier mails were so often the cause of complaint. "The blame, then, attaches to the Post Office Department," he judged. "Some of the Postmasters do not understand their duties; some of them do not attend to their duties at all; some are not impressed with the sacred nature of the contents of a mail bag; some are careless."[1]

Part of the problem lay in the department's adherence to the "way mail" system of delivery. Instead of allotting individual bags for each post office on the route served, the department used one or more bags of general "through" mail, with the items for the intermediate stops mixed in with each other and those for the terminal point on each coach's run. Thus, at each stop the resident postmaster would hunt through the bags in search of those letters and parcels addressed to his office. Since all the postmasters on a given route had keys to all the bags, the chances for loss, theft, or damage to their contents was greatly increased.

[1] *San Antonio Daily Herald*, Nov. 26, 1868.

Logan's solution to the problem was logical. "Every post office should have a bag exclusively to itself . . . all stage-drivers are already sworn officers in the postal service, each on relieving the other acknowledging on the way-bill the receipt of so many bags of mail . . . and . . . should allow each postmaster to open such bags destined further along the road as he might have matter to put therein, prohibiting him from taking anything out." With the driver retaining control of the bags and a complete set of keys while the postmasters had only their own keys, control and responsibility would be enhanced. "What we wish to effect on behalf of the people—soldiers and citizens—of the Texas frontier," stressed Logan, "is an inspection of the mail route and the adoption of some system, by which every man will get his own."[2]

But there could be no guarantee against a random meeting with violence on the road. On December 3 a stage rumbled into town from the northwest and the *Herald* learned why the earlier scheduled mail had never arrived. The coach had left Concho Station at dark on November 30 with only Mullen, the driver, on board. The next day a patrol from Fort Concho found his scalped and mangled body lying in the brush five miles below Kickapoo Springs. The coach stood nearby, mules and harness gone, its interior gutted. The mail bags were missing. Two army officers who conducted the subsequent investigation held that white men were probably to blame, not the Indians. The mail had been carried off intact, instead of being strewn over the plains, as was the custom among the warriors. Also, the driver had been lashed to the rear of the rig by one leg and then dragged through the brush for quite a distance. Whoever drove the coach had managed the team skillfully. It was hardly a comforting thought to know that yet another threat had been fielded against the mail company.[3]

Major George Gordon, Fort Concho's commander, also criticized conditions at Kickapoo Springs. He described the neighborhood as "a source of annoyance . . . a whisky hole." His teamsters and passing troops were continually getting drunk

[2] Ibid.
[3] *San Antonio Daily Express*, Jan. 13, 1869; *San Antonio Daily Herald*, Dec. 5, 1868; *Galveston News*, Dec. 15, 1868.

there. "As I passed up on Sunday night," he complained, "I found the stage agent so drunk that he did not know what he was about. When the stage mules were run off from there some three weeks ago, I am of the opinion that it would not have occurred if the mail employees had been attentive to their own business."[4]

The major's comments were largely accurate, but the root of the problem at Kickapoo Springs stemmed not from the stage line's employees, but from the other residents of the area. Ficklin did not yet hold title to all the land around his station and thus had trouble controlling the swarm of liquor peddlers and transients who drifted into the small settlement. It would be months before he acquired clear ownership of the entire tract. Until then all he could do was to threaten the bad element and fire any men he found drunk on company time.

Kickapoo Springs continued to attract unwelcome attention as December opened, with the Comanches launching a half-hearted raid on the eighth. Off to the west, and a week before, white outlaws had savagely murdered a lone traveler on the mail road between Camp Charlotte and the Head of Concho in another brutal reminder that cruelty recognized no color. The weather also turned hostile that month. The eastbound mail had to halt overnight at Mason when the team's ears became frostbitten. The icy winds did not slow the pace of Comanche raids in the least, for the braves struck a station just north of Fredericksburg, capturing all the stock.[5]

All of these incidents combined failed to create the shock and horror that a single piece of news from Fort Davis brought later that season. On January 5 driver James Bass helped Jarvis Hubbell climb aboard his rig in El Paso. Hubbell must have felt some chagrin at having to ask for his aid on that crisp winter morning. He had made the trip to Bexar scores of times with Skillman and Giddings. A seasoned frontiersman, he had never suffered a scratch from the Indians. Now he was gingerly taking his seat, a sore and swollen foot clad loosely in a carpet slipper.

 [4] Maj. George A. Gordon to Assistant Adj. Gen., Dec. 10, 1868, Letters Sent, Fort Concho, Texas, RG 98, NARS.

 [5] *San Antonio Daily Express*, Dec. 18, 1868, Jan. 10, 20, 1869; *San Antonio Daily Herald*, Dec. 20, 1868, Jan. 7, 1869.

Bass took his team downriver past San Elizario and Fort Quitman, making the dash through the canyons to the east in safety. Banks of lowering clouds were draping a gray caul of snow over the mountains as the coach left Eagle Springs for Fort Davis. Ice froze in the ruts of the trail even as it passed.

Two days later line agent Henry Morrell set out from El Paso on another coach with his driver and a lone passenger. Together they traced the road southward and to the east, confident that all was well on the route ahead. In such bitterly cold weather the Apaches were certain to be sheltering in some hidden valley and keeping close to their fires.

They had entered the long canyon that ran east from Eagle Springs and were only nine miles out from Van Horn's Wells when the mules shied at something that lay in the road. The driver swore as they broke stride and then began to gag on his morning coffee. The object was a battered human head. He halted the rig and Morrell dismounted to inspect the grisly piece of debris. He then joined the ashen-faced driver on the box as they urged the skittish mules past it.

The coach rolled on with all three men nervously scanning the brush and rocks to the sides of the road. A short distance to the east they found a severed arm, and not far beyond lay the body belonging to it. The Mescaleros' knives and the wolves who followed after had reduced it to a poor, tattered thing, but the line agent recognized the few shreds of clothing that littered the ground nearby. James Bass was dead.

They found the stage nearly half a mile from the road. Bloodstains marred the interior and arrows jutted from the side panels. Hubbell's slipper lay on the ground, but there was no sign of his body. Morrell attempted to search the area but withdrew and headed for Fort Davis when several groups of Apaches appeared.[6]

Upon arriving at the post he met Jim Spears and reported what he had found. Spears immediately requested an escort from the fort commander and headed west with a coach and driver to visit the ambush site. They had gone only thirty miles when the troopers' mounts began to lag from fatigue. Grain had

---

[6] *Galveston News*, Feb. 9, 1869; *San Antonio Daily Express*, Jan. 22, 24, 1869; *San Antonio Daily Herald*, Jan. 16, 19, Feb. 2, 1869; Jack Shipman, "Fort Davis and Indians," *Voice of the Mexican Border* 1 (Dec., 1933): 172–73.

been scarce at the fort that winter and they were in bad condition from poor feed. Spears told the escort to turn back and continued on his own.

By the time he reached El Muerto, his driver was openly opposed to continuing the expedition. The stationkeeper took malicious delight in assuring him that "there was no danger now . . . it might be eight or ten days before another driver would be killed." Spears calmed his anxieties and they warily drove on to enter the canyon and find the splintered wreckage where Morrell had left it. There was still no sign of Hubbell, and the wolves had been back at Bass's remains, leaving hardly enough to bury. Seeing that there was nothing left to salvage and despairing of ever finding Hubbell, the Texans headed back for Fort Davis. From that day on, the notch in the mountains west of Van Horn's Wells would be known as Bass Canyon.[7]

The loss of so prominent a figure as Hubbell and the sheer, animal ferocity displayed in the murder of Bass appalled men throughout the state. Ficklin had been pondering methods of protecting his coaches for a long time. Even before the news of this latest outrage reached San Antonio, he had announced an innovation on the route.

"There is one consolation, however, for future travelers on the stage line," reported the *Express*. "The proprietor having heard of gunboats running in a heavy sea . . . has concluded to iron-clad his stages. Kioways nor Comanches, outlaw nor renegade, can harm his patrons more—they have only to sit in the coach and await the arrival of relief, plying in the meantime the six Spencers with which each wagon is provided." The journal marveled that "the driver may be killed, mules run off, but the unharmed traveler has only to sit in his crennellated fortress and bid defiance to all the red men who attack."[8]

Little else was heard of Ficklin's mule-drawn juggernauts, and the silence of the press suggests that the experiment was painfully short-lived. The extra weight of the sheet-iron armor plate must have been enough to stagger even the strongest team

---

[7]Shipman, "Fort Davis and Indians," 172–73. Accounts of this incident varied. The author's version is a composite of them all.

[8]*San Antonio Daily Express*, Feb. 5, 1869; *San Antonio Daily Herald*, Jan. 7, 1869.

of Missouri-bred jacks, and such a coach was certain to bog down on muddy roads or at sandy river crossings.

Ficklin could not be blamed for taking an unconventional approach to his problems, for as the month of January continued, things got worse. An attempted mutiny among the troops posted at Pecos Station threatened the line's property briefly before it was quelled. Three days later a winter storm piled snow drifts high from Fort Davis east to Concho Station. To the south, rain left all the rivers running high, slowing travel to a crawl above San Antonio. Somehow the coaches made it through on the twentieth and twenty-seventh, only slightly behind time. The *Express* proudly claimed that "the El Paso Mail can only be stopped by the public enemy—the Indian, and only by actually killing the driver." Sadly enough, it was one of Ficklin's drivers who was soon listed as a public enemy by the army. On January 24, John Lutz allegedly stopped his rig between Camp Melvin and Fort Stockton and raped his woman passenger. The fort's commander issued orders for his arrest, but the records are silent on the outcome of the incident.[9]

Despite the turmoil, Ficklin bore ahead with his ambitious plans for the company. the postmaster general had granted an extension to the existing mail contract. The new leg connected San Antonio and El Paso with Fort Smith, Arkansas, by way of Fort Griffin, Fort Belknap, Jacksboro, Fort Richardson, and Sherman on a 625-mile weekly route. The terminus at Fort Smith was linked to St. Louis by another line.[10]

Ficklin acted quickly to support the company's expansion. On January 30 he purchased a 640-acre tract on the south bank of the Middle Concho, thereby gaining clear title to the site of his headquarters station and securing ample room for the construction of additional buildings. Contractors were summoned from Bexar and skilled workers came in from the German settlements that dotted the hill country to the south. New corrals and

---

[9] Grover C. Ramsey, "Camp Melvin, Crockett County, Texas," *West Texas Historical Association Yearbook* 37 (Oct., 1961): 138–40.

[10] *San Antonio Daily Herald*, Mar. 3, 12, 16, 1869; *San Antonio Daily Express*, Jan. 24, 1869. The postmaster general's report for 1869 made no mention of Ficklin in connection with any of these routes.

houses appeared. Wagon shops, paint, wheelwright, harness, and blacksmith sheds sprang up as well. Warehouses held grain and food stocks, in addition to spare items of equipment for the coaches and stations. A commissary provided meals and dry goods for travelers and expressmen alike. Hay contractors piled giant ricks of forage in the sheltered lees of the eight-foot corral walls while the stone masons hastened to finish their work. Local ranchers drove in small herds of beef cattle and other stockmen provided fresh mules and horses. The station began to turn into a bustling village.[11]

Ficklin could use all the help he could get in maintaining the new line between Fort Concho and the Pass. There were legions of details to anticipate and deal with on both that route and the other leg linking the line to Fort Smith. Although the expansion might well bring a jump in revenues, any tardiness of service or failure to deliver the mail would also earn the company a staggering load of government fines. Experienced men in the express business were at a premium on the frontier. Hostlers, guards, and drivers could be found at decent wages, but there was a continuing need for men with organizational ability, and the contractor was always alert for those with such a skill.[12]

A valuable new hand for the company came down from Kansas, where he had been scouting for the cavalry during General Sheridan's campaign against the Cheyennes. James H. White was a twenty-two-year-old Virginian. A veteran of Lee's army, he had drifted west at the war's end, driving cattle and fighting Indians by turns. Early in 1869 he joined Ficklin's line to serve as his forage agent on the road between Fort Concho and Fort Quitman. Although White's job was less glamorous than those of Spears and McLeod, it exposed him to his full share of danger and fatigue as his wagon trains rolled up and down the line in an unceasing effort to keep both the men and animals stationed at the lonely relay posts well supplied.[13]

[11] Mary Bain Spence, "The Story of Benficklin, First County Seat of Tom Green County, Texas," *West Texas Historical Association Yearbook* 22 (Oct., 1946): 28–31; Grace Bitner, "Early History of the Concho Country and Tom Green County," *West Texas Historical Association Yearbook* 9 (Oct., 1933): 9.

[12] Bitner, "History of the Concho Country," 9.

[13] "El Paso Pioneers' Sketchbook," Southwestern Collection, University of Texas at El Paso Library, 63–64.

Few people except veteran stagers or army quartermaster officers could appreciate just how big a job White had tackled. During the Civil War the Union army had settled on a standard ration of 14 pounds of hay and 9 to 12 pounds of grain for each mule or horse per day. By conservative estimate there were at least 150 animals kept at all the stations between Fort Concho and the Rio Grande. That meant the expenditure of 3,450 pounds of forage each day, or more than fifty-one tons each month.[14]

It was not an easy matter to procure and distribute that much feed. The amount sent out on the road had to be supplemented by a large reserve stock as well as adequate supplies for the animals that remained at Concho Station. The army computed that fifteen hundred tons of hay would break down for storage into eight stacks, each 230 feet long, 28 feet high, and 18 feet wide at the base. A hundred wagons would be required to haul it. Under ideal conditions a healthy six-mule team might be able to pull a four-thousand-pound load twenty miles each day. This meant that on a journey of twenty-eight days, an entire wagon full of forage would be required to feed each team in the train. Although the pasturage available en route might reduce some of this daily requirement, a significant amount of the load carried by each supply train had to be devoted to feed for its own animals. Even without the constant harassment by the Indians and the obstacles posed by rough roads and capricious weather conditions, James White faced an uphill battle to keep the feed troughs filled.[15]

Ben Ficklin put his new employees to work after a final check on the existing operations and left Concho Station on February 1 with the first mail bound for Fort Smith. He spent two weeks on the journey, buying stock and mustering workmen to build stations and repair the road. The towns along the route were uniformly pleased about the service and its portent for the future. The region had not known such excitement since the opening days of the old Butterfield mail in 1858.[16]

[14] John G. Moore, "Mobility and Strategy in the Civil War," in *Military Analysis of the Civil War*, 109–10.

[15] Ibid.; *San Antonio Daily Herald*, Nov. 12, 1868.

[16] *San Antonio Daily Express*, Jan. 24, 1869; *San Antonio Daily Herald*, Mar. 3, 12, 16, 1869.

After making additional arrangements in Fort Smith, Ficklin rode back to Texas and arrived in San Antonio late in March. Things had been surprisingly quiet in his absence, although the Comanches had paid another visit to Kickapoo Springs late in February. They lost the skirmish, and the Texans scalped a dead brave, sending his hair to San Antonio, where it was proudly displayed over the bar in Pat Caulfield's saloon.[17]

March passed with a strange tranquility. Ficklin was occupied with supervising the construction of a large stable for the company's stock and equipment in San Antonio. The building stood on the lot adjoining the south side of Vance and Brothers General Mercantile, directly across from the Menger Hotel. On the other side of the plaza stood the army quartermaster depot in the roofed-over ruins of the Alamo. The February mails had come in and departed with pleasing regularity, and news of a gold strike in the mountains near El Paso had helped to restore the volume of passenger traffic bound for the west after the shock of the January killings had faded.[18]

The air of tranquility endured through March, with few noteworthy events breaking the routine for drivers and line agents. At Fort Concho, surgeon William Notson obtained the skull of one of the three braves killed at Kickapoo Springs and shipped it to the United States Army Medical Museum in Washington, D.C., via the stage line. The carefully packed skull was one piece of freight that Ficklin's men were always delighted to list on their waybills.[19]

The *Daily Express*, not to be outdone by its rival, the *Daily Herald*, sent a correspondent westward on the stage line that April, and he furnished Ficklin with another testimonial on the mixed delights of stage travel. "Wanderer" found the journey entertaining, although the food served at the relay stations left much to be desired. The only real disappointment of the entire trip occurred when he reached El Paso and found that the celebrated gold strike was a myth. Ficklin's agent in town shook his

---

[17] *San Antonio Daily Express*, Mar. 2, Apr. 7, 1869.
[18] *San Antonio Daily Herald*, Feb. 21, 25, 27, Mar. 2, 1869; *San Antonio Daily Express*, Mar. 3, 21, 1869.
[19] Stephen W. Schmidt, ed., *Fort Concho Medical History, 1869 to 1872*, 9–11.

head sympathetically and cheerfully sold the correspondent's party return tickets for San Antonio. No one had any idea who had started the rumors that had drawn so many excited adventurers west on the nine coaches that had left Bexar since the news first appeared in the *Express*.[20]

A more shocking revelation soon roused the public in San Antonio. While being held in the Fredericksburg jail, a negro horsethief had confessed to a full slate of crimes. In November he had joined two white men and a fellow black who operated a gang of thieves in Llano County. Donning buckskins and warbonnets, they had ambushed the stage below Kickapoo Springs on the night of the thirtieth. When the wounded driver offered resistance they had dragged him through the brush behind his coach before scalping and mutilating the dying man.

There had been a strong suspicion from the start that outlaws had been Mullen's killers, but the black's confession contained details of a horrifying conspiracy. His gang was supposedly operating over the breadth of the frontier from the Brazos River in Texas to Monterrey, Mexico. When captured, he had been carrying maps showing the location of every station on the mail route. A letter of introduction included in the packet of maps bore the signature of William Haynes, a merchant in the town of Llano. The evidence was damning, and when bands of raiders attacked the stations at Boerne and Comfort on the nineteenth and twenty-first, men in Llano County went looking for Haynes with coils of rope slung from their saddles.[21]

Excitement mounted at Concho Station on April 23 when the Comanches waylaid the coach on the new branch line to the east and captured it. The driver escaped on foot and met one of Ficklin's agents east of the post. They backtracked to find that the Indians had wrecked the coach and paused to barbecue one of the mules. The other lay dead in its harness.

Indian troubles notwithstanding, relations between the company and the army still left much to be desired. A black hostler employed at Kickapoo Springs took a pistol bullet through

[20] *San Antonio Daily Express*, Apr. 8, 14, 16, 25, 1869.
[21] Ibid., Apr. 24, 1869; *San Antonio Daily Herald*, Apr. 24, 1869.

his arm in a dispute with one of the troopers posted there on guard duty. Ficklin was nettled by the army's casual treatment of the affair and was further angered when Captain Charles Hood, the acting post commander at Fort Concho, involved himself in a disagreement between the stage line and a local civilian contractor. Hood threatened to arrest George Needham, an agent at Concho Station, if he did not report to the post headquarters and explain his failure to pay the contractor. Needham's reply to this demand went unrecorded, but it was probably a pungent reprise of Ficklin's earlier response to Major Cram.[22]

It had been a hectic month to follow on the heels of so much trouble in the beginning of the year, and some of its turmoil spilled over into May. On April 21 the Indians had raided the new station at Fort Griffin, taking all the stock. They returned on May 7, and again on the twenty-first, exactly a month after their first strike. Like the other branch line to Eagle Pass, the Fort Smith service was going to be expensive to operate. The raids were bad enough, but it was doubly galling to have the officers at Fort Concho openly charging that the attack on the mail from Fort Griffin in April had been a ruse by the driver to conceal his theft of the cargo.[23]

The wet winter had brought good pasturage to the plains that spring, and the same grass that fattened Ficklin's stock also gave strength to the Comanches' ponies as they ranged down from the Llano Estacado and their sanctuary on the reservation at Fort Sill to the north. By June they were out in full force on the mail road, striking a freight train near Camp Johnston, overrunning the teamsters, and capturing better than a hundred mules. On the seventeenth nearly thirty braves attacked the Head of Concho, stampeding both mail company and army stock in the face of heavy fire from the picket guard at the station. They then swept downriver a short distance to strike a party of travelers, capturing their animals as well. Troops from Fort Con-

[22] Schmidt, *Medical History*, 12; Statement of Jessa Jones, Apr. 21, 1869, Letters Received, Fort McKavett, Tex., RG 98, NARS; Captain C. C. Hood to George Needham, Apr. 8, 1869, Letters Sent, Fort Concho, Tex., RG 98, NARS.

[23] *San Antonio Daily Express*, June 12, 1869; *San Antonio Daily Herald*, July 2, 1869; Schmidt, *Medical History*, 13.

cho pursued them unsuccessfully. Only nine days later the Mescaleros mounted an equally lucrative raid on Barilla Springs.[24]

Despite these interruptions the mail continued to go through on time, "with regularity second only to clockwork," at least until late in the month when the skies opened again as they had in November and continued to loose heavy rains for several weeks. With the roads mired and the rivers running high, the normal two-day run from Concho Station to San Antonio took eight.

The weather and the repeated Indian attacks made Ficklin's perpetually short fuse burn down to a stub. In July he took a Mexican freighter to court on charges of stealing some stock. The jury believed the man when he claimed that he had found the mules roaming free on the plains and ruled in his favor, leaving Ficklin with the court costs and an even worse case of bad humor. His men walked quietly around the Virginian until the mail was running smoothly again between Bexar and the Concho by July 20.[25]

While Ficklin was wasting time in court, his enemies had been causing trouble in the west again. This time they had the unintended aid of the company's erstwhile protectors in a tragic incident at Lipan Springs. The victim, David M. Mason, was another of the young southerners who were attracted to Ficklin's service. Mason had ridden with Mosby's guerrillas during the war and acquired a hunger for adventure. The skills of survival acquired during dozens of clashes with the Yankees in Virginia could not protect him from freakish circumstances.

On the night of July 8, Mason was at Lipan Springs, awaiting the stage from San Antonio so that he could catch a ride to Concho Station. As the time for its arrival drew near, Mason walked down the road in the sultry gloom to flag it down. Pri-

---

[24] *San Antonio Daily Express*, June 12, 1869; *San Antonio Daily Herald*, July 2, 1869.

[25] Schmidt, *Medical History*, 16; *San Antonio Daily Express*, July 6, 16, 1869; *San Antonio Daily Herald*, June 11, July 6, 14, 17, 18, 20, 1869. Ficklin's conduct in the court case was curious. Samniego, the accused, was widely known in the community, and his possession of the mules under the circumstances related was hardly suspicious. Political or business rivalries may have accounted for the clash with Ficklin.

vate George Washington, Company B, Ninth Cavalry, was riding guard on the driver's box as the rig came up the trail. Suddenly a shouting figure loomed up by the roadside. When the man tried to swing aboard the coach, Washington swung his Spencer carbine down and fired blindly. The .50-caliber slug tore through Mason's chest and threw him to the ground. He lived for a little over an hour before the wound claimed him. An investigation followed the incident, but under the circumstances the army felt that the soldier could not be blamed for his action. Ficklin had lost another good man to chance.[26]

There was more trouble on the road beyond Fort Concho that month, and though Ficklin's men were not the only ones involved, the entire chain of events bore worrying implications for the company. On July 26, Lieutenant Samuel Armstrong and a small detachment from the Forty-first Infantry at Fort Stockton were camped twenty-three miles west of the Head of Concho when the Comanches attacked and ran off their horses, leaving their wagons stranded by the road. Armstrong reported that "one person in the garb of a citizen, or dark clothes, mounted on a fine horse with elegant trappings rode along the hillside or slope in full view of our camp at a distance of some 800 or 1,000 yards, as if reviewing the operation, and afterwards rode slowly away to the main party." It was not the first time that white men or Mexicans had been seen in company with the raiders, and the possibility that the Indians were operating under some purposeful direction was disturbing.[27]

Armstrong's mysterious rider made another appearance soon afterward when a driver known as Dutch Jake was overtaken in the same area by a mixed band of Comanches and Mexicans led by a white. The stranger rode alongside the coach on a superb black horse and told Jake and his guard that if they abandoned the rig without a fight they would not be harmed. At the first clump of brush they passed the two men jumped clear of the

[26] *San Antonio Daily Express*, July 21, 1869; Capt. James Morse to Commanding Officer, Aug. 3, 1869, Letters Received, Fort Concho, Tex., RG 98, NARS; A. J. Sowell, *Early Settlers and Indian Fighters of Southwest Texas*, 2:751.

[27] Schmidt, *Medical History*, 16; Lt. Samuel E. Armstrong to Post Adjutant, July 29, 1869, Letters Received, Fort Concho, Tex., RG 98, NARS.

coach and took cover. The warriors seized the stage's reins and drove it off to be looted. Jake and his partner walked in to the nearest station to report the attack. The coach was later recovered and brought back to Concho Station for repairs. Such bands of thieves would not often be so chivalrous.[28]

The trouble continued as groups of up to 150 braves were seen roaming the country beyond the Head of Concho. On August 5 a war party jumped an army courier at the same place Armstrong had been robbed and almost ran the rider to ground before he escaped. In San Antonio the *Express* worried because "fears are entertained that some of these stations may be attacked and broken up by the Indians, and that the stage business will be seriously interrupted on the El Paso road if no movement is made by the military authorities on a large scale."[29]

Ben Ficklin and the army were confronting the practitioners of an ancient and dishonorable trade on the plains. The whites and Mexicans who rode with the Indians formed the brotherhood of the Comancheros. Since the mid-seventeenth century bands of traders had been venturing out from the New Mexico settlements to contact the tribes that roamed the bison country to the east. Liquor, guns, and trade goods were exchanged for cattle, horses, and slaves in a commerce that mushroomed when the Anglo-Saxon settlers began pushing westward into Texas.

The business hit its peak in the years immediately following the Civil War. Both the frontier settlements and the cattle herds that trailed west from Texas to New Mexico offered rich prizes to the Comanches and their Kiowa allies. In June, 1867, the *Santa Fe New Mexican* cited the loss of a thousand head of cattle from a single herd that was attacked near the territory's border with Texas. A year later it recorded the capture of three other herds on the same site. Pioneer rancher and traildriver Charles Goodnight estimated that in only a few years the Indians stole at least four hundred thousand head of horses and cattle from the Texans for sale to the Comancheros at such desolate rendezvous as Quita-

[28] Sowell, *Early Settlers*, 2:746–47. Sowell's account was based upon an interview with Charles Peters, who drove for Ficklin from Dec., 1868, through June, 1869. "Dutch Jake" was a personal acquaintance.

[29] *San Antonio Daily Express*, Aug. 10, 1869.

que, Las Lenguas, Las Tecovas, and Tascosa. Captives seized in raids on the settlements or emigrant trains also figured in their sordid dealings with such scoundrels as Jose Pied Tafoya, Juan Trujillo, Julian Baca, and literally hundreds of others whose names were never recorded. Usually the Comancheros were content to let the tribes bring their booty to them, but on occasion renegade whites and Mexicans would ride with their customers on raids and select the merchandise they wanted while the Indians did the fighting. For a man without a conscience, it could be a very lucrative enterprise.[30]

Even without these predatory merchants in the field, warfare in the region was unceasing. The next blow came from the Mescaleros. On August 13, Jim Spears was conferring with the station chief at El Muerto when four braves ran between the corral and the grazing mule herd. Despite firing from the station's guards, they stampeded the animals and drove them away into the mountains. By that time the company had lost a hundred mules since the first of the year. The line was crippled at El Muerto until a fresh herd could be driven in from El Paso or Fort Davis.[31]

One of the men charged with replacing the stock on that section of the road was another prewar veteran of the express business. Charles Bain had emigrated to Texas from Missouri during the 1850s and began driving a stage between Hempstead and Austin in 1858. He later handled the route between Austin and San Antonio with "Pap" Howard, another celebrated jehu among the fraternity in Texas. Bain was not content merely to handle a team, and eventually he owned the company. By the late 1860s he was one of Ficklin's chief lieutenants on the El Paso contract. Bain ranged up and down the road between Bexar and the Rio Grande, troubleshooting the line's operations. The first public reference to his role with the mail company came on September 7, when the *Herald* noted his arrival in town from El

[30]The best study of the Comancheros is in J. Evetts Haley, "The Comanchero Trade," *Southwestern Historical Quarterly* 38 (Jan., 1935): 157–76. Also of interest is Jack D. Rittenhouse, *Maverick Tales*, 135–54.

[31]*San Antonio Daily Express*, Aug. 21, 1969; *San Antonio Daily Herald*, Aug. 21, 31, 1869.

Paso. He was probably seeking more stock to replace the recent losses.[32]

Bain would have been wise to buy all the mules he could find at any price, for he had no sooner finished his business and begun driving the animals north for Concho Station when trouble flared again. By September 17 the Comanches had raided the station at Fort Mason twice in two weeks and had taken every horse and mule in the corral. The animals were doubtless already on the trail for New Mexico. Local stock thieves did not present too great a threat to the company's animals, for Ficklin had widely publicized his adoption of a specific set of brands for his teams. A wavy *M* appeared on the left shoulder or left side of each animal's neck, and a device resembling a Celtic cross was burned into the hide of its left hip. Such markings could not be easily altered or effaced, and their publication in the *Daily Herald* guaranteed that they would be easily recognized.[33]

Ficklin was taking other measures to eliminate some of the threats to his property. On November 1 he purchased the entire tract of land surrounding Kickapoo Springs and served eviction notices on the riffraff that had been plaguing his men at the station. In a brace of letters to the commander at Fort McKavett he identified the chief troublemaker in the settlement. David Young Walker had been responsible for turning the location into "the most notoriously infamous place in Texas . . . the scene of uninterrupted drunken rows . . . the rendezvous of outlaws." The contractor offered to give the army a permanent lease on the property for the grand amount of one penny if it would consent to post a standing guard detail there.[34]

Another major problem confronted Ficklin as winter edged closer. In August and September the Indians or their Comanchero allies had set widely spaced grass fires that destroyed most of the pasturage within a fifty-mile radius of Concho Station.

[32] Wilma Roberts, comp., *1880 Census of 13-County West Texas Area*, 24; *San Angelo Standard*, Mar. 24, 1894; Mary Bain Spence, correspondence with author, July 2, 1979; *San Antonio Daily Herald*, Sept. 7, 1869.

[33] Ibid., Sept. 25, 1869.

[34] Benjamin F. Ficklin to Brig. Gen. Ranald S. Mackenzie, Nov. 9, 12, 1869, Letters Received, Fort McKavett, Tex., RG 98, NARS.

Even with the reserve stocks of hay and grain on hand, it would be a strain to keep the line supplied with forage through the cold months ahead. Between the fires and the perpetual danger to grass cutters from Indian attacks, hay would become both scarce and expensive. Mules worked on reduced rations could put the coaches well behind schedule if they weakened or fell sick. There was little to do but buy more grain and scour the counties to the south for other feed supplies.[35]

Ficklin was not the only one trying to prepare for the winter as the nights grew chill. The Mescaleros had long considered barbecued mule a delicacy, and late in December they returned to El Muerto to replenish their larders. Fortunately, Jim Spears was on hand at the station, and he rallied Charles Babcock's staff to repel the attack. The Apaches almost succeeded in driving off the stock before Spears's determined sortie forced them to retreat empty-handed.

At virtually the same time as the raid on El Muerto, a small band of hostiles descended on Camp Johnston and ran off the company's mules as well as the cavalry guard's mounts. They had not counted on meeting so fierce a defense. "The soldiers retired to their stockade and burnt powder with a vim," chortled the *Herald*, "while the station keeper, 'Old Jimmy,' sallied forth, and charging the Indians alone, recaptured the mail company stock. . . . Too much cannot be said in praise of the brave old mountaineer, well known as 'Old Jimmy' for the gallantry he displayed. We hope Major Ficklin will find it to the interest of the Mail Company, to promote 'Old Jimmy,' as he has certainly won a brevet."[36]

Ben Ficklin was not one to award praise lightly, but with men like these on his payroll he knew that his enemies' knives would soon be blunted. It had been a costly year in both lives and property for his organization, but he had won another round with the calendar and the Indians. The new decade gleamed ahead as brightly as the brass sidelamps on a new Concord.

[35] Schmidt, *Medical History*, 19.

[36] *San Antonio Daily Herald*, Jan. 3, 1870; *San Antonio Daily Express*, Feb. 24, 1870.

CHAPTER 13

"Charges against the Service"

Bᴇɴ Fɪᴄᴋʟɪɴ probably celebrated New Year's Day in Austin, for his business kept him in the state's capital for most of January and February as he prepared for a crucial trip to Washington, D.C., and an encounter with a new set of foes. His innate optimism was doubtless tempered with some reservations as he watched the 1870s open. A decade before, he had been working himself to exhaustion for an employer who could muster grand dreams for himself, but little gratitude for the men who made them a reality for him. Now Ficklin was a partner and active director of a stage company that ran for over a thousand miles to link the Southwest with the rest of the nation. Despite his clashes with the army and continuing struggles against the Indians, he had established his business on a sound footing and won the respect and admiration of fellow Texans.

In the opening days of 1870 he had a strong team and a sound rig, but the road still held too many blind turns and deep holes to allow him to slacken his hold on the reins for a moment. His possession of the mail contract was disputed by far more powerful enemies employing subtler weapons than he had ever encountered before. The El Paso Mail Company had become a pawn in the game of Reconstruction politics, and Ficklin found himself with the most improbable allies imaginable in the bitter atmosphere of intrigue that permeated public life in the postwar years.

By 1870 Texas remained a conquered province after nearly five years of Union occupation. The Republican-dominated government was badly rent by a power struggle between the radical followers of Edmund J. Davis and the supporters of ex-Governor Andrew J. Hamilton. In late 1869 the two men ran against each other for the governorship, and through blatant manipulation of the black vote Davis won the election.[1]

On January 8, 1870, Davis began his new administration, and Ben Ficklin found that he was already deeply in trouble. In El Paso, W. W. Mills had held the post of customs collector and generally ran the town's political affairs as if it were his private Republican fiefdom. Mills was Hamilton's son-in-law, and when President Grant threw his support to the successful Davis in the gubernatorial race, Mills lost both his federal job and his position of dominance in El Paso politics.

Mills was desperate for an issue that would put his name before the public again in a favorable light, and he was keen to punish his Republican opposition in El Paso. Even before the elections and his banishment from the customs house, he had begun sniping at the mail company. As early as May, 1868, Mills and his cronies were complaining about erratic service on the route. Ficklin and Sawyer covered their flank by allying themselves with Albert J. Fountain, Mills's bitterest enemy in El Paso. Fountain had induced a former clerk of the customs station to publicly charge Mills with smuggling and misappropriation of government funds.

Frederick P. Sawyer allegedly commissioned a team of lawyers to assemble more evidence against Mills in El Paso in the spring of 1869. Sawyer planned to force Mills out of his customs position by presenting the evidence to the secretary of the treasury.[2] Mills responded by journeying to Washington with plans for a campaign that would destroy Ficklin and Sawyer's contract while embarrassing the Grant and Davis administrations. In company with James A. Zabriskie, El Paso district attorney, he won a hearing before the Joint Select Congressional Committee on Re-

[1] W. C. Nunn, *Texas Under the Carpetbaggers*, 3–14; Charles W. Ramsdell, "Reconstruction in Texas," *Columbia University Studies in History, Economics, and Public Law* 26 (1910): 55–287; Carl H. Moneyhon, *Republicanism in Reconstruction Texas*, 114–23.

[2] *San Antonio Daily Herald*, Apr. 15, May 8, 27, 1868; *San Antonio Daily Express*, May 5, 7, 8, 14, 16, July 23, 1868, Jan. 26, 27, Feb. 11, 1869; C. L. Sonnichsen, *Pass of the North*, 183–86; J. Morgan Broaddus, *The Legal Heritage of El Paso*, 89–94; W. W. Mills, *Forty Years at El Paso, 1858–1898*, 137–38.

trenchment and began an open battle with the mail company.

There is no reference to Ficklin's presence at the hearings, but Mills was confronted by Sawyer and his associates: Jere Black, a Maryland attorney; Judge George W. Paschal, a Hamilton Republican from Houston; and newly elected congressmen Edward Degener and William T. Clark, two Davis men. Evidently, Mills had enemies even among the ranks of his own faction of the party.

Appearing before Senator James W. Patterson and his fellow committee members, Mills and Zabriskie charged that the mail company had not only failed to fulfill the original terms of its contract, it had also extended it by fraudulent means and collected excessive sums of money for a miserable record of service. Their accusations specified that only ten of thirty-seven scheduled mails arrived in El Paso during a given period. The mail company had allegedly bribed the postmasters along the route to certify the arrivals of the missing mails. Between August, 1867, and January, 1869, charged Mills, the company had parlayed the original $33,000 annual compensation into payments of $333,617 from the government. This was done by pledging to "increase and expedite" service while adding the branch routes to Eagle Pass, Presidio del Norte, and Fort Smith, Arkansas. None of the secondary lines were opened to competitive bidding prior to their assignment to Ficklin and Sawyer, charged Mills.[3]

In his memoirs Mills claimed to have administered a smashing defeat to Sawyer and reduced him to tears in questioning before the committee. The only other published account of the hearings gave a different picture of what took place. The committee eventually decided in favor of Mills and Zabriskie to some extent, for the *Weekly Austin Republican* of May 11, 1870, summarized the findings against the mail company and noted that the committee recommended annulment of the contract. Mills recorded that the line was fined and suffered a major reduction in its contract fee. Surprisingly, the *Report of the Joint Select*

[3] Mills, *Forty Years*, 139–40.

Committee on Retrenchment, published in February, 1870, made no reference at all to the Mills-Sawyer case.[4]

The accusations made by Mills were supposedly the first in a long series of scandals that rocked the government periodically over the next several decades, yet Postmaster General John A. Creswell's *Annual Report* for 1870 made no reference to the incident. Eli Bates, Ficklin's agent, was still listed as the contractor on Route 8530 from San Antonio to El Paso, with the addition of branch lines to Eagle Pass and Presidio del Norte. An extension to Fort Smith, Arkansas, was granted on January 20, 1869, with total compensation listed at $235,286 on February 1, 1869.

The records of the period are mystifyingly devoid of references to Mills's great crusade and the mail line's disgrace. The poorly documented charges raised by Mills in the winter of 1869–70 simmered until 1872, when Joseph C. McKibbin, a disgruntled mail contractor and aspiring politician, published an article in the Washington *Patriot* that characterized the conduct of the government and mail contractors as "postal plunder." The resulting investigation revealed some evidence of collusion between the expressmen and the Post Office Department, but Postmaster General Creswell was exonerated of any wrongdoing. Sawyer was mentioned briefly in the report, but no evidence or charges were cited against him.[5]

Two years later Congress responded to more charges of abuses in the contract system with another probe of the Post Office Department, but nothing of importance could be proven. In the spring of 1876 the Committee on the Post-Office and Post-

[4] *Weekly Austin Republican*, May 11, 1870; U.S. Congress, Senate, *Report of the Joint Select Committee on Retrenchment Inquiring into the Expenditures in All the Branches of the Service of the United States together with the Testimony Relating to the Same*, House of Representatives, Feb. 21, 1870, Senate Report 47, 41st Cong., 2d sess., 1870.

[5] Marshall H. Cushing, *The Story of Our Post Office*, 32; Nathan Miller, *The Founding Finaglers*, 290–94; Dorothy G. Fowler, *The Cabinet Politician: The Postmasters General, 1829–1909*, 142–61; U.S. Congress, House, *Annual Report of the Postmaster General, 1870*, 41st Cong., 2d sess., 1870, House Exec. Doc. 314, pp. 396–97; U.S. Congress, House, *Management of the Post-Office Department*, 44th Cong., 1st sess., 1875, House Report 814, pp. xix–xx; Letterbooks of the Postmaster General, Series 2: Records of the Immediate Office of the Postmaster General, Letters Sent, July 21, 1850–Aug. 18, 1882, RG 28, NARS.

Roads staged yet another investigation of the department's management. Out of a welter of conflicting testimony and dissenting
minority reports from the committee findings themselves, a few
facts emerged in sharp relief.

Former Postmaster General Creswell acknowledged that all
of the Sawyer-Ficklin routes in Texas had undergone reductions
in payment following the charges made by Mills, but the total
reductions of $90,432 had been economy measures and not pun-
ishment for defrauding the government. Judge Paschal testified
that Mills and Zabriskie had initially tried to join the Ficklin and
Sawyer partnership but were rebuffed. Their accusations were
simply a means of gaining revenge. Then Paschal dropped a genuine bombshell. In response to a question from the committee,
he explained that several entries in the now deceased Sawyer's
account books that totaled $4,500 made in April, 1869, were
payments to the Washington law firm of Dent and Page for certain unspecified services. Frederick T. Dent, the attorney concerned, was President Grant's brother-in-law and a member in
residence of the executive household.[6]

Perhaps sensing that they were skirting territory that was as
yet best left unexplored, all of the committee members moved
on from the possible link to the White House and pursued other
lines of inquiry. There was still enough dirt to be uncovered.
Francis C. Taylor, Ficklin's chief subordinate on the El Paso line,
charged that John L. Routt, Creswell's Second Assistant Postmaster General, was an extortionist. Between 1871 and 1872
alone, claimed Taylor, Sawyer had been forced to pay Routt and
several other men of influence nearly $50,000 to prevent the loss
of his contracts.[7]

Investigations of the Post Office Department continued
through the 1870s and reached a climax in the scandals of the
next decade. In 1881, U.S. Attorney A. M. Gibson compiled a
report that detailed the history of the so-called star contracts
since their origin in 1845 and summarized the attending corruption. Ficklin and Sawyer were never mentioned in his study.

[6] *Management of the Post-Office Department*, xi, xvii, 490–91, 638; William S.
McFeely, *Grant*, 300–303.
[7] *Management of the Post-Office Department*, 465–70.

Twentieth-century scholars who examined the contract scandals found great voids in the public records. In the 1950s one historian determined that by order of Congress the Post Office Department had destroyed its files concerning the questionable routes and other types of contracts with private mail carriers for the period 1870–1914. The corruption surrounding these routes ran so deeply through the government by then that Congress may have preferred to have the entire issue safely put beyond the reach of the inquisitive.[8]

The clash between the stage line and W. W. Mills demonstrated nothing else if it did not show that the denizens of the Potomac River country could be just as predatory as those of the Middle Concho. Even honest men had to play the game by the rules that prevailed among those who held power in the government. Ficklin seemed remarkably unaffected by his supposed defeat by Mills upon his arrival back in San Antonio that May. The *Daily Herald* remarked that "he looks like he had been enjoying 'chicken pie' or something else not bad to take."[9]

It did not take Ficklin long to learn of what had been happening in his absence. The months past had spared the line any jarring losses like those of the preceding year, but there had been a steady succession of incidents to keep the frontier on edge.

Concho Station suffered a raid early in January, with the Comanches taking stock right out of Ficklin's main corrals. In mid-February two war parties struck in concert at Loyal Valley and Mason, and a third murdered a settler within sight of Fort Concho and the mail station. The raiders had carefully skirted the company's stables and corrals and laid their ambush without arousing either the mules or the packs of greyhounds that Ficklin kept for hunting antelope. The braves had made their point.[10]

[8] A. M. Gibson, *Report to the Attorney General on the Star Mail Service by A. M. Gibson, Esq., Assistant Attorney of the United States*; William S. Wallace, "Short-Line Staging in New Mexico," *New Mexico Historical Review* 26 (Apr., 1951): 92.

[9] *San Antonio Daily Herald*, May 14, 1870. The mail scandals have continued to arouse investigators' interest. See J. Marvin Klotsche, "The Star Route Cases," *Mississippi Valley Historical Review* 21 (Dec., 1935): 407–418; and Louise Horton, "The Star Route Conspiracies," *Texana* 7 (Fall, 1969): 220–33.

[10] Stephen W. Schmidt, ed., *Fort Concho Medical History, 1869 to 1872*, 23–24;

The tempo of the raids mounted as other bands struck to the west at Camp Johnston and to the east at Mountain Pass on the Arkansas road. Soon afterward, a party of 150 braves circled Kickapoo Springs and caught one of Ficklin's men on the trail, leaving his scalped body where the next coach was certain to find it. There was also a spate of thefts from the mail bags by a driver. Money, a brace of pistols, and a pair of boots bound for Fort Quitman were lost before the pilferer was discovered and left the country to escape Ficklin's wrath.[11]

Despite the dangers of travel and such minor internal problems, the mail company and its employees remained popular in San Antonio. Ficklin's contract had helped bring new prosperity in the war's wake by pumping hard money into the economy. "Although fewer people went hungry than in more settled and supposedly more advanced states of society," recalled driver Henry Daly, "the only employers of labor of any consequence in western Texas who paid regularly in hard money were Adams and Wickes, freighters and government contractors, and the Ben Ficklin stage line."[12]

They earned every penny of their pay that angry spring on the Middle Concho. Jim Spears was continually ranging the line to solve problems and clear obstacles before they threw the rigs off schedule. His lean frame became a familiar sight to the warriors who scouted the road from the bluffs along Centralia Draw, and they did not wait for long to test him again.

"In April Comanches attacked the stage at a spot between Fort Concho and Fort Stockton," Spears later related to a journalist. "The driver was A. J. Bobo, with two colored soldiers aboard as guards. As the Indians approached, I fired my Winchester. The Indians began riding around and yelling." Spears was not impressed by either the attackers or his escorts. "During the fight one of the colored guards was so paralyzed with fright that his gun dropped from his hands without a shot being

---

Joan D. Stevens, "Fort Concho Guardian of the Conchos, 1867–1874" (M.A. thesis, Angelo State University, San Angelo, Texas, 1975), 55.

[11] *San Antonio Daily Herald*, Feb. 24, Mar. 1, 1870.

[12] Henry W. Daly, "A Dangerous Dash Down Lancaster Hill," *Frontier Times* 30 (Apr.–June, 1953): 167.

fired. The other Negro soldier, after shooting once at an angle of forty-five degrees upward, subsided into the interior of the stage, showing a large surface of white about the eyes and mouth. None of us were hit in the encounter, and the Indians soon rode off." While the troopers' timidity was hardly typical of their comrades in the Ninth Cavalry, it still served to reinforce the latent antagonism that persisted between the expressmen and the black soldiers.[13]

Escorted or not, the coaches continued to make the run up the Concho to the Pecos against mounting interference. A gang of fifteen warriors jumped Henry Daly's rig just west of Flat Rock Holes and chased it all the way into Pecos Station, closing to within fifty yards of the coach at one point in the pursuit. At the end of the chase a wheel was about to fall off the front axle and the mules were covered in lather and blood. To Daly and his shaken passengers, the desolate little outpost looked as welcome as the main plaza in San Antonio.[14]

Ben Ficklin learned of Spears's and Daly's encounters soon after his May arrival in Bexar, which coincided with the climax of troubles that hectic season. Raids at the Fort Phantom Hill and Loyal Valley stations were followed by an audacious piece of effrontery by the Mescaleros. On May 25 four Apaches appeared at Barilla Springs and confronted station herder Domingo Polomio with a demand that he surrender the stock to them. The Mexican and his grazing mules were nearly five hundred yards from the station, and many men would have thought it prudent to cooperate with the braves. Polomio cooly let them ride closer before raising his rifle and opening fire. Vaulting into the saddle of his horse, the vaquero kept shooting into the surprised braves as they milled in confusion. His weapon jammed just as the guards charged forward and drove away the Mescaleros. Polomio calmly herded his animals back into the corral, leaving his attackers to spread the word that Jim Spears was not the only man on the line who could not be bluffed.[15]

    [13]*Galveston Daily News*, May 20, 1877; Herschel Boggs, "A History of Fort Concho" (M.A. thesis, University of Texas at Austin, 1940), 61.
    [14]Daly, "Lancaster Hill," 171–72.
    [15]*San Antonio Daily Herald*, June 7, 1870.

In June a strangely calm spell followed this minor victory, giving Ficklin time to visit Concho Station and check on the progress being made by an old friend and new employee. On March 20 Francis C. Taylor had arrived from Greensborough, Alabama, to take charge of the leg between Concho Station and El Paso. A veteran expressman on the Alabama routes, Taylor brought his wife, sister, and niece to Texas with him. While the newcomer set to work reorganizing the service and putting Ficklin's neglected account books in order, his family brought some of the refinements of civilization to the raw settlement.[16]

Within a short time the Taylor home became the finest residence north of Fredericksburg. Built of stone from the company's nearby quarry, its rooms were large and airy. The parlor boasted a piano and the floor sported a thick Brussels carpet, unlike the packed dirt or canvas sheets that were found in most frontier houses. What really marked the Taylors as people of culture were the shelves of books that lined the parlor's walls. Freely loaned to friends and company employees, the volumes provided a welcome supplement to the newspapers and journals brought in on the stage.

Mrs. Taylor quickly became noted for the quality of her table as well. The family retained a black Union army veteran named Sandy Polite as cook. Polite could astound visitors with the transformations he worked on buffalo and antelope steaks. His greatest triumph was to serve prairie owl in the guise of chicken. Polite probably could have named his salary at the Menger or Nimitz hotels, but he remained at Concho Station to brighten the stay of the company's guests.[17] Actually the Taylors had few rivals in their bid to make the station the region's cultural center. Though the officers of Fort Concho definitely qualified as gentry, many of them were still living in tents as construction proceeded fitfully on the post.

---

[16] *Management of the Post-Office Department*, 462, 470. Taylor's testimony placed his arrival in Texas a full year later than most other accounts of his life.

[17] Mary Bain Spence, "The Story of Benficklin, First County Seat of Tom Green County, Texas," *West Texas Historical Association Yearbook* 22 (Oct., 1946): 31–32; Susan Miles, "Francis Corbett Taylor, 1822–1879—Father of Tom Green County," reference file, Fort Concho Preservation and Museum, San Angelo, Tex.

Another settlement had also sprung up adjacent to the fort and mail station, but it hardly deserved the description of a town or even a village. A miserable collection of picket-log and adobe hovels sprawled along the river. A few honest merchants joined the whiskey peddlers and prostitutes to cater to the appetites of the soldiers and stagemen. Dubbed "San Angela" in a corruption of the Spanish language that mirrored the state of the community's morals, the denizens of the squalid hamlet were lawless. Doctor Notson could stand in the belvedere of his new hospital at night and watch the flash of pistol shots as cards and liquor sparked gun battles in the streets. "Within the last six weeks there has been seven murders in a population of less than a hundred men, women and children all told," he wrote, "and during the residence of the Post Surgeon over one hundred murders have taken place within a radius of ten miles from the Adjutant's office, in a population which has never at any time exceeded two hundred and fifty."[18]

Obviously not all of the killings cited by the doctor took place between white men. The Indians eagerly bid to add their fair share to the homicide rate. Late in July they ambushed a coach east of the post, leaving the driver and guard to escape on foot while they drove off the team. Another war party chased the El Paso stage into the Head of Concho with its boot studded with arrows, and "only the utmost exertions of the mules and the whip of the driver unsparingly applied saved it," the *Herald* breathlessly reported. Less than two weeks later the Indians struck the station itself and captured some stock before the herders drove them away.[19]

The savages chose their victims impartially that summer. Early in September the driver of the eastbound stage halted his nervous team when a reeling, bloodsoaked scarecrow of a man staggered into the road and collapsed. A few days before, he and two companions were returning from a cattle drive into New Mexico when the Comanches ambushed them in Castle Gap. One drover died instantly while another fought his way clear.

[18] J. Evetts Haley, *Fort Concho and the Texas Frontier*, 272–73.
[19] *San Antonio Daily Herald*, Aug. 4, 14, 1870; *Daily Austin Republican*, Aug. 22, 1870.

James Cummings was badly wounded and lost his horse but managed to crawl away and hide from his attackers. Somehow he limped and stumbled south to the mail road. The stage carried him into Fort Concho, but he died of his wounds soon after his arrival.[20]

The post morgue was seldom empty for long that month. On September 30 the mail from Fort Smith ran into thirty Kiowas and Comanches only twenty-two miles from the fort. Driver Alphonse Prairear and a soldier jumped free and escaped into the brush, but another trooper riding inside the coach was killed, scalped, and mutilated. The stage and his body were brought back to the fort, and Doctor Notson counted sixty-eight wounds on the man's body.[21]

Stage travel could hardly be termed a healthy experience that fall, with the bad roads and rough fare of the stations added to the Indian threat, but even as some men were dying on the plains others were boarding a coach to seek a cure for their ills. In one instance the jostling trip to Concho Station proved more beneficial than any treatment that a doctor could offer.

Thirty-two-year-old Orlando M. Smith had survived smallpox in New Orleans and a San Antonio cholera epidemic in 1866 before a lung infection and chronic "bowel stoppage" forced him to leave his clerical job in Bexar to find a healthier climate on the Concho River. His coach left the plaza in front of the Menger Hotel on September 21 and bore north through the hills to Pegleg Crossing on the San Saba, where Smith became too ill to continue the trip. He spent three days in helpless agony from an intestinal obstruction before stationmaster Henry Milam Taylor brought him relief with an injection of mineral oil from an old horse syringe.

Fearing that he might soon die without proper medical care, Smith crawled aboard the next stage for Fort Concho and spent a night in purgatory. "A little after midnight the stage came along and I took passage. Jim Spears, agent for the line, was on the

[20]Grace Bitner, "R. F. Tankersley and Family, Pioneers of the Concho Country," *West Texas Historical Association Yearbook* 20 (Oct., 1944): 105–106; Col. Alvin C. Gillem to Assistant Adj. Gen., Sept. 23, 1870, Letters Sent, Fort Concho, Tex., RG 98, NARS.

[21] *San Antonio Daily Herald*, Oct. 6, 1870.

stage and he drove part of the way to Concho," Smith wrote with a shudder of remembrance. "While he was driving he just put the mules over the road and I was thrown up and down, in fact all over the stage and when I arrived at Fort Concho at 7 P.M. I was so sore that I could not get out of the stage without help."[22]

When Smith left San Antonio he was an emaciated husk of a man, weighing less than a hundred pounds. When he arrived at Fort Concho, Doctor Notson examined him and estimated that he would live for only a few months longer. James Trainer, Smith's friend and the post sutler, actually laid aside lumber and brass trimmings for his coffin. Evidently Spears's rough ride had proved therapeutic, for Smith surprised everyone by thriving. Within a few months he not only was still alive, but also was well enough to return to San Antonio with his strength regained.[23]

While Smith grew stronger, Ben Ficklin arrived and spent several days in October conferring with Taylor on the company's finances before spurring off again to check on his expanded contracts with lines that ran through the Indian Territory and into Kansas. His business empire had grown so large that it barely left him time to visit each division's headquarters before leaving on another circuit of the lines. It was a grinding schedule even for one of Ficklin's energy, but he could take pleasure from the recent bid that had won him another branch route to provide daily service from Sherman, Texas, to the railhead at Neosho, Arkansas, via Fort Gibson. From Neosho, rail service was available to St. Louis.[24]

Ficklin probably took one of those coaches east that fall for a meeting with Sawyer in Washington. Despite the challenges from hostile political factions and the ever-present Indian raids, the company had survived with most of its interests intact. He had assembled an able team of men to supervise the El Paso line and felt that with another round of diligent lobbying they could keep a firm hold on their contracts. As the train bore him across

---

[22] Escal F. Duke, "O. M. Smith—Frontier Pay Clerk," *West Texas Historical Association Yearbook* 45 (1969): 45–50.

[23] Ibid., 51–52.

[24] *Management of the Post-Office Department*, 464; *Daily Austin Republican*, Nov. 4, 5, 1870.

Missouri, a fisherman on Chesapeake Bay daily cast and retrieved his nets, drawing the Virginian's fate up through the green depths and into the chill light of his last new year.

Early in March, 1871, Ficklin and Frederick P. Sawyer finished a day's work amid the offices of Congress and the Post Office Department and went out to dinner in a Georgetown restaurant. It was a pleasant meal until a fish bone became lodged in Ficklin's throat. For the next several days it stubbornly defied all efforts to remove it. On March 10 a doctor tried to ease the gristly splinter free from the inflamed throat membrane. The jagged tip of the bone slipped from his forceps and slashed into an artery. Ben Ficklin drowned in his own blood at the age of forty-three.[25]

Two days later the Masons of Charlottesville, Virginia, buried him next to his parents in Maplewood Cemetery. A simple stone slab bore the inscription: "Our Brother Benjamin F. Ficklin. Born December 18, 1827. Died March 10, 1871. He was the Orphan's Friend." Ficklin's war exploits, his gallant rescue of Jefferson's Monticello, and generous patronage of the town's orphanages led the Richmond *Dispatch* to call him "a remarkable gentleman . . . his virtues made him an honor to mankind." Across the Atlantic the *London Standard* compared the former Confederate agent to one of James Fenimore Cooper's epic heroes of the American frontier.

Certainly few men ever lived through so many adventures in such a brief lifetime. Hardly a basin or range beyond the Missouri had not borne the marks of his passage as surveyor, scout, freighter, and expressman. He had known his share of frustration and defeat, but the same brash elan that had carried him through the Virginia Military Institute won out over the challenges he faced on the frontier. Like Henry Skillman before him, Ficklin knew that never to dare was never to triumph. That simple truth was the axle upon which the wheel of human ambition turned all across the continent. When all the eulogies had

---

[25] Susan Miles and Mary Bain Spence, "Major Ben Ficklin," *West Texas Historical Association Yearbook* 27 (Oct., 1951): 75; Susan Miles, "Ben Ficklin," *San Angelo Standard-Times*, Mar. 14, 1971.

been spoken, surgeon Notson of Fort Concho summed up his legacy best when he called the scattered stations on the westering road "the entering wedge of civilization."

The brave captain had passed over, but his company still mustered on the banks of the Concho. Ficklin's death was a jarring blow to Frank Taylor, who had just completed his first year in command of the El Paso line. Amid a flurry of Indian raids and a typhoid fever epidemic at the nearby post, he had kept the schedules intact and the coaches on the road. His friend's passing was rightfully mourned, but the company hardly faltered. Slaughter Ficklin, the contractor's younger brother, had invested heavily in the business, and he inherited both Ben's $50,000 estate and his interest in the partnership with Sawyer. Thus the upper-level management of the firm remained intact, although both Slaughter Ficklin and Sawyer left the actual direction of the El Paso branch largely in Taylor's hands.[26]

The exigencies of the service permitted little time for mourning the Virginian's loss, and Taylor's hands were soon caught up again in the daily struggles imposed by their race against the clock. Once again Jim Spears was there to set an example in speeding the mail through despite all obstacles. On April 17 the eastern and western coaches met in the early morning hours about six miles east of the picket post at Centralia Station. The two parties halted to feed their teams and confer about conditions on the road. Spears, the two drivers, and a pair of soldiers brewed coffee and talked about the massive storm that had swept through the region only three days before.

They were preparing to start out again when the two troopers spotted an Indian spying on the camp from a nearby clump of brush. Ignoring Spears's warnings, they rushed forward to capture him. At that point thirty other warriors rose from cover and opened fire on them. One man bolted back to the stages while the other took shelter behind a small tree. He was about to be surrounded when Spears stepped out from between the rigs and rushed the braves, his right hand a white blur on the lever of his

---

[26] *Management of the Post-Office Department*, 493, 500.

Winchester. The .44 rimfire rounds swept through the Comanches' ranks like so many hornets, forcing them to retreat while
the frightened soldier ran back to his comrades.[27]

For the next two hours the whites kept up a continual fire
against the Indians, holding them at bay with their repeating
rifles. By the end of the action every man bore bullet or arrow holes in his clothing, but only one of them had been hit, and
that was a minor wound. When the warriors pulled back and
kindled signal fires to summon reinforcements, Spears quickly
got the teams hitched again and put both coaches on the road for
the Head of Concho. One Indian dogged their trail for most of the
way, but they met no more resistance.

Jim Spears won new praise for his daring in this encounter,
but the company continued drawing fire from other quarters.
Complaints persisted over the recurring mail thefts, although
the blame was generally placed on the postmasters and not the
stage drivers. The line did win an enduring enemy on April 24
when attorney James P. Hague climbed on the El Paso stage at
Fort Concho for a wretched passage to the border. The travelers
fought a sandstorm all the way to the Pecos, with Hague losing
his hat and his even disposition to the rasping wind. "In a slow
moving vehicle as a stagecoach, one has to jump up to get in,
jump down to get out, and keep on jumping to stay in," he complained in a letter to his wife. "The speed of the coach depends
upon how frightened the horses are, or how drunk the driver is,
and how many Indians we hope never to meet. Take those little
things into consideration, for it is only by the grace of God that
we arrived with our scalps on."

The trip had been a steady drain on Hague's nerves, and he
arrived in El Paso imbued with the angry conviction that there
must be a better way to travel than by one of Taylor's jolting rigs.
He became the town's leading advocate of the railroads and
deeded a choice tract of land that ran through the settlement to
the newly formed Southern Pacific Railroad in 1873 as a lure to
draw its tracks westward as quickly as possible. Obviously the

[27] Schmidt, *Medical History*, 39; *San Antonio Express*, Apr. 22, 1871.

stage line's contribution to progress in the region was sometimes oblique.[28]

Instead of carping about the hardships of stage travel, Hague should have been thankful simply to have arrived safely in El Paso. Just before his journey took place, the Comancheros and their allies had been scourging the trail beyond Fort Concho. The brigands attacked Pecos Station in mid-May and threatened an army paymaster's party a few days later. Taylor had to request escorts from Fort Concho for the stock and supplies that he sent west to his stations. By the end of June the hands at Head of Concho and Barilla Station had repulsed three attacks by the Mescaleros and Comanches.[29]

Taylor met with little sympathy from the commander at Fort Davis, Colonel William R. Shafter. "In fact except to guard the El Paso Mail I am unable to discover the necessity for a single soldier at this post," complained the infantry officer, "as there is not now or ever will be an honest permanent settler from the Head of the Main Concho to this post. Of the two or three hundred Mexicans and dozen or so Americans in the vicinity of this post there is not one that is not directly or indirectly dependent on the post or El Paso Mail Line and military travel for their support." The colonel seemed to have difficulty grasping the idea that both his troops and the embattled stage line constituted the cutting edge of civilization in the region.[30]

The express company confronted other problems as the summer arrived. A drought held on to the plains until August, and the daily temperature often hovered around 102. The Main Concho ran only a few inches deep at the fords, and prairie fires raged out of control, reducing the open country along the road to the south to a desert of charred stubble. The price of forage shot upward as the hay contractors had to travel farther afield to find enough grass to cut and cure. The heat and poor grazing even

---

[28] Lillian H. Corcoran, "He Brought the Railroads to El Paso—The Story of Judge James P. Hague," *Password* 1 (May, 1956): 47–49.

[29] Duke, "O. M. Smith," 52–53; F. C. Taylor to Col. Edward Hatch, May 23, 1871, Letters Sent, Fort Davis, Tex., RG 393, NARS; Schmidt, *Medical History*, 42.

[30] Col. William R. Shafter to Assistant Adj. Gen., June 5, 1871, Letters Sent, Fort Davis, Tex., RG 393, NARS.

slowed down the Comanches, for they made only one fitful pursuit of a stage about forty miles out from the post that August.[31]

The tribesmen were increasingly shy as autumn approached. November arrived to mark the twentieth anniversary of Henry Skillman's first contract mail west from San Antonio. There were still many men around who could remember that event, and they realized that very little had changed on the road since then. The miles remained as long and the trail just as punishing. Drivers were still dying at the reins and the Post Office Department was still ready to fine the company for any disruption of service caused by the Indians.

Perhaps it was only coincidence, but Frank Taylor chose that month for what might have been an act of defiant celebration. He sent men and stock beyond the Head of Concho to the western end of Centralia Draw to construct a station at the old cavalry picket post. It was the first permanent structure to be erected between the Concho and the Pecos on that road. The little stone fortress was a brazen challenge to the Comanche scouts who watched from the greasewood thickets nearby, as the walls rose. They would not let the challenge pass unanswered.[32]

The Indians let the new station be built without interference, but they stormed into Kickapoo Springs on November 22 and overran a government wagon train that was encamped there. The teamsters lost all their animals to the raiders. The mail company eluded their attention, but Taylor knew that eventually the braves would try their luck in Centralia Draw.[33]

The superintendent was having enough trouble that fall without the Indians. The dry summer had given way to heavy rains in October and November that kept the rivers running high and reduced the roads to a soupy morass. The coaches ran behind time from the south all month, and on some trips they failed to arrive at all. Taylor could only compute the money lost in government fines and wait for the skies to clear.[34]

---

[31] Schmidt, *Medical History*, 42–45; *Austin Democratic Statesman*, Aug. 10, 1871; *San Antonio Daily Herald*, Aug. 8, 1871.
[32] Schmidt, *Medical History*, 50.
[33] Ibid., 49.
[34] Ibid., 47–50.

By the new year the weather had moderated and things were returning to what passed for routine in that hectic business. In February a coach left El Paso carrying the company's most vocal critic. W. W. Mills and his wife were bound for Austin; he had no scruples about taking passage on the line he had tried so hard to destroy. Mills bore no grudges against Taylor's employees and left a vivid account of the journey that captured the character of the drivers in all their roughhewn panache.

The Mills, attorney Charles Howard, and a young St. Louis lawyer named Bowman were listed on the waybill. A. J. Bobo held the reins, and he was spelled by Uncle Billy, another company driver. Mills quickly warmed to the plainsmen.

"Your stage driver was usually of a serious, almost sad disposition," he observed, "inclined to be reticent, particularly about himself or his associates." While many of them had probably led checkered careers in the past, Mills found traces of gentility in their conduct. "Rough, profane and unclean of speech among their own sex, they were remarkably courteous to lady passengers and ever thoughtful of their comfort and feelings," he wrote, "and more than once, on arriving at a station where the drivers were to be changed, I have heard one whisper to another: 'Remember, Sandy, there is a little lady in the coach.' This was sufficient."[35]

As the journey proceeded, Mills became increasingly impressed with the maturity and professionalism of his drivers. "He possessed the courage of the soldier and something more. The private soldier goes where he is told to march, and fights when he is ordered, but he has little anxiety or responsibility; but the stage driver in those times had to be as alert and thoughtful as a General." The job carried heavy obligations with it, for "there was not only his duty to his employers but his responsibility for the mails (he was a sworn officer of the Government), but the lives of the passengers often depended upon his knowledge of the country and of the Indian character, and his quick and correct judgement as to what to do in emergencies. Like the

[35] W. W. Mills, *Forty Years at El Paso, 1858–1898*, 125–26.

sailor, he was something of a fatalist, but he believed in using all possible means to protect himself and those under his charge."

The trip went pleasantly for most of the eight days on the road to Fort Concho and Austin, with the exception of a brief moment of concern when the coach cut across the trail of a large party of Indians that had recently crossed the track. Bobo told his passengers to get their guns ready and whipped the team on for the next station. The real excitement came one afternoon east of the Pecos.

At "Head of Concho" we came upon a herd of buffalo, and, of course, we dismounted and wantonly fired into them, with what effect I do not know, except that someone wounded an immense bull so seriously that he became angry or sullen and refused to run away as the others did. We, with our deadly Winchesters, ceased firing at him, as he was of no use to us, but not so with the young St. Louis lawyer. He wanted to do something that he could tell about at home, and so he advanced upon the irate animal with his little thirty-two caliber pistol, firing as he went. He was encouraged and animated by the shouts of Bobo and Uncle Billy: "Charge him, mister," "You've got him," "The next shot will fetch him," etc.

Mrs. Mills said: "Why, Uncle Billy, that animal will kill the man! Call him back!" Uncle Billy said: "Why, *of course* he'll kill him. Now you just watch, and you'll see fine fun. He'll toss that little lawyer higher'n the top of this coach." And yet Uncle Billy and Bobo were not cruel men.

The drivers must have killed the buffalo before he could hook a horn into the lawyer, for all the passengers were safely in Austin by mid-February.[36]

It was fortunate for them all that the journey took place early in the year, for that spring of 1872 proved to be among the worst seasons for Indian raids in the company's history. The trouble started on April 12 with a raid on Menardville. The next day warriors fired on two stages only 6 miles from Centralia Station, badly wounding a guard in the skirmish.[37]

[36] Ibid.; *Austin Democratic Statesman*, Feb. 17, 1872.
[37] Stevens, "Fort Concho," 68–69.

The trouble continued into May, and once again the elusive Comancheros were involved. A cavalry patrol killed one of the renegades and captured another beyond the Head of Concho. The prisoner reported that 150 whites, Mexicans, and Indians were encamped on a branch of the Main Concho for the purpose of staging raids into the settlements. One war party had already caught Charles Bain on the road near Loyal Valley, giving up the chase only when he reached the station. The agent learned that the country nearby had been full of Indians for some time. Their presence prompted one soldier who was detailed as a stage guard to desert at Coghlin's Station, taking the driver's rifle with him.[38]

By June the Comanches were even bolder. They raided Concho Station and the fort on two successive nights, and ten days later an ambitious series of attacks struck the stations to the west. The road was filled with stock being driven to market in New Mexico by Texan cattlemen, who often halted their herds near Taylor's station for the night camp. The results were predictable. Johnston's Station was attacked twice in one morning, and that night the braves struck Centralia Station to find a rude surprise.

Jim Spears was at the station and led the hands in a spirited defense. At the height of the action the station chief's dog broke loose and attacked the raiders. The hound chased a Comanche through the waterhole while the Texans whooped and cheered excitedly. Bullets and arrows seemed useless against the angry mongrel, and the Indians decided that their medicine had gone bad. They gave up and rode away with at least one shamefaced warrior sporting a ragged breechclout.[39]

Other depredations followed as the Comanches stubbornly struck at any prey on the road. They captured a coach near Camp Johnston on July 14, although the guard and driver escaped. Two weeks later a large band hit Centralia Station again, driving off the stock before the guards could open fire. They paused to inso-

[38] Francis C. Taylor to Col. Edward Hatch, May 17, 18, 1872, Letters Received, Fort Concho, Tex., RG 98, NARS.
[39] Francis C. Taylor to Col. Edward Hatch, June 17, 1872, Letters Received, Fort Concho, Tex., RG 98, NARS; Stevens, "Fort Concho," 100–106; Schmidt, *Medical History*, 60; *Austin Democratic Statesman*, June 11, 1872.

lently water the captured mules at a pond some distance away before moving north to rendezvous with the Comancheros.

Travel continued on the road despite such interference, but the danger increased markedly early in September when a Comanche band disguised in army uniforms attacked a party of hay contractors near Camp Johnston. Two weeks later a mixed band of warriors and traders killed a settler at Head of Concho and mutilated him in full view of the soldiers and expressmen at the station. The angry whites did not have to wait very long for revenge.[40]

Colonel Ranald S. Mackenzie and the Fourth Cavalry were already in the field from Fort Concho on a determined campaign to disrupt the sordid commerce that had kept the frontier in turmoil for so long. An earlier scout had already located the Comancheros' routes of travel and rendezvous sites. This foray was aimed at punishing the Comanche bands that collaborated with the brigands.

On September 29 Mackenzie's troopers surprised and attacked a large village on the North Fork of the Red River. Nearly sixty warriors died in the rout, while the colonel captured their horse herds and over a hundred women and children. The prisoners were taken back to Fort Concho and held as hostages against the surviving braves' actions. The result was the quietest winter west of San Antonio in living memory.[41]

Taylor had other reasons to celebrate that autumn. The company had weathered many storms in the year and a half since Ficklin's death, but it had come through intact and showed even more promise as new branches were added. In June, Slaughter Ficklin and Frederick Sawyer had brought Samuel T. Scott into the partnership by adding his daily service between Austin and San Antonio. Another route had followed in August when the operation east of Concho Station was broadened to provide coaches on a run through Dallas to the railhead at Atoka, in the Indian Territory. The Texas Central Railroad was fast approaching the frontier as well, building out from Dallas, while the Missouri,

[40] Stevens, "Fort Concho," 108.

[41] Robert M. Utley, *Frontier Regulars: The United States Army and the Indian, 1866–1891,* 211–12; Haley, *Fort Concho,* 210–13.

Kansas and Texas line also hastened construction across the
northeastern part of the state. For the first time, points in Texas
as far apart as Austin and El Paso had through connections to the
railroad links with St. Louis.[42]

There was room for optimism, but there was still some confusion and uncertainty hampering the company's administration
that dated from the time of Ben Ficklin's death. In November,
1872, Taylor, Sawyer, Slaughter Ficklin, Scott, and another junior partner, F. K. Wright, met in Austin for a conference. They
examined the accounts of not only the Texas routes, but also the
services in Arkansas and the Indian Territory that Ben Ficklin
had undertaken. Approximately $260,000 changed hands among
the six parties as they strove to balance all the various debts and
credits that were due to each of them from the date of their first
association with Ficklin.

The discussions did not always proceed smoothly. Sawyer
had to spend a great deal of time explaining and justifying his
expenditure of large sums of company funds in the form of bribes
to the men of influence in Washington. Slaughter Ficklin was
outraged by this practice, insisting that Sawyer should not have
submitted to such extortion and voicing his concern over the
lack of records covering the money's use. It took a second meeting in San Antonio the next month before the company's affairs
were settled to young Ficklin's satisfaction. He then consented to
sell all of his brother's interest in the concern to Sawyer. Taylor
retained both the partnership and the supervision of the Fort
Concho–El Paso route. He had exercised complete control over
this branch of the line since the previous June, when Ficklin had
relinquished his active participation on the route to Sawyer.
Sawyer shared responsibility with Taylor for operating the leg
north from San Antonio to Fort Concho and continued to use
Elisha Bates, his brother-in-law, as agent on the line.[43]

Taylor's head was still buzzing with the talk of accounts and
contracts when January, 1873, arrived, bringing with it a visitor
to the Southwest that threatened to do more harm to the stage

---

[42] *Austin Democratic Statesman,* June 11, Aug. 17, 24, 29, 1872.
[43] *Management of the Post-Office Department,* 462–65, 502–504.

line than any Comanche or Mescalero who ever drew a bow-
string. In September a particularly virulent strain of equine influenza had appeared in the Atlantic states and spread rapidly.
Within a month thousands of horses and mules were stricken.
By December the virus had reached Texas and was soon raging
through the settlements. Commonly known as the "epizootic,"
the disease attacked its victim's eyes, nose, and throat. In severe
cases, lung congestion developed, which was often fatal. The
main treatment consisted of swabbing the affected areas with a
diluted carbolic acid solution and feeding the animal warm bran
mash. A partially filled bag of boiled oats was often fitted about its
nose. This kept the nasal passages clear to permit unobstructed
breathing. If the animal was strong and otherwise healthy, it
might survive and still be fit for work.[44]

The El Paso Mail Company suffered along with all the other
businesses that depended upon large herds of horses and mules.
By January 9 the line had been forced to suspend service between Austin and San Antonio. It was several weeks before the
epidemic ran its course. Operations along the entire line had
virtually ceased before then.[45]

By the early spring Taylor had gotten his teams fit for the
road again and advertised arrivals from El Paso in San Antonio
every Sunday and Friday, with departures scheduled for Fort
Concho and the west at 8:00 A.M. on Tuesdays and Saturdays.
Coaches came in from Concho every Sunday, Wednesday, and
Friday at 5:00 P.M., barring some disputed rendezvous with the
Indians or swollen rivers from the spring rains.[46]

There were still problems with the operation to the east
from Concho Station. The *Fort Worth Democrat* complained
that "not a week passes but for some cause or other they will fail
to bring us a mail." The journal intended to inform the postmaster general about the situation and advised its readers to
withhold their patronage from the company. Sawyer and Taylor

[44] Robert G. Carter, *On the Border with Mackenzie*, 398; Ernest L. Reedstrom,
Bugles, Banners and Warbonnets, 217–18.

[45] Carl C. Rister, *Southern Plainsmen*, 56; *Austin Democratic Statesman*, Jan. 8,
11, Feb. 5, 1873; *San Antonio Daily Herald*, Jan. 4, 9, 17, 24, 1873.

[46] *San Antonio Daily Herald*, Apr. 17, 1873.

must have reacted quickly to the criticism, for within three months the same paper was praising the line's courtesy and efficiency. Journalists had always been a great deal easier to placate than some of Taylor's less literate critics.[47]

Late in May the Mescaleros ended an unusually long period of quiet by attacking Eagle Springs. The raid seemed to signal a resurgence of trouble along the line. Pecos Station weathered a raid in July, losing one man to the Indians, while another band struck at Kickapoo Springs. Already the braves had lashed out at Menardville, El Muerto, and Coghlin's Station. As if Taylor did not have enough problems, one of his drivers quarreled with a guard on the road near Concho Station and emptied his revolver into the man. He sought refuge at Fort Concho, but the post commander had him ejected from its limits. An hour later someone found his body in the brush about a mile from the post. Due process had been served with powder and ball.[48]

The summer closed with repeated violent encounters before Taylor was allowed to concentrate on a new project to bolster the company's fortunes. Esther Taylor was nearly caught on the road to Fredericksburg by the Comanches early in August and sought refuge at the Loyal Valley station. The braves swung north to plague the traffic on the trail above Lipan Springs. Late in the month Barilla Springs stood off another Mescalero raid, the hands killing two Apaches in the fighting.[49]

Despite the virtually daily round of problems that assailed him, Frank Taylor managed to plan ahead in pursuing his interests. As early as that summer it was apparent to him that change was coming to the Southwest, and that his business concerns could not remain static in the face of its challenges.

Irrevocable change rode the locomotive that year. The Missouri, Kansas, and Texas Railroad had already crossed the Red River in 1872. The International and Great Northern linked

[47] *Fort Worth Democrat*, June 14, Aug. 30, 1873.

[48] Edith E. Grote, "Early Days Recalled by Veteran Mason Leader," *Frontier Times* 28 (Oct., 1950): 25; *San Antonio Daily Herald*, June 24, Aug. 6, 1873; *Austin Democratic Statesman*, June 25, July 12, Aug. 5, 15, 1873.

[49] *Austin Democratic Statesman*, June 5, Sept. 4, 1873; *San Antonio Daily Herald*, Aug. 8, Sept. 2, 1873.

Shreveport to Longview in the northeastern quadrant of the state, and it was laying tracks for Austin as quickly as possible. The Gulf, Colorado, and Santa Fe had been incorporated in Galveston that May, and its surveyors were marking a route north to Fort Worth, while the Houston and Texas Central ran through Dallas to Denison on the southern border of the Indian Territory. In California construction had started on a line to link Fort Worth and the Pacific via El Paso. The great days of the overland mail lines were clearly drawing to their close.[50]

Taylor sensed that Concho Station might occupy an enviable position in the path of oncoming events. With Fort Worth and San Antonio developing into rail centers, the company could serve as a feeder for traffic from the west for either point. The extension of rail service from the eastern United States in the settled areas of Texas would also have the effect of increasing the amount of travel to areas beyond the railheads as the speed and ease of movement to the western terminals encouraged people to endure the interval of discomfort that remained before they reached their destinations. For a while, the coming of the railroads might actually boost business on the stage lines.

There was also the distinct possibility that the eventual rail connection between El Paso and Fort Worth would follow the old emigrant road directly through the Concho country. Even if the stage business was doomed on the longer routes, Taylor's line and his settlement could still reap benefits from catering to the demands of a new environment. The railroad would bring more people to the towns that already existed on the frontier, and as others sprang up in the interior their residents would still need reliable commercial transportation to and from the depots. Concho Station could become an even greater crossroads than it was before the rails were laid.

That summer, Taylor and Charles Metcalfe staked out a townsite on a tract of land located a mile up the South Concho from the old station. The village was neatly surveyed in thirty-two blocks surrounding a central area for a courthouse and square. Streets were marked out and lots measured for sale. Tay-

---

[50]William C. Pool, *A Historical Atlas of Texas*, 164–65.

lor christened the embryonic settlement Benficklin in honor of his old friend. On September 30 the Post Office Department officially recognized its existence by granting it a postmaster's office.[51]

Benficklin showed promise from the start. By the middle of September a store, blacksmith, and carpenter's shops stood open for business while more structures went up to house the company's workers. Taylor had both Benficklin and Concho Station functioning with efficiency and surprising discipline. No liquor sales were allowed at either place, and drunkenness brought immediate dismissal for any employee. A visitor from San Antonio was greatly impressed with both establishments and asserted that "probably no stage line in the state is better managed than this—always coming to time when possible, and running even during the epizootic. . . . They have good coaches, good agents, good drivers, and generally good animals."[52]

Ben Ficklin would have been pleased by his partner's determined optimism. Neither Indians, epidemics, politicians, nor railroads would be allowed to efface the mark of the brash reinsman on that corner of the Southwest. Autumn came to the plains that October, but no frost ever blighted the ambitions of Francis C. Taylor for as long as he had left to live.

[51] Spence, "The Story of Benficklin," 35.
[52] *San Antonio Daily Herald*, Sept. 17, 1873.

CHAPTER 14

Concord Suffrage

W HILE the carpenters and masons were busy building the company's new headquarters at Benficklin, Frank Taylor's enemies applied great energy to their campaign to destroy what he had already created. That autumn saw some unexpected variations on the old, familiar theme of theft and destruction.

The raid that struck Centralia Station on October 1 was expected, but there was no way that Taylor could have anticipated the threat that materialized in the growing city of Fort Worth when a pyromaniac went on a rampage. On October 10 the arsonist ignited a huge haystack near the El Paso Mail Company's stables on Bluff Street. Luckily a brisk wind blowing out of the south kept the flames from reaching the buildings. The local hook-and-ladder company managed to contain the blaze, and the loss was limited to the feedlot. During the next week five other fires were set in the town, one of them almost destroying the post office. The pointless, irrational destruction was even more frightening than an Indian raid, for the culprit enjoyed the advantage of perfect anonymity on the crowded streets of Fort Worth.[1]

While the police hunted the firebug, there were scattered reports of more Indian trouble on the road beyond Fort Concho, but the company counted no more losses. Charles Bain kept on the road constantly that month, prowling both the main and branch lines from Benficklin to Fort Clark as he mounted a close watch on their operations. He informed San Antonians of the continuing growth of Taylor's settlement and the numerous farms that were springing up along the Concho as the village lured

---

[1] Sgt. Benjamin Stow to Post Adjutant, Fort Stockton, Tex., Oct. 2, 1873, Letters Received, Adjutant General's Office, RG 94, NARS; *Fort Worth Democrat*, Oct. 11, 18, 1873.

more settlers to the area. He predicted a mild winter, for the buffalo were late in arriving on the plains beyond the river that year.[2]

Bain's optimistic pronouncements were displaced by grimmer news in November when relations between the military and the stage line hit a new low point. Despite the incessant threat of Indian attacks, the black soldiers and white employees they were charged with guarding often spent their time feuding among themselves. Colonel Shafter had already protested from Fort Davis about the treatment his men had received at Leon Holes. The agent there had refused to provide them with food, shelter, or transportation back to Fort Stockton. "I shall be glad to furnish mail escorts as long as they are wanted," Shafter bristled in a letter to Taylor, "but they must be properly treated. They should either be fed by the company or allowed facilities at the stations for cooking their own rations and a decent place to stay while at the station and invariably brought back by the first return stage."[3]

The situation turned very tense when a soldier and a stageman clashed at Barilla Springs. The coach arrived late one night and Private Albert Stewart attempted to help unharness the team. The driver took offense at this and slapped him across the face several times while damning the soldier as a "black son of a bitch." When the Texan drew his pistol and opened fire, Stewart leveled his Springfield and killed him. The provocation had been clear and answerable only with violence. Even the stationmaster was willing to verify that the soldier had acted in self-defense, but the incident still created more antagonism between the two groups.[4]

Taylor was better off without the dead driver, for his men were coming under mounting scrutiny by the government. In June, 1872, Congress had required a certified oath from all mail contractors and carriers involved in any aspect of the service.

---

[2] *San Antonio Daily Herald*, Oct. 7, 16, Nov. 3, 1873.

[3] Lt. Col. William R. Shafter to Francis C. Taylor, [date illegible] Jan. 1872, Letters Sent, Fort Davis, Tex., RG 98, NARS.

[4] Sgt. John Means to Post Adjutant, [date illegible] Nov. 1873, Letters Received, Fort Davis, Tex., RG 98, NARS.

Drivers had to swear to "perform all the duties required . . . and abstain from everything forbidden by the laws in relation to the establishment of the Post Office and Post Roads within the United States; . . . and honestly and truly account for pay over and any moneys belonging to the said United States which may come into my possession or control: So help me God." Additionally, a county justice of the peace had to certify that the oathtaker was over sixteen years of age.[5]

The contractor had already noted how zealously attentive to their cargo his men had become since the San Antonio postmaster issued a public warning about the circulation of obscene picture-postcards through the mails. No postmaster ever lacked for witnesses while he sorted the mail for distribution after that announcement was made.[6]

The old year closed with a failed Mescalero raid on Eagle Springs, but Taylor paid little attention to the incident, for he was already planning a major coup of his own that he hoped would make Benficklin the keystone of all future settlement in the country west of the Concho and beyond to the Pecos. Taylor spent much of his time in Austin during the opening weeks of 1874 lobbying forcefully for legislative creation of a new county from the huge northwestern corner of the existing Bexar County. He proved persuasive, for on March 13 an expanse of 12,500 square miles was designated as Tom Green County. It was named in honor of a hero of the Texas Revolution and the Civil War, and consisted of land that had already been paid for in Texan blood many times over. The first step in Taylor's design for empire had been accomplished. The months ahead would be filled with many lethal distractions, but the Alabama frontiersman would never deviate from his course.[7]

The distractions did come thickly and furiously that spring and summer, as the Comanches saluted the new county by killing a stage driver named Charley Smith on the run from Fort

[5]Stephen W. Schmidt, ed., *News from the Frontier Fort on the Conchos* 3 (Dec., 1971).

[6]*San Antonio Daily Herald*, June 15, 1873.

[7]Grace Bitner, "The History of Tom Green County, Texas" (M.A. thesis, University of Texas at Austin, 1931), 18, 32.

Worth only a few miles east of Benficklin. By the end of March
the warriors had raided directly into the settlement to steal stock
after first lashing Kickapoo Springs with an attack.[8]

One traveler on the line that spring must have truly felt
that he had never been away from Texas at all in the past twenty
years. Zenas R. Bliss had returned to the state early in the 1870s
as a major in the Twenty-fifth Infantry and post commander at
Fort Davis. He retained vivid memories of his journey to that
post as a young subaltern in the 1850s, riding on one of George
Giddings's coaches. On April 14 Major Bliss departed the fort on
a leave of absence and found himself back in one of the rocking
coaches behind a span of bony-hipped jacks as he followed the
road eastward. Although the ride was too uncomfortable to elicit
any nostalgia, it did move him to devote more space in his memoirs to the ersatz romance of stage travel on the plains.[9]

Bliss was struck by the loneliness and privation that still attended the business of staging. "It was not a cheerful life, fifty to
seventy-five miles from a fort, surrounded by Indians, and liable
to be shot down every time they went to the door," he wrote of
the station hands. "Still, men were found for the place for about
thirty-five dollars a month."

He particularly admired the men at the reins. "Each driver
drove about a hundred to a hundred and twenty-five miles, day
and night, stopping at stations only long enough to swallow a
hasty meal. While the driver and escort were eating, the station
keeper and his helper hitched up a fresh team, and held them
till all were aboard, and then turned them loose, and they would
go upon the run for a mile or more, and then they would settle
down to a trot and go along peaceably. They were trained not to
stop or stand still on the road," Bliss learned. "This was said to
be on account of Indians, but whether it was done intentionally
or not, it was a very inconvenient thing for passengers who had
to get out of the stage between stations."[10]

The major recalled the plight of two travelers who found

[8] *Fort Worth Democrat*, Mar. 28, 1874; J. Evetts Haley, *Fort Concho and the Texas
Frontier*, 213–14.
[9] Zenas R. Bliss, "Memoirs," Zenas R. Bliss Papers, Barker Texas History Center,
University of Texas at Austin, 5:210–11.
[10] Ibid.

that the greasy bacon and leaden biscuits served at the stations hardly made ideal fare for the road. "I knew an officer who crossed the Staked Plains with his wife, who was sick and she had to alight from the stage several times. The lieutenant would notify the driver, open the stage door, and as soon as the mules stopped, he and his wife would jump out, and away would go the mules on the run." The emergency stops were frightening affairs for both of them. "It was raining hard, the night was pitch dark, and the driver would run the mules in a circle, and after awhile bring them back to where the lieutenant and his wife were standing, and they would jump in and go on again at a run. The officer told us that when the stage would leave him and disappear in the darkness, it seemed to him that it would never return."[11]

Major Bliss completed his journey without suffering similar inconveniences, although each time he stopped at a station he must have recalled the story of a line agent who paused at one of the relay points near Fort Davis and was surprised to see that the pack of dogs that had inhabited the place during his earlier visit was gone. He asked the station's chief what had happened to the hounds. "We ran out of venison," was the stoic reply.[12]

If the travelers and station hands found nothing more serious than the food to complain about that spring, they should have felt fortunate, for worse trials might still strike the line at any point. Late in March the Kiowa chieftain Lone Wolf led a raid into Texas to avenge the deaths of his son and nephew at the hands of the whites during an earlier incursion. The warriors struck at Johnston's Station, taking by surprise a company of the Ninth Cavalry that was encamped nearby. A brisk skirmish swirled around the station for over half an hour before the Indians succeeded in stampeding and capturing the soldiers' horses. The troopers were chagrined at losing the fight, but the men at the station could only thank God that they had been there when the Kiowas arrived.[13]

Lone Wolf's victory encouraged other raiding parties to

[11] Ibid.

[12] Francis C. Taylor reference file, Fort Concho Preservation and Museum, San Angelo, Tex.

[13] William H. Leckie, *The Buffalo Soldiers*, 115–16; Wilbur S. Nye, *Carbine and Lance*, 182–83, 188–89.

strike at Pecos Station and Barilla Springs. Not until the summer did relative quiet return to the line as the military mustered troops from Texas, Kansas, and New Mexico to sweep the plains clear of the hostiles in a campaign that became known as the Red River War. The offensive continued into the early months of 1875 and helped to give the mail company a welcome respite from attacks on the eastern portions of the route.[14]

The quiet spell came at the right time, for Taylor was summoned to Washington for a conference with Sawyer on the company's affairs. It was then that the senior partner confided in him about the bribery and corruption that permeated the government. Taylor was aghast at the sums of money being spent to protect their hold on the mail contracts and warned that the expense might eventually ruin them. Sawyer shared his fears but stressed that it was all part of the price of doing business with the Grant administration.[15]

As autumn approached, Taylor hastened to settle his business in Washington. Elections were scheduled for Tom Green County early the next January, and he wanted time to plan his strategy. The stage company had been the major economic force in the Concho country since 1868, and Taylor intended to see this fact reflected in its dominance of the new county's political affairs as well.

Taylor used the time to best advantage as he analyzed the situation and laid plans for an electoral campaign that would sweep the field. There were only five settlements within the county—San Angela, Benficklin, Bismarck Farm, Lipan Springs, and Kickapoo Springs. Though Fort Concho had a sizable population, its garrison was not a factor in computing the number of eligible voters. Lipan Springs and Kickapoo Springs were essentially stage stations, with a scattering of merchants and stockmen living in the area. Bismarck Farm, an ambitious irrigation project located a few miles upriver from Benficklin, was operated by the widow of former station chief Henry M. Taylor. Jim Spears and Frank Taylor both shared interests in the business, and it

---

[14] Robert M. Utley, *Frontier Regulars*, 225–41.

[15] U.S. Congress, House, *Management of the Post-Office Department*, 44th Cong., 1st sess., 1875, House Report 814, pp. 468–69.

was virtually a satellite of the stage company. That left San Angela to fill in the other half of the political equation.[16]

Despite its abundance of rather sordid businesses and generally raffish air, San Angela boasted a larger population than Benficklin, and its leading citizen, William S. Veck, was determined to win enough votes in the coming election to make it the county seat. Taylor knew that he had a worthy rival in the merchant and saloonkeeper. Veck had lived in California at the height of the gold rush. A string of varied adventures in both North and South America had followed until he arrived at Fort Concho as a wagonmaster in 1868.

Within two years Veck had acquired a ranch, general store, and saloon across the river from the post. His reputation as a man of energy and optimism was reinforced in 1872 when, at the age of forty-four, he married a fourteen-year-old girl. He was a popular figure in San Angela, and the impromptu banking service that he operated from his store gave him a great deal of influence with the other men of property in the community. As the election approached, he and Frank Taylor squared off for a determined contest.[17]

Both men had served on the original commission that oversaw the county's organization in March, 1874. When Taylor had foresightedly arranged to have Benficklin designated as the polling place, Veck should have sensed that something was afoot. The result was an operation that would have charmed Ben Ficklin with its guileful audacity.

Taylor opened his campaign with several gambits designed to put Veck on the defensive. He announced that the citizens of Benficklin would gladly concede the county seat to San Angela if Veck would agree to donate land for a courthouse, school, and public square. The merchant refused, and Taylor responded with a compromise appeal to locate the courthouse and public buildings at a point midway between the rival settlements. Veck refused this offer as well. The expressman was content, for he

---

[16] Grace Bitner, "Early History of the Concho County and Tom Green County," *West Texas Historical Association Yearbook* 9 (Oct., 1933): 14–16.

[17] William S. Veck reference file, Fort Concho Preservation and Museum, San Angelo, Tex.

had managed both to dominate the issues of the election and to make his opponent appear mean-spirited as well.[18]

There was increasing traffic from the west into Benficklin as election day approached. Taylor smuggled the clerk of the district court in El Paso into his store and then began stripping the line of every Mexican cook, hostler, and guard that could be spared. When they arrived he herded them into the clerk's makeshift office for naturalization and entry on the voting rolls. On January 15, 1875, Taylor marched his newly minted citizens to the polls and voted them as a block, decisively tipping the scales against Veck and San Angela. The angry merchant admitted that "Taylor slipped in a cold deck on us" and left his rival to claim not only the county seat but the office of judge as well. Concord suffrage and popular democracy had arrived together on the Concho country frontier.[19]

Frank Taylor was effectively installed as the leading figure in a county that sat astride the present and future arteries of travel for not only a large portion of Texas but the greater Southwest as well. Any man who knew the value of water and the symbols of a map realized that the next great thrust of railroad construction and settlement from the east would have to follow the narrow corridor along the Concho. To the northeast from Benficklin the growing towns of Fort Worth and Dallas continued to hold promise as major commercial centers. The financial panic of 1873 had stalled construction of the Texas and Pacific Railroad only 8 miles west of Dallas, but the Houston and Texas Central was already running trains through the town from the south and on to bridge the Red River for connections with the east. San Antonio endured as the hub of the old network linking the Gulf with Mexico and the American Southwest via Laredo and El Paso. The railroad was bound for El Paso as well, for the Southern Pacific's builders planned a line from New Orleans to California. The most densely settled portion of Texas was bounded by a triangle formed by Houston and San Antonio at the base with Dallas and Fort Worth forming the apex. All four towns were

[18] Bitner, "Early History," 17.
[19] Ibid.; Susan Miles, "Until the Flood; 1867–1882," *Edwards Plateau Historian* 2 (1966): 18–20.

being rapidly linked by railroads that would eventually connect them with the rest of the nation and enlist their people and resources in the continuing multipronged drive to the Pacific.[20]

Taylor may not have owned a single share of stock in a railroad company, but he was prescient enough to grasp that until this new transportation grid was completed, his business not only served the apex and western leg of the triangle but also anticipated the general route of the final line west to El Paso from the northeast. His senior partner in Washington was alert to the situation also, for he had already formed an expanded union with William D. Griffith, a Californian, to create the new Texas and California Stage Company. Though Taylor's operation continued to function as before, it was part of a larger service that provided coach mails from Fort Worth to San Diego by way of El Paso, Tucson, and Yuma. There was still money to be made before the last rails were joined, and any company land or property that was held in the regions served by the new industry was bound to appreciate in value as settlement increased. Frank Taylor saw himself in an ideal position to serve the end of one era with his company while prospering from the opening of another.[21]

The grand dreams of the future still had to be grown in the rocky soil of present realities, and the recurring problems on the line drew Taylor back to the daily concerns of the operation that February. There were complaints from Fort Davis about the mail service. Colonel George Andrews wrote to the postmaster general, protesting "gross carelessness or extensive speculation somewhere on the line." Whether it was negligence on the postmasters' part or the blame rested with the company's men, Taylor still had to sort out the problem and reply to the charges.[22]

Hard behind Andrews's complaints came more trouble with the Apaches. On April 8 fourteen braves ambushed the east-

[20] S. B. McAllister, "Building the Texas and Pacific Railroad West of Fort Worth," *West Texas Historical Association Yearbook* 4 (June, 1928): 50–53; John R. Hutto, "Pioneering of the Texas and Pacific," *West Texas Historical Association Yearbook* 12 (July, 1936): 124–25; Lewis W. Newton and Herbert P. Gambrell, *A Social and Political History of Texas*, 338–40; Donald W. Meining, *Imperial Texas*, 71–77.

[21] A. J. Hertz, "Arizona Expresses," *American Philatelist* 70 (Mar., 1957): 430–32.

[22] Col. George Andrews to Postmaster General, Feb. 8, 1875, Letters Sent, Fort Davis, Tex., RG 98, NARS.

bound stage as it left Bass Canyon and chased it through the evening twilight to Van Horn's Wells. Four days later at Eagle Springs the station head and a soldier were nearly killed when the Mescaleros attacked the grazing mule herd and drove it away. A patrol from Fort Davis pursued the thieves for over a week without catching them. Not long after this incident, the coach running east from Pecos Station met four Comanche scouts near Flat Rock Holes and quickly picked up speed to elude them. It had been nearly a year since there had been any serious Indian trouble on the road between Fort Stockton and Benficklin. The braves' presence was a bad sign, and as May arrived both Metcalfe and Bain were once again patroling the road in anticipation of renewed attacks.[23]

There was some good news for the company despite the complaints and Indian threat. In April, 1874, the state legislature had combined El Paso, Pecos, Presidio, and Tom Green counties to form the Twenty-fifth Judicial District of Texas. The new court was instructed to meet in El Paso County for three weeks each September, January, and May, beginning in the spring of 1875. It was to shift operations to Tom Green County for a week during October, February, and June. The result was increased business for the stage line, as lawyers and their clients shuttled back and forth between Ysleta and Benficklin.[24]

Taylor and his men had long been accustomed to dealing with the danger posed by Indians and renegade Comancheros, but in June a new menace appeared on the road above San Antonio. Five men rode into Max Aue's station and inn at Leon Springs at noon on the thirteenth. Although he did not know them by name, Aue recognized all of them as former customers. They suddenly drew their revolvers and announced a robbery. The settler and his guests were tied up after emptying their wallets. The bandits looted the store and then ordered the stage company's hostler to saddle fresh horses from those in the stable. The employee was a pugnacious Irishman named Sullivan, and

[23] *San Antonio Daily Herald*, Apr. 22, May 10, 15, 1875; Grover C. Ramsey, "Camp Melvin, Crockett County, Texas," *West Texas Historical Association Yearbook* 37 (Oct., 1961): 142.

[24] J. Morgan Broaddus, *The Legal Heritage of El Paso*, 119–21.

he told them in graphic terms what they could do with their saddles. He finally obeyed the demand when one of the outlaws put a pistol to his head and threatened to drop the hammer if he said another word.[25]

The robbers spurred off in the direction of Boerne while their victims spread the alarm. The next day the brigands ran into a posse near Kerrville and fought a four-hour battle with its members. Two of the felons were hit in the shooting. Coles, who was mortally wounded, told his captors the identities of the other men in the band after they abandoned him to make their escape. It was only a matter of time before the rest of them were apprehended.[26]

The trouble with the outlaws was only the prelude to more headaches for the contractors that summer. In June and July, Colonel Andrews complained repeatedly to Washington about the slipshod mail service. The San Antonio press joined in the criticism, echoing the protests of citizens that the subcontractor on the leg between Fredericksburg and Benficklin had failed to meet his responsibilities. By August the mail was reported running badly behind schedule on both the El Paso and Fort Clark routes.[27]

The root of the trouble could be traced to the turmoil in the Grant government. In June, 1874, the president suddenly fired Postmaster General Creswell and named Marshall Jewell to the office. Jewell, a former Connecticut governor, was serving as minister to Russia at the time. A loyal Republican but equally devoted reformer, he attempted to cut through the tangled intrigues of his department, and in so doing he antagonized many of Grant's allies. He also disrupted the mail service by withholding payment on routes that he deemed to be suspect in their manner of operation or methods of obtaining the contracts. The *New York Tribune* reported that Jewell had cut Taylor's compensation in half on the El Paso route, pending a review of Sawyer's

[25] *San Antonio Daily Herald*, June 14, 1875.

[26] Ibid., June 16–18, 1875.

[27] Col. George S. Andrews to Secretary of War William W. Belknap, June 8, 1875; Andrews to Assistant Adj. Gen., July 19, 1875, Letters Sent, Fort Davis, Tex., RG 98, NARS.

relations with the government. The sudden drop in funding and understandable damage to Taylor's credit must have affected his ability to keep the coaches running on a full schedule.[28]

The *Fort Worth Democrat* spoke up on his behalf. In January it had remarked that "during the unprecedented bad weather the El Paso Stage Company has managed to bring the mails once in every twenty-four hours. Sometimes they came in one conveyance and sometimes in another; but they always got here one way or another, for which the efficient offices of the company deserve credit." That summer the journal awarded the "blue ribbon of accommodation" to Sawyer and Taylor, defending the company against the charges stirred up by Jewell's actions. All this publicity was unwelcome in the White House, and Jewell's dedication to reform was gradually destroying his value to the administration.[29]

While the political cudgels were being lifted in print and in Congress, Taylor found himself under mounting pressure that August. The army was busily constructing a telegraph line from San Antonio to Fort McKavett and Fort Concho. It needed no great leap of imagination for him to predict the effect its commercial counterpart would have on the mail line's share of business. Worse yet, the Comanches were beginning to make their presence felt on the Concho while the Apaches plagued the road west of Fort Davis. In late June and mid-July they attacked two freight trains west of Van Horn's Wells, while the Comanches struck twice at Head of Concho in the first two weeks of August. Despite Mackenzie's victory of the last year, there were still many warriors willing to slip away from the reservation on minor forays, and the stations remained lucrative targets.[30]

The crowning blow came on August 20, when the telegraph into San Antonio from the east reported that Frederick P. Sawyer had died the day before. Taylor was left feeling like a man

[28] Dorothy G. Fowler, *The Cabinet Politician*, 151–75; *San Antonio Daily Herald*, July 9, 17, Aug. 6, 12, 1875, citing the *Galveston News* and *New York Tribune*.

[29] Fowler, *The Cabinet Politician*, 154–55; *Fort Worth Democrat*, Jan. 9, June 12, July 3, 1875.

[30] Corp. Gene Driscoll to Post Adjutant, Aug. 20, 1875, Letters Received, Fort Concho, Tex., RG 98, NARS; *San Antonio Daily Herald*, July 24, Aug. 16, 1875.

who has been cast adrift in a small boat with neither oars nor sail. His senior partner had left the company not only deeply in debt, but his secretive and eccentric methods of accounting had reduced its financial records to a shambles. It would be years before all the firm's affairs were settled, but in the confused weeks after his death Taylor could only struggle to preserve the business in Texas, leaving the rest of the Sawyer empire to shift for itself.[31]

By the time the storm generated by Sawyer's death had abated, a new alliance among the Texas routes had been formed by Taylor and two of the surviving partners of the old concern. On October 1 the branch line to Eagle Pass from San Antonio came under new management by the firm of Schott and Ashley, as the company sought to reduce its operations to conform with its straitened finances. Taylor, Charles Bain, and James T. Chidester combined to manage the San Antonio–El Paso route, as well as the eastern branch from Benficklin to Fort Smith, Arkansas. Taylor took responsibility for the Concho division, while Bain oversaw the Fort Worth–Fort Concho route, and Chidester assumed control of the rest of the territory. Bain also shared an interest in the division from San Antonio to Benficklin. Some idea of the company's assets can be gained from the inventory of a $12,000 deed of trust executed between the newly organized C. Bain and Company and Sawyer's administrator, J. H. James, in San Antonio on January 24, 1876:

8 teams of 4 horses each and their harness complete
8 teams of 4 mules each and their harness complete
4 teams of 2 mules each and their harness complete
3 teams of 2 horses each and their harness complete
3 9-passenger coaches
2 6-passenger coaches
1 6-passenger coach
3 4-passenger 2-horse hacks[32]

---

[31] *San Antonio Daily Herald*, Aug. 20, 1875; *Management of the Post-Office Department*, 462–78, 508, 19.

[32] Mary Bain Spence, "The Story of Benficklin: First County Seat of Tom Green County, Texas," Fort Concho Preservation and Museum, San Angelo, Texas; Deed Record Book B, County Clerk's Office, Tom Green County, Tex., p. 60.

Sawyer's death marked a turning point for the company in several respects. The organization survived his passing, but it was less of an empire than an appendage to the rapidly expanding railroads. Even though it still served the vital function of uniting El Paso and the country to the west with the settled portions of Texas, it was obvious by the fall of 1875 that there was no longer any question that the railroads would span the state; the only unanswered question was when the task would be completed. Chidester, Bain, and Taylor knew that the great times for their industry were past. The best they could hope for was a profitable leave-taking.

In the four and a half years between Ben Ficklin's death and Sawyer's demise, the stage line had endured enough turmoil for a decade. The intrigues and economies of the Post Office Department, the ceaseless depredations of the Indians and Comancheros, and even the scourge of the epizootic had failed to destroy the company. Although its finances and management organization were often strained, the coaches kept rolling with surprising regularity and speed. Even though people might complain that the mail was late, the very vehemence of their protests was proof of the valuable service being rendered by Taylor's men. As the El Paso Mail entered the final phase of its existence, there was still much to be proud of and little enough to regret. It had moved far beyond the role of a simple courier to act as a colonizing force on the frontier that was rivaled only by the military in its power to attract both people and government funds into the aching emptiness of the plains below the caprock ramparts of the Llano Estacado.

In the few years left to the expressmen they would continue to nurture the very expansion of civilization that guaranteed their industry's extinction. Change and progress may have brought a pang of remorse to many of the people who could yet remember the start of it all a quarter of a century before with Henry Skillman, but their passing remained as gallant as their coming.

CHAPTER 15

The Savage Recessional

T HE year 1876 marked the centennial of the nation's birth. It proved to be something less than celebratory for the stage line. From that point through the rest of the decade, the El Paso coaches would be caught between the oncoming nemesis of the railroads and the increasingly bitter assaults of Indians and white outlaws. Frank Taylor and his employees would wage a continuing battle to let their business live out the life left to it before the rails were joined between the Sabine and the Rio Grande.

Despite the admittedly uncertain outlook for the future, Taylor strove to keep the mail on the road and deny his critics any reason for more complaints. The trail was as rough and punishing on men and teams as ever; the schedules just as demanding. The *San Antonio Daily Herald* remarked admiringly on the addition of portable jacks and tool kits to the new coaches still entering service on the line. The management obviously meant to give its employees the ability to cope with any problem met on the road. It was an index to Taylor's character that he deepened his investment in an already moribund enterprise simply to insure that the agreement he had made with the government would be kept and the public would be well served.[1]

Throughout the first few months of the new year the coaches resumed the old clockwork regularity of their arrivals and departures, and there were no complaints recorded about the contractors. By late February the work crews had finished the telegraph line linking San Antonio to Fort Stockton. It was good news for Taylor in one sense, for though the wires represented the sort of progress that would eventually put him out of business, they also afforded greater security for his operation. Indian raids striking any portion of the line east of Comanche Springs could be

---

[1] *San Antonio Daily Herald*, Jan. 22, 1876.

quickly reported and troops dispatched from posts along the route to move in concert against the braves.[2]

The road was relatively quiet through the first half of the year, but the weather turned violently capricious. At least one late winter storm halted traffic through the mountains around Fort Davis in early March until the hurricane-force winds subsided. Any rig caught on the trail in such a blow could only run for cover or lock its brakes after turning the team's heads into the wind.[3]

By June, Taylor was eyeing the railroad's fitful advance from the east and judged that there was still reason to keep the company on the best footing possible. He purchased a trio of deluxe seven-passenger coaches, christening them the "John Hancock," the "General Mackenzie," and the "Alamo," with the names painted in gilt letters on their side panels. He put them on the run from San Antonio to Fort Concho with sleek new teams. The *Herald* called them conveyances "that for elegance and comfort, are in advance of the times . . . the annoyance and distress that usually accompanies staging will be reduced fifty per cent." The new stock on the road may have sold a few more tickets, but it also attracted unwelcome attention as well. In mid-August a gang of rustlers raided the station and settlement at Lipan Springs and drove their captured animals northwestward for New Mexico. A posse and army patrol caught up with them at the Head of Concho and recaptured the stock after a gun battle.[4]

By September other troubles were cropping up as the outlaws became even bolder along the eastern reaches of the line. On the twelfth they tried to rob an army paymaster at Jackson's Crossing of the San Saba, near Menardville. The troops routed the bandits, having received intelligence about the gang's intentions beforehand. This victory was counterbalanced by continuing reports of Comanches on the prowl in the hills near Mason and the destruction of long stretches of the telegraph lines west of Fort Concho. The Mescaleros were restive also. By early Oc-

[2]Ibid., Feb. 29, 1876.
[3]Ibid., Mar. 18, 1876.
[4]Ibid., June 3, 1876; *Fort Worth Daily Democrat*, Aug. 19, 1876.

tober they had raided the outskirts of El Paso and struck at Eagle Springs, killing two of Taylor's hands.[5]

Travelers had learned to take such occurrences in their stride as one of the expected risks to be endured on the frontier, although prudent men always went armed when they boarded a coach to ride west of Bexar. Traffic on the route hardly diminished that autumn, as one surviving waybill for the division between Fort Davis and Fort Stockton illustrates. Sporting the letterhead of the combined Texas and California Stage Company, the document listed three passengers departing Fort Davis that September 26. Letters and pieces of freight were catalogued by date of receipt, place of receipt, charge, and addressee. A space was also allotted on the form to record the stations en route, times of arrival and departure, number of mail sacks carried, and the name of each relief driver.

The management provided some detailed guidance for its employees as well. "Drivers are held accountable that each person and package on coach is entered on Way-Bill," it admonished. "Each driver and station-keeper will examine the Freight list on each Way-Bill, and take charge of Freight for their offices." No one was to be permitted to ride for free, as "Fare of Passengers is invariably to be paid in advance." The line agents were instructed to check schedules and monitor the drivers' conduct at all times. "Dogs," it was stressed, "are not allowed to be carried on the stage at any price."[6]

The dogs may have been fortunate. A pilgrim who took the coach west from Benficklin that year told of how the "headstrong, furious and ungovernable" mules swept the rig along at a brisk eight miles an hour over the rutted track. "It takes one who has the toughness of a light-wood knot to stand this," he complained.[7]

Taylor and Bain could shrug off the criticisms of those new to the rigors of frontier travel, and they still hoped that times

[5] Dorman H. Winfrey and James Day, eds., *Texas Indian Papers, 1860–1916*, 395.

[6] Waybill, "Texas and California Stage Company," Sept. 26, 1876, Fort Davis National Historic Site, Fort Davis, Tex.

[7] Nathaniel A. Taylor, *Two Thousand Miles in Texas on Horseback*, 373–85.

would improve for the line. Even with the El Paso contract facing its eventual demise, there remained a place for the short-line stages in serving the growing settlements. Although there had been problems with a lapse of service on the eastern leg to Fort Griffin from Fort Worth the year before, by that October the company could announce a new route from Fort Worth to Fort Concho by way of Granbury, Stephenville, Comanche, and Brownwood. The 170-mile run would be made on a semiweekly basis under the direction of agent C. K. Fairfax.[8]

There were other changes. Taylor yielded supervision of the line out of San Antonio to his partner, while he remained as general manager. Thus advertisements appeared in the newspapers, referring to C. Bain and Company, with its promise of a fifty-seven-hour passage to Fort Concho, "allowing eight hours rest at Fredericksburg." Bain's operation received additional publicity that month when the sheriff of Tom Green County led a posse into the station at Kickapoo Springs and killed two outlaws during a gunfight that lasted for five hours.[9]

It was an indication of the pace of change in those times that while men still died violently on the mail road to the west, others were laying out a streetcar system in Fort Worth and the railroad crept to within ten miles of San Antonio. The predictions of Taylor and Bain about the continuing utility of their business were borne out again in early February, 1877, when the *Daily Democrat* agitated for increased government support for the stage company. "The mail on the line is now transported three times a week, when it should by all means be six times. The amount is now very heavy," claimed the editor, "and is daily increasing." Six hundred pounds of mail went out on each coach, "which is far in excess of the amount of mail matter on many routes that have daily service."[10]

Bain remained optimistic enough to revive the service to Weatherford, Jacksboro, and Fort Griffin. While visiting Jacksboro he announced that new Concords would equip the route.

[8] *Fort Worth Daily Democrat*, Oct. 1, 19, 1876; *Jacksboro Frontier Echo*, Nov. 6, 1875, Mar. 10, 31, 1876.
[9] *San Antonio Express*, Jan. 11, 1877; *Fort Worth Daily Democrat*, Nov. 3, 1876.
[10] *Fort Worth Daily Democrat*, Nov. 3, 1876.

When the town's paper complained that his express rates were too high, the *Daily Democrat* dismissed the charge, replying, "There is not a better conducted line of stages in or out of the state than that of C. Bain & Co., none that has more careful agents."[11]

Charles Bain brooked no opposition from Indians, desperados, or journalists in running his business. When stock was reported missing from his Fort Worth stables, he and two companions took their shotguns down from the rack and searched every saloon and bordello in town for the thieves, prompting the *Democrat* to dub them the "Bloody Three" and publish an admiring, if humorous, poem about their exploits.[12]

Bain had good reason to take such militant action in defense of his property. A new campaign of theft and robbery had already been directed at the company. Late in January a gang of robbers had halted the stage near Pegleg Crossing. They had planned to catch the government paymaster for the garrison at Fort Concho, but he was not aboard. The brigands relieved the passengers of their wallets and escaped into the hill country. It was the first of many robberies committed near the station and ford on the San Saba.[13]

Bain would be faced with a spate of such incidents until the end of his service in 1881. Ironically, this new threat was the result of the same progress that was giving his business a last blush of prosperity before eventually dooming it. There were several reasons for the rise of this form of lawlessness. With the decline of the Indian threat to the settled tier of counties northwest of San Antonio, travel and population understandably increased. The roads in the region were safer and more lucrative places for the bandits to operate. Also, by 1877, the Southern Plains were being quickly depleted of their vast buffalo herds. The decline of the hide business threw men out of work, and for the luckless hunters and skinners, robbery was sometimes an attractive temporary occupation. The approach of the railroads also stimulated

[11] Ibid., Feb. 17, 1877.
[12] Ibid., Mar. 10, 1877.
[13] *Fort Griffin Echo*, Feb. 2, 1877.

settlement, and the criminal element that always form a part of any population grew accordingly.[14]

Bain and Taylor continued to capitalize on the growth in traffic in the face of the outlaw threat. On February 19 the first passenger train of the Galveston, Harrisburg, and San Antonio Railroad reached Bexar. The next day C. Bain and Company ran an advertisement in the *Daily Express* announcing a "Railroad Line," which was billed as the only line of coaches serving Fort Concho and intermediate points from a railhead. Six coaches a week ran from Alamo Plaza to handle the influx of travelers.[15]

The increase in receipts soon went to cover the cost of losses on the western road, as the rate of white and Indian attacks on the stages mounted. Early that spring Major John B. Jones and Captain Neal Coldwell of the Texas Rangers conducted sweeps of the San Saba and Llano river valleys, apprehending a fair number of wanted men and some generally suspicious characters in the process. For a while the stage route was cleared of outlaws and the coaches made the run north from San Antonio with little fear of being robbed. The calm did not last out the year.[16]

By May all the signs were pointing toward a resurgence of the Indian threat beyond Fort Concho. Captain Alex S. B. Keyes of the Tenth Cavalry spent most of April probing the country that stretched from the Head of Concho to Horsehead Crossing and Pecos Station. Bain's men at the lower crossing reported sighting Indians driving stolen stock along the river, and reports filtered in from New Mexico, telling of how the Comancheros were gathering to the north in Canyon Blanco to trade arms and ammunition to the braves for their plunder. Mackenzie's earlier campaigns had broken the main strength of the Kiowas and Comanches, but there were still enough incorrigibles left on the reservation at Fort Sill to make life risky beyond the settlements.[17]

[14] W. C. Holden, "Law and Lawlessness on the Texas Frontier, 1875–1890," *Southwestern Historical Quarterly* 44 (Oct., 1940): 192.

[15] *San Antonio Daily Express*, Feb. 20, 1877.

[16] James B. Gillett, *Six Years with the Texas Rangers, 1875 to 1881*, 69–70.

[17] Capt. Alex S. B. Keyes to Post Adjutant, May 1, 1877, Records of the Headquarters, Fort Concho, Tex., RG 393, NARS.

The farther west Bain looked, the worse things appeared. The Apaches were striking the road around Fort Davis again between March and June, killing at least three travelers. Colonel Andrews, the commander at Fort Davis, unwittingly identified one of the company's major dilemmas in a letter of complaint he sent to his superiors that July. "From *Fort Concho* to *El Paso* the stage company runs a buckboard or hack, twice and a stage once per week," he reported, "but the number of passengers between here and El Paso amounts to almost nothing, except during the session of the district court, during the spring and fall, of two weeks each term." Andrews was miffed at the rates charged for passengers and freight, for he remarked that "any manifestation of a desire to accommodate the members of the garrison at this end of the line, by the stage company, even at a reasonable compensation, would cause great astonishment."[18]

Andrews had put his gauntleted finger on the problem. The revenues were the lowest and the risks the highest on the leg between Fort Concho and El Paso. The contract bound the company to deliver the mail over the route, but the relative scarcity of passengers and freight generated little profit for it. El Paso remained a small, struggling outpost on the border while the shorter routes to the east serving San Antonio, Fort Worth, and Fort Concho bore the heaviest traffic. Once the rails advanced far enough to negate the value of those routes to the Post Office Department, the company would lose them and face reliance on the residual passenger traffic plus the El Paso mail contract until the railhead reached that town as well. By the summer of 1877 the end was well in sight for the line, but the last spike had yet to be driven.

It was already too late for some of Bain's men. On August 1 herder Henry Dill was shot to death at El Muerto and robbed by unknown persons. That same day another man was ambushed on the road four miles from the station. Colonel Andrews held that bandits, not Apaches, were the culprits.[19]

---

[18] Col. George L. Andrews to Assistant Adj. Gen., July 21, 1877, Letters Sent, Fort Davis, Tex., RG 98, NARS.

[19] Col. George L. Andrews to Assistant Adj. Gen., Aug. 13, 1877, ibid.

The trouble came in droves by autumn, as Apaches struck a train near Van Horn's Wells in late September and threatened to cut the line of communication to El Paso. On October 10, Luis Cardis, the company's agent in El Paso, was murdered in a political dispute that eventually brought in a company of Texas Rangers to quell the violence that followed in the valley settlements. Late that month driver John Sanders was ambushed by Indians at Flat Rock Holes. A patrol from Pecos Station found his mutilated body and the looted coach soon afterward. His death was quickly followed by another killing on the line, as the Apaches shot two men in Bass Canyon only a few days before Christmas. These incidents were climaxed by another outbreak of banditry south of Fort Concho.[20]

Lieutenant Harry Kirby, Tenth Infantry, boarded the stage in San Antonio for the last portion of his journey to Fort McKavett. Having heard of conditions on the road, he purchased a revolver for protection. His anxiety mounted when they met a wagon on the trail just a dozen miles from town. It carried the body of a man who had been bushwhacked on the road the night before. In Fredericksburg the subaltern changed to a canvas-roofed ambulance, a drafty conveyance for travel in such cold weather. Judge Allan Blacker of the El Paso district court shared the ride with him. At Mason they were joined by a company blacksmith and a Jewish merchant from New Orleans. The four men endured the biting wind with upturned collars as they settled down for the night's ride through the hill country.

At about one o'clock in the morning of December 15 the rig was bowling along not far west of Pegleg Station when driver James Brown suddenly halted the team. Two men stood in the road, the blued steel barrels of their Winchesters catching the beams from the sidelamps and throwing them back with an evil

[20] George Abbott to Post Commander, Oct. 1, 1877, Letters Received, Fort Davis, Tex., RG 98, NARS; 1st Sgt. Thomas H. Allsup to Post Adjutant, Nov. 4, 1877, Records of the Headquarters, Fort Concho, Texas, RG 393, NARS: John H. Nankivell, *History of the Twenty-Fifth Regiment United States Infantry, 1869–1926*, 28; *Record of Engagements with Hostile Indians within the Military Division of the Missouri, from 1868 to 1882, Lieutenant General P. H. Sheridan, Commanding, Compiled at Headquarters, Military Division of the Missouri from Official Records*, 75. The best account of Cardis's death can be found in C. L. Sonnichsen, *The El Paso Salt War of 1877*.

glitter. They ordered Brown to swing the stage off the track and drive it slowly into a nearby thicket. The bandits punctuated their demands with the snap of cartridges being chambered in their carbines. While the driver and his passengers were held at gunpoint, the coach and baggage were searched for money and other valuables. Kirby was ready to make a fight of it, but his companions dissuaded him, for the odds were too great. He did manage to hide his cash before the thieves searched him. As the outlaws released them, the gang's leader said, "You may tell the Menard people Dick Dublin has come back to stay awhile." [21]

Several hours later the travelers reached Captain Dan Roberts's camp of Company D, Frontier Battalion of the Texas Rangers. Roberts immediately led a patrol in pursuit of the robbers but had no success. They had simply melted into the rugged brush country that lapped the San Saba and Llano.

Pegleg Crossing continued to be the site of trouble. The road made an abrupt descent to the crossing of McDougal Creek after leaving the relay point and then hugged the south bank of the San Saba to a ford just short of Ten-mile Crossing, where it swung over to the north side of the river. A short distance before this crossing came the roughest part of the road for the teams. A narrow draw required a slow, straining pull up the steep cut through the face of the bank. Overlooking the road through the cut was a high hill with a curving downslope that gave a clear field of fire through the draw. This rise was known as Robbers' Roost, for the ground below it was an ideal ambush site for the road agents. [22]

Captain Roberts tried assigning men to ride shotgun on each coach that left Pegleg Crossing. The robberies halted for a time but began again when the guards were withdrawn. Roberts could not spare the men to serve as permanent mail escorts, and Robber's Roost once again hosted the outlaws. [23]

The Texas Rangers were needed on other portions of the line as well. Only a week before the year's end Bass Canyon

[21] Robert S. Weddle, "The Pegleg Stage Robbers," *Southwest Heritage* 3 (Mar., 1969): 4.

[22] Ibid., 3; Dan W. Roberts, *Rangers and Sovereignty*, 1–5, 29.

[23] Weddle, "Stage Robbers," 3.

claimed two more victims when the Mescaleros staged another ambush in its twisted gullet. The stripped bodies were left in the road for the next coach to find.[24]

The mounting pace of the killings on the route west of Fort Davis was particularly troubling to one of the company's men. William Mitchell, a transplanted Scot, drove the run between the post and Van Horn's Wells. Having worked on a construction crew for the Union Pacific Railroad a decade before, Mitchell was accustomed to privations and danger, but on a railroad crew there had always been the comparative safety of numbers. There were few occupations lonelier than that of holding the reins on a coach. One incident genuinely galled Mitchell while he drove the route. He had paid a seamstress at Fort Davis to make him a new shirt. Before he could wear the garment a fellow driver borrowed it to wear on the drive west. The jehu was later found by the side of the road, and Mitchell's new shirt was studded with arrows.[25]

The Apaches counted more victories in the region that winter, killing two more mail riders north of Fort Davis at Point of Rocks and slaying at least six men on the trail that led south to Presidio del Norte in January and February. There was a spell of calm in March, and then in April the Comanches jumped a stage twenty-one miles east of Fort Stockton, killing the driver and his passengers in a spatter of gunfire from the brush. A troop of the Tenth Cavalry futilely followed the raiders' trail to the north between the blue-hazed mesas. Even as that chase continued, the Apaches killed another man nine miles from the Fort Quitman station. The military responded by reinforcing the pickets at Van Horn's Wells and Eagle Springs, while sending escorts with each stage.[26]

That first quarter of 1878 brought some of the worst losses for the company in years, but the picture was not entirely bleak. Three years before, Colonel Benjamin Grierson had assumed

---

[24] *Records of Engagements*, 75.

[25] Civilian residents file, Fort Davis National Historic Site, Fort Davis, Tex., Mrs. M. T. Bennett, correspondence with author, Sept. 17, 1979. Mrs. Bennett is Mitchell's granddaughter.

[26] *Record of Engagements*, 76–77; J. Evetts Haley, *Fort Concho and the Texas Frontier*, 327.

command of Fort Concho and brought the post to a high level of efficiency. The cavalryman and Frank Taylor shared an interest in music and became fast friends. Taylor provided Grierson with free passes on the stage and the colonel responded by taking a personal interest in the mail line's welfare. It was all a far cry from the days of Ben Ficklin and Major Cram.[27]

In January, 1878, Grierson assumed command of the newly created Military District of the Pecos. His enlarged area of responsibility took in all of Texas west of the 101st meridian. He had six companies each of cavalry and infantry with which to police this largely uncharted country. In April and May, Grierson personally led an expedition out from his headquarters to scout the Big Bend region below Fort Davis. On the way he laid out a new road that struck south by west from Camp Charlotte for thirty-eight miles before reaching a recently discovered waterhole in a canyon that lay nearly eighteen miles south of the mail route through Centralia Station.

The improved road ran on from the waterhole for twenty-five miles to Pecos Station. Christening the oasis Grierson's Springs, he ordered a stone guardhouse and other structures built, and directed that the telegraph line be strung down from the north to tie the new subpost in with Forts Concho and Stockton. Eventually the stage company would route its carriers by the springs also.[28]

With Grierson bringing improvements to the western road, the Texas Rangers were stepping up their drive against the bandits on the trail above Fredericksburg. That May one of their patrols was scouting the South Llano when it captured Bill Allison, a member of the Dick Dublin gang. Allison was jailed in Austin on a number of charges and the bond was pegged high enough to insure that he would stay there until he came to trial. It would take some time, but eventually the outlaw would betray his comrades to the lawmen.[29]

---

[27] Susan Miles, "Until the Flood, 1867–1882," *Edwards Plateau Historian* 2 (1966): 21.

[28] Frank M. Temple, "Colonel Grierson: Builder on the Frontier," *Edwards Plateau Historian* 2 (1966): 30–31; Haley, *Fort Concho*, 328–29.

[29] Gillett, *Six Years*, 102–103; Weddle, "Stage Robbers," 4–5.

In the meantime there was still an abundance of trouble on the line. Bands of Indians were reported prowling the road near Pecos Station and Centralia throughout May. On June 27 a small war party attacked the westbound stage only 5 miles from Pecos Station. The rig escaped, but a passenger was so badly wounded that he had to be hospitalized at Fort Stockton. A little over a week later the coach from San Antonio met a bandit ambush two miles west of Pegleg Crossing. News of the robbery reached Fort Concho on the telegraph, and the Rangers took the field again in another unsuccessful search for the brigands.[30]

That summer's misfortunes came to an almost predictable climax in August when the Mescaleros stormed into El Muerto, killed a driver, and stole all of the station's stock. They fled northward for the Guadalupes, eluding a pursuing cavalry patrol from Fort Davis. Taylor and Bain responded to the attack with their typically dogged optimism. On August 8 the company agent in San Antonio announced the start of a new branch line offering service three times weekly to Laredo. Return tickets from any point on the road to either El Paso or Laredo were offered at half-price. Obviously the company planned to capture as much passenger traffic as possible before the rails began edging west from Bexar.[31]

For several years past the firm's relations with the military had been passably good, but in the fall of 1878 there was a minor crisis when the soldiers and stagemen clashed with each other again. Early in November the sergeant commanding the guard detail at El Muerto discovered the station's cook in the act of pilfering an express package from the boot of the westbound stage. A confrontation developed between the soldiers and the station hands. Sergeant Jenkins finally turned out the guard and arrested the thief at gunpoint, seizing the package as evidence at the same time. For a few moments it looked as though shooting might erupt. The driver of the stage coming down from El Paso

[30] W. P. Lockhart to Agent, July 6, 1878, Telegrams Received, Fort Concho Preservation and Museum, San Angelo, Tex.

[31] *Record of Engagements*, 82; *San Antonio Daily Herald*, Oct. 3, 1878; Robert H. Thonhoff, *San Antonio Stage Lines, 1847–1881*, 31.

was present, and he drove on to Fort Davis, where he accused Jenkins of interfering with the government mails.[32]

The incident touched off a furor, and when the news reached Fort Concho, Charles Bain and an agent of the Post Office Department immediately rode west to investigate the affair. The cook was subsequently fired, although the post commander at Fort Davis complained that he soon found another job with the company on the line between Eagle Springs and Van Horn's Wells. Resentment lingered between the black soldiers and the white expressmen, but they would soon have other enemies to face.[33]

Nearly six months of welcome quiet prevailed on the road after the incident at El Muerto. The garrisons beyond the Concho remained alert to the threat of Indian raids, and their vigilance was aided in May when the telegraph line extended beyond Fort Davis and Van Horn's Wells to close on Eagle Springs. Any depredation committed along the route would quickly be reported and the alarm spread for hundreds of miles along the border.[34]

The wires to the east of Fort Davis were soon humming with good news for the mail company that spring. Ranger James B. Gillett was delivering a prisoner to the Austin Jail when Bill Allison asked to speak with him. Gillett had known him in the days when he was still an honest man, and Allison trusted the peace officer to deal fairly with him. After spending a year in jail he had grown embittered after no word of comfort or help came from his comrades. He decided to tell the Texas Rangers everything he knew about the gang's membership and methods of operation.[35]

Dick Dublin, the felons' leader, had already been dealt with by the law. In October, 1877, the Rangers had almost killed him during a gunfight on the South Llano as he attempted to

[32] Lt. W. W. Landon to Sgt. Jenkins, Nov. 6, 1878, Letters Sent, Fort Davis, Tex., RG 98, NARS.

[33] Ibid.; Capt. L. H. Carpenter to Adj. Gen., Nov. 23, 1878, Letters Sent, Fort Davis, Tex., RG 98, NARS.

[34] Post Adjutant to Assistant Adj. Gen., Apr. 15, 1879; Post Adjutant to Lt. Syres, [illegible] Apr., 1879, Letters Sent, Fort Davis, Tex., RG 98, NARS.

[35] Gillett, *Six Years*, 103; Weddle, "Stage Robbers," 4–5.

escape with a herd of stolen cattle. On January 18, 1878, Lieutenant N. O. Reynold's company cornered Dublin in his stronghold, taking him completely by surprise. When the desperado tried to escape, Gillett dropped him with a fatal shot from his Winchester.[36]

Even with their chieftain dead, the remnants of the gang still posed a threat to the frontier settlements, and the lawmen were delighted with the information they gained from Allison. Captain Dan W. Roberts quickly led his men out from their Menard County camp to assault the bandits at their hideout in adjoining Kimble County. The bad men put up a stiff fight but finally surrendered. Role and Dell Dublin went into handcuffs along with Mack Potter and Rube Boyce. Potter and his friends received sentences of fifteen years each at hard labor for robbing the mails. Boyce made a daring escape from the Austin jail, was recaptured in New Mexico, and subsequently won an acquittal from the charges against him. With the capture of this gang, the organized stage robberies and stock thefts in the Pegleg Station and Menardville area came to an end. Bain's drivers could breathe a little easier each time they breasted the rise beyond McDougal Creek.[37]

The company did not have long to celebrate the bandits' defeat before another stunning blow struck it. In May, Esther Anne Taylor was stricken with typhoid fever and died at Benficklin. Within three weeks Frank Taylor succumbed to the disease and followed her into the flinty earth of the Concho country. Virtually the entire population of Benficklin, San Angela, and Fort Concho turned out for the funerals. Taylor's epitaph honored him with the title of "Father of Tom Green County," an appellation that ran very close to the mark. In less than a decade Taylor had helped revive the industry of commercial transportation in the Southwest, brought new population and resources to the cutting edge of the frontier, and created a county out of the endless leagues of caprock and buffalo grass. His death marked the mail company's entry into the final phase of its existence.

[36] Gillett, *Six Years*, 88–95.
[37] Ibid., 103–105.

The time of striving had not yet ended, but the days of building were irrevocably past.[38]

The effects of Taylor's death on the mail line are not documented. No records survive that deal with the company's affairs, and it can only be assumed that Charles Bain and whoever may have joined him as partners in the service took over full control of the routes radiating out of San Antonio and Fort Worth. Bain's name continued to appear on the company's letterhead in all of the advertising that was placed in the region's newspapers.

Bain turned from mourning his friend to contending with the unending flow of threats and challenges that faced the line. The western end of the El Paso route continued to offer only mounting losses and declining receipts. Lone travelers died on the road near Van Horn's Wells as Mexican bandits staged a foray across the border, and Mescalero raiders attacked ranches near Fort Davis while other braves killed two men within sight of the walls at Barrel Station. For a time that spring Bain pulled his coaches off the road and began using couriers to carry mail between Fort Stockton and Fort Davis, as well as to Presidio del Norte in the south.[39]

The troubles continued into late August, when Victorio and his band of Mimbres Apaches bolted the reservation at Fort Stanton, taking some of the resident Mescaleros with him. For the rest of the year and into 1880 the warriors rampaged throughout southern New Mexico and northern Chihuahua, slipping back and forth across the border to strike at will from their sanctuary in the Candelaria Mountains. The raids kept the entire region in an uproar for over a year. Bain's men did not escape the chieftain's attention, although they would have the eventual satisfaction of figuring in his defeat.[40]

At virtually the same time that Victorio was leaving the reservation, Lieutenant George W. Baylor was leading his company

[38] Miles, "Until the Flood," 23; Francis C. Taylor reference file, Fort Concho Preservation and Museum, San Angelo, Tex.

[39] *Record of Engagements*, 86; Capt. L. H. Carpenter to Adj. Gen., July 11, 14, 1879, Letters Sent, Fort Davis, Tex., RG 98, NARS.

[40] Dan L. Thrapp, *Victorio and the Mimbres Apaches*, 218–75; William H. Leckie, *The Buffalo Soldiers*, 210–15.

of Texas Rangers west from San Antonio to the Pass of the North.
James B. Gillett rode with the detachment, and in his memoirs
he left a perceptive account of the mail company's operations.
The lawman had nothing but admiration for the jehus, remarking, "There should be a monument erected to the memory of
those old stage-drivers somewhere along this overland route, for
they were certainly the bravest of the brave. It took a man with
lots of nerve and strength to be a stage-driver in the Indian days,
and many of them were killed."[41]

Baylor and his men had been in camp near El Paso for only a
few weeks when the Apaches struck the fringes of the valley
settlements. A band of renegades from New Mexico attacked
some Mexican hay cutters between San Elizario and the stage
station at La Quadrilla. Gillett and ten men quickly followed
their trail across the Rio Grande and joined forces with some local militia as they forged deeper into Chihuahua. On the morning of October 7 the Texans and Mexicans rode into an ambush
and fought the entrenched Apaches all day, finally breaking off
the action at dusk. The raiders slipped off to join their comrades
in the Candelarias.[42]

Victorio recrossed the border in January to raid New Mexico and fight several actions with pursuing detachments of the
Ninth Cavalry before fading south into the mountains. Coaches
coming down the line from Fort Worth found signs of Apache
scouts near Fort Quitman in early February, 1880, but the stage
company remained curiously immune to the Mescaleros' depredations for the time being. The Indian scare had done nothing to dull the enterprising spirit that was abroad in El Paso that
month.

Surveyor O. W. Williams arrived in town on the eastern
stage to find the citizens greatly excited over the oncoming railroads. Lots near the rumored site of the depot were selling for
one hundred dollars, and virtually all of the property in town
was increasing in value. What Williams saw in El Paso was the
first blush of anticipatory prosperity. A visitor to the town in
1876 had estimated its population at between fifty and a hun-

[41] Gillett, *Six Years*, 145–48.
[42] Ibid., 151–53; Walter P. Webb, *The Texas Rangers*, 396.

dred Anglos, remarking that half of the houses seemed deserted at the time. Despite its rather forlorn air, the town's inhabitants displayed an impressive optimism and fixity of purpose, pegging their fondest hopes on the certain arrival of the railroads.[43]

In San Antonio and Fort Worth the optimism was tempered by the patience of a people who already enjoyed the benefits of residing in established, growing towns. San Antonio had been the hub of Texas since the Mexican War, and Fort Worth was already linked to the east by the rails. It knew that another connection stretching to the Pacific was already assured. The region's growth to date and potential for further expansion may have been best represented by Tom Green County. It was fitting that the county's original settlements were spawned by the express business. At the time of its organization it had boasted only 160 qualified voters in a population of about 1,000 people, who were scattered along the mail road that cut across 12,500 square miles of frontier. By 1880 there were 3,609 people living in the communities serving the fort and stage line on the Concho. The high incidence of occupations relating to commercial transportation listed among them on the census rolls of that year was proof of the strategic role it played in the county's growth.[44]

Charles Bain had a good chance to judge the potential growth of the towns his company served, for he ranged up and down the line that April, meeting with a mishap en route that sent him back to Benficklin with his broken ankle propped on the seat of a rig. The accident came just as a final burst of tragic violence erupted on the road beyond the Pecos.[45]

On May 12 a small emigrant train left Van Horn's Wells and drove into a Mescalero ambush in Bass Canyon. The whites were forced to abandon their wagons and retreat to the wells. The Apaches paused to loot the train and then hurried south to join Victorio. Eleven days later another war party caught the stationkeeper at Barrel Springs on the road and nearly killed

[43] C. L. Sonnichsen, *Pass of the North*, 211–12; S. D. Myres, ed., *Pioneer Surveyor—Frontier Lawyer: The Personal Narrative of O. W. Williams, 1877–1902*, 104.

[44] Escal F. Duke, "A Population Study of Tom Green County, 1880," *West Texas Historical Association Yearbook* 52 (Oct., 1976): 49–61.

[45] San Angelo *Concho Times*, Apr. 24, 1881.

him in the chase that followed.[46] The tempo and direction of the raids led Colonel Grierson to think that Victorio was planning a major movement into Texas. He set out to bar the Apaches from entering the state by patroling the border crossings, guarding the mountain passes, and outposting the water holes. The Tenth Cavalry was soon raising dust on every trail between Limpia Creek and the Rio Grande. Grierson arrived at Fort Davis in July to take charge of the campaign. It was the beginning of the end for Victorio.

At Fort Davis, Grierson learned that a large force of Mexican troops was harrying the Indians northward toward the border. They were thought to be headed for Eagle Springs once they cleared the Rio Grande. The colonel and a small escort immediately rode west to check the outposts. By the twenty-third he was at Eagle Springs, receiving word that the braves were reported to be just fifty miles away and rapidly nearing the border. Grierson pressed on to check the guards at old Fort Quitman.[47]

On his return from the post Grierson met couriers from Eagle Springs, who told him that Victorio had crossed the Rio Grande not far below Fort Quitman. Knowing that the Indians would head for the nearest waterhole, Grierson planned to beat them to Tinaja de las Palmas and deny them access to the stone tank. Reaching the base of Devil Ridge on the twenty-ninth, the soldiers took a position on the same piece of rocky high ground where James E. Terry had stood off the Apaches nineteen years before. Grierson had only his son and eight troopers to hold the hill against Victorio.[48]

That night Grierson flagged down both the east- and west-bound stages to send messages to Fort Quitman and Eagle Springs requesting aid. When the Indians appeared at nine o'clock the next morning, Grierson's escort held them at bay until the reinforcements arrived and put the Apaches to flight for the Rio Grande. In four hours of fighting Grierson had blunted the chieftain's thrust into Texas. If Bain's men had been running behind

[46] Gillett, *Six Years*, 202; *Record of Engagements*, 95.
[47] Leckie, *The Buffalo Soldiers*, 223–24.
[48] Ibid.

schedule the Mescaleros might have overrun the outnumbered cavalrymen and escaped northward into the Guadalupes.[49]

Victorio withdrew back into Mexico, about sixty miles south of Fort Quitman. Parts of the band doubled back into Texas in small groups, and Bain's drivers were the first to feel the sting of their anger. On July 31, the day following Grierson's action, Captain Neal Coldwell of the Texas Rangers was riding the stage east for Fort Davis after visiting Baylor's Ranger company in Ysleta. Coldwell, the driver, a company hostler, and an army guard learned of Victorio's repulse at Quitman Station, but the men remained alert as they cleared Quitman Pass and swung south down the canyon. They expected to meet the coach for El Paso at Tinaja de las Palmas around dusk.[50]

On the way to the waterhole Coldwell sighted five riders moving along at a distance. They did not approach the stage, and he assumed that they were army scouts. When they reached the tinaja there was no sign of the coach. Three miles beyond the team shied at something in the road. It was the rig from Fort Davis. One mule was gone and the other lay dead in the traces. Nearby were the bodies of driver E. C. Baker and his passenger, F. C. Wyant. The Apaches had slashed open their abdomens and then stuffed the contents of the mail pouches into the gaping wounds.

Coldwell and his companions did not pause for long at the ambush scene but made the best time possible into Eagle Springs to report the killings. The cavalrymen posted there had earlier warned Baker not to make the westward run, but the jehu had driven on to his death. In Bain's service a man simply trusted to his luck until the string ran out.[51]

The Apaches had not finished with the company yet. By August, Victorio was probing the border crossings again, and Grierson was moving to block him. Ranger Baylor led a patrol east from the Pass to scout the road as far as Eagle Springs. On reach-

[49] Ibid., 224–25.

[50] Paul I. Wellman, *The Indian Wars of the West*, 384. Wellman's subsequent chronology of events was incorrect.

[51] Ibid.; Webb, *The Texas Rangers*, 400; A. J. Sowell, "Captain Neal Coldwell," *Frontier Times* 25 (Mar., 1948): 135–44.

ing the picket post, he found that the telegraph line from Fort Davis had been cut in Bass Canyon. The next day, August 5, the stage left Van Horn's Wells on a scheduled run. The driver had just topped a rise on the trail when he sighted Indians ahead and whirled the team about for a dash back to the station. That evening the coach set out again, escorted by a wagon from Van Horn's Wells, but when the caravan entered Bass Canyon the sound of horses on the trail ahead caused it to retreat again in fear of ambush.[52]

The military responded to the incident by placing guards on all the coaches running east to Barilla Springs and West to El Muerto from Fort Davis, but the post adjutant admonished the postmaster not to send the mail out lacking an escort under any circumstances. There were few enough troops to spare as guards, for Grierson was determined to bring the Apaches to battle and finish them. Victorio had managed to slip past his patrols east of Bass Canyon, and the cavalryman hoped to reach the next oasis at Rattlesnake Springs ahead of the braves. He succeeded and laid an ambush. On August 6, Victorio appeared and a vicious fight raged for most of the afternoon until the Indians broke away and fled for the border with the cavalry dogging their trail. Even as the yellowlegs and Baylor's Rangers pressed them, the fugitives paused to claim another victim.[53]

While the Apaches and soldiers stalked each other through the mountains to the east, the chief engineer of the Texas and Pacific Railroad Company was concluding some business in Ysleta and preparing to take a coach for Fort Worth. General James J. Byrnes knew that Victorio was running loose and recognized the risks involved in the journey back to the railhead. Pausing at the stage station, he wrote a letter to his young bride and gave it to the agent for safekeeping. He had a premonition that he would not survive the journey.[54]

Byrnes had survived bitter fighting in the Civil War, suffering at least one wound during his service. His old soldier's intui-

[52] Webb, *The Texas Rangers*, 400; Gillett, *Six Years*, 180; John F. Davis to Commanding Officer, Aug. 6, 1880, Letters Received, Fort Davis, Tex., RG 98, NARS.

[53] Leckie, *The Buffalo Soldiers*, 226–27.

[54] Sue Watkins, *One League to Each Wind*, 182–88.

tion was correct in telling him that the end was near. The coach carried him downriver to Quitman Station on August 8, and the next morning Byrnes and his driver, Ed Walde, set out for Eagle Springs. Walde was giving the team its head about four miles east of the station and nearing Quitman Pass when the Apaches swept out into the road, opening fire at once. Two bullets struck Byrnes, killing him instantly. Walde threw the rig about and made his whip sing over the mules' ears as they raced for the sanctuary of Fort Quitman. The braves screeched after him, and the dead man's body lay slumped halfway out of the coach, waving a macabre farewell to them as the vehicle swayed and jolted over the rocky trace at a flat run.[55]

Walde beat the Indians into the station, and they wheeled south past the whites to murder a Mexican herder and steal his stock before crossing the Rio Grande. Baylor's patrol arrived soon afterward, and James Gillett was incredulous at Walde's escape. "At old Fort Quitman I examined the little canvas-topped stage and found it literally shot to pieces. I noticed where a bullet had glanced along the white canvas, leaving a blue mark a foot long before it passed through the top," he wrote. "Three of the spokes of the wheels were shot in two and there were fifteen or twenty bullet marks on and through the stage." The Texans buried Byrnes in the abandoned post cemetery. A disgusted Ed Walde quit the stage company and enlisted in Baylor's company to seek revenge.[56]

After losing a driver and two passengers in the space of ten days, the stage line was hoping for calmer times when Victorio returned to Mexico. It was not to be, although the events that followed sometimes bordered on the farcical. On August 11 the adjutant at Fort Davis received a message from the guards posted at Barrel Springs. The Indians had raided the station and stolen all the stock, it reported. There was a flurry of excitement until it was learned that the soldier who sent the message had been drunk at the time he composed his dispatch.[57]

[55] Gillett, *Six Years*, 181–82.
[56] Ibid.; *Record of Engagements*, 96.
[57] Lt. Charles Nordstrom to Post Adjutant, Aug. 22, 1880, Letters Received, Fort Davis, Tex., RG 98, NARS.

This incident simply served as an irritant to other problems between the military and the stage company. The men at the mail stations and the troops who were assigned to guard them had conducted a long-running dispute over the responsibilities of the soldiers. The company employees expected them to help with the stock and perform other chores. The previous January, Fort Davis's adjutant had felt compelled to circulate a general order detailing the precise duties of the guards. They were instructed to stay away from the station houses, avoid disputes with the hands, and attend solely to their military duties.[58]

The disagreements continued between the soldiers and civilians. There may have been elements of racial animosity involved, for all of the units posted at Fort Davis were composed of black troops. On August 8, right in the midst of the frenzied hunt for Victorio, the adjutant informed Charles Bain that the guards detailed to Barilla and Barrel Springs had been told to perform no other duties besides those of securing the stations from Indian attack. The officer hoped to avoid future problems with the expressmen by strictly controlling his troops' contacts with them in the line of duty.[59]

The mail company was not solely at fault in the conflicts that arose. One soldier who rode as escort between Leon Holes and Barilla Springs repeatedly cursed and threatened the driver, James Shields. The abrasive Private Taylor was eventually barred from the coach by Shields, who preferred to risk Indian attack and ride without him. Taylor's conduct soon earned him a set of formal charges of misconduct from his harried superiors, who were not amused by his antics.[60]

The friction with the soldiers was soon forgotten in the wake of some very welcome news. In mid-October a force of Mexican troops caught up with Victorio at Tres Castillos, his mountain stronghold, and virtually annihilated the Apaches. For almost three months afterward Bain's coaches rode free from the

[58]General Orders No. 14, Jan. 19, 1880, Letters Sent, Fort Davis, Tex., RG 98, NARS.

[59]Lt. W. H. H. James to Mr. C. Bain, Aug. 8, 1880, in ibid.

[60]Corp. J. F. Ukkerd to Lt. W. H. H. Jones, Aug. 9, 10, 11, 20, 1880, Letters Received, Fort Davis, Tex., RG 98, NARS.

threat of attack. Their drivers would have been a great deal more cautious had they known that a small band of Indians had left Victorio shortly before the Mexican attack and were already riding north to claim new victims in Texas.

On January 8, 1881, driver Morgan was urging his team westward through Quitman Pass, while his passenger, a professional gambler named Crenshaw, slumped in his seat and tried to ignore the biting wind that slipped in through the curtains of the coach. They were threading their way through the roughest section of the gap when the rocks ahead erupted in a blaze of gunfire. A mule screamed hoarsely and dropped dead in the harness. The two men abandoned the rig and bolted for cover on the steep northern side of the track. They tried to make a fight of it, but within a few minutes the Apaches had killed them. The braves looted the bodies and left them sprawled in the concealing brush. After collecting the surviving mule, they fled eastward down the pass.[61]

When the stage failed to arrive on time at Quitman Station, agent John Ford took a few men out on the road to search for it. They found exactly what they had feared. Ford trailed the Indians for several miles but finally returned to the station and sent word to the Texas Rangers at Ysleta. The newly promoted Captain Baylor assembled twelve of his men and a trio of Pueblo Indian scouts for the pursuit. He also telegraphed Fort Davis to order Lieutenant Charles Nevill's company to head west in search of the killers. The Ysleta patrol cut the hostiles' trail about 25 miles below Fort Quitman and followed it into Mexico before it looped north again for Texas. The Rangers calculated that the Apaches were bound for the Eagle Mountains.

Baylor rendezvoused with Neville at Eagle Springs and they tracked the fugitives to Rattlesnake Springs, finding a fresh camp there and another ten miles to the north. By the night of the twenty-eighth they had trailed their quarry deep into the Sierra Diablo. At dawn the next day the Rangers closed on the Apache camp and attacked just as the braves were stirring in their blan-

---

[61] *Record of Engagements*, 100; Webb, *The Texas Rangers*, 402–403; Gillett, *Six Years*, 182–89; George W. Baylor, "The Last Indian Fight in El Paso County," *El Paso Daily Herald*, Aug. 10–14, 1900.

kets. Ed Walde went gleefully into the fight, his Winchester smoking. It was a complete victory for the Texans. The camp was overrun, with most of the Indians being killed or captured. Only a few braves escaped from the lawmen's well-executed assault. The last Indian fight in Texas had ended, and with it the threat to Bain's men from the doomed warriors.[62]

It would not be long before the coach and team followed the tribesmen into eclipse. After a fitful period of delay due to the nation's brush with a financial panic, the rails were starting to inch across the plains and deserts once more. The Texas and Pacific had reached Fort Worth in 1876, and then marked time for four years. The Southern Pacific began to build eastward from Yuma by the end of 1878, and by March of the next year it was in Tucson. Mid-December found the cars in Deming, New Mexico. On May 13, 1881, the last spike had been driven and El Paso found itself with a direct tie to the Pacific by rail.[63]

The Texas and Pacific had regained its momentum again by that spring. At the same time the Atchison, Topeka, and Santa Fe was coursing southward from Albuquerque to the Pass, and the Mexican Central laid rails between Chihuahua and the bordertown. As the railroads closed on El Paso, Bain's company enjoyed a last fleeting brush with prosperity. "It was obvious that the Great Day was at hand," an El Pasoan later recorded, "and as the railroads came closer the population of the town began to grow and multiply wildly. A stage line linked each end-of-the-track to the booming village, and every day another batch of strangers crowded in. By May of 1881, according to one estimate, the fifty citizens of 1876 had grown to fifteen hundred. Accommodations were at a premium. Prices skyrocketed. The streets were crowded day and night. El Paso was a dull and lonely place no longer."[64]

[62]Webb, *The Texas Rangers*, 403–406; Gillett, *Six Years*, 204–10; Baylor, "Last Fight"; Kenneth Goldblatt, "Scout to Quitman Canyon: Report of Captain Geo. W. Baylor of the Frontier Battalion," *Texas Military History* 6 (Summer, 1967): 149–59.

[63]Sonnichsen, *Pass of the North*, 212–14; Lewis B. Lesley, "A Southern Transcontinental Railroad into California: Texas and Pacific versus Southern Pacific, 1865–1885," *Pacific Historical Review* 5 (1936): 52–60.

[64]Sonnichsen, *Pass of the North*, 214.

If there was a jump in passenger traffic on the stages from the east it was soon to be offset by the loss of revenue Bain knew he would face when the railroads finally usurped his mail contracts with the government. The Post Office Department continued to regard the Texas contracts with an attitude that bordered on criminal negligence. In his annual report to Congress in 1881 the postmaster general listed the deceased Francis C. Taylor as the contractor on the routes linking Austin to Fort Concho and San Antonio to Fredericksburg, and assigned Charles Bain only the branch service from Bexar to Laredo. The route connecting Fort Worth with Yuma, Arizona, via El Paso was listed for Bain's associate, J. T. Chidester. Little is known of Chidester or the full extent of his influence on the line. To most Texans the man who had picked up the reins after Taylor's passing was clearly Charles Bain.[65]

The coaches kept up the run between the railheads and El Paso. The newcomers paid an ancient toll for the passage of their rails across that unforgiving country. In July the eastbound stage found a surveyor's wagon standing derelict at Tinaja de las Palmas. Nearby lay the bodies of two men. Renegade Apaches from Mexico or white outlaws had taken them by surprise at the waterhole.[66]

Such losses were still reckoned as part of the price of progress, and the construction crews labored on, reaching Toyah Springs to the north of Fort Davis by mid-September. In early November the station hands at Eagle Springs could look down from their aerie and see the steel bands flashing in the sun as they were laid in place on the railbed and lanced onward to Carriso Pass. By December 16 the work crews had reached the gap between Sierra Blanca and the Quitmans. After the end of that month the San Antonio newspapers ceased carrying advertisements for the overland stage lines. There is no record of when Bain's last coach made its run, but on January 1, 1882, a Texas and Pacific locomotive rolled into the depot by the Rio Grande.

---

[65] *Report of the Postmaster General, 1st Session, 47th Congress,* 516–17, 566–67.

[66] *Record of Engagements,* 100; Post Adjutant to Lt. R. D. Read, July 11, 1881, Letters Sent, Fort Davis, Tex., RG 98, NARS.

After thirty years and two months the game was finally up for the San Antonio and El Paso mail.[67]

Charles Bain had seen the end coming for a long time, and he was already seeking other business prospects. Writing to a friend from San Antonio in October, 1882, he mentioned a recent trip to St. Louis and remarked, "I have not quite sold all of my stage property, have a great many coaches and wagons on hand yet and likely to have for some time yet." He probably succeeded in disposing of most of his stock and equipment, even if at a loss, for short-line staging would continue in the state until well after the turn of the century. Bain, the last of the frontier Texas expressmen, entered the prosaic business of milling flour near San Antonio. His mill and ranch prospered. By the time he died in March, 1894, his estate was valued at over $100,000. A gleaming black hearse drawn by a plumed team carried Charles Bain through the streets of San Antonio on his last earthly journey. Somewhere in the funeral procession there should have been a dusty Concord and hitch of Spanish mules.[68]

[67]John R. Hutto, "Pioneering of the Texas and Pacific," *West Texas Historical Association Yearbook* 12 (July, 1936): 124–33; Clyde Wise, "The Effects of the Railroads Upon El Paso," *Password* 5 (July, 1960): 91–100.

[68]Charles Bain to Mrs. Joseph Spence, Jr., Oct. 20, 1882, Spence Family Papers, Ms. Mary Bain Spence, San Angelo, Tex.; *San Angelo Standard*, Mar. 24, 1894.

Afterword

It might be said that Coopwood, Ficklin, Taylor, and Bain had simply presided over an anticlimactic chapter in the story of transportation on the southwestern frontier. The years between 1866 and 1882 were filled with challenge for the men involved in the stage line, but when the long view is taken it seems that they were simply gallantly marking time until the railroads arrived to conquer space and bridle time. Certainly the locomotive brought prosperity and growth to the region that far exceeded anything achieved by the expressmen. Even then the towns and villages that had coalesced around the old stage stations and army posts remained primarily communities that were derivative of the surrounding countryside, existing to serve the needs of ranchers and farmers. The golden road never followed the ruts of the coaches or even in most cases the iron trail of the locomotive. El Paso and San Antonio grew along with Fort Worth, just as predicted, but D'Hanis and Uvalde remained as far from Cibola as ever.

It would be unfair to dismiss these men and their ambitions as inconsequential, for they had provided a valuable service between the closing of one era and the opening of another. Certainly only a definite need for the stagecoach mail service could have led to its revival in the lean years following the Civil War in the Southwest. Though it had been only locally important, the mail line was essential in the expansion of travel and settlement. There was no doubt that the dangers and obstacles faced by the contractors remained as terrible as ever.

The men who took up the reins in the postwar period faced an arrogantly resurgent Indian threat, a tumultuous political atmosphere in Austin and Washington, and a state economy that remained essentially colonial in nature until well into the next century. They were obliged to refight the same battles waged by Skillman and Giddings while being deprived of the support

those predecessors had enjoyed from the old planter and mercantile aristocracy that had dominated the state during the ante-
bellum years.

For over fifteen years the contractors kept the coaches moving between Bexar and the Pass of the North until the railroads'
arrival reduced them to serving the rural routes beyond the railheads. During that period they were the sole means of commercial transportation and communication across the state. If their
accomplishments did not lead to the realization of men's dreams
for the region, they at least served to whet the edge of their anticipation. As General William T. Sherman remarked in admiration, the mail companies were "the skirmish line of civilization."

It would be a mistake to portray the stage line as the tri-
umphant vanguard of the advance of unalloyed American values
into the borderlands frontier, for the land changed the newcomers much more than they ever succeeded in changing the
land. The Anglo-Saxon civilization that grew up in the desert
and mountain country marked that region far more deeply than
any of its predecessors, but it still had to confront and react to
the same set of harsh imperatives that had faced the Indian and
Spaniard.

Whatever cultural and political baggage they may have carried in the boots of their Concords, the expressmen and their
patrons did not hold to or practice a Jeffersonian ideal on the
borderlands frontier. Frederick Jackson Turner's twin gods of free
land and democracy grounded their sceptres at the Pecos, for
beyond loomed huge and abiding altars reared by the sun and
wind of the Chihuahuan Desert. It was a world that had little in
common with the lush cradle of the Appalachians.

Turner's frontier and the West could never be truly synonymous. The existence of abundant land did not necessarily beget
the growth of a democratic society of prosperous freeholders.
The land, even when free, dictated different responses and results to every human effort to occupy it. The dry-world expanse
of Trans-Pecos Texas marked a transition between climates and
cultures that could not be altered by theory or rhetoric. There,
an older Hispanic culture met a younger Anglo-American one,

and both trimmed their customs to accommodate the desert country.

Two hundred and fifty years of Spanish rule and occupation had brought not even a glimmering of democracy to this frontier along the entire arc of settlements from Bexar to Santa Fe. European civilization in the region clung to the few permanent water sources available, just as had the earlier sedentary Indian cultures. Only along the lush margins of the rivers was agricuture possible on a large scale. What little arable land that existed was claimed by the privileged classes of an authoritarian government that was no less intrusive for its distance from the Rio Grande country. It was not a society that fostered individual innovation or expansion. The ambitions and needs of the yeoman farmer meant little to its dominant elements. Ranching and irrigated farmland sustained the economy, and the average farmer or herdsman served a master, not himself.

The Iberians had never courted egalitarian notions, and the combination of an economy of scarcity, their own relatively small numbers, and the aching distances that separated them from the major outposts of Spain in the New World insured that these presumptuous conquerors would eventually become servitors of their desert world. "It was a civilization falling asleep," noted Paul Horgan, "remembering instead of creating. . . . Defeated by distances and time, the Rio Grande Spaniards finally lived as the Pueblo Indians lived—in a fixed traditional present."

In the 1820s a new element entered their world. The caravan captains and beaver hunters probed Santa Fe and Taos, eventually trailing southward to the Pass of the North and Chihuahua. The Anglo-American plainsman was warrior and merchant by equal turns. Skeptical of any aristocracy that was not based upon demonstrated merit and ability, he counted himself first among equals when dealing with folk of his own blood, but he was by no stretch of the imagination an egalitarian democrat, no matter what Jacksonian rhetoric might fill the air at election time to the east in Missouri or Kentucky. Indians and Spaniards took a lesser place in his eyes. The hard ranges and sere basins he had traversed fostered an aristocracy of talent within his ranks that was based simply on the stark ability to endure, survive, and prevail.

The early American settlers in El Paso brought a fresh spirit of commercial ambition with them. Freighters, merchants, and mechanics leavened the old Spanish communities in the river valley with their presence as they attempted first to capitalize on the Santa Fe–Chihuahua trade, and later on the flow of emigrants and gold seekers to California. Many of them married into the local gentry, and "with a baronical disregard for the little people (*los pobres*) they moved in the circle of the *ricos* and came in time to exercise all the rights of the aristocrats," remarked Rex Stickland in his insightful study, *The Turner Thesis and the Dry World.*

This dominant class of relative newcomers adapted itself handily to the existing order of things while trying mightily to improve its lot even more. By 1860 there were 165 recorded non-Hispanic residents of El Paso. Most of them, as Strickland discovered, were hired men. These wage earners worked largely for the military, the stage lines, and the merchant freighters. Not more than fifty of them were employers or independent men of property. Born the sons of Jacksonian America, they found the common man's goverment wanting in their new environment, for "the socio-political complex that they set up from Presidio del Norte to Santa Fe shows little evidence of democracy in action. The well-to-do traders, merchants and attorneys pre-empted the county offices and social leadership. From time to time 'public meetings' were held to discuss policy—open only to a small per cent of the total population, even Anglos, much less Latins." One need look no farther than Joseph Magoffin's 1854 "Salt War" against the native New Mexicans with the aid of Mexican employees and the resident Americans to see this attitude in practice. Thus the Harts, Magoffins, and Stephensons asserted their dominance in a distinctly non-Turnerian process of frontier settlement. "It was not a small farming frontier (except for native patch farmers); it attracted wage earners rather than landless poor in search of land; it was esentially an exploitative frontier," emphasized Strickland, "in which self-seeking and highly individualistic men sought to acquire wealth by merchandising, freighting or mining."

It was this class of men who were the earliest and strongest patrons of the stage lines. They realized, perhaps instinctively, that with their ambition and a reliable means of communication the whole axis of trade and population movement throughout the Southwest could be shifted in the mutual favor of El Paso and San Antonio. The lure of the California gold fields and the militant boosterism of the borderland commercial elite helped to create and sustain the overland mail service out of San Antonio to the Pass and beyond. "Thus at the very outset of American rule," recorded cultural geographer Donald W. Meining, "a latitudinal thoroughfare was suddenly imposed across the historic longitudinal lineaments of the Southwest." George Giddings and Henry Skillman, who were themselves of the mercantile-freighter class, pioneered the stage service through the region and laid out at least one leg of a new pattern of travel routes that would define a basic grid for such movement that endures into the present.

Thus Texan dreams of empire were kindled on the adobe hearths of Spanish El Paso, to send their sparks whirling east and west in the wake of the Concords. The expressmen pointed the way for the railroad builders, and a part of the continent that still yields little of value without due sacrifice was bound to the United States forever, carrying with it two cultures that still part and twine in uneasy union.

The coaches and their reinsmen bestowed another legacy beyond that of land. They added new charts and courses to the geography of hope. Over a decade after the last stage had run west with the El Paso mail, such veterans of the service as Bigfoot Wallace and Edward Westfall used to gather in San Antonio to tell the old stories and spend a little more of the coin of their youthful dreams. They had lived to see the frontier's passing, and many of them felt out of place in a world of telephones and streetcars. Despite the bewildering changes that had overtaken them, the old plainsmen remained imbued with the optimism that had so typified their era. After one such reunion Westfall echoed their thoughts in his journal:

All of the old stagers that I met up with here in course of the whole
day were all golly [jolly] for the reason that we don't know how to appreciate hard times. Long ago we made no calculations on carrieing
[*sic*] our scalps from one weeks end to another and now after thirty-five
or forty years it would be base ingratitude for us to loose [*sic*] confidence in providence or even ourselves . . . because we have learned
by long and at times sad experience that threats many times falls short
of the mark.

The courage and intelligence that Westfall possessed shone
through the irregularities of his grammar and spelling. He dis-
counted his own exploits as a frontiersman, agreeing with his
friends that their adventures would probably never be believed
by future generations, and thus, "its best they should drift down
the declivity of time among all other things forgotten." Despite
his professed disregard for posterity, it was typical that the man
who had so often risked his life to carry the written word to his
fellows willed his entire estate to the city of San Antonio for the
specific purpose of establishing a public library.

Westfall, Skillman, Giddings, Ficklin, and all the rest who
took the coaches west left an example of valiant aspiration behind them that far outweighed the material results of their efforts. Alan LeMay, a gifted novelist of the Texas frontier, might
well have been thinking of the old expressmen when he wrote
this tribute to all those who dared the free spaces and wild
horizons:

These people had a kind of courage that may be the finest gift of
man: the courage of those who simply keep on, and on, doing the next
thing, far beyond all reasonable endurance, seldom thinking of themselves as martyred, and never thinking of themselves as brave.

Chronology of the San Antonio–El Paso Mail, 1850–1881

February, 1850: Henry Skillman conducts unofficial courier service between San Antonio and El Paso.

April, 1851: William A. "Bigfoot" Wallace and Richard A. Howard unsuccessfully bid on a government contract to carry the mail between San Antonio and Doña Ana, New Mexico.

April, 1851: Mail arriving in Santa Fe from El Paso "as usual." This may have been an extension of Skillman's service.

September 20, 1851: Henry Skillman granted a contract by Postmaster General N. K. Hall to provide mail service from San Antonio to Santa Fe via El Paso, effective November 1, 1851.

November 3, 1851: Skillman departs San Antonio with first mail. He arrives in Santa Fe by November 24.

December 6, 1851: Skillman advertises addition of carriages for passenger service on the mail line.

January 2, 1852: First eastbound mail departs Santa Fe for San Antonio.

January, 1852: Second westbound mail from San Antonio ambushed by Indians in Quitman Canyon. No survivors.

January 25, 1852: Northbound mail from El Paso attacked by Apaches near Laguna del Muerto, New Mexico. Skillman's station at Fort Inge, Texas, raided by Indians.

February, 1852: Northbound mail from El Paso attacked by Apaches near Laguna del Muerto, New Mexico.

August, 1852: Skillman's station in El Paso raided by Apaches, the third such attack on the station in six months.

September 9, 1852: Bigfoot Wallace and westbound mail party attacked at Painted Cave on the Devil's River.

October, 1852: El Paso station raided by Apaches.

December, 1852: Skillman awarded new contract for monthly service. Fee increased from $12,500 to $28,000 per year.

April, 1853: Bigfoot Wallace and westbound mail attacked on the Devil's River.

June, 1853: Skillman writes testimonial to Sharps Rifle Company, lauding the breechloaders.

August, 1853: Skillman visits Washington, D.C., to win extension of contract to June, 1854.

August, 1853: James Magoffin hosts a convention in El Paso to discuss construction of a trans-Texas railroad.

November, 1853: Skillman establishes stage line from San Antonio to Indianola on the Gulf of Mexico.

January, 1854: Skillman in gunfight at Mexican cantina in Paso del Norte.

February 4, 1854: Skillman mortgages assets to James Magoffin for loan.

February 27, 1854: Leona Station at Fort Inge raided.

April 4, 1854: Frederick Law Olmsted meets the mail at Fort Inge.

April 22, 1854: Postmaster General Campbell revokes Skillman's contract. Grants new contract on route to David Wasson. Skillman's personal appeals unsuccessful.

May, 1854: Eastbound mail attacked at Eagle Springs, Texas. Troops from El Paso outpost the site soon afterward.

July, 1854: Wasson fails to begin service on schedule. Brevoort and Houghton secure temporary contract for service south of Santa Fe. They designate Skillman as their agent.

August, 1854: Wasson's agents secure authority to carry mail west from San Antonio. George Giddings brought into partnership with Wasson via an unsecured loan to his agents.

August, 1854: Louis Oge and eastern mail attacked at Howard's Well, Texas.

September, 1854: Frank Giddings and Johnson Thomas attacked at Howard's Well with westbound mail.

October, 1854: David Wasson surrenders contract to George Giddings. Giddings and Skillman form new partnership.

October, 1854: Fort Davis established in Limpia Mountains. Mail station constructed at "La Limpia," adjacent to post.

November 15, 1854: Skillman and Frank Giddings attacked by Apaches at El Muerto, Texas.

December, 1854: Leona Station at Fort Inge and Ney's Station at D'Hanis raided.

Januarh, 1855: Fort Clark station raided.

February 10, 1855: Giddings writes testimonial praising the Sharps rifles in use on the stage line.

April–June, 1855: Post Office Department fines Giddings for late deliveries. He is informed that his contract will expire on June 30, 1858.

June, 1855: Price Cooper and Santa Fe mail attacked near Laguna del Muerto. Coach and mail destroyed; two guards killed.

June, 1855: El Paso station raided.

August, 1855: Permanent camp established at Fort Lancaster on the Pecos.

October, 1855: Lt. Zenas R. Bliss records his journey from San Antonio to Fort Davis.

December, 1855: Price Cooper attacked at Point of Rocks on Jornada del Muerto. Apaches steal herd of stock near Eagle Springs, Stewart supply train attacked at Barilla Springs.

March 3, 1856: Giddings contract fee increased to $33,500 a year. Property losses to date total $54,465. Giddings confers with Senator Rusk in Washington.

April, 1856: Stewart's supply train attacked east of Eagle Springs.

June, 1856: Jack Gordon murders travelers on the mail route.

July, 1856: Eagle Springs station destroyed; three men killed.

August, 1856: Bigfoot Wallace attacked near Escondido Springs.

October, 1856: La Limpia raided; one man killed.

November, 1856: Price Cooper attacked on the Jornada del Muerto.

January, 1857: James Cook and mail for San Antonio attacked in Quitman Canyon at Cienegas. Stages burned; stock lost.

March, 1857: Station at Van Horn's Well attacked by Comanches.

June 22, 1857: Postmaster General Aaron V. Brown grants route from St. Louis to San Francisco, California, to the Butterfield Overland Mail Company. James Birch wins contract for service from San Antonio to San Diego, California, via El Paso. Contract gives Birch $149,800 a year for semimonthly deliveries to begin July 1, 1857.

July 9, 1857: Birch's first mail departs San Antonio for San Diego.

July 16, 1857: I. C. Woods, Birch's agent, hires Henry Skillman and Bigfoot Wallace to expedite line's operations.

July 24, 1857: Skillman departs San Antonio with second California mail.

July 29, 1857: Giddings enters partnership with Birch at Woods's request.

August 1, 1857: Woods departs San Antonio with supply train and El Paso mail coach.

August 2, 1857: Woods meets Wallace west of Castroville. Learns of Comanche capture of stock train on Devil's River.

August 16, 1857: Woods reaches San Elizario.

August 22, 1857: Woods departs El Paso for San Diego.

August 30, 1857: First San Antonio mail reaches San Diego.

September 8, 1857: Woods arrives in San Diego.

October 5, 1857: Fifth mail party from Texas reaches San Diego.

October 13, 1857: James Birch dies in maritime disaster.

October 23, 1857: Woods departs California for Texas. Learns of Birch's death at Fort Yuma on November 2.

November 7, 1857: Fort Clark station raided.

November 20, 1857: Woods fired by executor of Birch estate.

November 26, 1857: Woods reaches Mesilla, New Mexico. Arrives in El Paso to confer with Giddings soon afterward.

December 25, 1857: Woods and Giddings depart El Paso for San Antonio.

December, 1857: Fort Lancaster station raided; all stock lost.

January, 1858: La Limpia raided; all stock lost. El Muerto station destroyed by Apaches; two coaches destroyed. Van Horn's Wells destroyed in costly raid for the Apaches.

February–March, 1858: Birchville, Comanche Springs stations raided. Frank Giddings killed in El Paso. George Giddings purchases contract from Birch's attorney. Woods reinstated.

April, 1858: Lancaster Station attacked.

May 31, 1858: La Limpia attacked.

June, 1858: Stations established at Cottonwoods on Limpia Creek and Barilla Springs, north of Fort Davis. Others follow at Escondido Springs, Howard's Well, and Beaver Lake.

September, 1858: Station built at Leon Holes, 9 miles west of Comanche Springs. Fort Quitman established on the Rio Grande below El Paso. Butterfield Overland Mail Company begins service through El Paso.

October, 1858: Escondido Springs station destroyed. Giddings establishes new relay point to the northeast on west bank of Pecos.

December, 1858: Eagle Springs station destroyed by Apaches. Giddings loses Santa Fe–El Paso mail contract. Route between El Paso and Fort Yuma terminated in favor of Butterfield line.

January, 1859: Comanche Springs and Barrel Springs stations raided. Beaver Lake station destroyed.

February, 1859: Fort Stockton established as permanent post at Comanche Springs.

March, 1859: Post Office Department eliminates Giddings's route between El Paso and Fort Stockton, effective May 1, 1859.

March 23, 1859: Coach repulses Indian attack at Pecos Spring, northwest of Fort Lancaster.

April, 1859: Attack on Barrel Springs.

June 1, 1859: Giddings's service reduced to twenty-eight trips per year at $120,000. Raids on Mud Creek and Cottonwoods stations follow.

September 1, 1859: Attack on El Muerto.

October 7, 1859: Barilla Springs station raided. Van Horn's Well repulses Apache assaults soon afterward. Leon Holes also raided.

January, 1860: Comanche Springs raided. Giddings departs San Antonio for conferences with Post Office Department in Washington, D.C.

February 4, 1860: Postmaster General J. Holt eliminates Giddings's service between San Diego and Fort Yuma, effective April 1, 1860.

March, 1860: Giddings informed that he will lose the El Paso–Fort Stockton service on May 1, 1860.

May, 1860: Apaches raid San Elizario and burn station. Leon Holes attacked on May 7.

June 23, 1860: Howard's Well station attacked.

November–December, 1860: Raids on La Limpia, Van Horn's Wells, Beaver Lake, Leon Holes, and Fort Quitman stations.

January, 1861: Comanche raid destroys Howard's Well station. Pecos Station attacked.

February, 1861: Texas secedes from the Union.

March, 1861: Giddings in Washington, D.C., to win new contract for service to Los Angeles. Agrees to carry message to Governor Houston from President Lincoln. Butterfield Overland Mail ends service in Texas.

April 28, 1861: James Giddings and California-bound mail party killed by Apaches at Stein's Peak, New Mexico.

May, 1861: George Giddings and Parker Burnham attacked by Apaches east of Barilla Springs. Second California mail party wiped out at Cooke's Springs. Stations destroyed at Cooke's Springs, Mimbres River, Cow Springs, Soldier's Farewell, Barney's Station, San Simon, Apache Pass, Dragoon Springs, and San Pedro. Thirty men killed. Six coaches destroyed; 146 horses and mules stolen.

June, 1861: *Mesilla Times* promises early restoration of California mail service under direction of Skillman and Giddings. Eagle Springs station destroyed.

July, 1861: Confederate troops occupy El Paso. Skillman carries mail to California and back.

August 28, 1861: Giddings signs Confederate mail contract for service to San Diego, California. Apaches attack troops and stages in Fort Davis area. Captain James E. Terry and mail party ambushed in Quitman Canyon.

Janary, 1862: Pecos Station and Van Horn's Wells destroyed in raids.

August, 1862: Defeated Confederates evacuate El Paso before Union advance from New Mexico. Mail service ceases beyond Fort Clark.

December, 1863: Giddings and B. R. Sappington open branch line from Uvalde to Eagle Pass.

April 15, 1864: Henry Skillman killed by Union troops near Presidio del Norte.

April 24, 1866: Bethel Coopwood opens coach service to El Paso. The first party is attacked at Escondido Springs and arrives in El Paso on May 6.

July 7, 1866: Second mail east from El Paso destroyed at Barilla Springs.

November, 1866: Coopwood yields control of company to Sawyer, Risher, and Hall.

February, 1867: James Cook and western mail attacked by Kickapoos near Fort Clark.

March, 1867: Indian troubles cause suspension of service.

September, 1867: Benjamin Franklin Ficklin takes control of the mail line. Ficklin takes mail west for El Paso on the thirtieth.

October 11, 1867: San Antonio mail destroyed north of Howard's Well.

December 5, 1867: Attack on coach near Eagle Springs.

December 11, 1867: Attack on Eagle Springs.

December, 1867: Attack on stage near Fort Lancaster.

May, 1868: Attack on stage east of Fort Clark. Ficklin begins feud with Major Cram at Fort Concho.

November, 1868: Kickapoo Springs station raided. Coach from Concho Station ambushed near Kickapoo Springs on the thirtieth. Driver Mullen killed.

December 8, 1868: Kickapoo Springs attacked.

January 6, 1869: Eastbound mail destroyed in Bass Canyon.

February 1, 1869: Ficklin initiates branchline between Concho Station, Fort Griffin, Jacksboro, Sherman, and Fort Smith, Arkansas. Francis C. Taylor joins the company. Comanches attack Kickapoo Springs late in the month.

April 23, 1869: Coach captured by Indians east of Fort Concho on branch line. New relay station at Fort Griffin raided two days before.

May 7 and 21, 1869: Fort Griffin station raided.

June 17, 1869: Head of Concho station attacked.

June 26, 1869: Apaches attack Barilla Springs.

July 8, 1869: David M. Mason killed in accident at Lipan Springs.

July 26, 1869: Comancheros reported on the road west of Fort Concho.

August 13, 1869: Jim Spears repulses Apache attack on El Muerto.

September, 1869: Charles Bain joins the company.

September 17, 1869: Comanches raid station at Fort Mason.

December, 1869: Raids on El Muerto and Camp Johnston.

January–February, 1870: Ficklin in Washington, D.C., with partner Frederick P. Sawyer to defend the company against charges of inefficiency and corruption. Concho Station raided early in January, Employee killed near Kickapoo Springs late in February.

April, 1870: Jim Spears and A. J. Bobo repulse attack on coach between Fort Concho and Fort Stockton.

May, 1870: Ficklin back in San Antonio. Raids on Loyal Valley and Fort Phantom Hill stations. Apaches attack Barilla Springs on the twenty-fifth.

July, 1870: Coach destroyed east of Fort Concho.

August, 1870: Comanches chase stage into Head of Concho. Two weeks later they return to attack station.

September 30, 1870: Mail from Fort Smith ambushed 22 miles east of Fort Concho.

November, 1870: Ficklin opens another branch line connecting Sherman, Texas, with railhead at Neosho, Arkansas.

March 10, 1871: Ben Ficklin dies in Virginia.

April 17, 1871: Jim Spears repulses attack on two stages 6 miles east of Centralia Station.

May, 1871: Comancheros attack Pecos Station at Camp Melvin.

June, 1871: Head of Concho and Barilla Springs attacked repeatedly.

November 22, 1871: Kickapoo Springs attacked.

April 13, 1872: Coach attacked 6 miles from Centralia Station.

May, 1872: Comancheros roaming the Concho River area. Charles Bain attacked by Indians near Loyal Valley.

June, 1872: Concho Station raided twice in two nights. Camp Johnston and Centralia Station attacked.

July 14, 1872: Coach captured near Camp Johnston.

July 28, 1872: Centralia Station raided.

September, 1872: Raids at Camp Johnston and Head of Concho.

November, 1872: Taylor and partners meet in Austin to reorganize company.

January, 1873: Stage operations temporarily halted by equine influenza.

May, 1873: Apache raid on Eagle Springs.

July, 1873: Raids on El Muerto, Pecos Station, Kickapoo Springs, and Coghlin's Station near Menardville.

August, 1873: Raid on Barilla Springs.

September 30, 1873: Benficklin established by F. C. Taylor.

October 1, 1873: Centralia Station raided.

November, 1873: Soldier kills stage driver at Barilla Springs.

December, 1873: Apaches raid Eagle Springs.

March, 1874: Tom Green County organized. Indian raids on Camp Johnston, Pecos Station, and Barilla Springs. Stage driver killed by Comanches just east of Benficklin. Attacks follow on that settlement and Kickapoo Springs.

January, 1875: Benficklin designated seat of Tom Green County.

April 8, 1875: Stage attacked at Bass Canyon. Raids on Eagle Springs and Pecos Station follow.

June 13, 1875: Bandits rob Aue's Station at Leon Springs.

August, 1875: Head of Concho attacked twice in two weeks. F. P. Sawyer dies.

October 1, 1875: Company reorganized. Taylor retains control of route west of Fort Concho to El Paso.

February, 1876: San Antonio linked to Fort Stockton by telegraph.

August, 1876: Rustlers steal stock from Lipan Springs. Herd recaptured in skirmish at Head of Concho.

October, 1876: Apaches raid on El Paso and Eagle Springs.

November, 1876: Two outlaws killed in five-hour gun battle at Kickapoo Springs.

January, 1877: Stage robbed near Pegleg Crossing.

August 1, 1877: Herder killed at El Muerto.

October, 1877: Stage ambushed at Flat Rock Holes; driver killed.

December 15, 1877: Stage robbed near Pegleg Station.

April, 1878: Stage ambushed near Escondido Springs; driver and passenger killed.

June 27, 1878: Stage attacked 5 miles from Pecos Station.

July 6, 1878: Stage robbed near Pegleg Station.

August, 1878: El Muerto raided.

November, 1878: Dispute between employees and soldiers at El Muerto.

June, 1879: Francis C. Taylor dies at Benficklin. Charles Bain assumes control of El Paso route.

May, 1880: Station chief at Barrel Springs attacked by Apaches.

July 30, 1880: Grierson defeats Victorio at Tinaja de las Palmas.

July 31, 1880: Stage ambushed 3 miles east of Tinaja de las Palmas; driver and passenger killed.

August 5, 1880: Westbound stage sights Apaches in Bass Canyon.

August 6, 1880: Grierson repulses Victorio again at Rattlesnake Springs.

August 9, 1880: Stage ambushed in Quitman Pass, 4 miles east of Quitman Station. General James J. Byrnes killed.

October, 1880: Mexican troops kill Victorio at Tres Castillos.

January 8, 1881: Stage ambushed in Quitman Pass; driver and passenger killed.

January 29, 1881: Texas Rangers destroy last remnants of Victorio's band.

January 1, 1882: Texas and Pacific Railroad reached El Paso from the east. The San Antonio–El Paso Mail is put out of business.

March, 1894: Charles Bain dies.

Bibliography

PRIMARY SOURCES

Archival and Manuscript Materials

National Archives and Records Service:
Adjutant General's Office. Record Group 94. Returns from United States Military Posts, 1800–1916: Fort Davis, Fort Stockton, Fort Concho, Texas.

Bureau of the Census. Record Group 29. Federal Census Population Schedules. 7th Census (1850: Texas; 8th Census (1860): Texas; 9th Census (1870): Texas; 10th Census (1880): Texas.

Confederate States Post Office Department. Record Group 109. Chapter 11, Vol. 13, Mail Contracts, Texas, 1861–63; Vol. 26, Route Book, Texas, 1861–62; Vol. 27, Route Book, Texas, 1861–62; Vol. 31, Contract Bureau, Letters Sent, 1863–64; Vol. 44, Inspection Office, Letters Sent, June, 1861–February, 1862.

Court of Claims Section (Justice). Record Group 205. *George H. Giddings* vs. *the United States, Kiowa, Comanche, and Apache Indians* (Indian Depredation No. 3873). United States Court of Claims, December Term, 1891.

Interior Department. Record Group 48. Pacific Wagon Road Office, El Paso–Fort Yuma Road, Letters Received.

Office of the Chief of Engineers. Record Group 77. Cartographic Records Section, Civil Works Map File. Lieutenant Colonel Thomas B. Hunt, "Journal Showing the Route Taken by the Government Train Accompanying the 15th Regiment, U.S. Infantry from Austin, Tex. to Ft. Craig, N.M. and Returning to San Antonio July–December, 1869."

Office of the Quartermaster General. Record Group 92. Letters Received.

Post Office Department. Record Group 28. Letterbooks of the Postmaster General, Series 2: Records of the Immediate Office of the Postmaster General, Letters Sent, July 21, 1850–August 18, 1882.

U.S. Army Commands. Record Group 98. Letters Sent: Fort

McKavett, Fort Concho, Fort Stockton, Fort Davis, Texas; Letters Received: Fort McKavett, Fort Concho, Fort Davis, Texas.

U.S. Army Continental Commands, 1821–1920. Record Group 393. Records of the Headquarters, Fort Concho, Fort Davis, Texas.

Library of Congress:

Manuscript Division. Records of the Confederate States of America (Pickett Papers). Office of the Postmaster General. Letters Sent, March 7, 1861–October 12, 1863.

United States Government Publications

Congressional Globe. Washington, D.C., 1850–81.

Record of Engagements with Hostile Indians within the Military Division of the Missouri, from 1868 to 1882, Lieutenant General P. H. Sheridan, Commanding, Compiled at Headquarters, Military Division of the Missouri from the Official Records. Washington, D.C.: Government Printing Office, 1882.

Report to the Attorney General of the Star Mail Service by A. M. Gibson, Esq., Assistant Attorney of the United States. Washington, D.C.: Government Printing Office, 1882.

U.S. House. *Abstract for Offers for Carrying the Mails.* 35th Cong., 1st sess., 1857. House Exec. Doc. 96.

———. *Abstract of Offers for Carrying the Mails.* 36th Con., 2d sess., 1860. House Exec. Doc. 73.

———. *Allowances to Contractors for Fiscal Year Ending June 30, 1879.* 46th Cong., 2d sess., 1879. House Exec. Doc. 30.

———. *Contracts for Transportation of the Mails, April 14, 1872.* 42d Cong., 2d sess., 1871. House Rept. 38.

———. *Court of Claims Report No. 266.* 36th Cong., 2d sess., 1860. House Doc., unnumbered.

———. *Fines and Deductions from Pay of Mail Contractors, 1870.* 41st Cong., 3d sess., 1870. House Exec. Doc. 87.

———. *Fines and Deductions of Mail Contractors.* 33d Cong., 2d sess., 1854. House Exec. Doc. 92.

———. *Fines and Deductions of Mail Contractors.* 34th Cong., 1st sess., 1855. House Exec. Doc. 112.

———. *Fines and Deductions of Mail Contractors.* 36th Cong., 1st sess., 1859. House Exec. Doc. 40.

———. *Letters from Postmaster-General on Star Route Correspondence.* 48th Cong., 1st sess., 1883. House Rept. 372.

———. *Mail Contracts*, 32d Cong., 2d sess., 1852. House Exec. Doc. 62.

———. *Mail Contracts*, 34th Cong., 1st sess., 1855. House Exec. Doc. 122.

———. *Mail Contracts.* 35th Cong., 2d sess., 1858. House Exec. Doc. 109.

———. *Mail Contracts and Temporary Service, June 20, 1874.* 43d Cong., 1st sess., 1873. House Rept. 775.

———. *Management of the Post-Office Department, August 9, 1876.* 44th Cong., 1st sess., 1875. House Rept. 814.

———. *Offers and Contracts for Carrying Mails, Additional Allowances to Contractors, and Curtailment of Mail Service, 1861.* 37th Cong., 2d sess., 1861. House Exec. Doc. 137.

———. *Offers and Contracts for Carrying Mails, Additional Allowances to Contractors, and Curtailment of Mail Service, 1871.* 42d Cong., 2d sess., 1871. House Exec. Doc. 322.

———. *Offers and Contracts for Carrying Mails, Additional Allowances to Contractors, and Curtailment of Mail Service, 1875.* 44th Cong., 1st sess., 1875. House Exec. Doc. 191.

———. *Offers and Contracts for Carrying the Mails.* 36th Cong., 1st sess., 1859. House Exec. Doc. 86.

———. *Offers and Contracts for Carrying the Mails, Additional Allowances to Contractors, and Curtailment of Mail Serice, 1879.* 46th Cong., 2d sess., 1879. House Exec. Doc. 47.

———. *Offers and Contracts for Carrying the Mails, Additional Allowances to Contractors, and Curtailment of Mail Service, 1880.* 46th Cong., 2d sess., 1879. House Exec. Doc. 55.

———. *Offers and Contracts for Carrying the Mails, Additional Allowances to Contractors, and Curtailment of Mail Service, 1881.* 47th Cong., 1st sess., 1881. House Exec. Doc. 266.

———. *Offers for Carrying the Mails–Mail Contracts.* 33d Cong., 1st sess., 1853. House Exec. Doc. 125.

———. *Offers for Carrying the Mails—Mail Contracts.* 33 Cong., 2d sess., 1854. House Exec. Doc. 86.

———. *Relative to Discontinuance of Mail Service in Seceded States.* 37th Cong., 2d sess., 1861. House Exec. Doc. 55.

———. *Report of Captain Samuel G. French.* 31st Cong., 2d sess., 1850. House Exec. Doc. 1.

———. *Report on Delinquent Mail Contractors.* 35th Cong., 1st sess., 1857. House Exec. Doc. 81.

———. *Report on Mail Contracts.* 31st Cong., 1st sess., 1849. House Exec. Doc. 88.

————. *Report on Mail Contracts.* 32d Cong., 1st sess., 1851. House Exec Doc. 56.

————. *Report on Postal Claims.* 32d Cong., 1st sess., 1851. House Exec. Doc. 62.

————. *Report on Receipts and Expenditures of the Post Office Department.* 32d Cong., 1st sess., 1850. House Exec. Doc. 47.

————. *Report on the Claim of George H. Giddings, November 15, 1877.* 45th Cong., 1st sess., 1877. House Rept. 1.

————. *Report on the Post Office Department.* 31st Cong., 1st sess., 1849. House Exec. Doc. 55.

————. *Resolution of the Mail Service in Texas.* 41st Cong., 3d sess., 1870. House Misc. Doc. 81.

————, Postmaster General. *Annual Report.* 31st Cong., 2d sess., 1850. House Exec. Doc. 1.

————, ————. *Annual Report,* 32nd Cong., 1st sess., 1851. House Exec. Doc. 2.

————, ————. *Annual Report.* 32d Cong., 2d sess., 1852. House Exec. Doc. 1.

————, ————. *Annual Report.* 33d Cong., 1st sess., 1853. House Exec. Doc. 1.

————, ————. *Annual Report.* 37th Cong., 3d sess., 1862. House Exec. Doc. 1.

————, ————. *Annual Report.* 38th Cong., 1st sess., 1863. House Exec. Doc. 1.

————, ————. *Annual Report.* 38th Cong., 2d sess., 1864. House Exec. Doc. 1.

————, ————. *Annual Report.* 39th Cong., 1st sess., 1865. House Exec. Doc. 1.

————, ————. *Annual Report.* 39th Cong., 2d sess., 1866. House Exec. Doc. 1.

————, ————. *Annual Report.* 40th Cong., 1st sess., 1867. House Exec. Doc. 1.

————, ————. *Annual Report.* 40th Cong., 3d sess., 1868. House Exec. Doc. 1.

————, ————. *Annual Report.* 41st Cong., 2d sess., 1869. House Exec. Doc. 1.

————, ————. *Annual Report.* 41st Cong., 3d sess., 1870. House Exec. Doc. 1.

————, ————. *Annual Report.* 42d Cong., 2d sess., 1871. House Exec. Doc. 1.

————, ————. *Annual Report.* 42d Cong., 3d sess., 1872. House Exec. Doc. 1.

————, ————. *Annual Report.* 43d Cong., 1st sess., 1873. House Exec Doc. 1.

————, ————. *Annual Report.* 43d Cong., 2d sess., 1874. House Exec. Doc. 1.

————, ————. *Annual Report.* 44th Cong., 1st sess. 1875. House Exec. Doc. 1.

————, ————. *Annual Report.* 44th Cong., 2d sess., 1876. House Exec. Doc. 1.

————, ————. *Annual Report.* 45th Cong., 2d sess., 1877. House Exec. Doc. 1.

————, ————. *Annual Report.* 45th Cong., 3d sess., 1878. House Exec. Doc. 1.

————, ————. *Annual Report.* 46th Cong., 2d sess., 1879. House Exec. Doc. 1.

————, ————. *Annual Report.* 46th Cong., 3d sess., 1880. House Exec. Doc. 1.

————, ————. *Annual Report.* 47th Cong., 1st sess., 1881. House Exec. Doc. 1.

————, ————. *Annual Report.* 47th Cong., 2d sess., 1882. House Exec. Doc. 1.

————, Secretary of War. *Annual Report.* 32d Cong., 1st sess., 1850. House Exec. Doc. 1.

U.S. Senate. *Amounts Paid for Overland Mail Service, 1858 to 1868.* 46th Cong., 3d sess., 1880. Senate Exec. Doc. 24.

————. *Letter of Postmaster-General on Obtaining Certain Records of the Confederate States Pertaining to Mail Contracts.* 48th Cong., 2d sess., 1884. Senate Exec. Doc. 72.

————. *Memorial of George H. Giddings.* 36th Cong., 2d sess., 1860. Senate Misc. Doc. 15.

————. *Report of the Joint Select Committee on Retrenchment Inquiring into the Expenditures in All the Branches of the Service of the United States together with the Testimony Relating to the Same. House of Representatives, February 21, 1870.* 41st Cong., 2d sess., 1869. Senate Rept. 47.

————. *Report of the Texas Boundary Commission.* 47th Cong., 1st sess., 1881. Senate Exec. Doc. 70.

————. *Report on Claim of George H. Giddings.* 45th Cong., 2d sess., 1877. Senate Rept. 508.

————. *Report of Legislature of Texas for Establishment of Mail-Stage Route from Austin to Some Point on Overland Mail-Stage Route from St. Louis to El Paso.* 36th Cong., 1st sess., 1859. Senate Misc. Doc. 40.

———, Postmaster General. *Annual Report*. 33d Cong., 2d sess., 1854. Senate Exec. Doc. 1.

———, ———. *Annual Report*. 34th Cong., 1st sess., 1855. Senate Exec. Doc. 1.

———, ———. *Annual Report*. 34th Cong., 3d sess., 1856. Senate Exec. Doc. 5.

———, ———. *Annual Report*. 35th Cong., 1st sess., 1857. Senate Exec. Doc. 11.

———, ———. *Annual Report*. 35th Cong., 2d sess., 1858. Senate Exec. Doc. 1.

———, ———. *Annual Report*. 36th Cong., 1st sess., 1859. Senate Exec. Doc. 2.

———, ———. *Annual Report*. 36th Cong., 2d sess., 1860. Senate Exec. Doc. 1.

———, ———. *Annual Report*. 37th Cong., 1st sess., 1861. Senate Exec. Doc. 1.

———, Secretary of War. *Annual Report*. 32d Cong., 1st sess., 1851. Senate Exec. Doc. 1.

———, ———. *Annual Report*. 32d Cong., 2d sess., 1852. Senate Exec. Doc. 1.

———, ———. *Annual Report*. 33d Cong., 1st sess., 1853. Senate Exec. Doc. 1.

———, ———. *Annual Report*. 33d Cong., 2d sess., 1854. Senate Exec. Doc. 1.

———, ———. *Annual Report*. 34th Cong., 1st sess., 1855. Senate Exec. Doc. 1.

———, ———. *Annual Report*. 34th Cong., 3d sess., 1856. Senate Exec. Doc. 5.

———, ———. *Annual Report*. 35th Cong., 1st sess., 1857. Senate Exec. Doc. 11.

———, ———. *Annual Report*. 35th Cong., 2d sess., 1858. Senate Exec. Doc. 1.

———, ———. *Annual Report*. 36th Cong., 1st sess., 1859. Senate Exec. Doc. 2.

———, ———. *Annual Report*. 36th Cong., 2d sess., 1860. Senate Exec. Doc. 1.

———, ———. *Annual Report*. 37th Cong., 2d sess., 1861. Senate Exec. Doc. 1.

War of the Rebellion: A Compilation of the Official Records of the Union and Confederate Armies. 130 vols. Washington, D.C.: Government Printing Office, 1880–1901.

Maps

United States Geological Survey Topographic Map Sheets: Texas.
1/24000 scale.
Texas Highway Department. County General Map Sheets.

Newspapers

Austin Democratic Statesman, 1872.
Austin Statesman, 1907.
Austin *Texas Democrat*, 1848–61.
Austin *Texas State Gazette*, 1849–61.
Austin *Texas State Times*, 1854.
Clarksville *Northern Standard*, 1848–55.
Daily Austin Republican, 1870.
Dallas Herald, 1867–81.
El Paso (Daily) Herald, 1890–1957.
El Paso Times, 1957.
Fort Griffin Echo, 1877.
Fort Worth (Daily) Democrat, 1873–81.
Freie Presse feur Texas, 1867.
Galveston (Daily) News, 1848–77.
Houston *Beacon*, 1848–50.
Jacksboro Frontier Echo, 1875–76.
La Grange *Texas Monument*, 1851–52.
Marshall *Texas Republican*, 1849–61.
Mesilla Times, 1861.
Nacogdoches Times, 1848–61.
New Orleans (*Daily* and *Weekly*) *Picayune*, 1850–61.
New York Herald, 1858–59.
New York Times, 1857–61.
Sacramento Transcript, 1851–59.
Sacramento Union, 1851–59.
St. Louis *Missouri Reporter*, 1848–61.
St. Louis *Missouri Republican*, 1848–61.
San Angelo *Concho Times*, 1881.
San Antelo Standard, 1894.
San Angelo Standard-Times, 1971.
San Antonio *Alamo Express*, 1860–61.
San Antonio (Daily) Express, 1902–1903, 1949.
San Antonio Herald (*Daily* and *Tri-Weekly*), 1855–75.
San Antonio Ledger, 1855–61.

San Antonio Texan, 1855–61.
San Antonio *Western Texan*, 1851–54.
San Diego Herald, 1857–61.
San Francisco Bulletin, 1857–61.
San Francisco Call, 1852–59.
Santa Fe New Mexican, 1864–68.
Santa Fe Republican, 1847–68.
Santa Fe (Weekly) Gazette, 1851–64.
Tri-Weekly Austin Republican, 1868.
Washington, D.C., *Daily National Intelligencer*, 1851–61.
Washington, D.C., *Rural Free Delivery News*, 1917.
Weekly Austin Republican, 1870.

Periodicals

Harper's New Monthly Magazine, 1879.
Harper's Weekly, 1858.
[New York] *Crayon*, 1855.

Public Records

El Paso County, Texas. County Clerk's Office. Deed Record Book A.
Tom Green County, Texas. County Clerk's Office. Deed Record Book B.
Tom Green County, Texas. County Clerk's Office, Probate Court Minutes, Book A.

Private Collections

Henry L. Dexter Papers. Mr. Art Leibson, El Paso, Texas.
Rude Family Papers. Mrs. Joe Rude, Austin, Texas.
Manuscript Notes on Henry Skillman. Dr. Rex Strickland, El Paso, Texas.
Spence Family Papers. Ms. Mary Bain Spence, San Angelo, Texas.
Manuscript Notes on West Texas. Mr. Clayton Williams, Fort Stockton, Texas.

Special Collections

Emily K. Andrews, "Diary of a Trip from Austin to Fort Davis, September 8, 1874." Barker Texas History Center, University of Texas at Austin.

Zenas R. Bliss, "Memoirs." 5 vols. Barker Texas History Center, University of Texas at Austin.

R. F. Burges Collection. University of Texas at El Paso.

Frederic C. Chabot, comp. "Texas Mail Service and the San Antonio Post Office." United States Postal Service Library, Washington, D.C.

Martin L. Crimmins Collection. Barker Texas History Center, University of Texas at Austin.

El Paso Pioneers Biographic and Historical Sketchbook. University of Texas at El Paso.

Benjamin Franklin Ficklin. Graduate Record Files. Virginia Military Institute, Lexington, Virginia.

Fort Concho Preservation and Museum Archives. San Angelo, Texas.

Fort Davis National Historic Site Archives. Fort Davis, Texas.

Books

Abel, Annie H., ed. *The Official Correspondence of James S. Calhoun while Indian Agent at Santa Fe and Superintendent of Indian Affairs in New Mexico*. Washington, D.C.: Government Printing Office, 1915.

Andrews, C. C., ed. *Official Opinions of the Attorneys General of the United States Advising the President and Heads of Departments, in Relation to Their Official Duties*. Washington, D.C.: Robert Farnham, 1856.

Banning, William, and George H. Banning. *Six Horses*. New York: Century Company, 1930.

Bartlett, John R. *Personal Narrative of Explorations and Incidents in Texas, Mexico, California, Sonora, and Chihuahua, Connected with the United States Boundary Commission during the Years 1850–1853*. 2 vols. New York: D. Appleton, 1854.

Bieber, Ralph P., ed. *Adventures in the Santa Fe Trade*. Glendale, Calif.: Arthur H. Clark Company, 1931.

———, ed. *Exploring Southwestern Trails, 1846–1854*. Glendale, Calif.: Arthur H. Clark Company, 1938.

———, ed. *Journal of a Soldier Under Kearny and Doniphan, 1846–1847*. Glandale, Calif.: Arthur H. Clark Company, 1935.

———, ed. *Marching with the Army of the West 1846–1848*. Glendale, Calif.: Arthur H. Clark Company, 1936.

Boggs, Mae Helene, ed. *My Playhouse was a Concord Coach*. Oakland, Calif.: Howell North Press, 1942.

Carter, Robert G. *On the Border with Mackenzie*. New York: Antiquarian Press, 1961.

Connelley, William E. *Doniphan's Expedition and the Conquest of New Mexico and California*. Kansas City, Mo.: Bryant Book and Stationery, 1907.

Davis, W. H. H. *El Gringo*. New York: Harper, 1857.

Duval, John C. *The Adventures of Bigfoot Wallace*. Macon, Ga.: J. W. Burke, 1870.

———. *Early Times in Texas*. Austin: H. P. N. Gammel, 1902.

Eccleston, Robert. *Overland to California on the Southwestern Trail in 1849*. Los Angeles: University of California Press, 1950.

Edwards, Frank S. *A Campaign in New Mexico*. Philadelphia: Carey and Hart, 1847.

Ford, John S. *Rip Ford's Texas*. Austin: University of Texas Press, 1963.

Frazer, Robert W., ed. *Mansfield on the Condition of the Western Forts, 1853–1854*. Norman: University of Oklahoma Press, 1963.

———, ed. *New Mexico in 1850: A Military View*. Norman: University of Oklahoma Press, 1968.

French, Samuel G. *Two Wars: An Autobiography of General Samuel G. French*. Nashville: Confederate Veteran, 1901.

Froebel, Julius. *Seven Years Travel in Central America, Northern Mexico and the Far West of the United States*. London, 1859.

Gillett, James B. *Six Years with the Texas Rangers, 1875 to 1881*. Lincoln: University of Nebraska Press, 1976.

Gray, Andrew B. *Survey of a Route on the 32nd Parallel for the Texas Western Railroad*. Los Angeles: Westernlore Press, 1963.

Greene, A. C., ed. *The Last Captive*. Austin: Encino Press, 1972.

Gregg, Josiah. *Commerce of the Prairies*, ed. Max L. Moorehead. Norman: University of Oklahoma Press, 1954.

Hafen, LeRoy, ed. *Ruxton of the Rockies*. Norman: University of Oklahoma Press, 1979.

Hammond, George P., and Edward H. Howes, eds. *Overland to California on the Southwestern Trail 1849*. Los Angeles: University of California Press, 1950.

Heartsill, W. W. *Fourteen Hundred and 91 Days in the Confederate Army*. Jackson, Tenn.: McCowat-Mercer Press, 1954.

Hilton, William H. *Sketches in the Southwest and Mexico, 1858–1877*. Los Angeles: Dawson's Book Shop, 1963.

Hood, John B. *Advance and Retreat*. Philadelphia: Burk and McFetridge Press, 1880.

Johnson, Adam R. *The Partisan Rangers of the Confederate States Army.* Louisville, Ky.: George G. Fetter, 1904.

Johnson, Frank W. *History of Texas and Texans.* 5 vols. New York: American Historical Society, 1914.

Longstreet, James. *From Mannassas to Appomattox.* Philadelphia: J. B. Lippincott, 1896.

McCracken, Harold, ed. *Frederic Remington's Own West.* New York: Promontory Press, 1960.

Maury, Dabney H. *Recollections of a Virginian.* New York: Charles Scribners and Sons, 1894.

Mills, W. W. *Forty Years at El Paso, 1858–1898.* El Paso: Carl Hertzog, 1962.

Minot, George, and George P. Sanger, eds. *Statutes at Large and Treaties of the United States of America.* Boston: Little, Brown, 1859.

Minot, Theodore *A Jaunt on the Border.* Phoenix, Ariz.: Nugget Press, 1957.

Moore, Ike, ed. *The Life and Diary of Reading W. Black: A History of Early Uvalde.* Uvalde, Tex.: El Progresso Club, 1934.

Myres, S. D., ed. *Pioneer Surveyor—Frontier Lawyer: The Personal Narrative of O. W. Williams, 1877–1902.* El Paso: Texas Western Press, 1968.

Noel, Theophilus. *A Campaign from Santa Fe to the Mississippi, Being a History of the Old Sibley Brigade.* Houston: Stagecoach Press, 1961.

Oates, Stephen B., ed. *Rip Ford's Texas.* Austin: University of Texas Press, 1963.

Olmsted, Frederick L. *A Journey Through Texas.* Austin: University of Texas Press, 1978.

Ormsby, Waterman L. *The Butterfield Overland Mail.* San Marino, Calif.: Huntington Library, 1942.

Orton, Richard. *Records of California Men in the War of the Rebellion, 1861 to 1867.* Sacramento: State Printing Office, 1890.

Reagan, John H. *Memoirs with a Special Reference to Secession and the Civil War.* New York: Pemberton Press, 1968.

Reid, John C. *Reid's Tramp.* Selma, Ala.: J. Hardy, 1858.

Roberts, Dan W. *Rangers and Sovereignty.* San Antonio: Wood Printing and Engraving, 1914.

Rodriquez, Jose Policarpo. *The Old Guide.* Dallas: Publishing House of the Methodist Episcopal Church, South.

Samuels, Harold, and Peggy Samuels, eds. *The Collected Writings of Frederic Remington.* Garden City, N.Y.: Doubleday, 1979.

Santleben, August. *A Texas Pioneer.* New York: Neale Publishing, 1910.

Schmidt, Stephen H., ed. *Fort Concho Medical History, 1869 to 1872.* San Angelo, Tex.: Fort Concho Preservation and Museum, 1974.

Schurz, Carl. *The Reminiscences of Carl Schurz.* New York: McClure, 1908.

Smith, George G. *The Life and Times of George Foster Pierce.* Sparta, Ga.: Hancock Publishing, 1888.

Smithwick, Noah. *The Evolution of a State.* Austin: H. P. N. Gammell, 1900.

Sowell, A. J. *Early Settlers and Indian Fighters of Southwest Texas.* 2 vols. Austin: Ben C. Jones, 1900.

Sumpter, Jesse. *Life of Jesse Sumpter, The Oldest Citizen of Eagle Pass, Texas.* N.p., n.d.

Tallack, William. *The California Overland Express.* Los Angeles: Historical Society of Southern California, 1935.

Taylor, Nathaniel A. *Two Thousand Miles in Texas on Horseback.* Houston: N. T. Carlyle, 1936.

Tevis, James H. *Arizona in the '50s.* Albuquerque: University of New Mexico Press, 1954.

Thomas, W. Stephen, ed. *Fort Davis and the Texas Frontier: Paintings by Captain Arthur T. Lee, Eighth U.S. Infantry.* College Station: Texas A&M University Press, 1976.

Wilbarger, Josiah. *Indian Depredations in Texas.* Austin: Hutchings Printing House, 1889.

Wilhelm, Thomas, ed. *History of the Eighth U.S. Infantry.* New York: n.p., 1871.

Winfrey, Dorman H., and James Day, eds. *Texas Indian Papers.* 3 vols. Austin: Texas State Library, 1960.

Woods, Isaiah C. *Report to the Honorable A. V. Brown, Postmaster General, on the Opening and Present Condition of the United States Overland Mail Route Between San Antonio, Texas and San Diego, California.* N.p., n.d.

Articles

Abel, Annie H. "Indian Affairs in New Mexico under the Administration of William Carr Lane." *New Mexico Historical Review* 16 (July, 1941): 238–58.

———. "The Journal of Jacob Greiner." *Old Santa Fe* 3 (1916): 189–243.

Anderson, Hattie M., ed. "With the Confederates in New Mexico: Memoirs of Hank Smith." *Panhandle Plains Historical Review* 1 (1929): 65–97.

Barnes, Charles M., ed. "Memoirs of Colonel George H. Giddings." *San Antonio Daily Express*, May 4–27, June 1, 1902.

Baylor, George W. "Historical Sketches of the Southwest." *El Paso Herald*, January 20, 1900.

———. "The Last Indian Fight in El Paso County." *El Paso Daily Herald*, August 10–14, 1900.

———. "Memories of Old Days." *El Paso Herald*, December 18, 1899.

———. "Tragedies of the Old Overland Stage Route." *Frontier Times* 26 (March, 1949): 125–29.

Bieber, Ralph P., ed. "Letters of William Carr Lane." *New Mexico Historical Review* 3 (April, 1928): 187–94.

Clary, David A., ed. "'I Am Already Quite a Texan': Albert J. Myer's Letters from Texas, 1854–1856." *Southwestern Historical Quarterly* 82 (July, 1978): 25–76.

Daly, Henry W. "A Dangerous Dash Down Lancaster Hill." *Frontier Times* 30 (April–June, 1953): 165–74.

Duffen, William A., ed. "Overland via 'Jackass Mail' in 1858: The Diary of Phocion R. Way." *Arizona and the West* 2 (Spring, Summer, Autumn, Winter, 1960): 35–54, 147–64, 279–92, 353–71.

Duke, Escal F., ed. "A Description of the Route from San Antonio to El Paso by Captain Edward S. Meyer." *West Texas Historical Association Yearbook* 49 (1973): 128–41.

———. "A Population Study of Tom Green County," 1880." *West Texas Historical Association Yearbook* 52 (October, 1976): 49–61.

———. "O. M. Smith—Frontier Pay Clerk." *West Texas Historical Association Yearbook* 45 (1969): 45–58.

Edgar William. "One Wagon Train Boss of Texas." *Outing* 39 (January, 1902): 381–83.

Ellison, William H., ed. "Memoirs of Honorable William M. Gwin." *California Historical Society Quarterly* 19 (September, 1940): 256–77.

Faulkner, Walter A., ed. "With Sibley in New Mexico: The Journal of William Henry Smith." *West Texas Historical Association Yearbook* 27 (1951): 111–42.

Galloway, Tod B., ed. "Private Letters of a Government Official in the Southwest." *Journal of American History* 3 (1909): 541–54.

Goldblatt, Kenneth A., ed. "Scout to Quitman Canyon: Report of Captain Geo. W. Baylor of the Frontier Battalion." *Texas Military History* 6 (Summer, 1967): 149–59.

Grote, Edith. "Early Days Recalled by Veteran Mason Leader." *Frontier Times* 28 (October, 1950): 25–26.

Haley, J. Evetts. "The Comanchero Trade." *Southwestern Historical Quarterly* 38 (January, 1935): 157–76.

———, ed. "A Log of the Texas-California Cattle Trail, 1854." *Southwestern Historical Quarterly* 35 (January, 1932): 208–37.

Hall, Martin H. "An Appraisal of the 1862 New Mexico Campaign: A Confederate Officer's Letter to Nacogdoches." *New Mexico Historical Review* 51 (October, 1976): 329–37.

Hargrave, Maria. "Overland by Ox Train in 1870." *Historical Society of Southern California Quarterly* 26 (January, 1944): 9–37.

Hord, Ruth W., ed. "The Diary of Lieutenant E. J. Robb, C.S.A., from Santa Fe to Fort Lancaster, 1862." *Permian Historical Annual* 18 (December, 1978): 59–80.

Hunter, J. Marvin, ed. "An Early-Day Traveler's Description of Menardville." *Frontier Times* 27 (August, 1950): 323–26.

———, ed. "Karger Tells of Flood Loss at Benficklin." *Frontier Times* 6 (November, 1928): 83–84.

———. "Major James M. Hunter, Frontiersman." *Frontier Times* 28 (November, 1950): 43–47.

Laxson, Crawford. "Personal Recollections of Bigfoot Wallace." *Frontier Times* 12 (January, 1935): 166–67.

Moore, John H., ed. "Letters of a Santa Fe Army Clerk, 1855–1856." *New Mexico Historical Review* 40 (April, 1965): 154–62.

St. John, Silas. "Tragedies of the Old Stage Days." *Frontier Times* 28 (January, 1951): 102–108.

Sanderlin, Walter S., ed. "A Cattle Drive from Texas to California: The Diary of M. H. Erskine, 1854." *Southwestern Historical Quarterly* 47 (August, 1959): 397–412.

Schmidt, Stephen H., ed. "Fort Concho 1868–1872: The Medical Officer's Observations by William M. Notson." *Military History of Texas and the Southwest* 12: 125–49.

Sowell, A. J. "The Life of Bigfoot Wallace." *Frontier Times* 5 (November, 1927): 162–66.

Spofford, Harriet P. "San Antonio de Bexar." *Harper's Magazine* 55 (November, 1877): 831–50.

Stillman, J. D. B. "Wanderings in the Southwest." New York *Crayon* 5 (1855): 65–67.

Taylor, Frank H. "Through Texas." *Harper's New Monthly Magazine* 54 (October, 1879): 703–18.

Townsend, Everett E. "An Old Texan." *West Texas Historical and Scientific Society Publications* 33 (December, 1930): 48–51.

Tyler, Ronnie C., ed. "Exploring the Rio Grande: Lieutenant Duff C. Green's Report of 1852." *Arizona and the West* 10 (Spring 1968): 51–54.

Watson, Douglas S., ed. "To California through Texas and Mexico: The Diary and Letters of Thomas B. Eastland and Joseph G. Eastland, His Son." *California Historical Society Quarterly* 18 (June, September, 1939): 99–135, 229–48.

Williams, Clayton W., ed. "Excerpts from the Diary of George W. Wedemeyer." *West Texas Historical Association Yearbook* 46 (1970): 156–66.

Williams, J. W., ed. "Journey of the Leach Wagon Train Across Texas, 1857." *West Texas Historical Association Yearbook* 29 (1953): 115–77.

Woolford, Samuel, ed. "The Burr G. Duval Diary." *Southwestern Historical Quarterly* 65 (April, 1962): 487–511.

SECONDARY SOURCES

Books

Anhert, Gerald T. *Retracing the Butterfield Overland Trail through Arizona*. Los Angeles: Westernlore Press, 1973.

Auchampaugh, Philip G. *James Buchanan and His Cabinet on the Eve of Secession*. N.p., 1926.

Bauer, K. Jack. *The Mexican War, 1846–1848*. New York: Macmillan, 1974.

Beck, Warren A. *Historical Atlas of New Mexico*. Norman: University of Oklahoma Press, 1969.

Beers, Henry P. *Guide to the Archives of the Government of the Confederate States of America*. Washington, D.C.: National Archives and Records Service, 1968.

Bierschwale, Margaret. *Fort McKavett, Texas Post on the San Saba*. Salado, Texas: Anson Jones Press, 1966.

Billington, Ray Allen. *The Far Western Frontier, 1830–1860*. New York: Harper Colophon Books, 1956.

Binkley, William C. *The Expansionist Movement in Texas, 1836–1850*. Berkeley: University of California Press, 1925.

Bonsal, Stephen J. *Edward Fitzgerald Beale: A Pioneer in the Path of Empire, 1822–1903*. New York: G. P. Putnam Sons, 1912.

Borein, Edward. *Stagecoaches of the Old West*. Santa Fe: Institute of Fine Art, 1968.

Bowden, J. J. *Surveying the Texas and Pacific Land Grant West of the Pecos River*. El Paso: Texas Western Press, 1975.

Brannon, Peter A. *The Organization of the Confederate Postoffice Department at Montgomery and a Story of the Thomas Welsh Provisional Stamped Envelope together with the Activities of the Montgomery Postoffice in the Confederate Period*. Montgomery, Ala.: Peter A. Brannon, 1960.

Broaddus, J. Morgan. *The Legal Heritage of El Paso*. El Paso: Texas Western Press, 1963.

Broussard, Ray F. *San Antonio During the Texas Republic: A City in Transition*. El Paso: Texas Western Press, 1967.

Burkhalter, Louis, ed. *A Seth Eastman Sketchbook, 1848–1849*. Austin: University of Texas Press, 1961.

Cage, James C. *Fort Quitman*. McNary, Tex.: James C. Cage, 1972.

Carter, Kathryn T. *The Stagecoach Inns of Texas*. Waco: Texian Press, 1972.

Catton, Bruce. *The Coming Fury*. New York: Doubleday, 1961.

Clark, Mary W. *Thomas J. Rusk: Soldier, Statesman, Jurist*. Austin: Jenkins Publishing, 1971.

Conkling, Roscoe P., and Margaret B. Conkling. *The Butterfield Overland Mail, 1857–1869*. 3 vols. Glendale, Calif.: Arthur H. Clark, 1947.

Couper, William. *One Hundred Years at V.M.I.* 4 vols. Richmond: Garrett and Massie, 1939.

Crandall, Marjorie L. *Confederate Imprints*. 2 vols. Portland, Me.: Athenaeum Press, 1955.

Craven, Avery. *Civil War in the Making, 1815–1860*. Baton Rouge: Louisiana State University Press, 1959.

Cushing, Marshall H. *The Story of Our Post Office*. Boston: A. M. Thayer and Co., 1907.

Davis, David Brion. *The Slave Power Conspiracy and the Paranoid Style*. Baton Rouge: Louisiana University Press, 1969.

DeVoto, Bernard. *The Year of Decision, 1846*. Boston: Little, Brown, 1943.

Dietz, August. *The Confederate States Post-Office Department: Its Stamps and Stationery*. Richmond: Dietz Press, 1950.

———. *The Postal Service of the Confederate States of America.* Richmond, August Dietz, 1929.

Edwards, William B. *The Story of Colt's Revolver.* New York: Castle Books, 1957.

Egan, Ferol. *The Eldorado Trail.* New York: McGraw-Hill, 1970.

Eggenhoffer, Nick. *Wagons, Mules, and Men.* New York: Hastings House, 1961.

Emmett, Chris. *Texas Camel Tales.* Austin: Steck-Vaughn, 1969.

Everett, Donald E. *San Antonio: The Flavor of its Past, 1845–1898.* San Antonio: Trinity University Press, 1976.

Fehrenbach, T. R. *Lone Star: A History of Texas and the Texans.* New York: Macmillan, 1968.

Fowler, Dorothy G. *The Cabinet Politician: The Postmasters General, 1829–1909.* New York: Columbia University Press, 1943.

Frantz, Joe B. *Aspects of the American West.* College Station: Texas A&M Press, 1976.

Frederick, J. V. *Ben Holladay, The Stagecoach King.* Glendale, Calif.: Arthur H. Clark, 1940.

Friend, Llerena B. *Sam Houston: The Great Designer.* Austin: University of Texas Press, 1954.

Galluci, Alfred D., and Mary M. Galluci. *James E. Birch.* Sacramento: Sacramento Historical Society, 1958.

Ganaway, Louis M. *New Mexico and the Sectional Controversy.* Albuquerque: University Press, 1944.

Garber, Paul Neff. *The Gadsden Treaty.* Philadelphia: Press of the University of Pennsylvania, 1923.

Getlein, Frank. *The Lure of the Great West.* Waukesha, Wis.: Country Beautiful Corporation, 1973.

Giles, Janice Holt. *Six-Horse Hitch.* New York: Houghton Mifflin, 1969.

Goeldner, Paul., ed. *Texas Catalog: Historic American Buildings Survey.* San Antonio: Trinity University Press, 1975.

Goetzmann, William H. *Army Exploration in the American West, 1803–1863.* New Haven: Yale University Press, 1959.

———. *When the Eagle Screamed: The Romantic Horizon in American Diplomacy, 1800–1860.* New York: John Wiley and Sons, 1966.

Griggs, George. *History of the Mesilla Valley or the Gadsden Purchase.* Las Cruces, N.M.: Bronson Printing, 1930.

Hafen, LeRoy R. *The Overland Mail, 1849–1869.* Cleveland: Arthur H. Clark, 1926.

―――. *The Utah Expedition, 1857–1858*. Glendale, Calif.: Arthur H. Clark, 1958.

Haley, J. Evetts. *Charles Goodnight: Cowman and Plainsman*. Boston: Houghton Mifflin, 1936.

―――. *Fort Concho and the Texas Frontier*. San Angelo: San Angelo Standard-Times, 1952.

Hall, Martin H. *The Confederate Army of New Mexico*. Austin: Presidial Press, 1978.

―――. *Sibley's New Mexico Campaign*. Austin: University of Texas Press, 1960.

Hamilton, Holman. *Prologue to Conflict: The Crisis and Compromise of 1850*. Louisville: University of Kentucky Press, 1964.

Hamilton, Nancy. *Ben Dowell, El Paso's First Mayor*. El Paso: Texas Western Press, 1976.

Harlow, Alvin F. *Old Post Bags*. New York: D. Appleton Century, 1934.

―――. *Old Waybills: The Romance of the Express Companies*. New York: D. Appleton Century, 1934.

Harris, Benjamin B. *The Gila Trail: The Texas Argonauts and the Gold Rush*. Norman: University of Oklahoma Press, 1960.

Hart, Herbert M. *Old Forts of the Southwest*. New York: Bonanza Books, 1964.

―――. *Pioneer Forts of the West*. Seattle: Superior Publishing, 1967.

Heyman, Max. *Prudent Soldier: A Biography of Major General E. R. S. Canby, 1813–1873*. Glendale, Calif.: Arthur H. Clark, 1959.

Hollon, W. Eugene. *The Southwest: Old and New*. Lincoln: University of Nebraska Press, 1961.

Horgan, Paul. *Great River*. New York: Holt, Rhinehart and Winston, 1977.

―――. *The Heroic Triad*. New York: World Publishing, 1970.

Horn, Calvin. *New Mexico's Troubled Years*. Albuquerque: Horn and Wallace, 1963.

―――, ed. *Union Army Operations in the Southwest—Final Victory*. Albuquerque: Horn and Wallace, 1961.

Hughes, W. J. *Rebellious Ranger: Rip Ford and the Old Southwest*. Norman: University of Oklahoma Press, 1964.

Hunt, Aurora. *The Army of the Pacific*. Glendale, Calif.: Arthur H. Clark, 1951.

Jackson, W. Turrentine. *Wagon Roads West: A Study of Federal Road Surveys and Construction in the Trans-Mississippi West, 1846–1869*. Berkeley: University of California Press, 1952.

James, Marquis B. *The Raven*. New York: Paperback Library, 1971.

Keleher, William A. *Turmoil in New Mexico, 1846–1868.* Santa Fe: Rydal Press, 1952.

Kerby, Robert L. *The Confederate Invasion of New Mexico and Arizona.* Los Angeles: Westernlore Press, 1958.

Lamar, Howard R. *The Far Southwest, 1846–1912.* New York: W. W. Norton, 1970.

Lang, Walter B. *First Overland Mail.* East Aurora, N.Y.: Roycrofters, 1946.

Leckie, William H. *The Buffalo Soldiers.* Norman: University of Oklahoma Press, 1967.

Lucia, Ellis. *The Saga of Ben Holladay.* New York: Hastings House, 1959.

McFeely, William S. *Grant.* New York: W. W. Norton, 1981.

McGaw, William C. *Savage Scene.* New York: Hastings House, 1972.

Malone, Dumas, ed. *Dictionary of American Biography.* 22 vols. New York: Charles Scribner's Sons, 1932.

Meining, Donald W. *Imperial Texas: An Interpretive Essay in Cultural Geography.* Austin: University of Texas Press, 1975.

———. *Southwest: Three Peoples in Geographical Change, 1600–1970.* New York: Oxford University Press, 1971.

Merk, Frederick. *History of the Westward Movement.* New York: Alfred A. Knopf, 1980.

———. *Manifest Destiny and the Mission in American History.* New York: Vintage Books, 1963.

Miller, Nathan. *The Founding Finaglers.* New York: David McKay, 1976.

Moneyhon, Carl H. *Republicanism in Reconstruction Texas.* Austin: University of Texas Press, 1980.

Moody, Ralph. *Stagecoach West.* New York: Promontory Press, 1973.

Moorehead, Max L. *New Mexico's Royal Road: Trade and Travel on the Chihuahua Trail.* Norman: University of Oklahoma Press, 1958.

Nankivell, John H. *History of the Twenty-Fifth Regiment United States Infantry, 1869–1926.* New York: Negro Universities Press, 1969.

Newton, Lewis W., and Herbert P. Gambrell. *A Social and Political History of Texas.* Dallas: Turner Company, 1935.

Nichols, Roy F. *The Disruption of American Democracy.* New York: Macmillan, 1948.

Noll, Arthur H. *General Kirby Smith.* Sewannee, Tenn.: University of the South Press, 1907.

Nunn, W. C. *Texas under the Carpetbaggers.* Austin: University of Texas Press, 1962.

Nye, Wilbur S. *Carbine and Lance: The Story of Old Fort Sill*. Norman: University of Oklahoma Press, 1969.

Orton, Richard H. *Records of California Men in the War of the Rebellion, 1861–1867*. Sacramento: State Printing Office, 1890.

Park, Joseph H. *General Edmund Kirby Smith, C.S.A.* Baton Rouge: Louisiana State University Press, 1954.

Patrick, Rembert W. *Jefferson Davis and his Cabinet*. Baton Rouge: Louisiana State University Press, 1944.

Pierce, N. H. *The Free State of Menard*. Menard, Texas: Menard News Press, 1946.

Poole, William C. *A Historical Atlas of Texas*. Austin: Encino Press, 1975.

Potter, E. D. *Nimitz*. Annapolis: Naval Institute Press, 1976.

Powell, C. Percy. *Lincoln Day by Day: A Chronology, 1809–1865*. 3 vols. Washington, D.C.: Lincoln Sesquicentennial Commission, 1960.

Price, G. F., comp. *Across the Continent with the Fifth Cavalry*. 2 vols. New York: Antiquarian Press, 1959.

Raht, Carlyle G. *The Romance of Davis Mountains and Big Bend Country*. Odessa, Tex.: Rahtbooks, 1963.

Ramsdell, Charles. *San Antonio: A Historical and Pictorial Guide*. Austin: University of Texas Press, 1959.

Ramsey, Grover C. *Confederate Postmasters in Texas*. Waco: W. M. Morrison, 1963.

Reedstrom, Ernest L. *Bugles, Banners and Warbonnets*. Caldwell, Idaho: Caxton, 1977.

Reilly, Robert M. *United States Military Small Arms, 1816–1865*. Baton Rouge: Eagle Press, 1970.

Rhoades, J. F. *History of the United States from the Compromise of 1850*. 2 vols. New York: Harper and Brothers, 1896.

Richardson, Rupert N. *The Comanche Barrier to South Plains Settlement*. Glendale, Calif.: Arthur H. Clark, 1928.

———, et al. *Texas: The Lone Star State*. New York, Prentice-Hall, 1943.

Rideing, William. *The Overland Express, 1837–1875*. Ashland, Ore.: Lewis Osborne, 1971.

Rister, Carl C. *Southern Plainsmen*. Norman: University of Oklahoma Press, 1938.

———. *The Southwestern Frontier, 1865–1881*. Cleveland: Arthur H. Clark, 1928.

Rittenhouse, Jack D. *Maverick Tales*. New York: Winchester Press, 1971.

Roberts, Wilma, comp. *1880 Census of 13-County West Texas Area*. San Angelo, Texas: n.p., n.d.

Roland, Charles P. *Albert Sidney Johnston: Soldier of Three Republics*. Austin: University of Texas Press, 1964.

Root, Frank A., and William E. Connelley. *The Overland Stage to California*. Topeka, Kans.: privately published, 1901.

Russel, Robert W. *Improvement in Communication with the Pacific as an Issue in Politics, 1783–1864*. Cedar Rapids, Iowa: Torch Press, 1948.

Rywell, Martin. *Sharps Rifle: The Gun That Shaped American Destiny*. Union City, Tenn.: Pioneer Press, 1957.

Sabin, Edwin L. *Kit Carson Days, 1809–1868*. 2 vols. New York: Press of the Pioneers, 1935.

Scobee, Barry. *Fort Davis Texas, 1853–1960*. El Paso: Hill Printing, 1963.

————. *Old Fort Davis*. San Antonio: Naylor, 1947.

Sellers, Frank. *Sharps Firearms*. North Hollywood, Calif.: Beinfeld Publishing, 1978.

Settle, Raymond W., and Mary L. Settle. *Empire on Wheels*. Stanford, Calif.: Stanford University Press, 1949.

————, and ————. *Saddles and Spurs: The Pony Express Saga*. Lincoln: University of Nebraska Press, 1955.

————. *War Drums and Wagon Wheels*. Lincoln: University of Nebraska Press, 1966.

Shipman, O. L. *Taming of the Big Bend*. Austin: Von Boeckman–Jones, 1926.

Simpson, Harold, ed. *Frontier Forts of Texas*. Waco: Texian Press, 1966.

Sloane, Eleanor. *The Butterfield Overland Mail across Arizona*. Tucson: Arizona Pioneers Historical Society, 1958.

Smith, Cornelius. *William Sanders Oury: History-Maker of the Southwest*. Tucson: University of Arizona Press, 1967.

Sonnichsen, C. L. *The El Paso Salt War of 1877*. El Paso: Texas Western Press, 1961.

————. *The Mescalero Apaches*. Norman: University of Oklahoma Press, 1973.

————. *Pass of the North*. El Paso: Texas Western Press, 1968.

————. *Tularosa: Last of the Frontier West*. New York: Devin-Adair, 1960.

Strickland, Rex. W. *El Paso in 1854*. El Paso: Texas Western Press, 1969.

――――. *Six Who Came to El Paso*. El Paso: Texas Western Press, 1963.

――――. *The Turner Thesis and the Dry World*. El Paso: Texas Western Press, 1963.

Tarbell, Ida M. *The Life of Abraham Lincoln*. 2 vols. New York: McClure, Philips, 1904.

Taylor, Morris F. *First Mail West: Stagecoach Lines on the Santa Fe Trail*. Albuquerque: University of New Mexico Press, 1971.

terBraake, Alex. *Texas: The Drama of its Postal Past*. Federalsburg, Md.: J. W. Stowell Printing, 1970.

Thompson, Jerry Don. *Colonel John Robert Baylor: Texas Indian Fighter and Confederate Soldier*. Hillsboro, Tex.: Hill Junior College Press, 1971.

Thonhoff, Robert H. *San Antonio Stage Lines, 1847–1881*. El Paso: Texas Western Press, 1971.

Thrapp, Dan L. *The Conquest of Apacheria*. Norman: University of Oklahoma Press, 1967.

――――. *Victorio and the Mimbres Apaches*. Norman: University of Oklahoma Press, 1974.

Tyler, Ronnie C. *The Big Bend: A History of the Last Texas Frontier*. Washington, D.C.: Government Printing Office, 1975.

Unruh, John D. *The Plains Across*. Urbana: University of Illinois Press, 1979.

Utley, Robert M. *Fort Davis National Historic Site, Texas*. Washington, D.C.: Government Printing Office, 1965.

――――. *Frontier Regulars: The United States Army and the Indian, 1866–1891*. New York: Macmillan, 1973.

――――. *Frontiersmen in Blue: The United States Army and the Indian, 1848–1865*. New York: Macmillan, 1973.

Van Alstyne, Richard. *The Rising American Empire*. Chicago: Quadrangle Books, 1965.

Vandiver, Frank. *Ploughshares into Swords: Josiah Gorgas and Confederate Ordnance*. Austin: University of Texas Press, 1952.

Van Zandt, Lee. *Early Economic Policies of the Government of Texas*. El Paso: Texas Western Press, 1966.

Vestal, Stanley. *Bigfoot Wallace*. Boston: Little, Brown, 1942.

Walker, Henry P. *The Wagonmasters*. Norman: University of Oklahoma Press, 1966.

Wallace, Ernest. *Texas in Turmoil, 1849–1875*. Austin: Steck-Vaughn, 1965.

Warner, Ezra J. *Generals in Gray*. Baton Rouge: Louisiana State University Press, 1959.

Watkins, Sue, ed. *One League to Each Wind*. Austin: Von Boeckman–Jones, Printers, n.d.

Webb, Walter P., and Joe Bailey Carroll, eds. *The Handbook of Texas*. 2 vols. Austin: Texas State Historical Association, 1960.

———. *The Texas Rangers*. Austin: University of Texas Press, 1965.

Weddle, Robert S. *The San Saba Mission, Spanish Pivot in Texas*. Austin: University of Texas Press, 1964.

Wellman, Paul I. *The Indian Wars of the West*. Garden City, N.Y.: Doubleday, 1954.

Werst, J. L., ed. *The Reagan Country Story: A History of Reagan County, Texas*. Seagraves, Tex.: Pioneer Book Publishers, 1976.

White, Owen. *Out of the Desert*. El Paso: McMath, 1924.

Whitman, S. E. *The Troopers: An Informal History of the Plains Cavalry*. New York: Hastings House, 1962.

Wilkinson, John. *The Narrative of a Blockade Runner*. New York: Sheldon, 1897.

Williams, Clayton. *Never Again: Texas*. 3 vols. San Antonio: Naylor, 1969.

Williams, J. W. *Old Texas Trails*. Burnett, Tex.: Eakin Press, 1979.

Winther, O. O. *The Transportation Frontier: Trans-Mississippi West 1865–1890*. New York: Holt, Rhinehart and Winston, 1964.

———. *Via Western Express and Stagecoach*. San Francisco: Stanford University Press, 1947.

Wise, Henry A. *Drawing Out the Man: The VMI Story*. Charlottesville: University Press of Virginia, 1978.

Wiseheart, M. K. *Sam Houston: American Giant*. New York: Van Rees Press, 1962.

Woods, Edgar. *Albemarle County in Virginia*. Charlottesville: Michie, 1901.

Wortham, Louis J. *A History of Texas: From Wilderness to Commonwealth*. 4 vols. Fort Worth: Wortham-Molyneaux, 1924.

Wright, Louis, and Josephine M. Bynum. *The Butterfield Overland Mail*. San Marino, Calif.: Huntington Library, 1942.

Wright, Marcus J. comp. *Texas in the War 1861–1865*. Hillsboro, Tex.: Hill Junior College Press, 1965.

Wylie, Rosa Lee. *History of Van Horn and Culberson County, Texas*. Hereford, Tex.: Pioneer Book Publishers, 1969.

Articles

Amaral, Anthony. "Wild Horse Stageline." *Western Horseman* 29 (March, 1964): 56, 115.

Aston, B. W. "Federal Military Reoccupation of the Texas Southwestern Frontier, 1865–1871." *Texas Military History* 8 (1970): 123–34.

Austerman, Wayne R. "Arms of the El Paso Mail." *The Gun Report* 25 (January, 1980): 48–52.

———. "Bradford Daily, A Man of Many Epitaphs." *Password* 25 (Fall, 1980): 118–24.

———. "Identifying a 'Lost' Stage Station in Jeff Davis County." *Password* 25 (Spring, 1980): 3–11.

———. "'Old Nighthawk' and the Pass of the North." *Password* 27 (Fall, 1982): 115–32.

———. "Parker Burnham, an Expressman of Old El Paso," *Password* 27 (Spring, 1982): 5–14.

Baldwin, P. M. "A Short History of the Mesilla Valley." *New Mexico Historical Review* 13 (1938): 314–19.

Bender, A. B. "Frontier Defense in the Territory of New Mexico, 1846–1853." *New Mexico Historical Review* 9 (July, 1934): 249–72.

———. "Government Exploration in the Territory of New Mexico, 1846–1859." *New Mexico Historical Review* 9 (January, 1934): 1–32.

———. "Military Transportation in the Southwest, 1848–1860." *New Mexico Historical Review* 32 (April, 1957): 123–51.

———. "Opening Routes across West Texas, 1848–1850." *Southwestern Historical Quarterly* 37 (October, 1933): 116–35.

Bieber, Ralph D. "The Southwestern Trails to California in 1849." *Mississippi Valley Historical Review* 12 (1925): 342–75.

Bitner, Grace. "Early History of the Concho Country and Tom Green County." *West Texas Historical Association Yearbook* 9 (October, 1933): 3–23.

Boucher, Chauncey S. "In Re That Aggressive Slavocracy." *Mississippi Valley Historical Review* 8 (June–September, 1929): 13–29.

Bowden, J. J. "The Magoffin Salt War." *Password* 7 (Summer, 1962): 95–121.

Branch, E. Douglas. "Frederick West Lander, Road-Builder." *Mississippi Valley Historical Review* 16 (September, 1929): 172–87.

Brent, Robert A. "Nicholas P. Trist and the Treaty of Guadalupe Hidalgo." *Southwestern Historical Quarterly* 77 (April, 1954): 454–74.

Brooks, Clinton E., and Frank D. Reeve. "A Dragoon in New Mexico, 1850–1856." *New Mexico Historical Review* 12 (January, 1947): 51–97.

Callaway, Lew. "Joseph Alfred Slade: Killer or Victim?" *Montana: The Magazine of Western History* 3 (January, 1953): 5–34.

Campbell, T. N., and William J. Field. "Identification of Comanche Raiding Trails in Trans-Pecos Texas." *West Texas Historical Association Yearbook* 44 (October, 1968): 128–45.

Cheetham, F. T. "El Camino Militar." *New Mexico Historical Review* 15 (January, 1940): 1–11.

Clendenen, Clarence C. "Dan Showalter—California Secessionist." *California Historical Society Quarterly* 40 (December, 1961): 309–25.

Corcoran, Lillian H. "He Brought the Railroads to El Paso—The Story of Judge James P. Hague." *Password* 1 (May, 1956): 45–54.

Cotterill, Robert S. "Early Agitation for a Pacific Railroad, 1845–1850." *Mississippi Valley Historical Review* 5 (March, 1919): 396–414.

Crane, R. C. "Stagecoaching in the Concho Country." *West Texas Historical Association Yearbook* 10 (1934): 58–68.

Crimmins, M. L. "Colonel J. K. Mansfield's Report on the Inspection of the Department of Texas in 1856." *Southwestern Historical Quarterly* 42 (April, 1939): 351–88.

———. "Fort Lancaster, Crockett County, Texas." *Frontier Times* 10 (February, 1933): 196–98.

———. "The Last Fight on Texas Soil Between Apaches and Rangers." *Frontier Times* 27 (January, 1950): 113–15.

Cunningham, Olivia R., ed. "Helped to Make Boundary Survey in 1858–1860." *Frontier Times* 27 (September, 1950): 336–43.

Day, James M. "El Paso's Texas Rangers." *Password* 24 (Winter, 1979): 153–73.

Donnell, F. S. "The Confederate Territory of Arizona, from Official Sources." *New Mexico Historical Review* 17 (April, 1942): 148–63.

Duncan, S. Blackwell. "The Legendary Concords." *The American West* 8 (January, 1971): 16–18, 61–62.

Essin, Emmit M. "Mules, Packs, and Packtrains." *Southwestern Historical Quarterly* 74 (July, 1970): 52–63.

Ewing, Floyd F. "The Mule as a Factor in the Development of the Southwest." *Arizona and the West* 5 (Winter, 1963): 315–26.

Farris, Frances B., and C. L. Sonnichsen. "The Domestication of Bigfoot Wallace." *Southwestern Review* 29 (May, 1944): 429–36.

Fauntleroy, J. D. "Old Stage Routes of Texas." *Frontier Times* 6 (July, 1929): 420–23.

Fletcher, Henry T. "Old Fort Lancaster." *West Texas Historical and Scientific Society* 44 (December, 1932): 28.

Frizzel, John, and Mildred Frizzel. "Autobiography of the 'Old Overland.'" *Western Horseman* 35 (July, 1970): 58, 126–28.

———. "The Mud Wagon." *Western Horseman* 41 (May, 1976): 52, 140–44.

Ganaway, Loomis M. "New Mexico and the Sectional Controversy, 1848–1861." *New Mexico Historical Review* 18 (April, 1943): 113–47.

Garrison, L. R. "Administrative Problems in the Confederate Post-Office Department." *Southwestern Historical Quarterly* 19 (October, 1915–January, 1916): 111–42, 232–51.

Gilbert, Benjamin F. "California and the Civil War: A Bibliographical Essay." *California Historical Society Quarterly* 40 (December, 1961): 289–307.

Green, Fletcher M. "James S. Calhoun: Pioneer Georgia Leader and First Governor of New Mexico." *Georgia Historical Quarterly* 39 (December, 1955): 309–347.

Greenwood, C. L. "Opening Routes to El Paso, 1849." *Southwestern Historical Quarterly* 48 (October, 1944): 262–74.

Greever, William S. "Railway Development in the Southwest." *New Mexico Historical Review* 32 (April, 1957): 151–203.

Hall, Martin H. "The Formation of Sibley's Brigade and the March to New Mexico." *Southwestern Historical Quarterly* 61 (January, 1958): 383–405.

Hamilton, Holman. "Texas Bonds and Northern Profits: A Study in Compromise Investment and Lobby Influence." *Mississippi Valley Historical Review* 43 (March, 1957): 588–91.

Hess, Chester N. "Stagecoach Renaissance." *American West* 3 (Winter, 1966): 30–35.

Hodder, Frank. "The Railroad Background to the Kansas-Nebraska Act." *Mississippi Valley Historical Review* 12 (June, 1925): 3–22.

Holden, W. C. "Law and Lawlessness on the Texas Frontier, 1875–1890." *Southwestern Historical Quarterly* 44 (October, 1940): 188–204.

Hollon, W. Eugene. "Great Days of the Overland Stage." *American Heritage* 8 (June, 1957): 28–31, 101.

Holt, R. D. "Old Texas Wagon Trains." *Frontier Times* 25 (September, 1948): 269–78.

Hunt, Elmer M. "Abbot-Downing and the Concord Coach." *Historical New Hampshire* 3 (November, 1948): 1–20.

Hunter, J. M. "Bigfoot Wallace." *Frontier Times* 6 (March, 1929): 209–13.

———. "Bigfoot Wallace, A Lone-Star Hero." *Frontier Times* 7 (October, 1930): 11–12.

———. "Bigfoot Wallace, the Daniel Boone of Texas." *Frontier Times* 17 (July, 1940): 424–27.

———. "Bigfoot Wallace's Fight on the Nueces." *Frontier Times* 5 (April, 1928): 278–79.

———. "Early Day Mail Lines in Texas." *Frontier Times* 13 (February, 1936): 232–34.

———. "Fort McKavett Has Interesting Early History." *Frontier Times* 8 (November, 1930): 58–60.

———. "Old Stage Routes of Texas." *Frontier Times* 28 (April, 1951): 205–10.

———. "Passing of the Stage Driver." *Frontier Times* 11 (January, 1934): 143–44.

———. "The San Antonio-San Diego Mail Route." *Frontier Times* 25 (November, 1947): 55–58.

———. "Six People Drowned in the North Concho." *Frontier Times* 27 (November, 1948): 43–44.

———. "Thirty Day Mail Schedule to California." *Frontier Times* 26 (June, 1948): 219–22.

Hutto, John R. "Pioneering of the Texas and Pacific." *West Texas Historical Association Yearbook* 12 (July, 1936): 124–33.

James, V. L. "Old Times in San Antonio." *Frontier Times* 6 (June, 1929): 379–81.

Jones, Daniel W. "Letter from El Paso." *Password* 24 (Winter, 1979): 197–98.

Kellog, Stan. "History on Wheels—The Mud Wagon." *Western Horseman* 39 (November, 1969): 66, 170.

———. "A Queen of the Old West." *Western Horseman* 34 (March, 1964): 6–7, 102–104.

Kenner, Charles. "The Origins of the 'Goodnight' Trail Reconsidered." *Southwestern Historical Quarterly* 77 (January, 1974): 392–94.

Kielman, Chester V., and Emmie W. Mahon. "George H. Giddings and the San Antonio–San Diego Mail Line." *Southwestern Historical Quarterly* 61 (October, 1957): 220–28.

Liebson, Art. "A Page from El Paso's Past." *El Paso Today* 30 (September, 1978): 16–17.

Lesley, Lewis B. "A Southern Transcontinental Railroad into California: Texas and Pacific versus Southern Pacific, 1865–1885." *Pacific Historical Review* 5 (1936): 52–60.

Linceum, Hugh L. "Old Fort Davis." *Frontier Times* 6 (November, 1928): 88–89.

McAllister, S. B. "Building the Texas and Pacific Railroad West of Fort Worth." *West Texas Historical Association Yearbook* 4 (June, 1928): 50–57.

McCaleb, Walter F. "John H. Reagan." *Texas State Historical Association Quarterly* 9 (1905–1906): 41–51.

———. "The Organization of the Post-Office Department of the Confederacy." *American Historical Review* 12 (October, 1906): 66–74.

McKay, S. S. "Texas and the Southern Pacific Railroad, 1848–1860." *Southwestern Historical Quarterly* 35 (July, 1931): 1–27.

McMillen, Kathryn S. "A Descriptive Bibliography on the San Antonio–San Diego Mail Line." *Southwestern Historical Quarterly* 59 (October, 1955): 206–12.

Martin, Mabelle E. "California Emigrant Roads through Texas." *Southwestern Historical Quarterly* 28 (April, 1925): 287–301.

———. "From Texas to California in 1849: Diary of C. C. Cox." *Southwestern Historical Quarterly* 29 (July, October, 1925, January, 1926): 36–50, 128–46, 201–33.

Mayes, Edward. "Origin of the Pacific Railroads, and Especially of the Southern Pacific." *Publications of the Mississippi Historical Society* 6 (1902): 307–38.

Miles, Susan. "Until the "Flood: 1868–1882." *Edwards Plateau Historian* 2 (1966): 15–25.

Miles, Susan, and Mary Bain Spence. "Major Ben Ficklin." *West Texas Historical Association Yearbook* 27 (October, 1951): 58–77.

Miller, Darliss A. "Carleton's California Column: A Chapter in New Mexico's Mining History," *New Mexico Historical Review* 53 (January, 1978): 23.

Moore, John G. "Mobility and Strategy in the Civil War." In *Military Analysis of the Civil War*. Milwood, N.Y.: KTO Press, 1977.

Moorehead, Max L. "Spanish Transporation in the Southwest: 1540–1846." *New Mexico Historical Review* 32 (April, 1957): 107–20.

Nettels, Curtis. "The Overland Mail Issue During the Fifties." *Missouri Historical Review* 18 (July, 1924): 521–34.

Nichols, Roy F. "The Kansas-Nebraska Act: A Century of Historiography." *Mississippi Valley Historical Review* 43 (September, 1956): 187–212.

Ramsdell, Charles. "The Frontier and Secession." In *Studies in Southern History and Politics*, pp. 63–82. Port Washington, N.Y.: Kennikat Press, 1964.

———. "Reconstruction in Texas." *Columbia University Studies in History, Economics, and Public Law* 26 (1910): 54–84.

———. "Texas from the Fall of the Confederacy to the Beginning of Reconstruction." *Quarterly of the Texas State Historical Association* 11 (October, 1957): 199–219.

Ramsey, Grover C. "Camp Melvin, Crockett County, Texas." *West Texas Historical Association Yearbook* 37 (October, 1961): 137–46.

Read, B. M. "Ben Ficklin 1849 and the Pony Express." *VMI Alumni Review* 49 (1972): 13.

Reynolds, Cedric O. "The Postal System of the Southern Confederacy." *West Virginia History* 12 (April, 1951): 200–79.

Richardson, Rupert N. "Some Details of the Southern Overland Mail." *Southwestern Historical Quarterly* 29 (July, 1925): 1–18.

———. "The Southern Overland Mail, Conveyor of News, 1857–1861." *West Texas Historical Association Yearbook* 34 (October, 1958): 25–37.

Riegel, Robert E. "Trans-Mississippi Railroads During the Fifties." *Mississippi Valley Historical Review* 10 (1916–17): 153–72.

Riney, W. A. "Retracing the Butterfield Trail." *West Texas Historical Association Yearbook* 9 (October, 1933): 97–100.

Rippy, J. Fred. "Mexican Projects of the Confederates." *Southwestern Historical Quarterly* 22 (April, 1919): 291–317.

Root, George A., and Russell K. Hickman. "Pike's Peak Express Companies: Part II–Solomon and Republican Route—Concluded." *Kansas State Historical Quarterly* 13 (November, 1944): 211–43.

Ruhlen, George A. "Quitman, The Worst Post at Which I Ever Served." *Password* 11 (Fall, 1966): 103–14.

———. "Quitman's Owners: A Sidelight on Frontier Reality." *Password* 5 (Fall, 1960): 54–64.

Russel, Robert R. "The Pacific Railway Issue in Politics Prior to the Civil War." *Mississippi Valley Historical Review* 12 (September, 1955): 187–201.

Scannell, Jack C. "Henry Skillman, Texas Frontiersman." *Permian Historical Annual* 18 (December, 1978): 19–32.

———. "A Survey of the Stagecoach Mail in the Trans-Pecos, 1850–1861." *West Texas Historical Association Yearbook* 47 (1971): 115–26.

Scheiber, Harry N. "Coach, Wagon, and Motor-Truck Manufacture,

1813–1928: The Abbot-Downing Company of Concord." *Historical New Hampshire* 20 (1965): 3–25.

Shipman, Jack, ed. "The Price They Paid." *Voice of the Mexican Border* 1 (September, 1933): 39–46.

Skaggs, Jimmy. "Military Operations on the Cattle Trails." *Texas Military History* 6 (Summer, 1967): 137–48.

Smithers, W. D. "Mule Packs and Wagon Trains, Part I." *Western Horseman* 30 (February, 1965): 52–53, 102–105.

Sonnichsen, C. L. "Major McMullen's Invasion of Mexico." *Password* 2 (May, 1957): 38–43.

Sowell, A. J. "Captain Neal Coldwell." *Frontier Times* 25 (March, 1948): 135–44.

Spence, Mary Bain. "The Story of Benficklin, First County Seat of Tom Green County, Texas." *West Texas Historical Association Yearbook* 22 (October, 1946): 27–46.

Stein, Gary, ed. "Overland to California." *American History Illustrated* 12 (May, 1977): 26–36.

Stephenson, Nathaniel W. "California and the Compromise of 1850." *Pacific Historical Review* 4 (1935): 114–22.

Strickland, Rex. "P. T. Herbert: Ante-Bellum Resident of El Paso." *Password* 5 (April, 1960): 43–52.

———. "W. W. Mills, El Paso Politician." *Password* 7 (Summer, 1962): 83–94.

Tittman, Edward D. "The Exploitation of Treason." *New Mexico Historical Review* 4 (April, 1929): 128–45.

Wallace, William S. "Short-Line Staging in New Mexico." *New Mexico Historical Review* 26 (April, 1951): 89–100.

———. "Stagecoaching in Territorial New Mexico." *New Mexico Historical Review* 32 (April, 1957): 204–11.

Waller, J. L. "The Civil War in the El Paso Area." *West Texas Historical Association Yearbook* 22 (October, 1946): 3–14.

Watford, W. H. "Confederate Western Ambitions." *Southwestern Historical Quarterly* 44 (October, 1940): 161–87.

———. "The Far-Western Wing of the Rebellion, 1861–1865." *California Historical Society Quarterly* 34 (June, 1955): 125–48.

Weddle, Robert S. "The Pegleg Stage Robbers." *Southwest Heritage* 3 (March, 1969): 2–9.

Williams, J. W. "Butterfield Overland Mail Road across Texas." *Southwestern Historical Quarterly* 61 (July, 1957): 1–19.

Wilson, John P. "A *Mesilla Times* Returns to New Mexico." *El Palacio* 78 (1972): 2–9.

Winther, O. O. "The Southern Overland Mail and Stagecoach Line, 1857–1861." *New Mexico Historical Review* 32 (April, 1957): 81–106.

————. "Stage-Coach Service in Northern California, 1849–52." *Pacific Historical Review* 3 (1934): 386–99.

Wise, Clyde. "The Effects of the Railroads Upon El Paso." *Password* 5 (July, 1960): 91–100.

Zornow, William F. "Jeptha Wade in California: Beginning the Transcontinental Telegraph, 1860–1861." *California Historical Society Quarterly* 29 (December, 1950): 345–56.

Unpublished Papers

Ashton, John. "A History of Jack Stock and Mules." M.A. thesis, University of Missouri, 1924.

Bitner, Grace. "The History of Tom Green County, Texas." M.A. thesis, University of Texas at Austin, 1931.

Boggs, Herschel. "A History of Fort Concho." M.A. thesis, University of Texas at Austin, 1940.

McMillen, Kathryn S. "The San Antonio–San Diego Mail Line in Texas, 1857–1861." M.A. thesis, University of Texas at Austin, 1960.

Mahon, Emmie W. "George H. Giddings and the San Antonio–San Diego Stage Line." Seminar paper, University of Texas at El Paso, 1962.

Robertson, Robert J. "The Texas Delegation in the National Congress, 1851–1861." M.A. thesis, Lamar State College of Technology, Lamar, Tex., 1965.

Spence, Mary Bain. "The Story of Benficklin, First County Seat of Tom Green County, Texas." Research monograph, Fort Concho Preservation and Museum, San Angelo, Tex.

Stevens, Joan D. "Fort Concho: Guardian of the Conchos, 1867–1874." M.A. thesis, Angelo State University, San Angelo, Tex., 1975.

Utley, Robert M. "Utley's Scrapbook." Research monograph, Fort Davis National Historic Site, Fort Davis, Tex.

Index